between the lines
unconscious meaning in
everyday conversation

between the lines

unconscious meaning in everyday conversation

robert e. haskell, ph.d.

 INSIGHT BOOKS

PLENUM PRESS • NEW YORK AND LONDON

Library of Congress Cataloging-in-Publication Data

Haskell, Robert E.
    Between the lines : unconscious meaning in everyday conversation /
Robert E. Haskell.
        p.   cm.
    Includes bibliographical references and index.
    ISBN 0-306-46009-2
    1. Psycholinguistics. 2. Interpersonal communication.   I. Title.
BF455.H27169 1999
302.3'46--dc21   99-18667
                                                                     CIP

ISBN 0-306-46009-2

© 1999 Robert E. Haskell
Insight Books is a Division of Plenum Publishing Corporation
233 Spring Street, New York, N.Y. 10013

10 9 8 7 6 5 4 3 2 1

A C.I.P. record for this book is available from the Library of Congress

Printed in the United States of America

CONTENTS

FOREWORD

Robert Haskell suggests that humans communicate not only consciously, but unconsciously as well. We sometimes blurt out truths we meant to hide by way of unconscious puns, or by jumping to a new topic with unconscious relevance. Or a chance remark may have double reference: we may express anger about some remote event when we are really annoyed with a close friend. Haskell's "deep encryption" hypothesis is an important idea about human nature, with a good deal of everyday plausibility. It is broadly consistent with current theories of language generation, and there is some direct experimental evidence in its favor.[1]

Language gives us many vehicles for expressing multiple layers of meaning. Most words and idioms have more than one sense, and the ones we choose may be shaped by many unconscious factors. A thought may be conscious for an instant, and still influence the selection of words after it has faded into memory. The means to express multiple ideas in a single phrase are readily at hand.

This book is a wide-ranging survey of situations in which unintended meanings appear to be expressed. Robert Haskell provides a theory of the conditions under which subliteral meanings may occur. Additional hypotheses are generated in the process, such as the notion that humans are not just unconscious generators of meaning, but that they may also unconsciously pick up subliteral expressions from others. The result is the most complete statement arguing for subliteral meaning available today, providing a broad platform for future research.

This book also represents a personal intellectual journey, a lifelong pursuit of an intriguing set of ideas. Haskell has collected his ideas and examples over many years of work with T-groups, refining his understanding of the conditions under which "deeply encrypted" words are likely to appear.

---

[1]See Baars, B. J., Cohen, J., Bower, G. H., and Berry, J. W. "Some Caveats in Testing the Freudian Slip Hypothesis: Problems in Systematic Replication." In B. J. Baars (ed.) *Experimental Slips and Human Error: Exploring the Architecture of Volition.* (New York: Plenum Press, 1992).

Many of these conditions make good theoretical sense. While they resemble ideas expressed by Freud, Lacan, and Langs, they are not the same, and should be evaluated separately.

The author's Concluding Ethical Postscript is one of the most important parts of this book. The notion of unconscious meaning is both powerful, and as a consequence, vulnerable to misuse. For example, many memory researchers are convinced that the popular idea of unconscious traumatic memories has led to a spate of false accusations of child abuse against innocent people. Intellectually, deep ideas are essential in science, but we should be very careful about applying them prematurely in the wider world.

Scientists today should shout from the rooftops that there is simply no infallible technique for reading minds. Yet we all have powerful reasons for wanting to read the minds of others, and our attempts to do so sometimes lead to unfortunate results. Humans are rarely neutral observers. We tend to interpret others according to our hopes or fears, our animosities or suspicions. Therefore, it is easy to misunderstand other people. A man may become convinced that a woman loves him by reading her unintended signals, even though she denies it. An adult daughter may be convinced that her father abused her as a child, even though she can no longer quite remember the details and he denies it. A wife may try to read a husband's infidelity from his words. An employee may fear being fired when the boss makes an innocent comment. These examples are not unusual when people experience intense emotion. Indeed, wars can break out when countries read malicious intentions into each others' words. Ethnic conflicts all over the world are aggravated by such false mind reading.

That is plainly not the intention of this book, and it is what makes the ethical cautions at the end of the book especially important. As Haskell points out, science is often a double-edged sword, and it is vital to begin thinking about the possibility of harmful as well as beneficial applications early in the process of discovery.

Bernard J. Baars
Berkeley, California
January 1999

PREFACE

This book is the result of years of work that I have published in professional peer-reviewed journals. The time has come, however, to make my findings available to a wider audience. The question now arises, why do this? Like most things, the answer is not simple. An author's reasons for writing a book are numerous, some personal, some professional, some altruistic, some not. Aside from the more obvious reasons like ego gratification, monetary reward, and the sheer enjoyment of sharing with others what one has discovered—which really aren't entirely sufficient, I think—there is a more important reason for writing this book: To help people understand what others are really thinking and feeling during a conversation. By this, I mean what they are "really" thinking and feeling, not the public facade that's mostly presented while we are engaged in these social situations.

I remember wondering as a very young child when listening to adults talk, "What do they really mean?" Although their words literally said one thing, it often seemed to me that their words, tone of voice, and behavior, "said" something else. At first, I thought my confusion was due to some inadequacy on my part. Later, however, I heard adults say to other adults, "Well, you have to read between the lines." What did it mean to "read between the lines," I thought? Ever since those early days, I continue to find myself asking the same question, "What did they really mean by that?" Partly on a conscious level, and partly unconsciously, my entire career in psychology has been a quest to answer the question, "What's going on here?"

Certain books and people can be important ingredients in developing one's personal and professional interests. I owe a debt to an old high school friend, Dave Dyer, who perhaps unknowingly started me on my quest to understand the unconscious mind. Dave and I worked after school on the local newspaper in Bath, Maine, the town where we grew up. During our job of counting papers, cleaning up printers' ink, and sweeping the floor, I would wax philosophical about "meaning" and the mind. One day he gave me a book on hypnosis, which in those days, was quite esoteric. It was the first book that I read cover to cover. But more importantly, it started me on my more tutored investigation into the meaning of meaning.

Subsequently, in my quest I came across a book in the town library by an author I had only vaguely heard of at that point, Sigmund Freud. The book was his magnum opus, *The Interpretation of Dreams,* which, of course, is about meaning. But contrary to popular belief, his book is not just about the meaning of dreams. It's about how language "means." Disregarding his psychoanalytic orientation, the book significantly influenced me.

Then, there's my closest friend of more than twenty years, Dr. Aaron Gresson, who shared with me his writings, brilliant insights, and ever-so-keen perceptions of what people in our common social interactions and conversations "really" mean. His supportive but critical views on my method presented in this book also gave me much to think about during the years, especially around my interpretation of unconscious racial and ethnic references in conversations. Maybe this book will do for someone what Dave Dyer, Sigmund Freud, and Aaron did for me.

Now I know that the question I asked as child and continue to ask as an adult is an eternal one that most people would like to have answered. Of course, there is no single answer. Human meaning is more complex than that. It involves multiple meanings of what people are saying, and it also involves eternal concerns about the meaning of human relationships that are archetypal, concerns about what others are feeling toward us, about jealousy, rivalry, and authority.

To read between the words, as it were, we have to understand how language works and also how the mind works. Accordingly, this book is not just about understanding how language "means." It's about the way the "mind" makes meaning. Indeed, it's about consciousness itself.

Understanding how language means and how the mind works is a concern not only of psychologists and philosophers. On some level—everyday, in some way—most people try to understand how language means and how the mind works. They must because social living requires it. It's as basic as that. Survival and success in one's life goals depend on it. This book, then, was written to help people better understand language and unconscious meaning in conversation and also in so doing to assist in achieving one's life goals. An added "plus" is that along the way it's fascinating reading as well.

ACKNOWLEDGMENTS

I would like to acknowledge the many people who have influenced this book in some way. First, I must express my appreciation to my long time friend and colleague, Dr. Aaron Gresson, with whom I spent many hours at the inception of the material in this book. Though he was a most valuable critic, he was always supportive.

I also need to thank the many people who contributed examples. These include my former colleague, Mr. John Heapes, Mrs. Virginia Look, Sarah Look, my daughter Melyssa, and Claudette Haskell, and my many former students and other people who were not aware that they were providing me with examples.

Finally, I would also like to thank Dr. Joseph Kockelmans and Dr. Richard Gregg of The Pennsylvania State University for their early support.

between the lines
unconscious meaning in everyday conversation

INTRODUCTION

This book is an introduction to the way our unconscious mind creates hidden meaning in everyday conversations and is a new way to uncover these hidden meanings and the unconscious feelings that generate them. My method is practical and concrete and can be initially learned in less time than it takes to read this book. In the process, this book will take you on, what I, at least, think is a fascinating and pioneering trip through the mind, a trip that will take you through an intriguing web of meanings in social conversations created by feelings, pun-like sounds, double entendres, and other everyday uses of language. The ancient Greek philosopher, Plato, said that we don't learn anything new, we simply remember what we already know on some deep level.[1] Thus, because this book is about human feelings and about how we use sound when we talk, it will not be so much about learning something new and strange (though it's that, too), as one of startling recognition.

If nothing else is certain about most human beings, one fact is very clear: we like to talk a lot. But are we aware of the full meaning behind our talk? The research from various fields suggests that we are not. We take so much for granted in our daily lives, it's *as if* we are only half awake, unmindful of a great deal of the hidden meaning in our conversations. It's *as if* we're talking in our sleep.

As we engage in our daily activities, most of us take part in social conversations of one kind or another with family, friends, and with colleagues at work, and we are unaware of much of the hidden meaning in those conversations. It's no secret that language is highly symbolic, of course, but how symbolic it is, we have no precise idea. Talk has levels of unconscious meaning of which we consciously know nothing. It's perhaps disheartening, but apparently true, that much of the time we don't know what we're talking about.

If we listen with a trained ear to the words, phrases, and tones of voice people use, we can glimpse their hidden feelings and thoughts. This applies to adults and also to children. This book, then, is about training the ear, so to speak, to hear hidden and unconscious meanings in individual and social conversations. It's during coffee breaks and after meetings are over, where "free flowing" conversation is the rule, that many topics are thrown out for possible discussion. Some engender our interest, and we may stick with them for a while—and some don't. Why? Most researchers attribute this sort of "random talk" to a milling-around process whose function is simply to help members of a conversation get acquainted. But is such topic-hopping, in fact, random? The answer is "no," it isn't.

I've been researching unconscious meaning in conversations in my small group dynamics laboratory and have found some fascinating, indeed, often bizarre findings. For example, what does it mean and how do you explain a group of people discussing the topic of *skindiving* or the topic of *twins?* The literal answers to these questions are clear. They were simply talking about skindiving and about twin siblings. In fact, however, the topic of *skindiving* was a kind of metaphorical or encoded way of expressing their concerns about my *deep* analysis of a group member's behavior, i.e., the topic of *skindiving* is *an unconscious response to my deep analysis of members' behavior.* Likewise, the apparently literal topic of *twins* was a kind of metaphorical or encoded way of expressing concerns about the *two* trainers who were coleading the group, i.e., the topic of *twins* equates to *the two trainers in the group.*

This kind of unconscious or encoded talk has not been systematically observed or explained psychologically. Certainly, there are books that purport to explain how to interpret unconscious meaning, but the method typically advanced is so general as to be almost useless. This book, however, is based on a very concrete and specific set of rules for recognizing and analyzing unconscious meanings in everyday conversations. These examples of unconscious language are what I call subliteral conversations. The term subliteral simply indicates word meanings that are unconsciously attached to the conscious and accepted meanings of words, i.e., their literal or standard meanings.

We overlook a great deal of what's happening in our everyday life. When we look out at our lawn, we see a relatively homogeneous patch of green. But biologists who have specialized knowledge looking at the same lawn will see a whole lot more than just a patch of green lawn. The same is true for the psychologist or linguists looking at everyday conversations. This book will provide the language, concepts, and other tools that will allow you to see things you never saw before. And what you see will astonish you. It did me.

The implications of my findings for understanding how language and the mind work are themselves mind boggling—and I am not exaggerating here. The story of the origins of these findings is one of the more fascinating stories in the history of psychology (see chapter 2).

The question that may arise now is, why did I wait so many years to write this book? Again, the answer is not simple. However, there are two basic reasons. First, I wanted to wait until I had the research on my complete methodology published in peer-reviewed scientific journals. The second reason is that the time seems right for acceptance of my methodology by a general audience and by a wider professional community. For years the time was not right. When I first began developing this work in the early 1970s, the school of thought in psychology, called behaviorism, was still predominant. It emphasized behavior and a belief that the "mind" doesn't exist or at least that the mind is unstudyable. Overlapping this period, the up-and-coming cognitive psychology that viewed the mind as working like a computer (hence, called the computational view) was not friendly toward research on the "unconscious mind" or the study of subjective meaning. Both behaviorism and cognitive psychology—and the latter's broadened version called cognitive science, which includes philosophy, neurology, and artificial intelligence, e.g., programs for robots—studiously avoided anything even remotely resembling Freudian psychoanalysis (see chapter 8). One of the reasons why subliteral language has been avoided by cognitive science research is that the highly formalized, computer-like methods used by these sciences cannot analyze subliteral language.

Except for some psychotherapists, these biases generally spilled over into our high-tech culture at large and into various professional fields. In more recent years, however, there has been a shift and renewed interest in things unconscious that have subjective meaning. This shift was inevitable, for as Loren Eiseley, the anthropologist once noted, ever since ancestral humans entered their own heads and became conscious, they have been trying to adapt to what they found there. This book adds to what we humans have found in our heads and also hopefully will help us to adapt to what we have found, for what appear to be just interesting little stories in everyday conversations that have unconscious meaning in fact point to a shift that hasn't yet taken place in the way we think the mind works.

PERSPECTIVE OF THE BOOK

This book is about the way literal topics and language use in conversations have symbolic or unconscious meaning attached to them. In other words, talk about *twins* is considered literal when the talk is simply about twins, and does not have any added metaphorical, symbolic, or unconscious meaning. In my research during the past 25 years using T-groups ("T" stands for training) in controlled laboratory conditions and from everyday settings, however, I have found that a great deal of language and conversation considered only literal by both a speaker and a listener is actually a kind of "metaphorical" unconscious communication of which the speaker is unaware. But not always. As even Freud is reputed to have said, "Sometimes a cigar is just a cigar" (i.e., not a phallic symbol).

Generally speaking, during these times of informal chatter, unconscious meanings are most clearly visible. Thus, during highly structured conversations, like business meetings, for example, unconscious material may be difficult to recognize, but just before such meetings or during the first few minutes of "warming up" where ritual greetings and "small talk" are socially required, there is often a wealth of unconscious meaning being communicated.

Despite the fact that much of our life is spent talking to each other, surprisingly little is known about the complexity of meaning in our talk. Most people are usually just too busy talking to recognize what is being said unconsciously, and scientists are too busy focusing on grammar, semantics, rhetoric, and other more formal aspects of language. The full meaning of our words goes unheard.

In the group therapy and the small group research literature, however, occasional and brief instances of what I call subliteral conversations have been sporadically noted and generally called symbolic communication. Indeed there is no shortage of books and articles on hidden meanings. Such hidden meanings, however, are almost invariably explained in what has become clichéd Freudian terminology or some general variant thereof, with no method to verify that the talk is in fact "symbolic." Because Freud has become a household name in our culture, I should make it clear that although much of what is Freudian may be symbolic, not all that's symbolic is necessarily Freudian, especially the subliteral theory of language and mind that I present in this book.

Without a method, such Freudian analyses become simply intuitive interpretation, and "metaphorical" utterances become mere coincidence or random puns. Indeed, when I first began publishing my findings, reviewers almost immediately dismissed them as—at best—Freudian, as coincidence and—at worst—as "schizophrenic," as "wild puns," as "sheer fantasy," or as simply "ridiculous." Since that time, I have developed an extensive systemic method divided into fourteen major categories with over sixty separate cognitive and linguistic operations to analyze—but more important—to validate unconscious or subliteral conversation in everyday life (see Appendix). Although my approach to understanding the mind is to analyze the psyche, it is not psychoanalysis; my approach is based on a linguistic and cognitive framework.

USEFULNESS AND SCOPE OF THE BOOK

And so, of what use is all this understanding of unconscious meanings in talk, and to whom is it useful? First, it's useful for just about anyone because there are many situations in everyday social life and at work where information about what people may be "really" thinking or feeling is difficult or impossible to obtain. Listening subliterally can yield valuable and interesting information. The many illustrations throughout this book reveal the multifaceted nature of human relationships—indeed about human nature itself. The examples and illustrations I've gathered through the years confirm what we often suspect is going on beneath the polite surface of social relationships and also frequently reveal new and poignant insights into age-old and near-archetypal human concerns. These concerns include eternal issues revolving around gender, sexuality, sexual preference, race and ethnicity, age, authority, leadership, religion, communication, and the individual versus the group. Thus, they reveal a lot to us about human relationships in all their complexity, stereotypes, and prejudices (see chapter 9).

Second, this book is specifically useful for therapists and mental health counselors who conduct individual and group sessions to obtain information not consciously available to clients to observe unconscious psychodynamics.

Third, my method can be useful to those who attend the many support groups that meet to discuss personal issues and problems.

Fourth, it's useful for those who manage or lead the increasing number of small groups or teams in the business world.

Fifth, for those who conduct research on the dynamics of these groups and teams, it can be an important adjunct method for recognizing and uncovering otherwise hidden dynamics.

Sixth, many of the examples I present speak to cultural beliefs and rituals and their subliteral meaning.

Seventh, my findings cast new light on the nature of language and our use of it. And lastly, for anyone who is interested in how the mind works, this book has important implications.

Finally, a word about psychology books. There is no shortage of books on psychology written for a general audience. General audience books about psychology can be important. They disseminate valuable information about everyday life. They are important, too, for helping people understand psychology. There is often a downside to popular psychology books, however. For years I have railed, both in speech and in print, against some of these books that are what I call "pop psychology." Pop psychology books are characterized by wild speculation, based only on personal experience, not scientific research.[2] This is done by people who should know better. At least in psychology, personal experience is not a good basis for knowing how the mind or the world really works. Let me offer a glaring example.

It *appears* that the sun rises in the East in the morning and sets in the West in the evening. But it doesn't. If it did, this would mean the earth is the center of the solar system, and of course, it isn't. The Polish astronomer, Nicholas Copernicus (1473–1543) cleared this *appearance* up almost 500 years ago. Although operating on everyday appearances can often be useful, in scientific analysis it's most usually not. This is the problem with theories that are based on someone's everyday experience (it's what leads to pop psychology). Think about it. Where would our astronauts have ended up if NASA had based its astrophysical calculations of planetary orbits on the everyday appearance of the sun circling the earth? I rest my case.

This is why it's so important to understand scientific explanations of the world around us and not rely just on appearances. In using the obvious example of the sun *appearing* to rise and set, to make a point about everyday experience versus scientific explanations. If you think it was a much too obvious example, consider that although Americans have an interest in science, many are woefully uninformed. A recent study by the National Science Foundation found that *less than half of the population* knows that the earth goes around the sun once a year.[3]

Scientific explanations are typically more complex than *appearances* and require a little more patience to understand. They're worth it, however—or at least the astronauts think so. So did the late Carl Sagan, the well-known astronomer, author of a number of bestseller books, and Pulitzer Prize winner.[4] In his book, *The Demon-Haunted World: Science as a Candle in the Dark,* he pleads for books that inform the reader about science. I have tried to make this book informative about science.

To really understand an idea, it's necessary to go into some depth. But this doesn't mean it has to be tedious. Even the most complex scientific findings and theories can be explained without most of the specialized language (called jargon). But as in translating a poem from one language into another, something is always lost. In this book, I explain my ideas in some depth, but I hope I have succeeded in doing this in a readable and interesting way. It's important that I do this because anyone who puts forth novel ideas, such as the ideas in this book—which are outside the normal beliefs of the times about what is possible—had better be able to show clearly, far beyond what is normally expected, how the ideas are reasonable. As the history of science clearly shows, very few ideas—indeed, virtually none—are born without a heritage. And unless one is an incredible genius (which I am not), they need to show how the ideas evolved out of known ideas. And like understanding people, to really understand an idea, one has to understand its lineage (Can you imagine understanding female and male roles in our society without understanding the evolution of ideas about gender?). Anything less is pop psychology.

Finally, I would like to make it clear that I don't use the terms *valid* or *true* to describe many of the strange mental operations that I've found and will present in this book. Nor do I make such truth claims regarding the conceptual underpinnings that theoretically explain my findings. Even though I've developed an extensive method to validate subliteral conversations, scientifically speaking, it's too early to make any absolute claims. But this is not to say that the analysis of subliteral conversation is just a hypothesis. Given my methodology, the history of similar findings, and that many of the findings are compatible with other cognitive research and theory, the methodology constitutes something more than a hypothesis, but something less than accepted fact. And there is nothing wrong with this. Indeed, this puts subliteral findings in fairly good company in psychology and in other scientific areas of knowledge. Accordingly, research will undoubtedly continue to modify my findings.[5] In any event, while I believe this is more than a hypothesis, I recognize that others may not agree—and reasonably so. But, I hope by the end of this book I will have convinced you that something real is going on that we haven't recognized before.

THE STRUCTURE OF THE BOOK

Throughout this book, I show how to recognize unconscious meaning in subliteral conversations by examples from everyday life and from my small group laboratory. Many of these examples of unconscious meanings have been verified with my methodology. Others, however, are from everyday situations where it was not possible to completely verify them, but sufficient contextual information was available to establish at least a high probability that they are valid. In addition, their analyses were in keeping with those I have verified with my methodology. Still others with less exact verification can at least serve as hypothetical but probable examples of what they illustrate.

Some of my examples from TV talk shows and other situations are from the early times when I first began to develop my method and theory of unconscious meaning. Oddly, those were the days when I seemed to have more time to watch TV and listen to the conversations of others. If I weren't such a social recluse, I'd have many more examples from my own social conversations. In any event, the "time stamp," as it were, on some of the examples is not pertinent. Their value lies in their demonstrating interesting cognitive and linguistic operations.

Finally, I have packed this book with multiple examples that I've described and analyzed in some detail because the best way to learn to recognize and analyze unconscious meanings is to immerse oneself in concrete examples and let the mind absorb the patterns underlying them. Providing the complete word-for-word original data from which each illustration is derived would be ideal. Unfortunately, it would be much too cumbersome and tedious. The reason for describing the illustrations in some detail, however, is that the reader may find meanings that I have overlooked. I know that as I was rewriting some of these illustrations for this book, I discovered meanings that I had missed when I first analyzed them. Indeed, as you read the many examples in this book, you will begin to anticipate some of their meanings before I present my analysis.

The questions this book will answer, then, include, How is subliteral meaning possible? What are its mental mechanisms? How do feelings and emotions influence meaning? Why haven't the mechanisms of subliteral conversations been discovered before? Are there current data and theories that relate to subliteral meaning? What can the subliteral mind tell us that's new about the mind? What can slips tell us that's new about language? How is the subliteral unconscious mind different from that of Freud's and from the views of modern cognitive science? What does an unconscious mind that creates subliteral meanings look like, and what can it tell us about the nature of consciousness? Finally, what are the implications and practical applications of subliteral meaning?

I have divided this book into three sections. PART I, The Discovery of Subliteral Meaning, is a general introduction to unconscious meaning with explanations, examples, and themes. Chapter 1 has introductory examples, provides an overview and explains the usefulness of my method, and presents some basic principles for recognizing unconscious meaning. Chapter

2, the story of my discovery of what I term the subliteral mind, has some fascinating twists and turns. Chapter 3 presents numerous subliteral topics and themes which evolve out of timeless or archetypal human concerns about authority and leadership. Chapter 4 presents subliteral topics and themes that evolve out of timeless or archetypal human concerns about peer and interpersonal jealousy, rivalry, and other related issues. Chapter 5 demonstrates how numbers mentioned in conversations can have unconscious meaning.

PART II, How Subliteral Meaning Is Made, explains how feeling, and the subliteral unconscious creates meaning. Chapter 6 describes how deep feelings and emotions are fundamental in shaping unconscious language use in conversations. Chapter 7 describes how the pun-like sounds and playing with words in everyday language-use are responsible for designing subliteral phrases and sentences. Chapter 8 explains what it means to say that something is unconscious and outlines the various working parts of the subliteral mind.

PART III presents further specific applications of subliteral language. Chapter 9 presents many examples of racial prejudice and ethnic differences expressed in subliteral language. Chapter 10 presents examples of sex and gender prejudice and stereotypes expressed in subliteral language. Chapter 11 shows how what we know about dreams and dreaming figures into our understanding of unconscious meaning. Chapter 12 describes how subliteral communications can be used in psychotherapy by examining the work of the psychiatrist, Robert Langs, who founded a new school of psychotherapy based on unconscious communication that's similar to my own work.

A concluding ethical postscript addresses the issue of revealing subliteral meaning to others. Finally, for those interested in the systematic methodology underlying the illustrations given throughout this book, I've included an Appendix. The appendix is also a summary or overview of the subliteral approach to language, meaning, and the mind.

Robert E. Haskell
Old Orchard Beach, Maine 1998
email: rhaskell@javanet.com
alternate email: rhaskell@mailbox.une.edu

PART I

THE DISCOVERY OF SUBLITERAL MEANING

CHAPTER 1

SLIPS OF THE MIND

INTRODUCTION TO UNCONSCIOUS
MEANING IN EVERYDAY CONVERSATIONS

It's a fact hardly known only to professionals that in informal social conversation during coffee breaks, meetings, and other unstructured and informal moments that topics in the conversations seem to come and go rather haphazardly, apparently hopping from topic to topic in a nearly random way. Little or no meaning is ascribed to these fragmented bits of conversation. Most researchers attribute this sort of random small talk to a milling-around process whose function is to simply help members get acquainted, a kind of phatic communion, as it's been called, where people find their way around the social and conversational terrain. This small talk, then, sort of serves the same function as the scream of bats.

But is such topic-hopping, in fact, random, carrying little to no meaning? The short answer is, "no," and is what this chapter is about. The longer answer is what this book is about. In this chapter I present examples of conversations from my small group dynamics laboratory and from everyday life which illustrate that social conversation is not random but also that there is unconscious meaning in those conversations. The illustrations in this chapter are introductory and give just the flavor of more complex and important examples in the remaining chapters. After presenting these initial illustrations, I briefly explain how our mind and our unconscious use of language constructs these unconscious meanings and lay out the way my method can be applied in everyday life and professional situations. I also outline the importance of my method for understanding how our mind works. Finally I introduce some specific guidelines to help in initially recognizing unconscious meaning.

UNCONSCIOUS MEANINGS

IN EVERYDAY CONVERSATION

During the small-talk stage of conversation where we quickly hop from one topic to another, the important question is, why are certain topics brought into conversations at a particular time, and not others? Is it coincidence, for example, that in a conversation that's being openly tape recorded, there are repeated references to the *CIA* and *FBI*? Is it coincidence that the topics of *"God"* or *"policeman"* frequently selected into discussions whose members have concerns about a *leader, trainer, boss,* or *authority figure* who is also in the discussion? And is it coincidence that the topic of *child/parent* relationships is often selected into a conversation when members harbor concerns about the leader-authority relationship in the discussion. Or is it an accident that the topic of "state employment being a rip off to taxpayers" occurs immediately following my return to a group meeting I was leading after being absent unannounced for two sessions? No, it's no accident. The topic of "state employment being a rip off to taxpayers" reflects members' resentment at my being absent from the meetings and thus feeling they were not getting what they paid for—just as taxpayers often feel ripped off because of the benefits government workers receive and which many workers in business world do not get. Again, it's no coincidence that these topics are selected into the conversation at a particular time. The apparently literal topics of CIA, FBI, God, policeman, parents, and children are "metaphorical" expressions of members' unconscious concerns about being tape recorded and about the authority figure in the conversation. Unconscious concerns are metaphorically piggy-backed onto the meanings of what otherwise appear to be literal or conscious meanings. It's a kind of talking in tandem, as it were.

To further illustrate: How does one explain, for instance, the ostensibly innocent statement of a person who has just bought a new car and who says he bought it because he was tired of driving *old heaps*—meaning an old wreck of a car—when his last name is *Heapes?* Sounds like the wildest of coincidence, does it? Or perhaps it's simply just an unconscious pun or double entendre? Or what does it mean when a retired gentleman is standing in front of a door with a heavy package in his arms and his son-in-law offers no help, and the retired gentleman just happens to look over at a young child who is pretending to help its mother carry a suitcase and says to the child, "That's very thoughtful of you to help out"? Is this a conscious snide remark directed at the son-in-law? Again, the answer is, "probably not." What the gentleman's remark reflects is his unconscious feelings that this son-in-law is not very thoughtful.

Much of our everyday conversation, then, expresses more than the standard or literal meaning attached to it. A further example: Years ago my wife and I bought a small rundown summer cottage in Maine where I grew up and knew quite a few people. For the first couple of summers, we were so busy trying to make the cottage livable that we had no time to socialize. At last the cottage was decent enough to invite some old friends for an evening of conversation. Having not seen our guests for some years, the conversation was rapid fire and free-associative. The initial small talk finally got around to discussing the cottage, so my wife and I proceeded to give our guests the "grand tour." In the stream of conversation, one of our guests started telling us about attending a party given a few weeks before. It seemed that the people who gave the party had just finished redecorating their home. Sandwiched in between talking about the party, it was said *"they only had the party to show off their redecorating work."* Unconsciously—and I believe it wasn't a conscious snide remark—the speaker's feelings about our motivation for inviting them were perhaps clear.

It's widely recognized, of course, that in everyday conversations certain euphemisms are often consciously employed to talk cryptically about some out-group person or group of people. For example, students may want to talk about professors but may not want to say explicitly what they are feeling openly, parents may want to talk about children when they are present without them knowing they are being talked about, and one ethnic group may want to talk about another. Such euphemisms like "you know how *they* are," may be used. This is called "coded speech," where often everyone knows what's "really" being discussed. But this is *not* what this book is about. I'm not just talking about euphemisms, here. I'm talking about deep encryption.

Such talk occurs with intimates and with relative strangers. If we listen carefully to their talk, responses to the finer nuances of their feelings often become clear. One evening my former wife and I were taking our evening walk, and I was rambling on, half incoherently and stumbling over my words, mispronouncing them and repeating syllables. I had no sooner finished one of these broken sentences as we were passing one of those fences that look like they are woven, when my wife said — out of a myriad of things she could have said— *"There's a fence with a broken spoke."* She was, in fact, unconsciously, commenting on the fact that I *spoke*(en) in a broken manner. Hence, *"broken spoke."* Here we see the word spoke being used literally as a noun, referring to a connecting piece of wood in a fence and unconsciously as an adjective referring to my speaking (the archaic of spoke is a past participle of speak). This is perhaps not a very important example, but it is poignant, as are the two following personal recollections.

The unconscious mind of the child is much closer to consciousness than the unconscious of an adult, as the work of Jean Piaget,[1] the renowned Swiss psychologist, has clearly demonstrated. Thus one might expect that unconscious meaning is closer to consciousness in children than in adults. One Halloween evening, I was playing with my daughter, Melyssa. I was playfully squeezing, hugging, and kissing her. While doing this, she was trying to open her Halloween bag of goodies. As she opened it and spied something within, she exclaimed, "Oh, it's one of those doodady things" (i.e., an unnamed or nameless gadget or trinket). Unconsciously, she was acknowledging that I was engaging in those things that Daddy's do, i.e., doodady things.

The second example occurred in a restaurant one day. My former wife and I were discussing and explaining pregnancy to our seven and a half year old daughter, Melyssa, who had some questions she wanted answered. She had always been very curious about things. We explained it as well as we could to a seven and a half year old. When we seemed to have reached an appropriate end to our explanation, there was a slight pause and my wife and I began talking about the events of the day. Then my daughter tugged on my sleeve, turned herself toward me, and asked, "What do you think of my shirt, Dad?" On her shirt was a decal—at stomach level—of a banana that was depicted as a little child. In unconscious or subliteral terms, my daughter's question was pregnant with the meaning her question was about.

As I briefly explained in the Introduction, the term subliteral indicates word meanings that are unconsciously attached to the conscious and accepted meanings of words, i.e., their literal meanings. I coined the term subliteral for my approach to unconscious meaning, language, and mind for two important reasons. First, the concept replaces traditional psychoanalytic terms like "latent," "unconscious," and "symbolic" meaning. It also replaces the linguistic term "metaphorical" insofar as the term "metaphor" describes symbolic meaning in our language.[2] This name change is not just a semantic game, it's an important conceptual distinction. This is why.

Historically, the psychoanalytic approach has rendered the interpretation of unconscious meaning a mystery for all but highly trained practitioners. Although Sigmund Freud didn't invent the concept of the unconscious, Freud almost singlehandedly made us aware of the unconscious mind.

Freud's genius was to take the various notions of the unconscious that had been around for some time and organize them, connect new data to them (such as it was), and then to provide a new theory or framework of the unconscious mind. Seldom are discoveries made whole cloth, so to speak (see next chapter). In any event, Freud's classic notion of the unconscious is not adequate to explain the kind of linguistic phenomenon that I describe in this book. Even the many neo-Freudian reformulations of Freud's concept of the unconscious are not adequate. Freudian notions of the unconscious are much too vague, and psychoanalytic interpretations of an event often are all-meaningful. A subliteral framework demystifies the deep dark Freudian unconscious (see chapters 8 and 12).

To anyone who understands my method, it will be clear in a discussion about identical *twins* in a group that has *two leaders* which *twin* in the discussion unconsciously refers to which of the two leaders. Accordingly, it's no accident when a member of a conversation "just happened" to talk about an old brand of cough drops called *Smith Brothers*, which as a trademark had a picture of two bearded men, one who had a black beard and one a reddish beard on its packaging, when one leader in the group had a *black beard,* the other a *reddish beard.* No accident, indeed. Semantically, then, the topic of "Smith Brothers" like the topic of identical "twins," was a parallel or tandem talk that unconsciously referred to the two leaders. Just as to the theoretically informed physicist, certain marks observed in a bubble chamber mean the presence of a particular subatomic particle, so too, someone who is theoretically informed about my method can recognize that certain kinds of conversational cues and language mark the presence of unconscious or hidden thoughts and feelings.

Every intonation made, indeed, even some of the physical aspects surrounding a conversation are unconsciously registered on some level. Normally, however, neither the person listening nor the person speaking is privy on a "conscious" level to the way these events are processed in the mind. For example, my fiancee's mother recently visited her podiatrist to have her feet worked on. As she lay on his couch having her feet massaged, they were talking to fill an otherwise silent activity. As they did so, the podiatrist said that his clients often told him very personal things about themselves as they lay on his couch. My fiancee's mother replied that laying on a couch while having one's feet massaged is very relaxing and soothing. She said it was like being in a psychologist's office having therapy, so people would naturally have a tendency to "bare their souls" to you. When she said this, she immediately became conscious of the double meaning: they bare their *souls* means they bare the *soles* of their feet to him. This may appear to be a simple pun, but it's not (see chapter 7 for further analysis of this example).

Think about it for a moment. We must ask, why these particular words were combined into this particular phrase? There were many other words and phrases that could have been used (i.e., selected) to express the meaning she was expressing: that his patients tell him lots of personal things about themselves. The similar sounds then used in her narrative are not simply puns. Their meaning is created by using similar sounds. Indeed, it's the sound of meaning. Puns have been given a bad rap.[3] They can, in fact, be a window into the complex tandem workings of our minds (see chapter 7). There are levels of meaning, one literal in which each single concern creates a number of unconscious or subliteral variations that can be mapped (see below) and stacked upon each other in a mental matrix (see Figure 1).

These unconscious meanings may begin unconsciously and slip into conscious awareness, just as in slips of the tongue (Freudian slips), or what, in this chapter, I call slips of the mind. Just as with the concept of the unconscious, that slips of the tongue have meaning wasn't invented by Freud. They were long noted in literature, and he acknowledged this fact. Often, it seems, a person or a circumstance comes to nearly usurp the identity of a idea or the meaning of a word. Freud's genius was in recognizing their importance for a study of the mind. Despite this historical reality, the terms unconscious mind and slips of the tongue have become welded to Freud's name.

The phrase slips of the mind first occurred to me when I was pondering puns and slips of the tongue in relation to the unconscious mind. Then the analogous idea, *slips of the mind,* occurred to me. Indeed, what I have come to call subliteral language is a kind of slip of the mind. The question is, why did this concept occur to me at this particular time?

The semantic association based on the similarity of pun-like sounds and slips of the tongue is reasonably clear. There were other conditions, however, that precipitated my association as I soon found out when I started thinking about it. At the time the phrase *slips of the mind* occurred to me, I was thumbing through the many little yellow 2 × 3 inch *slips* of paper that I always kept with me to write down ideas and insights which often popped into my head at the oddest times. Indeed, I was physically working with "slips" of the mind. Because I have a computer and personal digital memo pad now, I no long need to keep those slips of paper.

Yet another crazy slip of the mind, as it were, occurred while I was a graduate student. While taking graduate seminars, I frequently had these

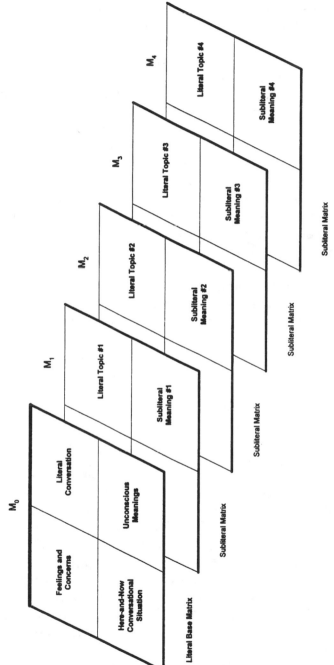

FIGURE 1. General transformational topic matrices.

little yellow slips of paper spread in front of me. I was constantly shifting through them and springing forward to write something down before I forgot the idea. From time to time, I was aware of the other students and the professor looking at me rather strangely. One day, seemingly out of nowhere and apparently unconnected to his lecture, the professor began to talk about a crazy colleague he once knew. It seemed that whenever anyone went to his office his desk was strewn with pieces of paper that he wrote upon—even while people were talking to him. The professor's story was a subliteral reference to my little slips of paper. Indeed, the professor's story itself was a slip of his mind. Although it may seem that the professor's remark was conscious, from the context of the situation, it didn't seem to be.

These double meanings can't be explained as simply slips of the tongue because slips of the tongue are merely the physical delivery mechanism for expressing slips of the mind. Now it's perhaps becoming clear that talk has meaning other than the apparent and intended literal meaning of the speaker and by listening subliterally you can recognize the hidden feelings and opinions that people have but won't tell you. This can be very useful. But fair warning: Some of what you will hear may be things that "even your best friends won't tell you." Indeed, some things you many not want to hear (see Concluding Ethical Postscript at the end of this book).

What may not be clear at this point is how our mind uses language to create these slips of meaning. To explain these slips of the mind, we need to take a brief excursion into understanding the nature of language, not Freudian psychoanalysis, for it's here that we will find the operations that make subliteral meaning and create slips of the mind.

HOW SLIPS OF THE MIND ARE MADE

As a general introduction to the way the mind uses language to make meaning and to produce these slips of the mind, we need to understand the three basic components of language, semantics, phonology, and syntax.

Semantics is the study of the relationships between words and their meanings. We have a large store of words and their meanings, which we have learned through the years, called a lexicon. A lexicon is a dictionary in our minds from which we select the appropriate word to express an intended meaning. Most words have many meanings. This is called polysemy. Words come to have meaning by being repeatedly connected or associated with past experience. Some word concepts acquire meanings by comparing their meaning to other similar concepts and situations. Typically this is called metaphor. Other words have acquired meaning by their similarity of sound. This similarity of sound brings us to phonology.

Phonology is the study of the elementary sounds (like "ba" for the letter b) that make up a language and the rules of their distribution and patterning that govern pronunciations. On a less elementary level, the sound of an entire word can be similar to a word that has a different meaning. For example, words like *knight* and *night* are called homophones. Semantics and phonology mutually influence each other (as I explain later). How we put meaning (semantics) and sound (phonology) together involves syntax.

Syntax is the study of the rules by which words or other elements of sentence structure are combined to form what we call grammatical sentences (the term grammar is a broader term including the arrangement of words, the combination of their component parts, and sometimes includes pronunciation and meaning).

I should point out that in applying the linguistic concepts of semantics, phonology, and syntax to explain how slips of the mind are created, I have extended the rather narrow and traditional meaning given to them by the field of linguistics. Strictly speaking, although the concept of phonology deals with elementary sounds and their permissible combinations, these elementary sounds carry no semantic meaning. I have raised the concept of phonology to a higher order or level, however, to include the sounds of whole words as in homophones and the sounds involved in puns.

Similarly, I have extended the concept of syntax to include what I have termed syntactic metaphor.[4] In the structural linguistics of Noam Chomsky, is there is no such concept as syntactic metaphor, nor is there any recognition of metaphor except as a deviant form of language. Typically a metaphor is called a figure of speech in which a word or phrase that ordinarily designates one thing is used to designate another, as in the phrase "an ocean of lies" or in Shakespeare's famous example, "All the world's a stage." After constant use, metaphorical meaning fades and comes to be seen as literal language. The phrases, "I *see* your *point,*" or "I *caught* your meaning," are considered literal language. No one (except some schizophrenics, and others with damage to the language areas of their brain) would actually take these phrases to mean that the listener physically "saw" or reached out and "caught" the meaning as it flew by.

What I call syntactic metaphor can be illustrated by taking the Dutch proverb, "We are too soon old and too late smart," and using its form or structure to say, "a metaphor is too soon worn and too late appreciated." I call this syntactic metaphor because in this statement I have transferred the syntactic structure, not the meaning of the Dutch proverb, to my statement. In syntactic metaphor, our unconscious accesses structure not meaning. I show later how subliteral meaning uses syntax metaphorically.

Traditionally, semantics, phonology, and syntax were all considered separate and therefore did not interact and influence each other. As I discovered early in my analysis of subliteral language in my small group laboratory, semantic meaning influences syntax.[5] In recent years, linguists, such as Ronald Langacker, George Lakoff, and Mark Johnson,[6] have also shown that meaning (semantics) affects syntax. This is now generally accepted by most linguists. Moreover, philosophers of language, such as Paul Ricoeur,[7] also maintain that these three components of language affect each other and also operate on the levels of meaning that I am suggesting.

I should point out here that much of what we think we are just discovering about the way language works is, in fact, not entirely new. As I show in Part II of this book, along the way to becoming what we think of as rational, logical, and high tech beings, we either lost, ignored, or misplaced valuable knowledge that we now have to reconstruct in order to understand subliteral meaning and conversations. "Progress" often doesn't proceed in a straight line. Sometimes, as a recent movie title indicated, we have to go back to the future.

So, how does all of this apply to slips of the mind? Semantically, the examples I gave about the topics of *CIA, FBI, God, policeman,* and *child/parent* relationships can be seen as unconscious *metaphors* about authority relationships. In other words, a CIA or FBI agent, a, boss, a policeman, a parent, or a God, all carry the same meaning: They are authorities. Within our semantic lexicon each of these particular words is linked to a higher order or superordinate category. On this level they are interchangeable semantically. Thus, we can use any one of them in describing any other one. Similarly the topic of identical *twins* is unconsciously connected to lexical items that refer to sets of "twos." Having two trainers in a T-group is unconsciously connected to the lexical item "twins" in our mental dictionary. The item *twins* can be broken down into subcategories each of which contains certain descriptions of things double, like pairs or duets, which then can be further broken down into particular descriptions of a given pair. Then, these unconscious templates can be matched or mapped (see later) onto people in one's surroundings. This is exemplified by the illustration given previously where the physical description of the two *Smith Brothers* on the cough drop package, where one has a reddish beard, and one a black beard, matched the description of myself and my cotrainer.

In terms of phonology, the example of my fiancee's mother at her podiatrist's office accessing similar sound meanings, allowed her unconscious mind to equate baring ones *soul* to baring ones *sole*. A more complicated example is that where my wife remarked on a fence with a *broken spoke*. This was a subliteral comment on my stumbling over words, mispronouncing them, and repeating syllables. Like homonymous terms, the word *spoke* can also mean speech, as in "he *spoke*." The semantic selection of the word *broken* was used "metaphorically" to refer to my stumbling, mispronouncing, and repeating syllables. The particular order of the words in my wife's statement are an example of how syntax creates meaning. Instead of saying, *"There's a fence with a broken spoke,"* she could have said, "There's a slat broken in that fence," or "Look at that busted fence," or "Look at that busted fence spoke," or a host of other word orders. But these arrangements of word order would not have done the job of the intended subliteral meaning. Thus, a particular phrase is selected from our semantic and phonological lexicon, and ordered in a particular way because it best expresses an unconscious thought or feeling. Puns are a paradigm that serve as a model for creating subliteral meaning.

I was recently watching a program called "Burden of Proof," on CNN.[8] Roger Cossack, one of the hosts of the program, made a slip of the tongue or speech error. In talking about President Clinton testifying before a grand jury, he meant to say that it was "unprecedented," but he slipped and clearly began to say, "unPresidented." Linguists would say that this is caused by confusing the similar sound and spelling of the two words which interfere with each other. Look closely at the spelling of "unprecedented," and "unPresidented." This not a meaningless speech error caused by the similar sound of the two words. The slip has meaning. The context of the program and the previous number of programs were about the possible impeachment of Clinton because of charges of perjury. The slip "unPresidented" in this case refers to being removed from his office or impeached, that is, unPresidented, as in "unseated" or coming "unhinged." Without access to the personal views of Roger Cossack, however, there is no way of assessing the deeper subliteral motivations of this slip, i.e., whether Cossack believes that Clinton should or will be impeached as the result of the scandal (see chapter 7 for more detail).

On another recent CNN program,[9] Wolf Blitzer reported that President Clinton's team of lawyers was about to launch an attack on Ken Starr's grand jury report that Clinton's lied about his affair with a young White House intern. Wolf meant to say that Clinton's team was about to go on the *offensive* against the material in the report, but he slipped and said they were about to engage in *offenses*. Is this just a simple slip of the tongue, or is it a slip of the mind? I suggest it's the latter. Given the continuous reportage of Clinton's alleged sexual behavior that many people find *offensive*, Wolf's slip was perhaps clear about what he was really thinking about Clinton's behavior. They were *offenses* that were *offensive*. Wolf, of course, immediately caught what he had really said.

Looking back on it, in my coining the term "slips of the mind," both semantic and syntactic considerations were operating. Most everyone, of course, has heard of slips of the tongue and Freudian slips. As I described above, conceptually, I combined slips of the tongue, Freudian slips, and an unconscious pun on the word *slips*. My unconscious lexicon includes slips as slipping on a banana and, of course, slips as in slips of the tongue. It also includes slips as in slips of paper. But it gets even deeper. A slip also means a particular piece of women's undergarments, which are often made of silk. In writing on my little slips of paper, I was making notes about subliteral sexual examples. Then, as I was thinking about Freudian slips, a joke popped into my mind, that Freudian slips are made of silk and lace. Syntactically, the question is why did I not first come up with "mind slips?" The answer is that a mind slip doesn't mean the same thing as a slip of the mind. First, the phrase *slips of the mind* is what I called previously a syntactic metaphor based on the same word order as *slips of the tongue*. Slips of the tongue in the popular vocabulary has come to mean (thanks to Freud) unconscious meaning slipping out by a "mistake" of language.[10] The concept mind slips associate more with accidents, as in the popular youth vernacular of a short time back, "mind skips." Thus unconscious semantics influenced unconscious syntax to create the exact meaning my mind evidently wanted. This is, indeed, the stuff of poetry.

But slips of the mind don't just inform us of other peoples' unconscious feelings and thoughts. As I just demonstrated, by understanding what I call the subliteral mind, it can also help us understand our own unconscious thoughts and feelings. Another example of learning about oneself using subliteral analysis occurred when a colleague and I were discussing the validity of a piece of subliteral talk. He was quite skeptical and was advancing what I considered were irrelevant arguments. My feeling was that he just didn't understand, that, unlike myself, he was new at it, but I didn't say this to him. In frustration, I decided to show him part of an article I had written that outlined some of the principles for establishing the validity of my subliteral material. So, I said to him, "Look, let's start over again. For beginners, let me show you an article of mine on the issue of validity."

Again, the question is why did I select the particular phrasing, "For beginners?" The phrase *"for beginners"* literally meant, "to start with" or "for openers." Subliterally, however, it revealed my feelings that he was new at understanding subliteral material, a novice, *a beginner.* I could have said, "to begin with" or "to begin" or "beginning again," but these phrases would not have expressed my feelings as did the phrase, "For beginners."

Unconscious meaning in conversations can be heard almost everywhere at almost any time. An interesting place to see and hear unconscious meaning is on TV news and talk shows. In a TV news item about the former executive producer of a program called "Police Story," the announcer said that in filming the show the producer *shot for 104 straight days.* It's no accident that the title "Police Story" is followed by the sentence, *shot for 104 straight days.* "Police Story" conjures up the association with guns, hence, *shots.* Although the title "Police Story" is literal, it might be asked why the numerical phrase *104 straight days* was selected for the news item? Is it coincidence that "Police Story" frequently signed off by hearing a voice over a police radio using the code *10-4?* I think not. Whether or not the writer of this piece knew it, notwithstanding, the language exuded subliteral processing. Unlike other examples, however, the meaning that resulted from this analysis was not exactly profound. Not all subliteral narratives are profound in communicating information. Nevertheless, they are important. Their importance is that they show the subliteral mind working, albeit perhaps with no particular place to go. In not going anywhere meaningful, they still demonstrate the operations by which subliteral meaning is made.

Unlike news programs where the language is scripted, talk shows are verbally unstructured, or at least the tele-prompts leave a great deal of latitude for conversations to occur spontaneously. This spontaneity creates conditions for unconscious meanings to seep out. In the give and take of talk show conversation, egos may get hurt and strong feelings that are socially taboo to express openly may show themselves in the unconscious and double meaning of the talk. Indeed, talk *shows.*

A case in point: One evening the comedian Steve Allen was guest host on the Johnny Carson *Tonight Show.* When I tuned into the show, Steve was talking to a young male concert violinist. The violinist said he had been playing violin since he was seven years old. It was evident that the young violinist was a virtuoso. It was also evident that he was trying to project an image of a normal male and not a virtuoso geek. One of the guests asked him to display his hands. The guest said that the violinist's hand looked just like everyone else's hands, except that the muscle between the thumb and forefinger seemed larger as a result of playing the violin everyday for years. The young violinist quickly retorted that he had strong arm muscles, too, and proceeded to flex his biceps in the traditional macho way. All this was done quite seriously. The young virtuoso was probably too used to having his masculinity impugned.

In response to the virtuoso flexing his arm muscles, one of the guests, who was a well-known comedian (I believe it was Don Rickles), then said *"Gee, wouldn't it be awful to have to tell someone that you'd been beaten up by a violinist."* The put-down, of course, was that violinists are somewhat less than masculine. Strong feelings were obviously being generated. There was a slight anxious pause, as no one wanted to deal any further with this statement. At such times people quickly change the topic. Then, the young violinist turned to Steve Allen and asked, *"Were you ever made fun of when you were in school, like for wearing glasses?"* This was undoubtedly meant as a change in the topic of conversation. And in a sense it was. But just as undoubtedly, it contained unconscious meaning. The question, *"Were you ever made fun of when you were in school, like for wearing glasses?"* unconsciously meant, *"I have just been made fun of."* Because Steve Allen is an accomplished pianist, the young violinist obviously identified with Steve, selecting Steve's "other deviation," his thick eyeglasses.

Always watch for what immediately follows an embarrassing silence. After such silences, what appears to be a change of topic is not really a change of topic at all. The unconscious meaning of the original topic continues beneath the apparent topic change. Such a topic change is frequently an unconscious comment on the preceding discussion. So what we have is a change of literal language, not a change in the unconscious meaning of the topic. At this point, you may have noticed that the young violinist's question to Steve Allen, *"Were you ever made fun of when you were in school, like for wearing glasses,"* in response to the comedian's *"Gee, wouldn't it be awful to have to tell someone that you had been beaten up by a violinist"* may not have been an unconscious statement. Rather, the young violinist may have been quite aware of what he was saying, but I don't think it was the case.

Words are vague and ambiguous, always leaving room for other meanings. This is true even for understanding meaning in literal conversations. Unlike words, however, numbers are quite precise and much less open to interpretation. I have repeatedly found that, like words, numbers that are selected for topics of conversation also can represent unconscious meanings. For example, it's no coincidence that the repeated occurrence of the number 5 occurs in a conversation where only *five* members are extremely active or dominant or the repeated occurrence of the number *14* when the conversational situation is composed of *fourteen* members, only to have the number change to *13* after a member leaves the conversation for an appointment. Unlike words, these literal "figures of speech" have precise and concrete referents for their unconscious meanings. In this example, the referent is the subgroup of five. This is not the stuff of ancient or New Age numerology; it's verifiable (See chapter 5 and Appendix).

Unconscious meaning is often consciously programmed into advertisements, too. I recall a rather cute ad for dog food. But as I'll suggest, if my analysis of the unconscious meaning in the ad is correct, it ends up not being quite so cute. Many pet owners want the best for their pets. In a TV commercial about dog food, a little old lady who looked like everybody's hot-apple-pie-home-made-bread grandmother was extolling the virtues of a particular brand of dog food that looked like hamburger. The white-haired grandmother says, "It's better than hamburger." At the close of the commercial she adds in a surprised tone of voice, "Better than hamburger, my word!"

Now, aside from the more obvious association of the product with an all-American grandmother figure that leads to the conclusion that the dog food is better than hamburger, and also thereby more patriotic, the ad is a masterpiece of construction. The literal meaning of the phrase "better than hamburger, my word!" translated, would be "my goodness, it's better than hamburger." And how are we to know it's better than hamburger? We know that because hot-apple-pie-grandmothers are true to their word, as indeed is indicated by the last words of the ad. Thus, there is a subliteral level meaning of the phrase "better than hamburger . . . my word." The only thing better than this hamburger is her *word*. But there's another subliteral meaning that the advertiser is communicating. With just a little thought, now the question arises, how does she really know the dog food is better than hamburger—unless, of course, she has eaten it! Now, before you say, "this is ridiculous," consider the contextual fact that when the ad appeared, there had been news stories about poor elderly people eating dog and cat food to survive. Was this ad for dog food then subliterally directed at the elderly?

As I indicated at the opening of this chapter, ostensibly random or small talk has been considered by most researchers as a kind of "quantum" process, that is, that such talk is not subject to a Newtonian-like lawfulness as is most of the universe around us, including our biological, chemical, genetic, neuronal, and linguistic selves. There is no *a priori* reason, however, why the human mind and our conversations should be any less structured and lawful than the rest of nature. Indeed, as in physics, why should there not be cognitive "quarks" of the mind, fundamental meaning-structures from which all others are generated? Indeed, this book is based on the Einsteinian assumption that "god does not play dice," that our mental universe is just as ordered as our physical universe and is not the result of chance.

SUBLITERAL MEANING

Now, increasing research on unconscious processes is beginning to emerge from the study of language and from cognitive science research that points to unconscious meaning. I describe this fascinating story of understanding the psychoanalytic and the cognitive unconscious mind in more detail in chapter 8. In the meantime, let me illustrate the linguistic framework for what I call subliteral meaning.

LANGUAGE AND MIND

To avoid endless interpretations, I have adapted the framework of modern linguistics, called generative grammar, that was created by Noam Chomsky (b. 1928), the renowned linguist. Chomsky revolutionized the study of language in his book, *Syntactic Structures,*[11] and its relationship to cognitive psychology in his book, *Language and Mind.*[12] According to Chomsky, language is made possible by innate structures that generate all languages and all possible grammatically correct sentences.[13] More important, for subliteral meaning, however, is his notion of the surface and deep structures of sentences and their multiple cognitive or semantic representations. For example, the following classic sentences demonstrate such multiple internal representations and meanings that underlie a single surface structure of a sentence:

1. *Surface structure:* The shooting of the hunters bothered him.
   Representation 1: The killing of the hunters bothered him.
   Representation 2: The sound of the hunters shooting their guns bothered him.
2. *Surface structure:* Flying airplanes can be dangerous.
   Representation 1: Flying in airplanes can be dangerous.
   Representation 2: Airplanes flying in the air above you can be dangerous.

Many sentences have this surface structure and multiple deep structures or internal representations—what Chomsky has called deep structure ambiguity—from which multiple meanings are generated. Thus, sentences have a surface or literal meaning and a deep structure that in my adaptation may generate subliteral meaning.

In the example cited previously, where my wife and I gave our guests the "grand tour" of our newly renovated cottage, and one of the guests told a story about attending a party a few weeks previous, saying that the hosts of that party that *"only had the party to show off their redecorating work,"* my interpretation of the guest's subliteral meaning of that statement was that my wife and I just had the party to show off our renovations. Put into the previous linguistic framework, this statement looks like this:

Surface structure: they had the party only to show off their redecorating work.

Literal Representation 1: The hosts of the party we had attended a few weeks ago had the party only to show off their redecorating work.

Subliteral Representation 2: You are having this party only to show off your newly renovated cottage.

In addition to the parallel situation of hosts having a party after completing renovations, the pronoun *they* is the ambiguous element in the sentence that can be cognitively used to link two different representations (see Appendix, 6.6. Pronoun Operations).

In adapting Chomsky's linguistic framework, I should mention a number of very significant differences. First, structural linguistics does not deal with metaphorical language and symbolic meaning very well. Second, underlying representations do not reflect intentional and motivational (psychodynamic) processes. Moreover, unlike structural linguistics, my adaptation takes issue with the standard distinction between literal versus figurative language. I address this latter issue in more detail later.

THE SUBLITERAL UNCONSCIOUS

In addition to my concept of the subliteral to replace the linguistic term metaphor and the psychoanalytic concepts of latent and symbolic, I developed the concept of the subliteral unconscious to carve out a more concrete and specific set of processes from the the nearly all-meaningful notion of an unconscious mind.

That much of our linguistic processes are unconscious is not new. It's universally accepted, for example, that most of our normal use of language is not conscious. As we speak, we are unaware of the hundreds of rules of grammar that we use. Nor can most of us render them conscious if we tried—mainly because we didn't learn most them consciously. The grammar we learned in school is only a minute portion of the total number of syntactic structures. But there is more to unconscious language processes than mere syntactic rules.

In the subliteral mind, these unconscious language processes are linked to emotional and feeling processes. But these feelings are not simply raw feelings. They exhibit primitive cognitive structures (see chapter 6). Together, subliteral language and an underlying specific set of unconscious perceptions and cognitive operations that I have found in my research constitute what I call the subliteral mind. So the subliteral mind is not a vague black hole in the mind as much theorizing about the unconscious is. Moreover, and contrary to most cognitive science research and classic psychoanalytic theory, the subliteral unconscious "thinks" and "reasons" just like our conscious mind.

Accordingly, I would like to point out that though this book is clearly about hidden meaning in everyday language and how to recognize it, in describing this process my intent is to introduce linguistic and cognitive operations that have not been generally recognized, and also, more importantly, to introduce a new view of the mind. I would like to note that the purpose of my research and findings about small group conversation have always been secondary to their implications for perception, cognition, and the way the mind works. As we will see later, even conscious conversation is not so simple.

INTERPRETATION: OF HERMENEUTICS AND HERMENAUTS

At this point, I need to say a few words about the way we understand what words mean in everyday conversations. In the beginning, we are told in *Genesis,* was the Word—but unfortunately, its meaning didn't come with it. Meaning creation is born of our interpretation of the word. Spoken words, by themselves, are simply arbitrary sequences of sounds in search of meaning. Similarly, written words are merely a sequence of arbitrary marks or scratches in search of coherence. Only through constant and consistent association and social agreement do arbitrary sounds and scratches come to have consensual meaning. Even so, the everyday agreed upon meaning taps only a small proportion of those associations and agreements.

Furthermore, the socially agreed upon meaning of those sounds and scratches is not all that precise. We make our meaning, as the conversation between Alice and Humpty Dumpty in Lewis Carroll's *Through the Looking Glass,* suggests,

> "When I use a word," Humpty Dumpty said in rather a scornful tone, "it means just what I choose it to mean—neither more nor less."
> "The question is," said Alice, "whether you CAN make words mean so many different things."
> "The question is," said Humpty Dumpty, "which is to be master—that's all."[14]

Thus, the meaning of the words that we use in conversation are in constant need of interpretation in the specific context in which they are used. Males mean one thing by certain words, and females may mean another. Similarly, people in different socioeconomic classes and ethnic groups may mean different things by the same word.

A particular profession, too, may mean specific things when using certain words compared to people who are not members of the profession. When writing this book, my editor kept e-mailing me to be less "clinical." I didn't understand what he meant. Although I talked about Freud a little, I used no examples from psychotherapy. So I removed most of the psychological jargon. He still e-mailed me back, saying, "don't be so clinical." I was becoming very impatient. At that point, I went to the dictionary, thinking, "I'll fix him, I'll send him the definition of clinical." Lo and behold, one of the meanings was being too objective and analytical. Now I understood what he meant. When someone says "clinical" to a psychologist, it is automatically associated with a psychotherapeutic issue.

The specific context—the unique situation—in which a given piece of talk occurs acts as a rule that tells us its meaning in a particular context. Though we are typically not aware of it, we have to interpret the simplest everyday statements. For example, the statement, "I am going to get into the *pool*" means little by itself. It can mean (a) I am going to get into the *swimming pool,* (b) I am going to join the *football pool,* or (c) Join the *car pool,* etc., depending on the context in which the statement is made. When we utter such a sentence, the conditions surrounding the conversation act as a rule to inform us which meaning should be selected out of the many possible meanings. Obviously, if it's 98 degrees outside and you are sitting beside a private swimming pool, you can safely assume that the person who made the statement is not talking about a baseball pool. Or take the statement, "Well done." What does this statement mean? Without context, it means nothing. Now, what if we know that the statement was made in the context of discussing food. It could still mean two different things. First it could mean "well done," as in "you did a good job." Or it could mean, "I would like my food cooked nicely," or that I want my meat cooked thoroughly. We are always interpreting meaning.

On an everyday level, the rules that allow us to make interpretations are taken for granted. We interpret automatically, using our own frame of reference. Usually it's only when nonstandard meanings are derived from a piece of talk that we become aware of the process of interpreting that meaning. Thus, all of our talk requires interpretation, and interpretation requires that we know the context in which the words are spoken. It has always been so since the beginning of language.

Since ancient times, layman and researchers alike have been concerned with the meaning of the spoken and written word in terms of its so-called surface meaning and also in terms of "hidden" or "symbolic" meaning. The discipline of interpretation is called hermeneutics. The word had its origins in biblical exegesis with the interpretation of Christian scriptures. More precisely, hermeneutics is the study of the rules of establishing the "correct" meaning of a text. Hermeneutic comes from the Greek word *hermeneutikos,* which means to interpret. In Greek mythology Hermes was a minor god who carried *The Word* from on high down to the people. He was a messenger of meaning, hence, hermeneutics.

In a very real sense we are all messengers of meaning. We interpret the words we hear. We are hermenauts exploring semantic space. Understanding everyday conversations is not a simple process, especially when we leave the standard expectations and assumptions surrounding a piece of talk. In leaving the security of standard, consensually agreed upon meaning, the ambiguity of a piece of talk becomes evident, and the awareness of the complexity by which we derive meaning also stands out in bold relief. Then, the problem is figuring out the rules to interpret correctly what we are hearing. For example, how do we know that the literal meaning of the word "twins" in a conversation also subliterally refers to the two dominant members in the conversation? Or how do we know when a seemingly literal conversation of "movie personalities" is subliterally about certain people in the conversation? How we can know these meanings is what this book is about.

Each conversation, then, requires a hermeneutic journey into a meaning universe, it's a trip into the far reaches of the associative orbits of our semantic space. Like Hermes, we all must be linguistic astronauts traveling unchartered subliteral universes in search of meaning. We are constantly engaging in a kind of intersemantic navigation. But we will not be able to find our way among the myriad of meanings if we analyze conversation in modern linguistic terms. Even though the small group function is primarily oral, research on group conversations has been analyzed as if it were "written," that is, as if it were regulated by "correct," well thought out, and logical rules of traditional grammar. As I show throughout this book, my subliteral method requires analyzing verbal utterances from the perspective of oral tradition (see chapter 7).

This bias to understand oral discourse as if were written speech is, however, not universal. It's generally true of Western/European culture, the highly educated, and certainly of academics and scientists. But certain subcultures may be returning to a kind of oral tradition. Perhaps beginning with the first TV generation of youth, we are seeing the effects of an oral tradition of sorts. These youths are weaned on thousands of hours of visual and oral material, not to mention teenage music, where meaning orally delivered in the lyrics resembles a kind of oral tradition poetry. Many of these youths find reading difficult and simply don't understand the printed word very well. Other subcultures remain largely within an oral tradition.

Let me illustrate with a story from my small group dynamics course, where 10–15 students learn about the dynamics of groups by functioning as a discussion group and where students verbally interact to a high degree. With one exception, the group membership was composed of middle-class, white students. The one exception was a bright young Cherokee female from a reservation in Oklahoma. When she would talk, most of the group could be seen rolling their eyes—nonverbally saying, "oh, here she goes again." What the group was reacting to was her constant storytelling during group conversation. The group became bored whenever she engaged in storytelling.

Because I understood why she told stories, I intervened at an appropriate time and asked the group to analyze and discuss this dynamic. The group members' first response was that they didn't see what "all these stories have to do with interpersonal communication and group dynamics." At my request, the Cherokee student proceeded tell the group that a great deal of teaching, learning, and relating in her culture was done by using stories and that if they would look at the stories they would see that they were like metaphors and analogies about the group and its interaction. In the oral tradition, stories are the instructional method of choice. Even knowing this, the group had a difficult time "translating" these stories into something that they could understand. Now the question is, so what? What use is all this clever analysis of subliteral stories, anyway?

THE USEFULNESS AND IMPORTANCE
OF THE SUBLITERAL MIND

IN EVERYDAY LIFE

Other than perhaps finding unconscious meanings fascinating, the phenomenon is useful in everyday life for understanding how the mind works. As I briefly mentioned in the introduction, there are many situations in everyday life where information about the social situation is difficult or impossible to obtain. Information regarding individual concerns, feelings, and attitudes may be intentionally (or unintentionally) withheld because of social taboos and the many rules of social etiquette. At work, fear of the "boss" or certain co-workers or the reward system may lead to withholding the true feelings that people have about one another.

Subliteral communications are a kind of coded message, and learning to understand and decode them can function as a kind of personal "surveillance" system that gathers interpersonal "intelligence" data. Our subliteral brain/mind is a bioelectronic detection device for picking up and monitoring people's underlying feelings and concerns. In addition, you can also learn to tune in on your own unconscious feelings and attitudes about people and situations by listening to yourself talk. As I noted previously, our conscious, literal talk leaves traces of underlying feelings and concerns. It's a psychological equivalent of the physicists "bubble chamber" where traces of unconscious particles of thought and meaning can be tracked and analyzed, just as physicists track subatomic particles. Thus, it is useful in finding out what's going on, in finding out what your spouse, your boss, or your friends are not saying, or what they are "really" saying and feeling. In short, my method is a new and useful interpersonal and cognitive skill.

IN THERAPEUTIC SETTINGS

My subliteral method can also be used to train mental health therapists and counselors, engaged in individual cognitive-behavioral, psychodynamic, or group therapy. The importance of the metaphors that clients use in psychotherapy have been recognized for some time.[15] As in everyday life, the method can provide therapists with valuable information about patients' unconscious attitudes, feelings and thoughts that patients may not want to reveal or of which they are not even aware. To use a phrase from Freud, the subliteral method can be a "royal road to the unconscious."

Freud originally used dreams and hypnosis to access a patient's unconscious but soon gave up on this method. Then, he switched to free association, which some psychoanalysts still use. Compared to my subliteral method, free association is like trying to put together the scrambled pieces of an abstract painting puzzle. More importantly, perhaps, recognition of these unconscious processes may also turn out to be a unique and powerful therapeutic method. I address this latter possibility in chapter 12 where I explain the new psychotherapy of the psychiatrist Robert Langs.

A great number of social and psychological support groups have sprung up over the years. There are literally thousands across the country. Most of these groups have conversations about problems and issues that their members have. These range from Alcoholic Anonymous groups, to single parent groups, to just simply people who want to talk about life and hear others do the same. These groups are made to order for applying my subliteral method. Whether as a counselor or as a member, listening subliterally in these groups can reveal a wealth of useful information not revealed consciously that can help individuals. Likewise listening subliterally can be useful for those who manage, lead, or take part in the increasing number of small groups or teams used in the business world

IN PRACTICAL RESEARCH

In addition to the everyday importance of subliteral phenomena, the discovery of the subliteral mind has rich research implications for understanding and discovering aspects of language and mind that we didn't know and as a method for unobtrusively acquiring information. For example, one of the long-standing problems in social psychology (and other areas) involves the use of questionnaires to assess people's attitudes and preferences. Responses to questions are notoriously unreliable measures of what people really think. People often give answers that they think are expected. In addition, what they think their attitudes or beliefs are often do not reflect what they actually do. For example, who are going to admit—perhaps even to themselves these days—that they have racial and gender prejudices? As a consequence , social psychologists have begun to develop what are called "unobtrusive methods" of measuring attitudes, i.e., methods that assess attitudes without the person being aware that they are being assessed.[16] My subliteral method is, in fact, an unobtrusive method for assessing what people "really" think without them knowing that they are revealing anything, and thus their "answers" are less subject to conscious distortions.

Another important area involves research into everyday phenomena, not just laboratory experiments. Cognitive science has virtually ignored everyday phenomena. Despite the lack of such research, some cognitive scientists have recognized this need. For example, Donald Norman, the well-known cognitive scientist at the University of California at San Diego, suggested years ago that "cognitive scientists as a whole ought to make more use of evidence from . . . cognitive sociology, and anthropology and from clinical studies of the human. These must be accompanied, of course, with the study of language."[17]

More recently, Jerome Bruner of Harvard University, one of the grand figures in psychology, notes in his book *Acts of Meaning*, that "The cognitive revolution as originally conceived virtually required that psychology join forces with anthropology and linguistics, philosophy and history, even with the discipline of law."[18] He also calls for studying everyday language, emphasizing that "I have been at great pains to argue (and will argue further later in this chapter) that one of the most ubiquitous and powerful discourse forms in human communication is narrative,"[19] that is, conversations. The linguistic study of subliteral narratives can provide important data for the future understanding of the way the mind works. It basically remains, as Blumenthal once put it, that "Today, the 'psycho-' has too often been left out of psycholinguistics"[20] and, it might be added, out of the study of language and mind.

Colin Martindale, too, a cognitive psychologist at the University of Maine, has suggested that "a viable science of cognition cannot restrict itself to explaining the mental activities of waking rational subjects in psychological laboratories. . . . we need mental activity in all its forms," including the "irrational thought of the poet."[21] In this regard, Bernard Baars, in his book reviewing what has come to be called the cognitive revolution in psychology emphasizes that psychology is a "natural bridge" to the humanities. He concludes by saying, "Scientific psychologists must have a commitment to hard evidence, but at the same time they are interested primarily in the content of the humanities: human knowledge, consciousness, feelings, imagination."[22] And Howard Gardner, psychologist and author of many well-known books, has asked "whether various forms of human irrationality—those documented by clinicians . . . or by anthropologists . . . can be elucidated by the methods of cognitive science."[23] Despite these pleas, the situation in cognitive science hasn't changed much since these early statements. There is virtually no mainstream cognitive science research on these everyday issues—and certainly none on subliteral language. Subliteral phenomena are still viewed as too anomalous, not to mention, weird.

Although subliteral narratives strain common sense and standard understanding of language and mental processes, so do many other anomalous phenomena that we yet do not comprehend. As the developmental psychologists Heinz Werner and Bernard Kaplan[24] pointed out in their classic book, *Symbol Formation,* ostensibly anomalous and atypical phenomena are often theoretically important. An example is the role of optical illusions in the field of perception or speech error in psycholinguistics. Research on both of these atypical phenomena have provided grounds for extending our knowledge about perception and language.

Only in abnormal states, such as schizophrenia, are strange verbal processes similar to those presented in this book occasionally recognized as lawful.[25] But even there, they are usually viewed as somehow different from normal processes. Subliteral analysis suggests that these linguistic anomalies, though atypical, are not anomalous but are rather clear cases through which the general underlying processes of mind and language can be seen.

Such uncommon pieces of language have been considered anomalous because there has been no systematic explanation or method for analyzing and validating them. In terms of language performance, subliteral narratives use many of the mechanisms involved in speech errors and action slips but suggest an underlying intentionality—in at least this class of subliteral "errors" and "slips." Recognizing this connection could provide grounds for beginning to integrate cognitive science and the field of linguistics with some long-established issues in psychodynamics, which involves conflicting thoughts and feelings that occur on a preconscious or unconscious level.

Virtually all linguists and cognitive scientists believe that Freudian slip type phenomena are linguistically lawful and therefore devoid of unconscious meaning. One notable exception is Bernard Baars, editor and author of *Experimental Slips and Human Error,* and his colleagues who have conducted some fascinating laboratory experiments on Freudian or unconsciously motivated slips. While he remains cautious, he leaves the door open on unconscious meaning. Baars, says, "From some of our findings. . . . the most immediate conclusion might be that the Freudian hypothesis is just plain wrong. But that is too simple."[26] He leaves the door open for possible new methods that may be less "blunt" (as he puts it) than current ones. I would, of course, strongly argue that my method is a new and less "blunt" method for investigating unconscious meaning.[27]

The findings, based on my methodology, suggest new knowledge about the mind, that reveal fundamental cognitive structures, which have not been generally recognized except in quasi-pathological states, such as dream processes, poetic thinking, slips of the tongue, and in the pathological language of schizophrenics. From a theoretical standpoint, an adequate explanation of human thought processes should simultaneously explain "abnormal" and the "normal." There should not be two different theories, one for abnormal functioning and one for normal.

A major theoretical implication of subliteral phenomena is the role of emotion (or affect) in cognition. The role of emotion in cognitive science research has had a controversial history.[28] Generally, emotion has been seen as separate from thinking. Jean Piaget, however, recognized that one of the most significant concerns of the social and behavioral sciences is "trying to characterize affective life in relation to cognitive functions [in so far as they relate to structure] and especially of defining their interrelation in the actual functioning of behavior."[29] As we will continue to see, the role of feelings in creating subliteral meaning is central.

Further methods and theoretical frameworks need to be developed in cognitive science to expand our understanding of subliteral phenomena and their relationships to areas already developed.[30] The approach to analyzing narratives presented here and some of the mechanisms discovered relate to the work of the philosopher Ernst Cassirer[31] and the anthropologist Claude Levi-Strauss[32] and to the general study of myths and mythological thinking found across various cultures. In addition, subliteral phenomena bear on the linguistic distinction between literal and figurative language. My findings suggest that the strict literal/figurative distinction is not psycholinguistically tenable, just as it's not tenable in much of poetic language.

Indeed subliteral narrative shares a commonality with the field of poetics and thus serves as a bridge to the humanities. We have much to learn about the mind. As the cognitive researchers Walter Weimer and David Palermo[33] observed in 1974, "the enormity of our ignorance conspires against us all. Perhaps the most important thing we can learn . . . is how little we know about the mind and its place in nature."

Finally, an area of significance is the research question of "ecological validity."[34] Ecological validity simply refers to research findings that are clearly related to everyday life, not just limited to the scientific laboratory. The subliteral data that I present in this book naturally occur in everyday sit-

uations and in the training or research setting of the small group laboratory. They, thus are ecologically valid.

In preparation for the many examples of subliteral talk in the following
chapters, it will be helpful to conclude this chapter with some initial principles and methods of recognizing when a conversation is subliteral.

RECOGNIZING SUBLITERAL CONVERSATIONS

INTRODUCTORY PRINCIPLES

Before proceeding to the rest of this book, it will be helpful to present
some introductory principles for recognizing and assessing whether the
subliteral material already mentioned and the wealth of examples in the
chapters to follow are "real" or are simply due to coincidence. During the
past twenty years, I have developed a systematic qualitative method divided
into fifteen major categories that have more than seventy separate cognitive
and linguistic procedures for parsing, analyzing, and validating subliteral
language and stories. This methodology provides the rules for parsing or
breaking down the components of the stories and the language used to tell
them. It also provides the rules for analyzing the parsed components, and
for establishing the validity of the parsing and analysis.[35]

In presenting the many illustrations in this book, however, it is impossible to apply my complete methodology to each one. To do so would make
this book too unwieldy, complex, and tedious. When it flows smoothly, I
note how the example given illustrates some aspect of this methodology.
I have included an outline of the complete methodological procedures
and operations for analyizing and validating of subliteral language in the
Appendix.

Although it's necessary to apply the methods carefully to each subliteral occurrence for research and to establish the validity of subliteral material, for everyday use, however, this may neither be possible nor necessary.
Once the principles and methods are understood, many subliteral instances
can be quickly evaluated.

Principle # 1: Conversational Conditions The optimal conditions for
generating subliteral material is one of low social structure, ambiguity, uncertainty, and anxiety. The more conversation floats freely, the more likely

it is that unconscious processes are activated and subliteral meaning is involved in the literal topics.

Principle # 2: Knowledge of the Situation   The more one knows about the conversational situation, i.e., the context, about the people in the situation, the issues, conflicts, expectations, etc., the better one can recognize subliteral talk.

Principle # 3: Affective Arousal   Under the previous conditions, when affective arousal levels are elevated, they create a cognitive state in which nonconscious affective schemas are activated that merge with and shape conscious literal linguistic schemas.

Principle # 4: Affective Loading   In addition to general affective arousal, subliteral material is optimally generated from specific, emotionally loaded issues and concerns.

Principle # 5: Social Censoring   The more social taboos, rules of etiquette, and other social rules that preclude the open expression of feeling and ideas, the more likely subliteral talk occurs.

Principle # 6: Silences   The more awkward silences and pauses in a conversation, the more likely subliteral talk occurs.

Principle # 7: Conflict   The more conscious or unconscious conflict that exists between or among members of a conversation, the more likely subliteral talk occurs.

Principle # 8: Association   A topic is often subliteral if it's associated in time, i.e., merely comes after another topic (especially after a silence or pause in the conversation)

Principle # 9: Topic Selection   Subliteral topics are "selected-in" because they relate to participants' feelings that occur in the conversation. It's important to recognize an incredible number of topics are possible in any conversation. The question is, out of all the possibilities, why are particular topics selected?

Principle # 10: Lexical Selection   In addition to the selection of topics, the selection of a given word or phrase also constitutes a choice from a large number of possible equivalent lexical (i.e., our mental dictionary of words with their associated morphemes and sounds) or semantic choices.

Principle # 11: Mapping   Subliteral material is present in a piece of literal discourse when it can be demonstrated that the talk has a dual structure which can be mapped onto the conversational setting (see Appendix, 1.1. Analogical Matching Operations, and 1 .2. Isomorphic Mapping Operations). For example, a literal conversation about

Representation 1.
(a)   four people in a bar,
(b)   two of whom are male and two female, who
(c)   are being boisterous, and who
(d)   are dominating the social interaction

can be hypothesized as subliteral when the membership composition and interaction in the conversation corresponds to the ostensibly literal story:

Representation 2.
(a')   four group members,
(b')   two of whom are male and two are female, who
(c')   are being boisterous, and who
(d')   are verbally dominating the group interaction

Having presented the general principles of how to recognize subliteral language, I now can turn to the next chapter. But first, a couple of important concluding points:

CONCLUSION

It's probably clear by now that there is always the danger of imputing unconscious meaning where it doesn't exist. Although this is true of analyzing the meaning of all linguistic communication, it's especially true for subliteral meaning. Admittedly, many of the illustrations presented and those still to come strain—almost to the breaking point—the bounds of what we think is reasonable and, also indeed, what we think is cognitively possible. I developed my methodology to guard against reading too much into the meaning of a piece of talk. Skeptics and critics of slips of the mind have to earn their naysaying by countering this methodology. It's not acceptable simply to say that it's all just a wild bunch of coincidences. I might note in this regard that the methods and procedures I have developed provide many more rules for analyzing subliteral meaning than we consciously have for analyzing the conscious meaning of everyday language.

As you read through the myriad of illustrations in this book, they can be read according to one's interest. *First,* they can simply and generally be read as interesting demonstrations of subliteral meaning. *Second,* they can be read as revealing, in important new ways, how we creatively use language. *Third,* they can be read as revealing group dynamics that might otherwise go unnoticed. *Fourth,* the subliteral meanings can be read as revealing a great deal about the underlying dynamics of social life. *Fifth*—and this is their seminal importance—they can be read as revealing how the subliteral unconscious mind works.

Finally, although some of the narratives are inherently humorous with others styled in a light-hearted manner, don't be fooled by this entertaining motif, for you will be witnessing some of the most profound operations of the human mind yet recognized.

CHAPTER 2

THE DISCOVERY OF SUBLITERAL MEANING

A PERSONAL AND SCIENTIFIC ODYSSEY

The discovery of the subliteral mind is one of the more fascinating—and it may turn out to be one of the more important—stories in the history of cognitive psychology. This chapter describes that discovery. There are a number of reasons for doing this. First, and most important, tracing its origins and development can help to understand subliteral phenomena. Contrary to much popular thinking, knowing the history of an idea is important to understanding it. Second, it's central for tracing the development and the evolution of the reasoning that gave rise to the subliteral mind, and thus to the history of ideas and the psychology of science, areas that have always fascinated me.

THE HUMAN SIDE OF DISCOVERY

The third reason to recount the discovery of the subliteral mind is to show that scientific discovery is often not the systematic and rational process that most textbooks make it out to be. Somewhat over simplified, the description of scientific discovery usually goes something like this: first develop a hypothesis (an educated guess, for example, as to how something works), then test it, and if it's confirmed, add it to an existing body of confirmed hypotheses, which then are used to formulate a theory. Once a theory is developed, then further hypotheses can be derived from the theory which then can be tested, and so on. It's in this step-by-step, methodical, and rational manner that scientists make great discoveries. This scheme is only generally correct, as historians and philosophers of science have shown.[1] If scientists simply thought up hypotheses and tested them one by one, important discoveries would be a long time in coming.

At best, standard textbook views actually describe what is called "normal science," not the process of making important discoveries. Normal science is what happens after an initial discovery, the hard work of testing and formulating a theory. The process leading up to significant discoveries is frequently a very personal and sometimes messy business. One only has to read the notebooks or the biographies of scientists like Darwin or Freud to see the actual process of discovery.

The fourth reason for recounting the process of discovery is to show the human side of science. In the Introduction, I noted that although Americans have an interest in science, they are woefully uninformed. A recent study by the National Science Foundation found that less than half of the population knows that the earth goes around the sun once a year.[2] This is serious. To many people, the picture of scientists in their laboratories, still often conjures up images of Mary Shelley's Dr. Frankenstein. I need only note the recent images of scientists who conduct research on gene therapy, fetal and organ transplants, including transplanting the human brain—which we legally prohibited in the 1960s.

Granted, the public image and status of psychologists as scientists is not like that of physicists. We don't have visually impressive instruments, like cyclotrons, that smash atoms apart, electron microscopes that magnify a bacterium millions of times, or laser beams used in industry for cutting metal and other important applications in communications and eye surgery, not to mention reading bar-codes in the supermarkets. Nor are psychologists even in the running for the Nobel prize, though we sometimes piggyback on the status of those who do become Nobel laureates. One example of piggybacking is the neurobiologist Roger Sperry whose work on the organization and functioning of the brain won him the Nobel prize. He is most well known, however, for his pioneering work in what is called split-brain research, where the corpus callosum, which connects the two cerebral hemispheres of the brain, is severed.[3]

Psychological discoveries are equally important, however, for the survival of the human species. Unfortunately, the public image of "the psychologist" is that of a "shrink," a psychotherapist, who with great intuitive powers discovers how the mind works. This image is a legacy from Freud, and nothing could be farther from the truth. First, most psychologists are not therapists. Secondly, most labor long and hard in the scientific trenches for their hard-earned knowledge.

In particular, the discovery of the subliteral mind is important for revealing things about the way the mind works that we didn't know before. Accordingly, the implications are enormous, as demonstrated by the strange set of cognitive operations that created all of the illustrations presented in this book. Like other innovations in psychology and science, the subliteral mind was not discovered sui generis, i.e., out of nothing. Although the historical and evolutionary roots of the subliteral mind go back to early philosophy and into the primal evolutionary history of the species, of which I only subsequently became aware, I begin in more modern times with my personal journey of discovery. In this journey, there are some rather interesting human twists and turns, some of which were important in the discovery of subliteral meaning or in its later development. Others are without theoretical significance, but they are just plain interesting.

THE QUEST AND DISCOVERY

IN THE BEGINNING

About 1972, I began to notice certain global "analogic" or "metaphorical," themes, as I first called them, being used in group conversations.[4] As I described in chapter 1, in conversations that were being openly tape recorded, I noticed repeated stories about the *CIA* and *FBI*, or the topics of *God* or *policeman* were frequently selected for discussions when the group was concerned about my *authority role* as trainer, or that the topic of *journalists* was selected for the conversation when the group was concerned about my *taking notes*. It soon became clear to me that these "metaphors" were unconscious communications about feelings and concerns. Group members were not conscious of the real reason they had selected these topics. In fact when I explained this to group members and asked them, they usually laughed and attributed it to coincidence. I thought to myself, "this is fascinating stuff."

I didn't discover these subliteral conversations by methodically forming hypotheses and then testing them. The ingredients for this discovery go back a long way into my personal history and professional experience. These themes grew out of two interests of mine, one in cognitive psychology (i.e., the study of how the mind works) and the other in metaphorical and analogical reasoning which I saw as windows into the workings of the mind. Of course, in conducting T-groups ("T" stands for training), I was always asking the question: What's going on here? I began to view such topics as a kind of "metaphorical code" that could be deciphered. The question was, however, was this "metaphorical" meaning real, or was I reading too much into them, too much beneath the words, or between the lines? When I confided in my colleagues about these observations, some thought I was going off the deep end, so to speak. Mostly, though, they just laughed at such bizarre, but worse, unscientific interpretations, calling them simply wild coincidence. As my sophistication for analyzing the subliteral talk developed, the subliteral structure of the discussions became even more intricate, and as they became more intricate, even I sometimes found it difficult to believe what I was finding. I was aware, of course, that psychotherapists had noticed brief instances of "metaphors" in therapy that they considered parallel to the therapeutic situation,[5] but nothing to compare to what I was—or thought I was—discovering.

I had to know if what I was perceiving was real. I became obsessed with a way to verify the phenomenon, otherwise there was no way to contain speculative "interpretations," and my colleagues could continue—at best— to laugh. More importantly, unless I found a way to prove that what I was observing was real, I certainly would never be able to convince journal editors to publish such bizarre material. What I needed was a systematic methodology, but one did not exist. I began with the scientific assumption that the brain/mind is structured in an orderly fashion and that there would be a natural system underlying what I was finding. So I started a search for an orderly set of cognitive and linguistic operations that would serve as a systematic method for analyzing and validating what I thought I was observing. The question was, where would I look? A Freudian approach didn't appeal to me. It's much too messy.

When I had group discussions transcribed into printed protocols, it became increasingly clear that language was the key. So, I began to analyze these transcripts for linguistic and cognitive operations that would help me to decode, test, and validate my hypotheses about the meaning of these "metaphorical" topics. I began to notice some very strange—and this is important—but *consistent* cognitive and linguistic operations. For example, I noticed that subliteral topics were introduced only by members who had an emotional involvement in the concern that the topic was about. For example, members who were not concerned about *my taking notes* did not generate topics about *journalists*. Such topics were generated only by those whom I knew were concerned about my taking notes about them. This important finding led me to still other discoveries (see Appendix 3, Psychosociometric Operations).

Another strange operation was that literal stories whose structure matched the status of members present in a conversation could be consistently tracked by spatial or prepositional markers. Those in the literal stories who were said to be either *up, down, left,* or *right,* would match the status of group members in the conversations, that is, the characters in the literal stories were consistently described as "down in back" or "on the left" as opposed to "up front" or "on the right." The significance of this kind of spatial tracking is that being "up" and "right" consistently related to positive/high status members, and being "down" and "left" with low status members.[6] (see Appendix 4.2., Dimensional Evaluative Vector Operations). There's more.

I found that names used in literal narratives were often like puns. For example—and please bear with me on these examples until chapter 8—the name *Harry* would unconsciously mean /*hairy*/.[7] What is more, I found that the initials of the first and last names in literal narratives would match a person's initials in the present conversation. For example, in a narrative about Walt Disney the name may be a subliteral reference to a person in a discussion whose initials are W.D. But then it got even stranger. Then, I discovered that often, the initials in the name of the person in a narrative would be the reverse of the person's initials in the conversation, e.g., Walt Disney may represent a person whose initials are D.W. I wasn't trying to have it both ways. This finding was based on rules. This is the rule that I found in the reversal of initials: When both the narrative and the subliteral meaning are congruent, the initials are not reversed,[8] that is, when a narrative is about something positive and the subliteral meaning refers to a person in the conversation who is viewed positively, the initials are not reversed. Conversely, when a literal narrative is about something positive and the subliteral reference is to a person in the conversation who is viewed negatively, then the initials are reversed. This reversal of the initials is the way the mind indicates the negative aspect of the subliteral meaning. I also discovered that names in narratives may be unconsciously "misremembered" or that unconscious "mistakes" would be made so that the literal narrative would match the situation subliterally referenced. For example, if the name of a well-known journalist wouldn't fit the subliterally meaning being communicated, then the journalist's name would be altered to make the name fit the subliteral intent. Believe it or not.

The situation became even more disturbing when I discovered that numbers used in conversations were also frequently "metaphoric" or subliteral. For example, if *four* members in a conversation were dominant, the number "4" would repeatedly occur in the discussions (see chapter 5). In other words, these numbers corresponded to a subgroup in the present conversation that was composed of the exact number of people as in the literal narrative. What is more, the story in which these numbers were used didn't simply refer to 4 members. The gender composition in the literal story of 4 people matched the gender composition of the 4 members of the present conversation. In other words, if the social conversation was made up of 3 females and 1 male, the literal story would be about 3 females and 1 male—again, consistently.[9] It became even more bizarre.

I also discovered that complex numbers matched the present situation. A literal number, say, "*10*,000," may be selected for a narrative of a group composed of *10* members. Subliterally the *10*,(000), represents the *10* members in the social conversation and the three zeros in (10,) *000* represented a subgroup of *3*. As a first check on this finding, I discovered that the numbers in subsequent literal stories would change to match the absent member or members for that day. I further discovered that within a narrative all of the different stories were variations on the present situation. It is important to note that these findings were consistent within a conversation and also across many different conversations composed of different member and situations. I discovered many other cognitive "encoding" operations (see Appendix, 8. Mathematical Computation Operations and 8.2. Cipher Operations). Certainly these were rather bizarre findings, So bizarre that I compulsively checked, rechecked my findings, and then checked them again.

At this point, I found myself suspecting my observations—and my sanity. So were other people whom I knew. After all, I observed that group members were talking to me in code, as it were. This is the stuff that paranoid schizophrenia is made of. Many paranoid schizophrenics have what is called delusions of reference, for example, where they think people on TV are really talking about them, or when they overhear a conversation, they think it's about them. And seeing numbers in the talk as symbolic communication—well, this is the stuff of occult numerology, isn't it?—where numbers have a symbolic or cosmic meaning?

OF CODES AND CONVERSATIONS

Developing a method to decode conversation is one thing, but developing a theory to explain the code is another matter entirely. Suffice it say for now that the propensity of humans at least to encode secret messages *consciously* goes back to almost the beginnings of written history.[10] As early as the Bronze Age (3500 B.C.), people in the Near East were being trained in the art of deciphering coded texts. One of the earliest and simplest forms of encoding is called an acrostic. Using acrostics, a hidden message can be deciphered by selecting the first letter of each line or verse in a text. An example of an acrostic was found in a clay tablet from the Iraq of the mid-second millennium B.C. The text on the tablet is a religious poem of twenty-seven verses but was written to be read by someone who knew the "key" as an acrostic in which the initial syllables of each verse combine to reveal a separate or hidden message.

In any event, as I began to discover these strange cognitive operations for decoding subliteral meaning, I began to feel like what I imagined the French Egyptologist, Jean Francois Champollion (1790–1832), must have felt as he began to decipher the famous Rosetta stone, or Michael George Ventris (1922–1956), the English linguist, when in 1952 he deciphered Linear B, a syllabic Mycenaean script generally thought to be from the fourteenth to the twelfth century B.C. The rules of Linear B are so complex that a word spelled in Linear B may be interpreted and spelled out in many different ways within the western European alphabet. The Rosetta stone, found in 1799 by Napoleon's soldiers near the city of Rosetta in Egypt, is a basalt slab that was inscribed with both Greek characters, hieroglyphs, and other strange characters. It provided Champollion and other scholars with the key for translating Egyptian hieroglyphics. Having spent years studying the hieroglyphics inscribed on the stone tablet, Champollion discovered that the inscriptions were made up of both sound signs (phonograms) and sense signs (ideograms). He proved that hieroglyphs have symbolic meaning and also that they are alphabetic for a spoken language. The language in literal narratives has been awaiting their subliteral decoding, like the Rosetta stone and Linear B.

Even with my method of validation, however, I knew too much about the history and philosophy of science and epistemology (the study of how we know what we think we know) to feel secure. Was it possible that I had simply constructed an elaborate—but consistent—system, which was not valid? I painfully recalled the Ptolemaic theory of the solar system from the history of astronomy. In the second century A.D., the Greek astronomer, Claudius Ptolemy, constructed a planetary system that had the earth at the center of our solar system, not the sun. With its elaborate system of imaginary and ad hoc orbital epicycles, it consistently predicted very well the movement of the planets and their respective positions at any given time. Now, we know, however, that the Ptolemaic system was *reliable* but not *valid*. Had I constructed a similar psychological system? I wondered if I had merely created a kind of methodological alchemy, a pseudoscience that only gave the appearance of changing literal meaning into subliteral ones, like the medieval alchemist who sought to turn base metals into gold or silver by mysterious methods.

CONNECTIONS

Then, I discovered that the literature on small group dynamics, group psychotherapy, and other areas of research and practice was interlaced with brief snippets of what I was calling subliteral narratives. The most developed was the work of Robert Bales, a social psychologist at Harvard University who was well known for his research in small group processes. He had labeled such symbolic talk "fantasy themes."[11] Other researchers working with him had noticed and written about such phenomena in small group discussions. For example, in group dynamics research, Richard Mann, Theordore Mills, Philip Slater, and others had variously labeled such subliteral language "learning by analogue," and "symbolic equivalences."[12] Except for a chapter by Bales, there was no method for analyzing or validating examples of subliteral communication like those I was finding. The intricate extent or the cognitive importance of such "symbolic" communications was not recognized, and phenomena were not understood or explained, except in general Freudian terms.

Continuing my search of the literature, I discovered that very rudimentary subliteral phenomena had been lying around as unexplained curiosities in other academic disciplines.[13] In the group therapy literature, occasional and brief instances of what I term subliteral conversation had been sporadically noted and generally referred to as "symbolic communication." In both the individual and group psychotherapy literature, subliteral talk was recognized by Irving Yalom, and by others, like the psychoanalyst Harry Stack Sullivan. Not surprisingly, these "metaphorical" communications were recognized especially by those of a psychoanalytic bent, who have variously called it "parataxic distortion" or "transference."[14] In transference, patients or group members are said to transfer their feelings about their fathers or mothers onto the therapists or trainers. In short, when talking about parents, the patient may be considered to be "metaphorically" talking about the therapist or trainer. I recently learned that the psychoanalyst Sandor Ferenczi briefly noticed what he called "hidden communications."[15]

Finally, I knew I was no longer alone in my perceptions. If I was suffering delusions, then I was in quite good company, at least for my observation of general "metaphorical" meaning—and there was some comfort in this. Even so, I experienced great difficulty in having professional journals accept my research. Reviewers called my findings, "schizophrenic," "paranoid," "ridiculous," and in their kinder, gentler moments, referred to them as "wild puns" or as "simply coincidence." Some of my early articles were published in journals that catered to research on psychotherapy. Even there, however, it was not easy going. The international journal that published my first article that contained only a rudimentary methodology rejected a later article in which I had begun to lay out a systematic method. I finally published in journals that specialize in small group dynamics research. Although this was progress, I had always really considered my findings primarily as a contribution to cognitive psychology.

Then in 1997, I was contacted by Piers Myers, a psychotherapist in England, who inquired if I was familiar with the work of the psychiatrist, Robert Langs. Myers had become aware of my work on subliteral communication and said it was very similar to what Langs had discovered independently, and that Langs had pioneered a new school of psychotherapy based on what I was calling subliteral communication. It is sometimes the case that discoveries in science are independently discovered by more than one person, either at a much earlier time or at nearly the same time. Perhaps the classic example of this is Charles Darwin's (1809–1892) theory of evolution, which was anticipated by his grandfather, Erasmus Darwin (1731–1802). More importantly, there was the English naturalist, Alfred Russell Wallace (1823–1913) who almost beat Darwin in establishing priority to the theory of evolution based on natural selection. Though, as I mentioned previously, I had been aware of an increasing literature about using "metaphors" in psychotherapy, I hadn't given much thought to subliteral narratives for therapeutic applications. This added another whole dimension. In part, I think my personal experiences were important early influences in discovering subliteral meaning. The more specific question remains, why was I able to discover these strange findings?

EARLY INFLUENCES

With hindsight, I think I understand now why I may have been predisposed to recognize subliteral language and meaning. Although retrospective recollection is fraught with problems of distorted memory and bias in selecting events for their importance in explaining the present, as historians well know, sometimes it's all we have to go on. With this caveat, now let me begin again.

ANALOGICAL REASONING

I mentioned in the preface that, as a child, I often wondered what people "really meant" by what they said. Later, as a young man, I began writing poetry and fancied myself a budding creative writer. The metaphorical language in my poems and the way the words were juxtaposed fascinated me and opened up my mind. Understandably enough, I became somewhat obsessed with metaphor and analogy. Though analogy and metaphor differ, they also are similar. With a metaphor like "the meaning of a stream of words is merely the surface current of a deeper meaning," the meaning has to be interpreted. The reader has to decipher it. Metaphor is closer to an encrypted code than analogy. Analogy is more clear-cut, as it were. The classic form of analogical reasoning is of the sort,

A is to B as C is to D (typically notated as, A:B :: C:D),

where B stands in relation to A as D does to C. More simply put, an analogy or metaphor can be characterized by saying, "it's *like.*" But unlike analogy, metaphorical meaning is not as clear-cut. Both, however, are based on the important psychological concept of *similarity.* Almost since humans started to think systematically, philosophers like Socrates, Plato, and Aristotle, have extolled the importance of similarity in thinking.[16]

In both my undergraduate senior thesis and in my master's thesis I researched metaphorical and analogical thinking which were then largely considered literary devices. Then, I found an article by J. Robert Oppenheimer (1904–67), the American physicist who had headed the U.S. Atomic Bomb (Manhattan) Project and who had been the Director of the Princeton Institute for Advanced Study. His article about the use of analogy in science made an impression on me.[17] Although it was no secret among physicists that they made extensive use of analogies, this was not the image of them from textbook descriptions of how "real" scientists went about their work. Oppenheimer's article brought the physicist's use of reasoning by analogy "out of the closet."

One such well-known analogy is the English physicist, Ernest Rutherford's (1871–1937) early formulation comparing the structure of the atom to the solar system, where the nucleus of the atom is like the sun and the electrons revolving around it are like the planets. In science we call this type of thinking model building. Even a cursory glance at the history of science demonstrates the extensive use of analogic reasoning.[18] This further expanded my thinking about analogical reasoning. At this point, I began even more clearly to view them as cognitive processes, not as literary devices, as they were largely viewed then.[19] Cognitive researchers began to understand the importance of metaphorical and analogical reasoning. Cognitive science, however, is still preoccupied with simple and surface aspects of analogies in science and analogical reasoning, continuing with endless analyses, for example, of Rutherford's early analogy of the atom to the solar system.[20]

I consider the cognitive mechanisms that underlie my subliteral material to be the fundamental processes giving rise to what we normally call metaphorical and analogical reasoning.[21] A subliteral narrative can be seen as an analogy to, or is like, what actually is occurring in a conversation. Thus my early interest in analogical and metaphorical reasoning provided the beginnings of what I had been discovering.

Finally, perhaps, I was hardwired to understand "metaphorical" meaning. I have come to believe that our brain has become hardwired through evolution to create invariances of meanings.

SIGMUND FREUD

Another influence in developing an interest in hidden meanings was my early experience of reading Freud. Although I was not overly impressed—even then—with psychoanalytic theory in general, what did intensely influence me was his book, *The Interpretation of Dreams*.[22] What fascinated me about Freud's book was how Freud described the way the mind works during dreaming, not dream interpretation. Later, I realized that *Interpretation of Dreams* was a precursor to modern cognitive psychology. It's quite different from the rest of his work. Freud himself considered it his masterwork. Indeed, it is one of the great books of Western civilization. In his chapter on *Dream Work,* his discovery of language and cognitive encoding operations, including the cognitive aspects of puns, slips of the tongue, and double meanings, are seminal, though he really did not fully know what he was doing. After all, it was not his purpose to study the cognitive deciphering process, per se. Rather, his goal was therapeutic, his method was intuitive, and he constructed his entire system on very general symbolic/psychoanalytic meanings and free associations. Nevertheless, I (and much of cognitive psychology) owe a considerable debt to the cognitive and linguistic aspects of Freud's *Interpretation of Dreams,* his *Psychopathology of Everyday Life,* and his *Jokes and Their Relation to the Unconscious.*[23] Moreover, one can't read Freud carefully and fail to see his talent for metaphorical and analogical reasoning. He was a master at them, and so are most psychoanalysts.

As I showed in my first article,[24] published as I was about to work on my Master's degree, the various psychoanalytic systems that derived from Freud's are analogical extensions of his basic system.

DECIPHERING "ENEMY" CODES

My quest to decipher hidden meaning was perhaps also influenced by my experience in the U.S. Army. In the days when young men were subject to involuntary draft into the Army, I volunteered shortly after high school so that I might have more of a choice in the job assigned to me. After testing me for my aptitudes and abilities, the Army tests indicated that I had aptitudes in electronics and in cryptography—the decoding of secret messages. I chose cryptography, of course, not because I thought it had anything to do with analogical reasoning—at that point, I knew nothing of analogical reasoning. I chose it simply because it sounded exciting. So I was assigned to an Army intelligence unit and was trained in breaking secret codes (now almost all decoding is done by computer) at the supersecret National Security Agency (NSA).

My job involved analyzing information obtained by electronically eavesdropping and typing out the coded communications that were intercepted from the "enemy." I was given this material to decipher. Just as in understanding the meaning of words you have to understand the grammar and logic of the sentences as well as the context in which the words are spoken, so too in deciphering codes there are the internal and the contextual aspects. For example, knowing the history and whereabout of the unit from which the codes came helped in decoding them. It was also important to recognize the style of the person sending the code. Each had a "fingerprint" that identified them. It was hard tedious work that sometimes yielded important information about the unit. But sometimes after hours of exhausting mental work, the message would read: "Merry Christmas, Americans."

There is little doubt that my Army training in deciphering codes was a factor in imprinting me to decipher subliteral language. After all, subliteral communication is a kind of encoded secret message. So, from an early interest in poetry, I went to code breaking. As it turned out, I was a better code breaker than poet. But the odyssey in discovering the subliteral mind is not yet finished.

LATER INFLUENCES

At the time I first began discovering subliteral cognition and language, I was teaching at a community college. I had my Master's degree, but knew I had to earn a doctorate if I wanted to be taken seriously by journal editors, especially with such seemingly bizarre material. So, I decided to work on my Ph.D. at Penn State. When I started working on my doctorate, I already had published a few articles, but not on my subliteral material, though I had most of my method worked out.

GIAMBATTISTA VICO AND THE DISCOVERY OF THE METAPHORICAL MIND

Because of my academic interest in metaphor, my mentor, Joseph Kockelmans, a renowned scholar in the philosophy of Martin Heidegger, told me about an eighteenth century Italian philosopher who wrote on the origins of metaphorical language. Interestingly, Heidegger maintained that we are not the masters of language but that language is the master of us. Kockelmans referred me to a faculty member, Donald Philip Verene, who had written about this Italian philosopher, Giambattista Vico (1668–1744). Now, if you have never heard of Vico, don't despair, neither have most people, including academics—outside of a relatively small esoteric cadre of Vichian scholars. Oddly, I remembered as an undergraduate first reading about Vico in a very brief paragraph in my Introduction to Sociology text. Vico, however, was known then almost exclusively for his ideas on history and social theory. Though most of my work on subliteral language was completed before I became aware of Vico, his story, nevertheless, is fascinating for further understanding the mind and subliteral language (see Chapter Six), and for me it was also "moral support" to know that if Vico were alive, he would instantly understand what I was discovering about the processes undergirding the mind and our system of language. Reading Vico also stimulated further nuancing of my developing method.

Giambattista Vico would have understood because he discovered that the psychological origins and functions of the human mind are based on metaphorical reasoning. But because he didn't have the advantage of modern cognitive research, he couldn't speak about the processes underlying what he called metaphor. About 1725 he set forth his views in his book, *The New Science.*[25] Of course, metaphor as a figure of speech was known long before Vico by the ancient Greek philosopher Aristotle (384–322 B.C.) In

Vico's time (and beyond, for that matter), metaphor was considered simply a figure of speech, a simple linguistic comparison. It's section two of Vico's Book, interestingly entitled, "Poetic Wisdom," which is the tour de force for his cognitive theory of mind.

Vico's near contemporary, the French philosopher Rene Descartes (1596–1650), held that clear, distinct, and logically precise ideas and categories are the only methods for assessing what is real and rational, not logically messy metaphors (see chapter 6). Vico believed that he demonstrated, however, that our clear and distinct, logically precise ideas and categories are merely the end result of an older more primary metaphorical or "poetic" process.

For Vico, then, what we call metaphor was not a mere linguistic figure of speech. It was a primary process of cognition responsible for creating our entire edifice of language and thought. I should note, too, that Vico's theory is not idle philosophical speculation: It's grounded in empirical data, something quite remarkable for a philosopher of his time. His data were the ancient fables, myths, and the epic poetry of the ancient Greek, Homer. His method was the linguistic analysis of those fables, myths, and poetry. He saw in those myths, poetry, and fables—all written in different historical times— a series of cognitive, structural, and linguistic transformations that changed throughout the different periods in which they were written. His assumption was that the changes he observed in the surface language of those fables, myths, and poetry indicated changing developmental psychological functions. In this respect, Vico's method was not too different from that of anthropologists like Levi-Strauss,[26] the classicist scholar, Bruno Snell,[27] the psychologist Julian Jaynes (see later),[28] and my analysis of group narratives.

According to Vico, primitive humans could speak only in what he called "poetic sentences." These sentences are generated from a feeling and sensory base, what he called "sensory topics," which resulted in "poetic sentences" that are felt more than they are intellectually thought out. What better description of subliteral narratives? As I read Vico, it became immediately apparent to me that in studying ancient fables and myths he discovered the general origin of some of the cognitive functions that I was discovering in my study of spoken language. It was as if Vico were talking to me through the centuries. Unlike the literature about small groups and the psychoanalytic literature, Vico presented a complete philosophical theory of mind lying beneath my subliteral theory of communication. His theory of metaphor and especially his theory about feeling/emotions, what he called sensory topics in the construction of poetic sentences, was so parallel to what I was discovering about the subliteral language of conversations that it was nothing short of astounding. Vico's views lent further credence to my discoveries.

JULIAN JAYNES AND THE BICAMERAL MIND

Then there was Julian Jaynes. Around 1981, I bought a book published in 1976 by the psychologist Julian Jaynes (1923–1997) entitled *The Origin Of Consciousness in the Breakdown of the Bicameral Mind.*[29] By that time, it was a well-known book in psychology and also in the humanities. After briefly scanning it, I put it on my bookshelf until 1985 when I met Jaynes at a conference. After having a few beers with him at a local pub and talking about his work, I was motivated to read his book in depth when I returned home. After the conference, he visited me briefly a couple of times on his way to his family residence in Nova Scotia. Then, I invited him to present a lecture on campus in 1991. When I carefully read his book, the similarities to Vico's work stood out in bold relief.

Jaynes's controversial theory of the origin of consciousness and the breakdown of the bicameral mind can be essentially summarized as follows. Like Vico, Jaynes said that human beings were not always conscious in the sense we think of being conscious today. Before becoming conscious as we understand it, the "mind" was bicameral, i.e., by analogy with the term as it's used in political science, divided into two "houses" or parts. Like Vico, consciousness (as we understand it now), says Jaynes, arose from interaction with culture and society. And like Vico, Jaynes maintained that our consciousness is fundamentally formed by language, particularly by metaphor and analogy. Unlike Vico, Jaynes dates the origin of modern consciousness. According to Jaynes, we became conscious in the modern sense somewhere around 1400 to 600 B.C. During what Jaynes calls the bicameral stage, like Vico, Jaynes believed that early humans hallucinated voices in their heads that they took to be the voices of gods.

Also like Vico, Jaynes's developed his theory by a historical analysis of ancient texts of myths and poetry that describe historical events, which he considered valid historical documents, and studied the history of language and its development. Unlike Vico, what he discovered in ancient texts was supported by data on the functions of the brain's left and right cerebral hemispheres. In addition, he found that many pathological and other anomalous cognitive phenomena (like hypnosis) were similar to what he found in the ancient texts, and thus had their origins in the bicameral stage.

In his book, Jaynes asks, it is possible that there "existed a race of men who spoke, judged, reasoned, solved problems, indeed did most of the things that we do but who were not conscious at all,"[30] and that "most men at one time, throughout the day, were hearing poetry . . . composed and spoken within their own minds,"[31] and that "poetry . . . was the language of the gods."[32] For those who are familiar with Vico's *New Science*, these words almost seem to be Vico's very words. But they're not. Apparently, Jaynes never read Vico. In the beginning of humanity, say Vico and Jaynes, human perception emanated from within and was based on bodily sensations. The first men, says Vico, "were all robust sense and vigorous imagination"[33] who "at first feel without paying attention."[34] So, too, Jaynes says, "Bicameral men did not imagine; they experienced."[35] Both Vico and Jaynes maintain that figurative or poetic language evolved first. On this Vico says that, "These expressions of the first nations later became figurative when, with the further development of the human mind words were invented. . . ."[36] And Jaynes says, "In early times, language and its referents climbed up from the concrete to the abstract on the steps of metaphors, even, we may say, created the abstract on the bases of metaphors."[37] Metaphor for Vico and Jaynes, then, was a cognitive operation before it was a linguistic device.[38]

One important difference between the two men should be mentioned. Despite Jaynes' use of ancient texts as data, unlike Vico, Jaynes was an empiricist in the sense that he valued empirical data, sound methodology, and clear, distinct and intelligible ideas. Given this, the similarities become even more poignant.

FINAL TWISTS AND TURNS

There are a couple of more interesting twists to my story. While still working on my doctorate at Penn State, the late Bob Di Pietro, then Chair of the Linguistic Department at Delaware State University and editor of a linguistics news letter, who had an interest in Vico, suggested that I write to Giorgio Tagliacozzo who was organizing a conference on Vico in Venice, Italy, to inquire if he might be interested in a paper for the conference on my view of metaphor and Vico. I contacted Tagliacozzo. In the summer of 1978, I presented my paper in an old monastery on the Island of San Giorgio in the waters off the Venetian shores.

The summer I was to present my paper in Venice, I was with my family on the coast of Maine at our summer cottage. One afternoon, I went down to the wharf just to gaze at the water and think. A man and his wife, who also had a cottage near ours, were there. Though we both had owned our cottages for a few years, we had never met. As the man and I began to talk, we learned that we both taught college. I ask him what he planned to do during the summer, and he replied that he was presenting a paper at a conference. This was not unusual, and I responded that I, too, was presenting a paper at a conference. To continue to make talk, I asked him where the conference was and what his paper was about. He replied that his conference was in Venice, Italy, and his paper was on a rather esoteric philosopher, named Giambattista Vico, of whom I probably had not even heard. When I informed him that I was also presenting a paper in Venice on Vico, needless to say, we were taken aback at this coincidence.

Another interesting twist is this. It's often the case that papers given at a conference are later published as the conference proceedings. My paper and the paper of another psychologist at the conference were not selected for publication in the proceedings. Perhaps my view of Vico's translators misrepresenting Vico didn't endear me to most of the Vichian scholars at the Venice conference. Well, I was a little upset, and assumed that it was because we were just the "token" nonphilosophers at the conference or that my paper was just a little too wild for this group of classical European scholars from "the old school." I continued, however, to be intrigued by Vico's work but did not continue my contact with these Vichian scholars.

Then, ten years later, I received a phone call from Giorgio Tagliacozzo, then Director and founder of The Institute for Vico Studies and editor of a series of books on Vico. He invited me to write an article on Vico and metaphor. He said that he had been told about the chapter on Vico that I wrote years after the conference but which was based on the paper I presented on Vico in Venice. He also said he knew that I was interested in metaphor because he was looking at the letter I had sent him regarding the Venice conference more than ten years ago. He actually had that ten-year-old letter.

I told him that I would consider writing a piece on Vico for him, but that I would have to think about it. Tagliacozzo called me about every three months after that until I finally accepted his invitation. However, I informed him that I wanted to write a paper relating Vico to a psychologist at Princeton, Julian Jaynes, who had written *The Origins of Consciousness and the Breakdown of the Bicameral Mind.* I told him that I was fascinated by the many similarities I found between Vico and Jaynes. He agreed, and I wrote an article somewhat esoterically entitled "A Comparative Analysis of Vico and Jaynes: Neurocultural and Cognitive Operations in the Origin of Consciousness."[39]

A final twist: About 1980, I had transformed a newsletter which Bob Di Pietro had handed over to me, into a journal format. As editor, I published an article by a linguist, Marcel Danesi, on the subject of language and brain lateralization. Years later, we reestablished contact. In the interim—and unbeknownst to me—he had become a well-known Vichian scholar.[40] He also knew Bob Di Pietro, Giorgio Tagliacozzo, and Donald Philip Verene. It's a small world. I'm not sure what these many strange twists and turns mean, other than that they are strange twists and turns.

POSTSCRIPT

Subliteral language has been awaiting its own method and theory to explain what it is, how it works, why it occurs, and how it evolved. After writing a culminating article on my subliteral methodology in 1991,[41] for a number of reasons, I put my research material in a file and closed the drawer for a few years. I was always alert, however, for related material and for research on the brain that someday I planned to use in developing a neurological theory to explain how subliteral operations are possible. Although the initial story about the discovery of the subliteral mind is now complete, the story will continue. Much work remains to be done. The next steps involve developing a brain-based theory that explains how subliteral language is possible and conducting some experiments. Writing this book is a part of that continuation because it has forced me to reanalyze my material along the way. After more than twenty years of working with subliteral material, I find that it still fascinates and intrigues me.

CHAPTER 3

OF CRYSTAL BALLS
AND THE MIND OF GOD
AUTHORITY AND LEADERSHIP CONCERNS

Throughout the course of human history, certain everyday topics and themes have been of universal concern. Indeed, this universality of human existence provides the emotional source for the enduring Greek tragedies, for the works of Shakespeare, and for other great and enduring literature around the world. The great works of literature speak to us from this common emotional experience of the conflicts and troubles in the everyday life of the human species. These enduring themes and topics have been called archetypal, i.e., a kind of universal prototype or template of human experience. Universal and archetypal, however, don't necessarily mean existentially profound. Some universal concerns are quite mundane, even petty. Alongside the grand archetypes of God, Earth Mother, and the Greek heroes Achilles, Hercules, and Odysseus are the mythical concerns about werewolves, vampire bats, and dwarfs. Given these nearly universal concerns, it's not surprising that many of them are expressed and can be observed in everyday conversations—both literally and subliterally. One major human theme is leadership.

Some of the more profound examples of these universal concerns can be found in the Christian Bible, in the works of Joseph Campbell[1] on myths around the world, and in the works of the anthropologist, Claude Levi-Strauss.[2] The T-group is a microcosm of the larger world, a miniature or microworld that reflects many of the mythic issues, concerns, and dynamics of the larger world that surrounds it. In the study of small group dynamics, Philip Slater in his little known—and now out of print—book about T-group dynamics, entitled *Microcosm: Structural, Psychological and Religious Evolution in Groups*,[3] describes many of these universal human concerns: authority, God, heroes, leadership, revolt, parenting, sibling rivalry, and many others, which he framed in Freudian and ancient Greek mythological terms.

In this chapter, I illustrate many of these themes and many others that have occurred in my T-groups which reflect concerns about leadership. In his book, *Interpersonal Styles and Group Development,* Richard Mann, one of the original researchers at Harvard who worked with what they called fantasy themes (see previous chapter), opens his book by saying, because the leader is the major figure in most groups, "The primary focus of this book is upon the relationship of the member of the group and its leader."[4] Understanding the subliteral meaning of these stories about authority and leadership can be valuable in recognizing individual and social dynamics that might not be evident or obtainable otherwise. Because the T-group is a microcosm, the concerns and subliteral meanings apply to most other social situations, whether they are groups in business, education, mental health, or in everyday social conversations.

In the course of human interactions, some of the concerns that people have are legitimate, but some seem just plain irrational. Either way they are based on peoples' perceptions of what they think is happening. Rightly or wrongly, these perceptions can tell us a great deal. Some of the perceptions that I have found repeatedly revolve around such eternal concerns as being spied upon, the competence of a leader, not being given what people think they deserve or should be receiving, leader influence, and being singled out from others.

Let me clarify once more the typical conditions that lead to subliteral expressions of concern about an authority. In T-groups, there is a constant concern with the trainer because typically the trainer is relatively nondirective, allowing members to experience a "naturally" evolving group and to develop their own internal leadership structure. The leader or trainer's role is more consultative. The trainer may intervene and clarify, but basically does not lead the group or participate in it. Whether they are laymen or professionals, most T-group members find this situation disconcerting because people expect "a leader" in the groups to which they belong. Thus, in the nondirective atmosphere of the T-group, concern about the trainer is often a foremost concern. Any remarks a trainer may make are felt emotionally and unconsciously. This condition applies to any social situation that's relatively unstructured and where there is at least one person who is socially dominant by assigned role or by their personal style.

One final point before beginning to look at these leadership concerns. Seldom do discussions reflect only one issue or concern. Often discussions weave related concerns into a primary topic. Accordingly, the examples presented in this chapter about leadership contain material about peer relationships, which I discuss in the next chapter. Although logicians may create mutually exclusive categories, the human mind doesn't naturally work that way.

CONCERNS ABOUT SECRET KNOWLEDGE AND SURVEILLANCE

We humans have an enduring interest and concern with secrets and with the secret powers that we suspect some people possess which allow them to gain access—without our knowing it—to our most hidden feelings, desires, and thoughts. Perhaps the basic template for this concern comes from a widespread experience in the Western cultural family. It's a common experience of children that their parents know everything they do and are thinking. It's also common for children to be told that Santa Claus also knows everything we do, that he "knows if you've been bad or good," and if we weren't good, we wouldn't receive presents from him. But even more seriously, many of us were led to believe in a God, high in the heavens, who is all-seeing and all-knowing, a kind of pretechnological great spy satellite in the sky.

A more mundane example of these concerns is the common belief that "psychologists can read your mind." This belief is, of course, not correct. Nevertheless, the belief persists on various levels of conscious and unconsciousness. The belief is so widespread that I have always been reticent to tell people that I am a professor of psychology, even though I am not a clinical psychologist or "shrink." A related concern that people have about psychologists is that of being experimented with. It should come as no surprise, then, that these concerns are expressed subliterally.

OF CRYSTAL BALLS AND SECRET KNOWLEDGE

The concern about spying and surveillance extends to the belief in magic, fortune tellers, and crystal balls. In one early recognition of subliteral meaning in conversation in his book, *Here Comes Everybody*, the psychologist William Schutz[5] tells of a time he shaved his head bald like Yul Brynner while he was conducting training groups. After he shaved his head, he noted that references to *crystal balls* subsequently appeared in the conversations. On the surface, this "metaphor" of a crystal ball for his shaved head is perhaps obvious. The references to crystal balls, however, go deeper than the mere physical relationship of a smooth (crystal) ball and Schutz's smoothly shaven head. From a subliteral perspective, the group's reference to crystal balls has triple meaning. In addition to the relationship between the physical characteristics of a crystal ball and Schutz's shaved head, on a second level it's a pun on the words "ball" and "bald." The third level is expectations and concerns on the part of group members that psychologists have special knowledge, that Schutz had "magic," powers, as it were, and therefore can "read their minds" and predict the future of the group, like a fortune teller with a crystal ball.

Though I already noted that psychologists can't read minds, understanding unconscious meanings by subliterally examining the words, phrases, and sentences that people use is a kind of mind reading. At least, it's about as close as we will ever get to reading other people's minds.

BEING SPIED UPON

Similarly, I have found that people's suspicions of being experimented with—especially by psychologists—are often expressed subliterally. These subliteral references regularly occur in my T-groups, where I inform them that I will be videotaping them from time to time and openly tape recording the sessions mainly for educational purposes. I also inform them that I will be taking notes, that all members should also take notes, and that they can have full access to the tapes. In addition, my T-groups are usually conducted in a room with a one-way mirror. Even though I inform them of these conditions, topics that involve the FBI and CIA frequently emerge in the conversations. In the initial stages of one group, the topic of conversation was about *"speakeasies"* (an illegal place to drink during the early 1900 prohibition against selling alcohol). The reference to "speakeasies" reveals a concern with the tape recorder, i.e., subliterally meaning *speak easy* so the tape won't record what they are saying. On a conscious or literal level, I've even had members act out by whispering and pointing to the tape recorder. On an unconscious level, in another group the literal topic of the game "Charades," a game in which communicating is done nonverbally in pantomime, just happened to become a topic of discussion.

These concerns about secret surveillance and experimentation are in part precipitated by my sitting silently and writing notes about the dynamics of the session. Groups are frequently concerned about my using these notes to write a book or article about them. Sometimes they overtly verbalize this concern along with a belief that I am experimenting with them. And, of course, the one-way mirror in the room generates conscious and unconscious images of spying and experimenting on them, even though I make it clear that I am not experimenting with them.

REVEALING SOURCES AND SURVEILLANCE

It's widely believed in our culture that tape recording and spying on people is illegal and also unethical. Accordingly, I have found that subliteral references often reflect this belief. In one group, the session began with my having difficulty with the tape recorder. The discussion began by a member asking if anyone had been following the legal hearings about the journalist, Daniel Schorr, who wouldn't reveal the confidential sources of his news story. A member responded, "Yes, and do you know that there are *three journalists* already in jail for not revealing their sources." A discussion of the "pros" and "cons" of the various reasons for not revealing sources ensued, followed by a brief silence. The silence was broken by a topic about a conference held by mayors of big cities who testified that crime rates decreased when cities were given sufficient money by the federal government and that after the conference a reporter countered all of the mayors' testimony with statistics from the FBI. It was further said that, "The reporter made fools of all the big mayors." Again, a silence. Seemingly changing the subject, a member then said, "I've been thinking about this group, and it seems to me that we've been trying to counteract what happened on the videotape of us the other day. It seems like the group didn't do much, and so today we're being very active." The group had been making attempts to develop rules for structuring the group process and was beginning to be concerned with being productive.

What does this literal conversation really mean? I mean, subliterally? Along with a continuing concern over being recorded, my bungling the restarting of the recorder once again brought the concern about being tape recorded to a semiconscious level. This served as a stimulus for the initial part of the session. Hence, the reference to the journalist, Daniel Schorr who wouldn't reveal his sources which was equivalent to me not revealing my notes. The ensuing discussion of the "pro's" and "con's" of the issue of confidentiality of a reporter's source reflects a continuing concern and ambivalence that the group is being recorded and over the confidentiality of the material.

The remark about "three journalists in jail" is a double reference to illegalities. On one level, illegal means that secret surveillance is not morally right. On another level, it's a reference to recording and withholding the information which group members unconsciously believe may be illegal. I find that behaviors or situations that members don't like or that are considered outside the expected norms are often subliterally referenced as either being crazy or illegal. On yet another level, the reference to "three" journalists in jail may indicate the three black members in the group, who have continually been sitting together and who are an unknown quantity in this group of white members. Thus, they constitute a threat like the trainer and the tape recorder. Indeed, later in the session there was an open abstract discussion about racial concerns in the group (see chapter 9).

The topic about mayors who said that crime went down when cities were given increased funds subliterally meant that the group would be more productive if I would give them more information, i.e., the information in my notes. The remark about a reporter who countered the mayors' assertion (refers to members) with statistics, is a reference to my suspected scientific research). Further, the reporter is equivalent to the videotape. The comment about making fools of the mayors represents themselves. That they were all made to look like fools refers to the videotape that showed them not functioning very well. The ostensible change of topic about the remark that the group was now trying to counteract its image shown on the video tape is equivalent to the reporter countering the mayors' actions.

SECRET FILES

The concern about an authority who secretly tape records or keeps secret records or notes about people is often permuted into various related topics, all of which constitute variations on a single subliteral theme, with each topic reflecting a particular aspect of the general emotional concern about secret surveillance. For example, in groups concerned with my *taking notes* about them, the concern may be permuted into the topics of (a) *journalists,* if the aspect of concern is collecting information for *publication,* into talk of (b) *FBI and CIA files,* where the aspect of concern is my *spying on them,* into (c) *novelists,* where the concern is whether what I am writing about them is untrue, i.e., a "novel" which represents fiction, or into (d) *archivists,* where the aspect of concern is that what I am writing about them is to be stored away for future researchers, or finally, into a topic about, (e) the *Dr.s writing prescriptions that patients cannot read,* where the aspect of concern is the feeling of being diagnosed by me. The prescriptions that the patients (the group members) *cannot* read, on the literal level, is a reference to the fact that a medical doctor's handwriting is unreadable. On a subliteral or

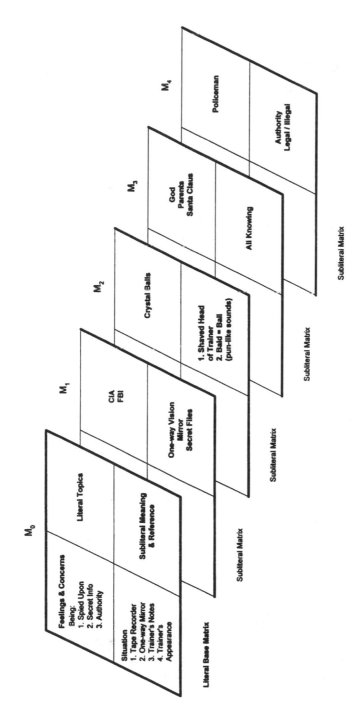

FIGURE 2. Transformational matrices.

poetic level, it's a reference to the fact that my notes were unavailable to them. Indeed, they "couldn't" read them. In addition, like not understanding undecipherable handwriting, they don't understand what I am doing writing notes. Finally, it's a reference to the fact that if they had my notes, i.e., the Dr.'s prescription, it would "cure" the group of its ills (see Figure 2).

An interesting aspect of these subliteral communications about spying and surveillance is that even though I informed members about being videotaped, about the one-way mirror, about my talking notes, and even though the tape recorder was in plain view, they remained unconsciously concerned. There seems to be a disconnect between reason and feeling, between what they consciously believe and what they unconsciously feel (see chapter 6). Subliteral meaning emerges out of this disconnect.

LEADERSHIP AND AUTHORITY THEMES

Throughout the years that I've been conducting T-groups, I've consistently found concerns with leadership and authority that are subliterally represented by a number of surprisingly consistent stories. Frequently, in the nondirective atmosphere of the T-group or other similar unstructured situations, the stories are about authorities who are incompetent and who abuse their subordinates. Topics are often about (a) governmental heads of state and how they mismanage their jobs, (b) about policemen and how they mistreat citizens, (c) about psychologists and their abuse of patients, (d) about teachers of retarded students, (e) about bosses who maltreat their workers, (f) about parents and how they abuse and batter children, and of course (g) about the ultimate authority figure God, and whether He is benevolent or malevolent. Whether authority figures are represented as benevolent or malevolent is determined by how members perceive they are treated by a leader or an authority figure. Let's now see how some of these concerns are subliterally expressed.

LEADER INCOMPETENCE

A universal concern about leaders is their competence, especially when they don't seem to be doing their jobs. The concern about the competence of leaders runs emotionally deep and probably has its earliest origins in the family. Parents are, after all, leaders. The group situation often precipitates the activation of these early emotional familial templates. After a silence in one group, a male member asked, "how many live at home with their parents?" Most of them responded that they still lived at home. The male member then went on to tell of his mother "who treated him as an incompetent." The older women in the group asked him if he ever told his mother how he felt, and he replied that he had. She went on to say that frequently parents are only trying to help and that "she spoke from experience" about this issue. She continued with, "children can benefit from parents' experience, and parents should help their children." Another member responded that "some families are close, some are not." Then, the male member said, "I am a psychology major and I am constantly analyzing my family."

Following this, there was much talk of parent–child generation gaps. Then, the older woman said, "Children may think certain ideas are good, but if parents suggest them, they may be rejected." Then, the male member asked if anyone had "heard of Timothy Leary," the former Harvard professor who, during the 1960s, advocated taking drugs to expand one's consciousness. Being too young, most responded that they hadn't. He went on to explain that Leary "was an advocate of learning by experience no matter what the cost" and that he agreed with Leary. Then, another member told of a child who learned to read by watching TV (Sesame Street); "that his parents didn't help him at all." Then, the discussion went to child development and the stages of learning.

The group was composed of mostly very young females, one older female, and one male who was slightly older than the young females. It was an extremely dependent group which waited for me or some member to take a strong leadership role to guide them. (In fact, however, peer leadership tends to be rejected or resented. This dynamic, too, harks back to family dynamics of sibling rivalry.) This was the fifth session of the group, and the members were still sitting with their chairs in rows, not having developed sufficient leadership even to arrange the chairs in a circle, as I typically suggest in my first and only introductory lecture at the beginning of the sessions. So, again, what does all this talk mean, I mean, subliterally?

The first remark regarding "living at home" refers to the group feeling dependent on authority figures, i.e., meaning myself and the older woman who represented a parent figure. Even the older woman, however, experienced dependency in this situation, as reflected in her statements about "parental experience" and that "parents should help their children" which subliterally reflected her feelings that I should offer my knowledge and experience to the group. The male member's remark that "I am a psychology major" equates with his identification with my role, as does his statement "I am constantly analyzing my family" meaning that he is analyzing the group.

His statement about agreeing with the philosophy of Timothy Leary is a further subliteral announcement to me that (a) he identifies with me and (b) he is learning by the experience. In fact he had been assuming the leadership of the group and was analytically watchful. The older woman's remark regarding "children rejecting parental suggestion" subliterally refers to the group's rejection of a suggestion I had made a couple of sessions previously. Just as adolescents are often in a state of conflicted ambivalence, where, on the one hand, they are dependent and want direction, it's often rejected on the other.

The male's reference to "Timothy Leary and his philosophy of learning by experience no matter what the cost" reflected my nondirective T-group educational philosophy of experiential learning. The clear semantic linkage is the term *experiential*. Both my initial lecture and the reading materials emphasized learning by experience, which is called *experiential* learning. The remark "no matter what the cost" also indicates the males's feelings that the T-group method has a high cost emotionally. The reference to the child who "learned to read by watching TV" subliterally refers to their feeling that not only am I like the parents in the story, not helping the group to learn, but it's also a double reference to the previous session when the group watched a video playback (equal to TV) of their session, i.e., they were learning by watching TV, not directly from me.

Finally, group members were actually living out their subliteral concerns. The older woman advocated my helping the group, just as she thought parents should help their children. Similarly, the male member was an "advocate" of learning by experience as expressed by Timothy Leary. The younger females, on the other hand, behaved in the group as if they were children learning to read without their parent's help. The last ironic dynamic is that the older woman's remarks about "children rejecting ideas that they would otherwise agree with just because it's suggested by a parent" was also happening in the group. Individuals and groups often enact that the older woman (equals a parental figure) described, i.e., rebelling against authority by not acting on the advice from me and my instructional material. The group members continued their discussion about the stages of child development. This topic, too, was in fact a subliteral discussion of the stages of group development.

BEING RIPPED OFF BY AUTHORITIES

When leaders, bosses, or other professionals are perceived as incompetent or simply not doing their jobs, people often feel cheated, or ripped off, as the following analysis of a group session shows. As part of my instructional philosophy, I absent myself from two or three group sessions each term. These are unannounced absences. I do this for three reasons. First, I want to see if the group has developed to a stage where it will meet if I am not present. Second, I want to see how members function without me. Third, I want members to experience the different dynamics in my absence.

The following session took place during my third absence, two weeks before the course ended. After waiting for about five minutes, the group's concern about my impending absence was expressed by wondering "Will he be here today?" After waiting a while longer, the group decided that I would not be there that day. As a part of a concern about me secretly spying on them, it was said, "He may be behind the (one-way) mirror." Then, the group attempted to look behind the mirror. After satisfying themselves that I was not "spying" on them, they decided that I was "home in bed, or having a good breakfast" (it was an 8:00 A.M. class). Then, the group began talking about problems with other classes and instructors.

The next topic was life in general. This led to a lively discussion of "store owners" and how they "ripped off the public with high prices, defective goods and false advertising." Subliterally, the "store owner" refers to me; "the public" is the group. The group felt that I was "ripping them off" by my absences. The "high prices and defective goods" stood for their feelings of not getting what they had paid for. The "false advertising" refers to the catalogue description of what they would learn in the course, which, in their view, was false advertising.

The topic of other problems with other classes and instructors is what I call a transitional topic. It's transitional because (a) it belongs in the same category as the actual here and now situation, and (b) it leads into the following topic about store owners who rip people off. Transitional topics are often links between present concerns and the subliteral expression of those concerns (See Appendix, 6.10. and 6.11.)

RECEIVING A SECOND-RATE EDUCATION

A variant on the theme of being ripped off is the following. The group began after one of my infrequent instructional interventions. I had put an outline of the various stages of group development on the blackboard. While members briefly glanced at the outline, they neither acknowledged nor discussed what I had put on the board. Then there was considerable talk of midterm examination week. Pause. In response to whether a member had a good weekend, a male who was slightly older than most of the members said, "No, I'm tired of this school, its midterm week." He continued with, "This school is really bad." Another said, "We're getting a second-rate education." Others denied it was so. "OK," the first member said, "Maybe it's not too bad, but I can't stand being treated like an adolescent, being talked down to." When an older female added that she did not find this so, it was argued that this was because of her age. The male who said that he was tired of the school, continued with, "Most [students] don't even know that they're being talked down to," further adding, "it might not be in the tone of voice, it may be in the structure of the teaching." Then, he told of a creative writing class where "the instructor outlined the whole story of what he thought was the right view of the story, and if you don't write exactly what he says, then it's wrong." Then, the member said, "It's disgusting, this school. I'm even afraid to go on to [name of an adjacent college], it's nothing but a branch of this school." Silence.

Again, the remark, "This school is really bad," is an expression of unconscious feelings about my nondirective style of teaching the course. This is indicated by the remark that "being talked down to" may be "in the structure of teaching." This is indicated, too, by the story "of a creative writing class where "the instructor outlined the whole story of what he thought was the right view of the story." This narrative about the creative writing teacher is a subliteral reaction to the outline of group stages I had put on the blackboard at the beginning of the session. In other words, the story about the creative writing instructor is *felt* to be parallel to the here-and-now group situation. The remark about the teacher, "If you *don't* write exactly what he says, then it's wrong," is likely a reaction to my stating that the order of group stages had been established by research, which was perceived as my saying authoritatively that the group stage scheme that I outlined was the correct one. This is indicated by his statement, "It might not be in the tone of voice," (meaning also that it might be in the tone of voice), but in the structure of the teaching that created the feeling that they were being "talked down to."

The remark that, "We're getting a second-rate education," is a double reference. First it refers to my nondirective style of teaching the course, and secondly, literally it refers to the college itself as a second-rate school. Contextually, this is indicated by the fact that the school was a two-year community college, and it was a common perception that the education was second-rate compared to a four-year school. This is indicated by the remark, "It's disgusting, this school. I'm even afraid to go on to . . . [name of an adjacent four-year college], . . . it's nothing but a branch of this school."

These subliteral messages make it clear that not all members felt so harshly about their situation. That not all members felt as he did, was indicated by the older female subliterally disagreeing that students are treated like adolescents, talked down to, and are getting a second-rate education. Further, it can be seen that even the slightly older male hadn't totally convinced himself of his negative view. In fact, on some level he was identifying with the older female, or at least disidentifying with the younger members of the group. This is indicated first by his statement that the older female didn't agree because she was older, and second, by his statement "I can't stand being treated like an adolescent," and thirdly, by his statement, "Most do not even know that they're being talked down to," implying that unlike the younger members, he does know. Finally, his ambivalence is indicated by his qualifying comment, "Maybe it's not too bad."

WAS DR. SPOCK RIGHT?

A variant on the theme of leader incompetence is the following. A widespread perception about college professors is that our research and books are really not practical, that we create theories in isolation from the "real world" that don't apply to everyday life. Hence the well-known phrase, "ivory tower" to refer to the academic environment. In my courses, I use a textbook that I wrote, along with a number of booklets. Following some small talk, there was a discussion of marriage and the problems of two people getting together. Then a discussion ensued about sibling rivalry and the problems of developing an identity in large families. One member said he "knew about identity problems" as he was a "twin." He proceeded to say that "psychologists don't know anything about twins. All the books I have read don't agree with my own experience." He further suggested that "psychologists write books that don't work. That makes me wonder," he said, "just how valid Dr. Spock's book really is." (This is a reference to Dr. Benjamin Spock's famous book on child rearing.)

"Psychologists" of course refers to me. The "books that don't work" are my book and pamphlets, and the reference to "Dr. Spock's book" is again my book. In addition, the reference to "just how valid Dr. Spock's book really is" again, is wondering just how valid my book is. It also links the parent/trainer in relation to children and to the general topics of marriage, family, and child development. The topic of "problems of developing an identity in large families" equates with the problem of developing a role/identity in the group.

ON FAIRNESS AND LEADERSHIP

In the first session of another group and after a silence following the previous topic, a member began talking about "community-living programs" for "mental patients" and "criminals." The group was composed of approximately eight students from a Human Services/Mental Health Program and seven from other curricula. The other members picked up on the topic and began discussing the pros and cons of "whether it was fair to those people who need help to put them out into the community. The new policy of emptying out the hospitals of people, who are used to their security and help, makes them have to do it all themselves." Then, it was said that they were put there in the first place because they couldn't handle life, stressing that "Society made them dependent and cannot expect them to all of a sudden function without help," and that "They should be eased into functioning on their own." It was said that there were some group homes for this purpose, "But most of the psychologists don't teach them anything." One member said "I know of one psychologist who does actually teach them skills—assertiveness training, etc. Some of these patients and convicts are going to school *here now*." The session ended.

The subliteral meaning of this discussion was: "community-living programs and group homes" refers to the group; "mental patients and criminals mean group members; "most psychologists" refers to me. Again, the concern is with my nondirective style and their perception that I do not teach them skills. Like the mental patients who have been made dependent on the hospital, the members feel that throughout their educational lives they have been conditioned to be dependent on teachers. Then, they, too, cannot be expected to function on their own in the group. Like the mental patients and criminals, they feel that they should be "eased into this type of life or situation." Further, the comment about a psychologist who teaches skills is a message to me that I should teach them skills directively.

Combining mental patients with criminals is also significant. Despite the feelings that, like mental patients and criminals, they have been conditioned to be dependent, they still feel that they are doing something wrong, and/or that they are defective. Finally, it is significant that the phrase "are going to school *here now*" in the statement that "Some of these patients and convicts are going to school *here now*," is a linguistic linkage connecting the literal with the subliteral situation (see Appendix, 6.5. Temporal Shift Operations).

Subsequently, this topic held the group's attention for the next three sessions, though it never "came up" as the same topic, nor was it ever explicitly continued. It usually evolved from other topics. In fact when I pointed this out, most members were only vaguely aware of the repetition of the narrative variations on their basic concern. Finally, the fact that it kept recurring indicates the group's continuing concern with my nondirective style of leadership.

DON'T JUST SIT THERE

This episode was identified by a colleague whom I was training to conduct T-groups and to recognize subliteral material.[6] On the particular day this episode occurred, I was absent from the group. This was the fourth session. The group was composed of a mixture of hippie types, middle-class students, and two state troopers who made their identities known immediately. The members were just getting to know each other and were expressing their frustration, anger, and confusion over the apparent lack of purpose and over what they perceived as the trainer's lack of leadership. During this session, the group discussed police and courts of law, rape, alcohol, drugs, and dentists. In discussing drugs, most of the hippie-type members said that drugs should be legalized. The group also talked about how "the quality of service was down," and how "big companies like Upjohn [pharmaceuticals] ripped people off."

It is particularly significant that the drug company "Upjohn" was selected, The first name of my colleague, who was the only trainer that day, was John. On one level the statement indicated that they thought the T-group experience was "a ripoff," that is, that my colleague was ripping off students just like they perceived the drug company "Upjohn" ripping off customers. Because they didn't feel comfortable directly asking John for help, subliterally Upjohn equals "get *up, John*, and start leading us."

REACTION TO A LEADER'S INFLUENCE

As usual, the members of this group expected a directive type of leadership, and as usual, despite these expectations, there is often ambivalence toward receiving direction from a trainer. The session began with a call for "rules and direction." Then, the group discussed structuring the group versus just letting it evolve naturally, but stopped when conflict over the issue became apparent. Then, one member asked me why I "don't talk more." I explained the dynamic that usually—especially in the first few sessions—when a trainer even implies a suggestion, groups often take it as the truth and enact the suggestion. Silence ensued. The next topic was "TV shows" and "Norman Lear" who produced many successful shows on television (notably, *All in the Family, Maude, Sanford and Son, Good Times,* and *Mary Hartman, Mary Hartman*). It was asked if it was "right for one person to have so much power and influence on the mass media." Then, it was explained that TV brainwashes people, and then people only want the types of shows by which they were brainwashed. Then, he emphasized that the process was just "all one big circle"—moving his hand spontaneously around the perimeter of the group. It was further suggested that "Kids learn what they see."

The "mass" media is the tape recorder, and probably the course itself. Norman Lear is myself, and the reference to the "rightness of Norman Lear having such influence" is a reaction to my explanation of the influence of a trainer's suggestions on a group. The remark about "kids learn what they see" represents me not showing or demonstrating to them by my own behavior how to function as a group. The implication is that if their model (i.e., me) is incompetent then, like children, they will behave in the same way. Moreover, the reference to it's just "all one big circle" is a subliteral statement about my not being a model, so they can't be expected to act appropriately (just like TV audiences who have been brainwashed). In addition the actual phrase "all one big circle" is a subliteral reference and linguistic linkage to the circular seating arrangement in the group.

Directly linking the literal topic with the here-and-now group situation is indicated by the speaker's physical hand movement pointing around the circular seating arrangement of the group while telling his literal story. Hand and eye movements also express subliteral meaning (see Appendix, 5.2. Gestural Operations). The literal statement that it's just "all one big circle," also directly links the literal topic with the here-and-now group situation.

DEVALUING THE LEADER

Resentment against an authority is often subliterally expressed by stories that devalue the leader. Having met for only the third time, the group was still quite dependent, though the members had formed their seating arrangement into a circle. Like most T-groups at the beginning, they were concerned about my behavior or more correctly, my nonbehavior. I had just bought a rather distinctive leather jacket that both colleagues and students commented on, and it was obvious that group members took particular notice of it, too.

After a brief silent period, a group member asked another member to pass her the "Styrofoam cup on the floor to use as an ash tray." After a pause, a male member then, apparently changing the topic again, and glancing at me, said, "Have you noticed in the student center that all of the plants are plastic. Even the "dirt" they are in is plastic."

The comment about "plastic plants" is a subliteral reference to my leather jacket. Imitation leather (plastics/vinyl) were popular, and from a distance it was difficult to distinguish leather from plastic. The discussion about plastic plants, which are artificial, occurred after some brief comments by members about the "artificiality" of the T-group situation. Thus, this brief comment was the trigger for the discussion of plastic plants. Moreover, the reference to even the "dirt" being artificial probably referred to the tape recorder because the development of the group is "planted" (i.e., recorded) in the tapes. The group situation is often viewed as artificial. The member who made the remark was relatively counterdependent, as indicated by his behavior in previous sessions. He had repeatedly talked about teachers in terms of their "worth" and how some "don't teach you anything." Being the only male in the group besides myself, his remark about plastic plants and the dirt they are in also being plastic functioned to subliterally devalue me (the only other male) in the eyes of the females, thus giving notice of his competition for leadership. Accordingly, the subliteral interpretation is congruent with my psychosociometric assessment of validity (see Appendix, 3.2. Sociometric Operations).

FEELING LIKE MENTAL PATIENTS

This session opened with the topic of "mental patients and community-living programs." It was said that "While it's a good idea, it's not handled well." A member said that one of the problems with these programs is that "They can't have psychologists there all the time, so volunteers must be trained to help." It was further explained that "Usually the volunteers and interns are not qualified and are not supervised adequately in their training." Then a member told of her work with the "mentally confused and senile," and how "It's hard work to work with these people." Then, she went on to talk about how "Open wards are nicer than closed wards." Following this, she said that the "Peons (i.e., nonprofessionals) treated the patients better than the people in higher positions." It was said that there is a need to "get on the people in higher places, to get them on the ball." Then, it was suggested that the "Patients should cooperate with each other." It was pointed out that "Interns only provide cheap labor."

Finally, a story was told of how the head of the California Mental Health Department had been kicked out of similar positions in Massachusetts and New York for his policy of releasing patients back into the community, ending with "And *here* he is doing it again." Another member replied that "the idea of community living is a new idea, so it will take time to make it work. But until it's worked out patients will have a hard time of it." He went on to say that he was "optimistic." "In some places," he continued, "patients do have someone to call if they need help," adding "It's working to a degree." This discussion encompassed a number of feelings and concerns about the T-group experience, some negative and some positive. The topic of "community-living programs . . . not being handled well . . . as they can't afford psychologists all the time" reflects their ambivalent feelings about the group and the apparent lack of my contribution to it.

The discussion about "volunteer help not being qualified" represents group members having to help teach themselves, their concern over their lack of qualification to do so, and therefore not learning anything from each other. The remark that "Volunteer interns are not even supervised reveals their feeling that I was not even supervising them in learning from each other. The reference to "mentally confused and senile" people and "how hard it is to work with them" represents group members who are confused about the functioning of the group. The discussion about "open wards" and "closed wards" refers to the group as an open class as opposed to the traditional teacher-centered classroom. Open and closed wards are probably also a double reference to "quiet" and talkative members (wards equal words). That "Peons treat patients better than higher-ups" means that members treat each other better than I treat them. To "get on the higher-ups" is a demand that I become more involved. That "Patients should cooperate" means group members should cooperate. The view that "volunteers and interns are cheap labor" indicates that members feel they are doing my job for me. The story of the "Head of the California Mental Health Department being kicked out of other jobs" is a threat to me if I insist on running this course the way I've been conducting it. Probably, it also expresses thoughts that I may have been fired from previous teaching positions because of my (incompetent) teaching method.

On a more positive note, the members who maintained that "Community living is a new idea and will take time" indicates their recognition that T-group type of learning is a new idea and therefore will take time to make it work. The comment that "Until then, patients will have a rough time of it," indicates that the members will continue to experience frustration. The reference to being "optimistic" about such programs means that some members are optimistic about the eventual outcome of the group experience. As confirmation of the subliteral connection between his views on community programs and the here-and-now group, later in the session, when a member asked the person who made this remark how he felt about the group, the person replied that he was confident that the group experience would work out. Thus, the parallel between the subliteral and the literal here-and-now group.

Finally, the male's comment "It's working to a degree," reflects that he thinks the group is partially successful and also that there is another level of meaning to the statement, that because the course is required to earn a degree in Human Services, it's working toward a degree, i.e., a diploma.

RESPONSE TO LEADER INTERVENTION

As I've already noted, a leader's comments and interventions are always experienced as important, especially in a nondirective atmosphere like the T-group. A group had been discussing an enjoyable/emotional topic before I gave my interpretation of the topic. The group was at the stage of becoming independent of me and did not like me "butting in." Some members voiced their dislike by saying, "Your comments are always so intellectual." They also complained about me "always spoiling our fun," to which they were referring to their enjoyable level of interaction—which is not usually very productive for learning.

I offered a subliteral interpretation of what was happening in the group, which was the second interpretation I had made during the course of the group. As is typical, a member commented that my interpretation was "pretty wild," and "funny." Another member said that "It's maybe a good analogy, but it's just an analogy." A long group silence ensued and members eyed each other and grinned. Then, a member reached behind her for her coat and bought forth a little booklet that had a picture of a dandelion on the front of it. Below the picture was a printed line which read, "Help Kill Dandelions." Then, she said how "awful it is to advertise this. Dandelions are flowers—and they're good to eat."

Then, most of the group began discussing this topic. In so doing, they spent time talking about the "white fluff" of the dandelion and how the fluff spreads the flower to other places. The topic ended and the group fell silent again. Then, a smile came over the face of the girl who introduced the booklet, and she looked at me and said challengingly, "OK, let's see you relate this topic by analogy," smugly sitting back in her seat.

My response was that a dandelion being a flower refers to members' feelings, as opposed to intellectual matters. The printed line Help Kill Dandelions was a response to my intellectual interpretations killing their feelings. Dandelion probably also means me, i.e., I am a dandy lion. Lions *kill* living things (equals feelings) as I kill their "fun." Furthermore, I am a dandy (lion) because my "aggressive" and "killing" interpretations are secretly admired, i.e., they are dandies. Also, the lion, like me, is the King of the jungle as I am "king" of the group. In addition, Dandelion represents the group in two other respects. First, the group had been operating on a "feeling good" level. Secondly, this had began to wane, i.e., die, as symbolized by the discussion of the dandelion's "white fluff," which indicates the dandelion's life cycle. The group did not laugh at my interpretation this time, but looked astonishingly at each other. At this point the session ended.

When comments are experienced as critical, they are often unconsciously experienced emotionally and are transformed into subliteral expressions. This transformation process is called holophrastic expression. An everyday example of this is when someone linguistically transforms a reaction of an intense insult into a feeling "just like they slapped me in the face." I've already noted one such reaction to a comment I made that resulted in the topics of "pierced ears" and "skindiving." The HELP KILL DANDELIONS is such an expression.

The next session began with a long period of silence. A member looked over toward another member who had on a jacket with the name of a high school athletic team. The jacket happened to have a fold in it so that the entire name of the team was not visible. All that could be seen was MARCH/INDIA. The member said "With that fold in your jacket, the name on it looks like something other than what it is. It looks like MARCH INDIA." The owner of the coat unfolded her jacket and revealed the full name: MARCHING INDIANS. The group laughed. The remark was made by the female who challenged me in the last session to subliterally interpret the title of the booklet she pulled from her coat entitled, "Help Kill Dandelions."

She was interested in mythology, and during the previous session I had suggested that she could look at some of the group stories as myths. But at that time, when her own behavior was being so interpreted, she "just couldn't see it." During this session, before interpreting her comments regarding the letters on the jacket, I asked her why she had commented on the folded over letter on the jacket. She responded with "I just happened to notice it. And anyway it was something to talk about." Then, I asked if she saw any relationship to her observation of the jacket printing, MARCH . . . INDIA with her booklet entitled, Help Kill Dandelions. She thought for a moment, then exclaimed, "Oh, no! You don't mean . . ." I said, "yes, I do mean . . ."

The previous session had evidently made an impact on her unconscious despite her conscious words to the contrary. My interpretation in the previous session was still psychologically present in the current session. Her comment on the folded over "letters" on the jacket subliterally indicated her agreement with the type of interpretation I gave in the previous session, even though she thought it was quite arbitrary and wild. Her mention of the MARCH . . . INDIA embossment on the jacket was her subliteral way of telling me that she had been thinking about it and was beginning to see and understand its logic. In subsequent sessions, some of the members began to offer their own subliteral interpretations. Our unconscious understanding of something often precedes our conscious understanding of it.

LEADERSHIP AND THE GOD TEMPLATE

For people raised to believe in a God who designed the universe in which we live, who is able to see everything that we do, and who sits in judgement on us, such a God becomes, by definition, the ultimate authority figure. This image of God, then, becomes a very deeply rooted emotional unconscious archetype, or template, for any authority figure. Accordingly, if authority figures resonate on an unconscious level to this unconscious God template, then we as subordinates are God's children, often wondering what God is thinking. I have found that the God template is quite prevalent in groups whose members are concerned with me as the authority.

THE MIND OF GOD

This group was nearing its final session. A number of members, who were absent in previous sessions, were also absent from this session. The topics briefly discussed were divorce, aging, and death, followed by discussion of the pros and cons of religion. Some felt that church was terrible because "Ministers and priests don't answer questions in church, and they should." It was also mentioned by a few members that their philosophy instructor didn't "really like to have questions asked in his class." Others felt that "you just have to 'believe,' for mortals cannot understand the workings and complications of the world." And "At any rate, when you're young, you couldn't understand religion, anyway."Another remarked that he could "not believe in God when He let little children die." In response, it was then said "Men can't understand what God is doing." Some maintained that "religion was too commercial," and that "Billy Graham types make money by helping others but withhold their wealth." Finally the topic of religion petered out, and the topic switched to divorce.

The group had been split into two factions: (1) those who wanted the group to be more highly structured and who wanted me to provide the structure, and (2) those who were more independent and who wanted the group to evolve naturally (this is a standard split in T-groups). The former made frequent eye contact with me and directly attempted to elicit answers to their questions from me. From time to time, they would find ways to hurl little innuendos at me about not helping them. Analyzing this piece of conversation subliterally reveals the God template at work and also reveals that different members have different levels of understanding the purpose and goals of the T-group philosophy.

The talk about God was subliterally about me, the authority. The "church," is the classroom, and "priests and ministers," also represent me. That ministers and priests "don't answer questions in church, and they should" is a clear reference that I was nondirective and did not answer their questions. The semantic and associative link to the here-and-now group was the transitional topic about a philosophy instructor who didn't like them to ask questions in class. Thus, some members still didn't accept my T-group philosophy of instruction. On an unconscious level, this was *felt* as I "didn't like questions asked in class." The statement, "you just have to 'believe,' for mortals cannot understand the workings and complications of the world," indicated that although some members did not really understand my philosophy and the group process, they felt that it just had to be taken on faith that my nondirective stance had a valid purpose behind it.

The statement that they are too young to understand religion is a subliteral reference to not having my years of experience that enable me to understand the group dynamics. Like the previous statement, it also reflects some members accepting on faith that I know what I am doing. Others, however, are not of like opinion. The remark of the member who said, he could "not believe in God when He let little children die," reflects this different opinion. Letting children die, subliterally means because the members were not learning anything from me, they were "educationally" dying. But, again, other members were willing to stand on faith. The statement that "Men can't understand what God is doing" means that, like mortals (i.e., novices) who can't understand God's purposes, they can't understand the purpose that I have in mind. The member who was a total disbeliever who maintained that "religion was too commercial," and that "Billy Graham types make money by helping others but withhold their wealth," means that although their tuition is paying my salary, I am not giving them anything in return. Some groups who access their God templates are much more disbelieving.

DISBELIEVERS

A variant on the leader as incompetent and the ivory tower themes is the following. This group had been discussing the increased conflict that occurred during the previous session. When unproductiveness or conflict reaches a certain level, I intervene. I asked the group members if they had read Albert Ellis' book, *A Guide to Rational Living*, that I had assigned. I suggested that Ellis had some important things to say and that reading the book would help them. Then, I explained that conflict in a group was not undesirable but was in fact necessary for growth, that the problem was managing it, not eliminating it. There was a very brief discussion, then silence. Following this silence, a member brought up the topic of religion. They became involved in this topic.

It was immediately clear that there were members who were religious and members who professed not to be. It was said by the disbelievers that "God never helped anyone and that the Bible was only the work of man and not to be taken as the last word." Then someone said that you "don't have to go to church to be religious," and that "these great cathedrals that look like . . . (name of a college) . . . are just to brainwash you." It was further asserted that "when you missed church, you were made to feel guilty." Finally, it was said that "Many Christians were hypocrites, who coveted their neighbor's wives and husbands."

In this conversation, God represents me, the authority. That "God never helped anyone," is again, a reference to me not helping them. And that "the Bible was only the work of Man and not to be taken as the last word," is a reference to Albert Ellis's book that I said would help them. It's also a negative reference to the other course readings that I assigned. The statement that "You don't have to go to church to be religious," probably is a reference to the widespread belief that a person doesn't have to go to college to learn about life. The statement that "these great cathedrals that look like . . . [name of a college] . . . are just to brainwash you," means that colleges are places of brainwashing. The statement, "When you missed church, you were made to feel guilty," is equivalent to a remark I had made about absenteeism in an earlier session. Finally that, "Many Christians are hypocrites, who covet their neighbor's wives and husbands," subliterally refers to a member who told earlier in the session of going with a married man, and who said that she was religious but did not go to church. It's also a reference to the various sexual tensions present in the group. Finally, the entire topic is a positive aspect of this session in that it reveals that some members are gaining independence from me, the authority.

THE CHOSEN ONE

In the history of humankind, one of the most enduring concerns is that someone else will get more than you will. This is illustrated in the Christian Bible numerous times, beginning with Cain and Abel. This episode illustrates in detail how such concerns are subliterally expressed. Throughout the previous eighteen sessions, I had limited my interventions to brief clarifying remarks, which always focused on a group level, never on an individual or a content level. In the previous session, however, I spent a great deal of time pointing out the implication of how people perceive each other using the member who was being criticized as the example. (There was a colleague in this group who I was training.)

After a few preliminary questions to me regarding a required paper, the group members began discussing whether or not they had been too hard on a member during the last session. At this point the member who was being discussed entered the group and sat in the vacant seat on my left. A couple of members asked him if they had "come down on him too hard," and he responded, "no, I really enjoyed it." Then, the member returned the tape of the last session to me, saying that he had not finished listening to it. I told him he could keep the tape until next session. Then, the member asked if he could borrow my pen, and I said "sure."

He had been outspoken in past sessions about his religious convictions. In response to further questioning by the group, he said, "If I seem that way, it's because I have God and I go by it. You really roasted me last time. I know I can't expect all of you to act like me just because I am that way." Another member said, "You really had to stand against the onslaught . . . of the devil." Much laughter ensued.

Then, the member said, "You've all seen that TV program where people are roasted and called names. That's how you all got to me Thursday." Then a member said, "It's hot in here," to which another member responded, " Last week when this was mentioned, I said we were going through The Change." Much laughter.

When someone questioned whether the group was adhering to the here-and-now rule, a member responded, "I think it's a here-and-now situation . . . you know, how we each project to others . . . am I being received the way I say things." At this point I suggested that groups frequently use an individual as a symbol of wider concerns, as a scapegoat for concerns that are present in the group as a whole but which the group doesn't want to deal with. Whenever a group spends session after session concentrating on a particular individual, it's usually an indication of scapegoating. Then, a lengthy silence followed.

An older member who also made no secret as to his religious convictions, said to the member of whom the group had been critical, "I've been seeking clarification of your Christian views." Then the member with whom the group had been preoccupied said, "I know for a fact that I am the only one in here that is apostolic, that probably I'm the only one who has been baptized in Jesus' name. I am quite sure." Some members immediately objected. But he went on to say, "You have been baptized Father, Son, and Holy Ghost, or sprinkled, but not in Jesus' name." A heated discussion ensued, in which the member then replied, "I was baptized underwater in Jesus's name." He went on to say that regular baptism was not the same, that "Just because you were baptized Father, Son and Holy Ghost . . . those are just titles. When Jesus arose from the dead, he told his disciples that all power is in the name of the Father, *comma,* the Son, *comma,* and the Holy Ghost. He did not say 'in the names' with an 's' on it, he said name." Another member replied that he was hung up on words. Once more I asked if the conversation had any here-and-now significance. I was ignored.

The member being criticized reiterated, " I know that I'm the only one in here that has been baptized in Jesus' name. Just because I am different. . . ." At this point, a member interjected with, "If others had been baptized the same as you, you're saying they would have known it?" The member replied, "Right." Another member responded, "If we were all baptized underwater, then would we all be the same?" He responded that "if you got the Holy Ghost, we would all be alike." It was objected that "first you say Jesus, now it's the Holy Ghost. Which is it?" He responded, "Those two scriptures went together. If you would all go to the Bible, then we would all have the same goals."

In a delayed response to my question about the here-and-now relevance of the topic, a member who had previously supported him, said, "There is the same process happening in here. Jesus was scrutinized, stoned, and called crazy. It's a parallel." There were some joking references that the member whom they were criticizing was like Jesus Christ. He denied it, of course, as did the other members—and, I might add, quite vociferously. Then a member said that perhaps he was "Jesus' son." A member interjected, "What's this got to do with the here-and-now?" "It's the way you are coming off to the group," another responded, "putting yourself above us." Then, someone asked, "Because I haven't gone through the same process that you have gone through, can I be accepted in this class?" The member being focused on responded, "on that train of thought, dealing with this class, yes."

The member who was asking if he could be accepted, continued, "Whatever goal we as a group have, as a class, can you accept us?" Referring to me, a supportive member said, "he is our leader," to which two other members responded, "He's not my leader. He has taught me nothing in here." Then, the supportive member interjected, "You'll change your mind when you hit the gates." Silence. Then, I asked, "What side of Jesus did Judas sit on at the Last Supper?" Much laughter ensued. The member sitting next to me put his arm around and on the back of my chair. Silence. A couple of members said they thought Judas sat on the left of Jesus, at least according to artists' conceptions. The member being criticized added, "He sat close to Jesus because Jesus said 'whosoever shall sup with me on bread—and he put something in Jesus' cup—shall have everlasting life.' And then Jesus told him [Judas] to go and do what he had to do and to do it quickly."

Then, the discussion revolved around whether the biblical quote about where Judas sat was correct. Silence. Then, a member directed the group into their perceptions of each other. The member, who has been the center of discussion up to this point, got up and *quickly* left the group, leaving his coat and books behind. A few minutes later, he rushed back into the room out of breath and announced that he looked up the quote and that he was right about what side of Jesus Judas sat on. The group continued giving their perceptions of each other until the end of the session.

Now, what does all this mean subliterally? First, it's important to note that whenever a member is perceived as having been singled out by a leader, it's often unconsciously felt—both by the member and by the group—that the member is somehow special (as if the member had been specially anointed). Thus the member's remark, "I know for a fact that I am the only one in here that is apostolic; that probably I'm the only one who has been baptized in Jesus' name. *I am quite sure*" means he is quite sure because he is the only member of the group who has in fact been directly focused on by me, to whom in fact I loaned my pen, and who I singled out by suggesting that the group was using him as a scapegoat.

His assertion that "You have been baptized Father, Son, and Holy Ghost or sprinkled, but not in Jesus' name," means that the other group members have been only the recipients of general remarks by me (the Father), the cotrainer (Son) and by the group as a whole (the Holy Ghost), but in a "personalized " way by me (reflects that he was baptized in Jesus' name).

His remarks about "I was baptized underwater," mean that by being focused on, he was submerged in the group process compared to the rest of the members. "Just because you are baptized Father, Son, and Holy Ghost . . . these are just titles," means that each member has received only general remarks from me, the cotrainer, and the group as a whole. "When Jesus arose from the dead . . ." means my finally becoming active (alive) in the group. "When Jesus arose from the dead, he told his disciples (the group) that "all power is in the name of the Father, *comma,* the Son, *comma,* and the Holy Ghost."

That he did not say in the "name*s* of . . ." with an 's' (denoting a plural noun) indicates that all power in the group, all action, derived from me (the Father/Jesus), not from the cotrainer (the son) or the group. They do so only in Jesus' name (i.e., "name" singular) equates to myself because my name does not end with an "s," i.e., Haskell. The cotrainer's name, however, Heapes, did have an "s." Further, his statement, "If you had the holy ghost, we would all be alike," means that if the trainer had focused on them in the same way they would all be equal.

Moreover, although the Holy Ghost (i.e., also the perceived messages by the trainer) did not tell the member how he should behave, it was *perceived* that he should behave in a certain manner. In response to the charge by another member that, "First you say Jesus, now it's the Holy ghost, which is it?" the member responded, "Those two scriptures went together," reflects me and my word and/or my textbook. "If you would all go to the Bible, then we would all have the same goals" says that if the group would all go by my textbook, then the group would all work smoothly.

The inquiry whether they could be accepted in the class even though they had not gone through the process that he had, elicited the member's response: "On that train of thought dealing with the class, yes," means that from the viewpoint that this is a class (i.e., on that train of thought means my thought) they can be accepted," but they are still not "equal" because they have not been favored like they perceived him to have been. The remarks "He's not my leader. He has taught me nothing in here," means that I have taught them nothing and they are not going to act like me or follow me (i.e., be disciples). Finally, the member's comment that, "You'll change your mind when you hit the gate," says you'll change your mind when grades are due, i.e., the time of Judgement.

CONCLUSION

All of these subliteral topics were transformations of basic concerns about leadership and authority, and each different topic was a permutation or variation revolving around a single complex of emotional concerns. We saw (1) concerns about authority figures who have special powers, concerns about being secretly taped and spied upon that were transformed into stories about crystal balls, speakeasies, the game of charades, the CIA, the FBI gathering information, and concerns about journalists writing about people; (2) concerns about the competence of leaders and authority that were transformed into stories about psychologists, parents, teachers, policeman, bosses, and God, who did not know what they were doing or who maltreated their subordinates; (3) concerns about authorities who ripped off, cheated, or otherwise engaged in false advertising, who were insulting and wrote books that were useless. The topics about leadership and authority presented in this chapter do not, of course, exhaust the list. Far from it.

We also saw that these subliteral transformations were carried out using various cognitive and linguistic operations. We saw (1) pun-like sounds being used to create meaning, as in the crystal *ball* being equated with *bald* head; (2) holophrastic transformations, as feeling like their ears had been *pierced;* (3) double meanings, where "it's working to a degree" was meant as "working toward a degree," i.e., a diploma; (4) the single name, "Upjohn" was subliterally used to mean, "get up, John;" (5) topics and phrases used as linkages, as a kind of clue, linking the literal topic with the here-and-now situation, e.g., the phrase "it's all one big circle," being subliteral for the circular seating pattern in the group; (6) the use of nonverbal hand gestures linking the literal topic to the here-and-now, e.g., pointing around the circular seating arrangement of the group while telling a literal story; (7) temporal tense shifts by specific use of nouns and pronouns that linked the literal topic to the here-and-now situation, e.g., using *this, here,* when *that* and *there* should have been used; (8) plural shifts used similarly; and (9) we saw that subliteral topics created by a person were consistent with their underlying concerns and views in the literal conversation.

Finally, we saw that much can be learned from listening subliterally. In addition to learning about particular unconscious feelings and thoughts, the subliteral stories revealed much about the dynamics among individuals and between the group and the leader. In the next chapter, I show similar kinds of subliteral operations in relation to peer and interpersonal dynamics.

CHAPTER 4

MARKS OF CAIN AND ABEL
PEER AND INTERPERSONAL CONCERNS

In the last chapter, I illustrated how archetypal human concerns about authority and leadership are expressed subliterally in social conversations. In this chapter, I illustrate archetypal concerns about interpersonal and peer relationships that occur in social situations. Many of these concerns, like those about leadership, have provided the emotional source for the enduring—and the not so enduring—literature around the world. As humans we have a range of deep emotional needs. We experience jealousy, betrayal, greed, love, fear, and a host of other feelings that are played out in our everyday dramas. Just like concerns with authority and leadership, archetypes of peer and interpersonal themes, too, range from the existentially profound to the mundane and petty.

One of the archetypal stories in Western society that describes the depth of feeling about rivalry and competition and the extreme consequences that ensue from these feelings is the Biblical story of Cain and Abel, the two sons of Adam and Eve. Cain kills his brother Abel out of jealousy. Then, God put a physical mark on Cain for all the world to see. I have drawn the title of this chapter from that story and use the murder of Abel by Cain as the basic template for the problems and feeling that are ever present in everyday conversations.

Through the years, I have observed a consistency of subliteral themes that reflect the eternal conflicts in human affairs. These themes include competition, rivalry, jealously, double standards, separation and loss, and others that are more positive—the positive ones, however, don't seem to be as abundant as the negative ones. Many of these interpersonal themes revolve around gender and racial or ethnic concerns. I present these last two concerns in separate chapters.

INTRODUCTORY ILLUSTRATIONS

As we carry on our conversations, our conscious and also our unconscious minds are always vigilant for any sign of perceived insult, bragging, injustice, or signs of behavior or attitudes that are just plain outside the norms of our expectations or what we think is acceptable behavior. Our unconscious picks up on these violations that our conscious mind misses. For example:

SPEAKING OF SPEAKERS

On one evening, my former wife, my friend and colleague, Dr. Aaron Gresson, and I were having an evening of engrossing conversation, as we often did. On the day before, we had bought a new stereo system with very nice stereo speakers. Now, Aaron is a very knowledgeable and verbal person. On this occasion, he was talking at great length about some subject, and we found it difficult to get a word into the conversation. Aaron and I would often carry on long discussions. My wife had no interest in many of them. My wife was casually looking around the room, obviously bored with Aaron's extended monologue. At this point and totally unrelated to what Aaron was talking about, she interrupted, asking, "Where's the other (stereo) speaker?" Subliterally, this question clearly meant, why is Aaron doing all the talking? Why isn't someone else talking, too? In short, she was asking, where are the other speakers in this conversation?

SPEAKING OF HEAVYWEIGHTS

When meeting someone for the first time, we often notice how they look and take particular note of any distinguishing characteristics. Sometimes we express our reactions to these characteristics subliterally. On a TV talk show some years ago,[1] the host Merv Griffin was introducing the actress, Virginia Graham, who was rather plump and large-framed. He began by describing her long career and distinguished list of credits in show business, as he often did when welcoming people, adding, "She's a real heavyweight." He no more than had spoken these words when he realized the implications of what he had subliterally said.

UNWITTING BRAGGING

One of the most egregious social faux pas recognized in most cultures is to be perceived as bragging about oneself. People usually pick up immediately on such ego trips. The problem is that we don't have control over how others perceive whether we may be bragging or not. Case in point: While sitting on my porch one day sorting through my note cards, a former student, who happened to be driving by, stopped to chat with me. Because I am not an especially talented conversationalist when it comes to superficial conversation, he did most of the talking. He really didn't have much to say, so he talked in a free-associating or near stream of consciousness manner, as much of this kind of meaningless chitchat tends to be. In between breaths he paused for a moment, looked at all my note cards, and asked what I was doing—was I "writing a book, or something?" With a matter of fact tone, I tersely replied, "Yes" that I was working on a number of things, a book, a professional article, and a talk for a conference. "Oh," he said. Pausing for a moment, he slipped back into his stream of consciousness talk. He began by telling the story about "a man he knew who was always bragging about the things he was doing." Subliterally, he obviously perceived me as bragging. Taken somewhat aback at this, I thought to myself, "Oh, is that what you think I was doing—bragging? I thought you were the one who asked me what I was doing." So much for being able to control what others perceive.

THE WORLD'S GREATEST AUTHORITY

Another instance of being perceived as bragging. I had sent a manuscript of mine on "Metaphor" to a colleague for his comments. The manuscript was written in metaphor and wasn't written for publication. Rather it was a "study" of metaphor in much the same manner that artists do "studies" with a particular technique they are developing.[2] Moreover, I roamed quite widely in the study, taking various authors to task. A great deal of my paper dealt with double meanings, plays on words, and how just the form or structure of a sentence could make it appear as if the sentence made sense when it in fact did not. In the last pages I dedicated the study to Professor Irwin Corey, a comic entertainer whose verbal nonsense is made to sound grammatically meaningful by the way he put words together. Professor

Corey always talked authoritatively on all subjects. He was one of my favorite comedians.

The manuscript came back to me with a letter attached which said in part, "I also liked the dedication to Professor Irwin Corey, who, if I am right, is the 'World's Greatest Authority,' is he not?" Indeed Professor Corey was frequently billed as the "World's Greatest Authority." What my colleague was doing was subliterally commenting on the tone of my manuscript which could lead one to believe that I was the world's greatest authority on metaphor. First, "authorities" are by definition "right." In the phrase ". . . if I am right . . ." (which he felt he was), my colleague was asserting his authority, too. What is more, the interrogatory phrase ". . . is he not?" also has a double meaning. In common usage, the phrase "is he not?" is a positive statement meaning "this is so, right?" Now, to understand what my colleague was really saying, you need to know about his background. He is a specialist on the German philosopher Hegel, who dealt with "logical negations," and furthermore who considered his philosophical system the culmination of all philosophy! Hegel thought that he was the world's greatest authority in philosophy.

Subliterally, the "World's Greatest Authority" equates to myself and Hegel. The "not" in the phrase ". . . is he not?", then, also meant "no he [meaning me] is not" the world's greatest authority. Now why was my authority negated? The answer is that my colleague thought he was the world's greatest authority, as he was working on a philosophical theory related to metaphor which took a different view from mine. Hence, if I am right, he is not right. And so it goes. We are all egotists if we dig deep enough. We would all like to be first. It's frequently the case that people may be unconsciously thinking something about you but for a number of reasons choose not to let you know. Usually, when people choose to hide their feelings about you, it's because the feeling is negative. But positive feelings may remain unsaid, too, for a number of reasons, some having to do with their egos. Listening subliterally, we can often hear these compliments.

A BEGRUDGING COMPLIMENT

As a doctoral candidate, I was sitting in my committee chairman's office discussing an issue regarding my dissertation, when a fairly well-known professor of small group communications appeared in the open doorway.

Seeing that there was a discussion in progress, there was a brief awkward silence. My chairman said to the professor, "Come on in, we're just sitting here talking." The professor briefly looked at me, and there ensued another, but shorter, awkward silence as I merely looked at him and then turned away. The professor fidgeted uncomfortably for a moment and then said, to my chairman, "Oh, did I tell you we have one of the very bright graduate students of Dr. _____ (a well-known scholar) joining our department? She left him; told him just where he could go, too. No one has ever done that. You really have to respect her for not bowing down to him." Then, the professor's eyes ever so fleetingly glanced over at me, as sometimes occurs in those little micro moments of eye contact. After some small talk with my chairman, the professor left.

Now, what did this conversation really mean? Was it simply a "literal" piece of information that the professor of small group communications came to tell my chairman, or was it merely a piece of small talk generated by an obviously uncomfortable social situation? Or was it a piece of subliteral talk? How is one to interpret this verbal exchange? Because words only *mean* something in a context, to understand the full meaning you need to be aware of the context to which this piece of talk belongs.

This professor had been my graduate major advisor for a brief period, until I refused to be his disciple, at which point I told him that our relationship was not going to work. This professor of small group communication was a well-known scholar in the field, just like the professor about whom he was telling in his story, and like the professor in the story, he wasn't accustomed to having graduate students refuse to work with him. Indeed, most graduate students considered it an honor to be selected to work with him.

With the telling of his story about a very bright graduate student of Dr. _____ (a well-known scholar) who left him, telling him just where he could go, noting that no one had ever done that, and saying that the graduate student had to be respected for not bowing down to him, my former professor was subliterally acknowledging to my chairman that, like the student who defected from the famous professor to his department, I had defected from him to my chairman. Moreover, he was subliterally informing me that although I did not assent to his wishes and defected, he nevertheless respected me for my independence. Again, I have no doubt that he was not aware of what he had said subliterally.

WHAT'S IN A NAME

One of the more interesting ways by which the subliteral mind communicates is with names and initials. When listening to conversations, careful attention should always be paid to names and initials. Name and initials are often used subliterally to communicate unconscious feelings, concerns, and issues. The cognitive operations often used to transform literal names and initials into subliteral references are (a) the pun-like use of sounds or phonetics, (b) similarly spelled names, (c) combining or embedding the name within an existing name or title, and (d) associations of name to other people's names. These subliteral operations can reveal what others may be unconsciously thinking and feeling about us.

SPECIAL EFFECTS IN HUMAN AFFAIRS

A brief introductory example of using similar sounding names to express a thought or feeling subliterally about a person occurred in a group concerned about a male member who was experimenting on them by his trying out different interpersonal techniques. The member seemed to be very good at adopting the different techniques mentioned in the reading material for establishing good interpersonal feelings among members. But at times, it seemed a bit artificial. Following a slight pause in the conversation, a member began talking about movies. In particular the member talked about the *"special effects"* used by the movie director Stanley *"Kubrick,"* who is well known for his movie *Dr. Strangelove,* among others. Now, what's interesting in selecting the name Stanley *Kubrick* is that the last name of the member they were having concerns about was *"Kulick."* The group was subliterally commenting on the special effects-like quality of the member's interpersonal techniques. Perhaps the member who selected Stanley Kubrick's name to comment subliterally on the male who was trying to create warm feelings in the group, felt that his engaging in interpersonal techniques was a strange kind of love.

BEING FOOLHARDY

Sometimes names combine pun-like sound relationships and embed a name within another name. This cognitive operation is exemplified by the following. On one afternoon, I was at a friend's house for an in-ground bar-beque. When the time came to begin putting the food in the pit he had dug, someone noticed that the pit was far too small for all the food that needed to be cooked. Many of the people, who were gathered around, agreed. Others just laughed. Then someone said, "Yes, this was fool*hardy*," literally meaning that it was *foolish* to have dug such a small in-ground bar-beque pit. The subliteral point, here is that my friend's last name is *Hardy*.

BEING *Rh* NEGATIVE

It's sometimes the case that only initials are used to refer subliterally to a person. In a group where I intervened to analyze and diagnose the dynamics of what just occurred in the group, a heavy silence followed. Members often experience these interventions as criticism, as a sign that "something is wrong." I have already mentioned one subliteral response to criticism felt where the topic of "pierced ears" followed a deep analysis I made about a group's behavior. Following an intervention I made, members then began discussing medical doctors and health conditions. The particular medical condition that preoccupied them was: *Rh negative blood*. Why did this specific condition emerge in the conversation? The answer is that, in addition to the topic of medical problems being subliterally equivalent to my (i.e., a Dr.) diagnosis and analysis of them, more tellingly, the topic of *Rh negative blood* was a specific subliteral reference to my initials, *R.H*. The *negative* in the phrase subliterally indicated their feeling that my remarks were perceived as critical of them. A further indication that *Rh negative blood* was a reference to me was that the approximate color of my hair was red.

MR. ROBERTS, I PRESUME?

A more extensive example of the subliteral use of names occurred in a group that I videotaped in the previous session for playback during the current meeting. The videotape machine and the television monitor were standing by, waiting for members to arrive. During this session, a member brought her small child to class. A member who was absent from the previous session entered the room and looked at the television, paused for a moment and said, "What are we going to watch, Mr. Roberts!" This was a subliteral reference to me. Out of a nearly infinite number of possible phrases the member could have used and out of at least hundreds of possible television programs, why was the particular name, *Mr. Roberts* selected?

The name was selected because it combined the member's basic and immediate feelings about me and the group. Let me explain.

The history and context of the situation created a Selection-Response Field that constrained and influenced the member choice of phrases (see Appendix 2.5. Selection-Response Field). *First,* the member unexpectedly confronted a television and a microphone, hence, increasing the possibility of narrowing the Selection-Response Field to a remark about television. *Secondly,* the member was surprised at seeing a child in the group, further narrowing his response-field to children's television programs. *Third,* the member had been counterdependent and considered the group process childish. *Fourth* was his concern with me as authority, hence, narrowing his response-field to a program which has a clear and distinct male leader. And *fifth,* my name being "Robert," narrowed the response-field to a television children's program that has a leader whose name begins with an "R," hence, *Mr. Roberts.*

Somewhat more peripherally, was perhaps a stereotypic racial factor involved in selecting the name prefixed with *"Mr."* Roberts. Both the child who came to the group and its mother were black. In past sessions, the child's mother always referred to me as "Mr." Haskell, whereas the member who made the remark usually referred to me as "Robert." The area of the country in which the group was conducted was quite racist. The stereotype involved here is the historical black and Southern linguistic style of referring to whites by the prefix "Mr." or "Miss," followed by a first name, as in "Mr. John," or "Miss Jane." Hence, the phrase, "Mr." + Roberts! Although the literal name was a last name, subliterally, it referred to my first name. All of these concerns and factors were fused together in the member's selection of the name Mr. Roberts.

This practice of using the titles "Mr." or "Miss." with a person's first name, instead of their last name, is most interesting. As explained in the illustration, the practice was historically connected with slavery and with Southern linguistic style. First, slaves often referred to the slave holder in this manner—as Mr. John, or Miss Emily. It was also sometimes used by members of the lower socioeconomic class when addressing the aristocracy. Because one of the members of the group was black and she had her little child with her, the title, Mr. Roberts, was thus probably more associatively linked to the racial aspects of its historical usage than to reflecting the status difference. It's also possible that the title Mr. Roberts reflected a status difference, especially given that the black female's child was in the group and the association with the children's program, *Mr. Rogers*.[3] In any event, the remark was no accident or chance statement.

Finally, this subliteral episode reflects the cognitive operation of strategic misremembering. There was, in fact, no TV program with a Mr. Roberts. The member literally meant the children's program, *Mr. Rogers*, but this name would not have subliterally referenced his specific feelings about me (see Appendix, 8.7. Memorial and Perceptual Operations).

JABBERWOCKY TALKIE

A very cognitively interesting—albeit more complex—illustration of using names is the following. A group began to discuss and repeatedly emphasize that plants should not be placed in *direct sunlight*. The phrase *direct sunlight* was tonally stressed. Just before this conversation, two dominant group members had been actively directing the group by talking about techniques to facilitate the group's growth (development). On a group level, not putting plants in *direct sunlight* means that the group is not comfortable always analyzing the dynamics and using techniques. The word sunlight, then, was a subliteral vehicle for expressing the group's disdainful concern about analyzing and using techniques. They thought it stunted their development.

The word *sunlight* was constructed out of two members' names, one of whom was a female who was older than the other female members. Her name was *Firestone* (equals sun, i.e., a big stone of fire), and a young male who was young enough to be her son (equals sun), whose name was *Wright* (i.e., phonetically or by rhyme equates to light;). Hence, *Firestone + Wright = sunlight*. The adjective *direct* in the phrase *direct sunlight* comes from the fact that these two members were *direct*-ing (i.e., leading) the group by analyzing and using various techniques to facilitate the *growth* of the group (group equals plants). Thus, the group was being subjected to *direct sunlight*, i.e., analysis.

My analysis of the word sunlight is no mere schizophrenic-like association. The word *sunlight* is a subliteral form of what is called a portmanteau word. A portmanteau word is formed by merging or combining the sounds and meanings from two different words, like the word *slithy* (from Lewis Carroll's poem Jabberwocky) formed from the words *lithe* and *slimy*. Only in this case the combining was accomplished unconsciously (see chapter 8).

As with all subliteral examples, we must ask why the particular word, topic, or phrase was selected instead of the many possible alternatives. In this case, why not have just said *sunlight* and not qualify it by the adjective *direct*? Why not have simply said *sun* instead of *sunlight*? Or why not have just simply said *light*? Again, the answer is that these alternatives would not have expressed members' subliteral feelings, perceptions, and concerns.

Linguistically, new words or neologisms and meanings are sometimes formed by condensing or assimilating elements of already existing words and their meanings. It's often the case that this standard linguistic process determines the selection (not the new creation) of a particular word or phrase to be used in a given piece of subliteral talk

INTERPERSONAL COMMUNICATION

Communicating with each other is a difficult and complicated process. Think about it for a moment. Each of us is confined to our own minds. We have no way to see into another person's mind or to feel their feelings. As the German philosopher and mathematician, Gottfried Leibniz (1646–1716), said, we are individual monads, completely sealed off units, floating around the universe with no way of seeing into other people's worlds. We often don't know, for example, when someone to whom we are talking is bored, is competing with us, or a host of other interpersonal things that are happening in social conversations. We don't know because all too often the other people may not have conscious access to what they are feeling, or because they simply won't tell us. Either way, listening subliterally can help to find out what's going on in another person's universe.

BORING CONVERSATIONS

A group had been in session for about half an hour, engaging in considerable small talk, when a member who developed into a "leader" in the group commented on the dynamics that were occurring and went on at great length expressing his feelings and giving suggestions. The group only very briefly discussed his suggestions. Then another male began to offer his ideas to the group. He prefaced his remarks with "I won't bore you with a long history of my feelings, so I'll make it short and to the point." He stated his point, and the group continued.

The male, who had become a leader, conducted groups as part of his job, and this group was aware of his background. Although the group liked him, his rather strong leadership frequently made him the target of subtle attacks and innuendos. While he was talking on at length, it was obvious that many members mentally "tuned out." The other male who said he didn't want to bore people had been in competition with him throughout the term, though he was not a serious threat.

The male's statement that "He did not want to bore the group," clearly may seem to be one of those conscious snide remarks, but it wasn't. It was in fact a subliteral comment on the other male's lengthy speech. In short, he was expressing (a) his own feelings and (b) those of the group regarding the male who talked a lot. In effect, he was telling him, "you were boring me and the whole group."

To check whether this remark was a conscious snide remark, later in the session, I asked the male who said he didn't want to bore people if he saw any significance in his statement. He said "No," he didn't. Continuing, I asked him why he prefaced his statement the way he did. Again, he replied that he didn't know. Then, I asked him if he was bored when the other male was talking and he replied "Yes, I was." A surprised look of insight came on his face. Now, he understood the subliteral meaning of his statement.

This clearly points out that in many of these subliteral illustrations, it may seem that the person must know what they are really saying, that statements like "I don't want to bore you," reflect one of those occasions when the speaker consciously makes such a statement to indirectly insult a person. As this analysis shows, however, in many situations people are not aware of the subliteral meaning of what they are saying.

HIDDEN THOUGHTS OF APPRECIATION

I noted in the introduction to this chapter that not just insults are subliterally expressed. Sometimes there are expressions of appreciation, as the following illustration shows. Members of a group were discussing their frustration with what they perceived as a lack of progress. One of the members suggested that "We need to read more of the text material." As typically occurs with a suggestion to read my textbook material, a silence followed. Then, I intervened saying that groups often didn't read and apply the material in the text because of a norm against not "showing each other up," that the group had what is called a "rate busting" norm. Silence. Then, the group went on to some small talk. A member suggested that the group examine its interpersonal structure, but this, too, soon ended again in silence. Then, an older woman in the group, said, "Why can't people be nice to one another? Why can't we say nice things to people when they do something good?" A heavy silence ensued. What did her statement mean? I mean, subliterally?

In previous sessions, the older woman had complained of the lack of structure in the group and in particular my failure to contribute to the sessions. Although she complained that she didn't understand the dynamics without help, she was always polite and courteous in doing so and was not as counterdependent as the younger members. During the previous session, I had drawn a diagram on the blackboard explaining the major dynamics of groups. I had done this quietly during a period of much small talk. Without saying anything, I returned to my seat. As is typical in a stage of group development when the members are becoming independent, the group totally ignored this instructional event. Only a couple of members took brief notes on what I had put on the board, and only the older woman took extensive notes. Even into the next session, no one mentioned my active contribution.

The older woman's inquiry, "Why can't people be nice to one another? Why can't we say nice things to people when they do something good?" was her way of subliterally thanking me for my direct suggestions as to what were some of the dynamics in the group.

As in the previous example, I later asked the woman if she could explain why her comment came at this particular point in the discussion because it seemed to have no connection with the previous comments. She replied she didn't know why she said it at that point. Then, I asked her how she felt when I put the diagram on the board. She replied, "grateful." I asked her how she felt when I commented on the group dynamics earlier this session. She replied, "I was relieved." Then, I asked if she saw any connection between her remark and my instructional contributions before her remark. Even with this hint, she shook her head, "No." When I shared my complete interpretation with her, her eyes opened wide, and she gasped "Oh, my God, that's right."

COMPETITION FOR KING OF THE MOUNTAIN

In most social situations there is an element of competition and rivalry of one kind or another. This group began with members discussing interpersonal relationships. They talked about competition amongst themselves in relation to making an impression on each other and to impress me. They went on to discuss the reasons for competition, namely, to get a grade, and perhaps to vie with me, the authority. Then, a male said that "Competition is what life is all about." Meanwhile the various members squirmed in their chairs, and changed body position while the male continued his speech from his position on the top of the back-support of his chair. He continued saying, "Life is competition to reach the top of the mountain." This male member had been uncooperative and counterdependent during most of the group sessions, and had openly challenged me numerous times.

His sitting atop the backrest of his chair, thus physically placing himself above everyone else, especially me, was subliterally congruent with his declaration, "Life is competition to reach the top of the mountain." Being on the top of his chair, he had subliterally reached the top of the mountain (See Appendix, 5.3. Body-Positioning Operations).

When asked if he saw any connection between his words and his actions, he stopped, literally looked at himself and said, "No." As obvious as this may seem, when I suggested this subliteral analysis, he was stunned, as was the rest of the group. There was a complete disconnect between the literal and subliteral levels of his consciousness.

DEMOCRACY IN ACTION

Like other narratives, listening to stories about politics and political leaders often reveals hidden feelings in a conversation. Years ago a group which had been recently formed, began with some of its members voicing concern over the meaning and usefulness of such a course. Other members attempted to justify the course. It was asked, "What topic shall we discuss?" Then there was talk about the quiet members not contributing to the discussions. After some small talk, one member—an older woman—suggested discussing the national presidential election between the Republican incumbent Gerald Ford and the Democratic nominee, Jimmy Carter. "Most students and teachers, I've found are Democrats," she said, "but I'm for Ford." She then talked about "voter apathy." The woman went on to say that although she was for Ford, she thought he had "accomplished nothing," adding, "though I am not really up on it." Another member said "I don't know whether to vote or not, I don't know anything about the candidates." Then during a discussion about politics in general, a member said "No matter what you do, politics is always present," to which another member responded, "Yes, there are always political favors." This episode reveals a concern with leadership and authority dynamics and also with member-to-member and member-to-trainer dynamics.

The older woman's suggestion to discuss the presidential election between the Republican incumbent Gerald Ford and the Democratic nominee,

Jimmy Carter stood for the divisions in the group between (1) myself as the trainer and the rest of the group, (2) the older woman and the rest of the younger members, and (3) specifically between her and myself. This is evidenced by her next statement "Most students and teachers, I've found are Democrats." Thus, Democrats are equal to myself and the younger members. On another level, however, both of the references to Republicans and to Democrats are equal to me. I say this first, because a President and a nominee for President is a leader and authority figure. As I indicate in my one and only lecture during the first meeting, my role in the group was dual. I'd be a member but not a member at the same time. Thus, I was both authorities, President Ford, and nominee (not yet President) Carter. The general context for the topic of politics is to be found in my initial lecture and in the texts, where I repeatedly refer to T-group functioning as a democratic process.

The older woman saying that while, "I'm for Ford," she thinks "he has accomplished nothing," reflects that although she identifies with me—being older and being the authority—she thinks I have done nothing to help the group. She is not sure, however, because she adds, "though I am not really up on it," which means she doesn't really know much about T-group functioning. Her remark about "voter apathy" represents (1) the quiet members who are not actively participating and (2) many of the other members who don't seem to be helping the group progress, i.e., she thinks they are apathetic—perhaps even pathetic.

The comment by another member in the discussion on politics who says, "I don't know whether to vote or not, I don't know anything about the candidates," means that he doesn't know enough about the group members to engage them productively. The remark by another member that, "No matter what you do, politics is always present," to which another member responded, "Yes, there are always political favors," represents concerns about rivalry among members, currying favor (otherwise known as "brown-nosing"), and being favored by me.

Finally, if you haven't already noticed, the comment by another member in the discussion on politics saying, "I don't know whether to vote or not, I don't know anything about the candidates," subliterally means that he doesn't know enough about the group members to productively engage them, and it is an especially interesting item. It's an unconscious response to the subliteral meaning of the older woman's charge that members are apathetic. In short, it demonstrates unconscious or subliteral conversations between members. Let's be clear on this. I mean that a listener's unconscious mind understands the subliteral level of meaning in the literal narratives spoken by another person.

DOUBLE STANDARDS

In social life we are always watchful for the rules and norms used to regulate interaction among people. We seem to be especially watchful for double standards where one person or group is favored and someone other than ourselves is selected as the "chosen one."

The group began with an older woman talking about her internship and the fact that she "is going to be running therapy groups." Another member asked if they were "voluntary or involuntary" to which she added as an afterthought and half under her breath, "like in here where we are forced to take it for credit." Silence. The topic returned to the previous session where a member revealed his recent arrest for selling drugs and the possibility of his being sentenced to prison. Then, the discussion centered around "police," "laws," and "rules." The member who was arrested explained that there is no crime in his township [meaning very little crime], so the "cops sit around and look for something to do." Shortly thereafter in the middle of a conversation and looking at two members and myself who were sitting together, he interrupted with, "As a matter of fact, I saw three police cars all parked together in one neighborhood." At a later point, he said, "If you were busted, they take you down to the station and wire you up [i.e., plant a microphone on you] and turn you into a stoolie." At the end of the conversation about the cops who busted him, the same member said that the police actually take drugs themselves and then added, "There's a double standard here." Further discussion. End of session.

About ten minutes into the session, I changed my seat so I could have a clear view of all members. Now, I sat between the older woman who mentioned she was going to be "running therapy groups" and a younger female member who had been an active leader in the group and who had mentioned in the first session that she was familiar with therapy type groups, too. About fifteen minutes after I had changed my seat, the younger female changed her seat to the one I had formerly occupied.

The topic of "voluntary and involuntary therapy groups" represent the present group because the course was an elective for half of the members (i.e., voluntary) and was a requirement (i.e., involuntary) for the other half. This link is clearly indicated by the member's afterthought in answering whether the therapy groups were voluntary or involuntary, saying somewhat under her breath, "like in here." The statement, "like in here," is a clear link to the here-and-now group topic.

The comment about cops taking drugs themselves and the subsequent complaint that, "There's a double standard *here*" has multiple subliteral meanings. First the "three cops" represent me, the older female, and the younger female who are the "leaders" in the group, i.e., the authorities. "Double" also means me and the older woman who were sitting together; and also includes the other female who moved to the chair that I had previously sat in, i.e., she is now in my role as a kind of "double" as an actor in a movie who "sits in" for the main actor. When members are absent, their spirit or presence is often considered to be occupying their empty chairs. This is especially so for the chair that belongs to the leader. My chair, then, becomes personified and thus is like a member of the group. In addition, double represents the male/female split in the group and the voluntary/involuntary split among the members. Finally, "double" means the double standard that the trainer shows by acting one way (no leadership) but expecting members to act in another way (i.e., to show leadership behavior).

The "here" in the "there is a double standard *here*" subliterally means here in the group. It's a link (only on a less conscious level) that belongs to the same type as the conscious link mentioned previously in the afterthought "like in here." That "cops sit around and look for something to do" represents the three leaders sitting around and looking for something to talk about, something "inter(ar)resting?" This analysis is supported by the statement, "I saw three cars all parked together" again, representing me and the two female leaders. At this point we were still sitting together. Finally, "being wired up," refers to the tape recorder, i.e., group has a tape recorder and microphone symbolically strapped to it, which makes them (self) stoolies.

TRAFFICKING IN IDENTITY

When becoming part of a group, a concern that many people in our individualistic culture have is losing their independence. Groups often exert pressure for conformity. This is often felt as psychologically and emotionally engulfing and as a threat to one's identity.

The following episode spans four sessions and comes from the same group as the "On Fairness and Leadership" subliteral narrative that I described in the last chapter. After considerable topic hopping, the group discussed "marriage" and its attendant problems of "getting together," "keeping a separate identity," "sharing," and "communication." The next session centered around discussion of rules in the group like "saying what you feel," and "sessions should be planned," and "whether notes should be taken during the session or after," etc. In an apparent complete change of topic, during the next session the group was preoccupied discussing "the traffic problem on campus," and how "people should not have to be told how to politely conduct themselves in traffic." Then a brief discussion about the quiet members of the group followed.

The topic of "marriage" and its problems of "separate identify," "sharing," and "communications" represent the group problems of the same nature. The topics of "traffic problems on campus and how "people shouldn't have to be told what to do, i.e., politely conduct themselves in traffic," are a continuation and reaction to the previous session on "rules" where conflict arose as to structure versus no structure in the sessions. It also indicates a continuing concern about order and cooperation in the group. The topic of "marriage" is further concerned with self-help and probing communication problems and other barriers to communicating. The "rules" session also indicates an increased work orientation. Thus the topic of "traffic problems" psychologically fused concerns of (a) real traffic problems, (b) group interaction rules, (c) competition, (d) conformity, (e) authority relationships, and (f) self-regulation, all revolving around personal identity.

SEPARATION AND LOSS

From the very early days of our childhood, we are all eternally concerned with separation and loss of a significant other. This concern plays out on many levels in many different situations and to varying degrees throughout our lives. Often, people wonder why the loss is happening to them. We like to have reasons for what happens to us, otherwise our lives seem meaningless and random.

A group session began with a member who had been absent for quite sometime announcing that she was going to drop out of the group. In an earlier session, the group had persuaded her not to do so. After announcing this for the last time, she left, and the members said their goodbyes to her. There was a long silence. Then, a male member said that the group seems to have stabilized to 10 members. Silence, again.

A female member broke the silence by telling of an interview on the morning TV program, the *Today Show,* where 3 people gave their opinions on whether or not legal records should be made available to those who were adopted as children. She told of a young woman who gave up her child for adoption 10 years ago but who wanted to know about the child because it was still a part of her emotional life. She said another person on the show had been adopted and had been looking for his parents for 30 years. A third panelist maintained that, once given up for adoption, that should be it; there should be no more communication between the biological parent and the adopted child. Then, the male in the group told of children who had been abused but had been given only to foster parents, not given up forever. The idea was eventually to keep the child with its natural parents. Long silence.

The male broke the silence relating religion to the previous topic. He said that he "wondered about a God who lets terrible things happen like child abuse," etc. On the other hand, he said, maybe God is "nondirecting," maybe he created mankind and let it "naturally evolve." I interjected, saying that I agreed, explaining that "we are a microcosm of the larger world." I again, interjected with "you mean just like in here!" The group reacted to this as if it were blasphemous. The male, half under his breadth, said "Hmm, God, just like an instructor?" To which he added "On a much, much, much, much smaller scale." Silence.

In this brief set of exchanges, a number of unconscious feelings are revealed. The first is the group's concern about separation and loss. They are more concerned about losing a member than their surface reaction indicates. We can see this deep concern in the topic of parents giving up their children for adoption, that is, the group had lost a "child," so to speak, as indeed I had, because I was perceived as the parental figure in the group. Group members often feel guilty when a member drops out. But often they secretly or unconsciously blame a trainer, thinking that the trainer could have avoided it. This blame was subliterally referenced by some members who "wondered about a God who lets terrible things happen like child abuse." Other members, however, see the loss as not necessarily due to a mean God but rather in terms of their not being able to understand God's reasons for the loss. That I am equal to God is reflected in the particular characterization of God's motives as seen in the statements that maybe God is "non-directing" and maybe God created humankind and "let it 'naturally evolve'." These references to being nondirective and naturally evolving, subliterally linked the literal topic to my philosophy of conducting T-groups. A further lexical link is the use of the pronoun "it" in referring to letting humankind naturally evolve. In terms of linguistic norms, it would be more normative grammatically to refer to "a group" as an "it" than to human beings (even though used collectively as in mankind). Thus "it" is a subliteral link to here-and-now feelings (again, see Appendix, 6.6. Pronoun Operations).

That the group was not entirely conscious of their equating of me to God is indicated by their responding to my subliteral interpretation of the topic, "you mean just like in here!" as blasphemous. Yet another linkage to the here-and-now group is that the topic came from the "Today Show," which represents *the show today* in the here-and-now group. Still another linkage that supported the topic subliterally referring to the group, it's not by randomness or coincidence that there are "3 people" on the Today Show, as there have been 3 very dominant members in the group. Similarly, it's no accident that the female on the show gave up her child "10 years ago," the exact number of the remaining membership of the group.

Like most subliteral conversations, this conversation, too, reveals some of the differences among the ways members viewed the group. The topic of losing children to adoption reflects a member's negative reaction to losing a group member. On the other hand, the male who introduced the topic of a mean God causing it all, at least has some doubts about understanding God's (meaing my) motivation. This is supported by the fact that in the here-and-now group the male had been understanding the group process better than most of the other members, so on some level, he understood that it wasn't my fault.

ARE WE TALKING ABOUT DEATH HERE?

Certainly one of our deepest concerns in life is about death. A group began with a member expressing a need to talk about a personal concern. She said that she had a friend, though not a "boy friend," who had just found out that he had only five months to live. A heavy silence came over the group. Then a great deal of talk about death ensued, mainly related to "not knowing how or what to say to people who have a terminal illness" and about the fact that in our culture one was not supposed to talk about death, especially to people who were dying. It was said that, "People don't like to talk about death." Silence, again. Then a member said that "We should use our time here in the group more wisely." Once more, silence. Then the discussion returned to the topic of the previous session about those in the group who talk and those who don't. After a pause, there was talk of boy friends. The member who had opened the group attempted to reintroduce her concern about her dying friend by saying "how hard it is to talk" to her dying friend unless "he was constantly pressured," and how "uncomfortable the relationship" was now. In an attempt to support her emotionally, other members tried to relate it to their boyfriends. A member talked about her boyfriend and how "hard it is to talk to him, sometimes." Then, the member who had the dying friend, fell into line by dropping the topic of death and started to talk about her problem of talking to her boyfriends on the telephone and "how difficult it is to talk to anyone on the telephone." Some members agreed.

Like most groups in an initial stage of development, members reduced the emotional discussion of death to a superficial and abstract level, largely because little interpersonal rapport had yet been established. Moreover, the member who told of her dying friend had joined the group only two sessions previously, having missed the introductory lecture and one group session. It's also because, as the group makes clear, talking of death in public is generally unacceptable, and the topic makes people feel uncomfortable, especially when they don't know how to deal with it. The basic concerns in the group were (1) establishing interpersonal rapport, (2) the quiet members, and (3) procedures for facilitating more communication among members, especially the quiet members.

The topic of the member's dying friend was personally—and in terms of subliteral meaning—too close to the "deadness of the group" to be discussed. This was indicated by the statement "We should use our time here in the group more wisely," as a link to the here and now. Because "People don't like to talk about death," the group didn't want to talk of the quiet (i.e., dead) members or about the deadness of the whole group process. The talk of boyfriends not communicating, however, suggests subliterally that they wanted to establish closer relationships with each other. The reference to "how hard it was to talk to her dying friend unless he was constantly pressured and how uncomfortable the relationship was," is a subliteral reference to the quiet members who had to be pressured into talking. Further, like talking to the dying friend, talking to the nonparticipating members about their quietness was similarly uncomfortable.

The discussion of talking on the telephone also explained subliterally (and told the quiet members) that their behavior was creating discomfort, i.e., talking on the telephone is like relating to quiet members. Like the normal bodily cues that people receive when talking face-to-face which are missing when talking on the telephone, so too, nonparticipating members offer insufficient information on which to base a relationship (conversation). In essence they were talking over a "dead telephone line" because no one appeared to be listening at the other end.

When the topic seemed to have reached closure, I asked the member who introduced the "telephone" topic if she saw any connection between her topic and the previous one of quiet members. She said she didn't see any connection. After I explained it in more detail, then the group understood the interpretation and discussed it. I didn't try to connect the topics directly with the member's problem of talking to her dying friend because I didn't consider it appropriate (see Concluding Ethical Postscript at the end of this book).

GENERAL STAGES IN CONVERSATIONAL LIFE

Whenever people assemble regularly for some purpose, they are forming a group. This is true whether the group plays cards, has an extended business meeting, is a support group, or is a committee meeting. There is a developmental pattern to the lives of these groups. Just as with an individual, groups too go through stages of growth. And just as in the stages of an individual's life (i.e., childhood, adolescence, adulthood, old age, and death) where there are concerns relatively peculiar to each stage, so too the same is true of the stages of a group's life. One useful and easily remembered scheme for understanding the developmental stages of a group's life is: *Forming, Storming, Norming,* and *Performing.*[4] A stage omitted from this scheme is the final stage, the ending of the group. I call this stage, *Ending and Termination.* The literal topics that occur during this final stage often subliterally demonstrate the concerns that are present about endings. Now, let me present brief subliteral examples from using the above scheme, after which I illustrate how the subliteral mind expresses concerns about *Ending and Termination.*

Forming Stage: Once again, it's no accident that discussions of *"a new job"* or *"being newlyweds,"* "periods of adjustment," or other topics having to do with "beginnings" most always occur in the initial stage of a group's life. Indeed, talk of newlyweds or a new job in the initial stages of a group is a subliteral way of expressing the here-and-now concerns of getting to know each other, including intimacy, communications, and problems around maintaining a separate identity while merging into a social group. Once these issues are resolved, a group moves into the next stage.

Storming Stage: Just as in many marriages, once the honeymoon is over, groups typically move into a period of conflict revolving around what the rules are going to be, indeed, if there are going to be any rules at all, and about the emerging leadership structure. At least in T-groups, these concerns are seldom discussed openly. Even when they are, the deeper feelings underlying them are not expressed. During this stage, literal topics are about competition and conflict. Movies may be selected as topics. Out of all the possible movie themes, the movies selected in one group was *Star Wars.* The word *Star* in the title represents the emerging leaders, and the word *Wars* refers to conflict and competition over leadership in the group. At other times the topics used to subliterally express feelings may be about *disaster movies* where groups of *people are dependent* on each other, or about rock *groups breaking* up. Once this stage is successfully negotiated, the group moves to the next stage.

Norming Stage: In this stage, members are ready to establish rules and group norms. This process may begin, however, with discussions about *traffic problems* and the need for rules to regulate the traffic flow, i.e., need for rules to guide group interaction or about how Congress works out a compromise on a bill. When this stage is resolved, the group moves to the next.

Performing Stage: When the group finally gets down to working through their unconscious or hidden feelings, then the members can begin doing their real work. The topics then, may be about how to *"grow plants* successfully," about *"building houses,"* or *"remodeling"* projects.

The lesson to be learned from these stories about group stages is that by listening subliterally a leader can begin to work with these issues (either directly or indirectly) to help the group move more quickly through the stages and thus function more effectively. To the extent issues remain unresolved, they limit the group's performance, whether they are business or therapy groups.

I should point out, too, that in groups that aren't T-groups (and often even in T-groups), these stages are not as sequential or as mutually exclusive as they appear. It's possible for some of the stages to be operating at once but to varying degrees and on different levels. In a group, for example, where the task is clear from the group's very inception (as in business meetings), members may appear to begin *Performing* immediately, but the underlying issues often reduce their performance. Individual members, however, may be experiencing the feelings and concerns of each stage. In other words, the issues underlying these stages may be operating in any given stage. Thus, the stages may not be recognized by the actual literal behaviors. This is where understanding subliteral narratives can reveal the true, i.e., emotional, stage the group is in or the stage toward which it's heading.

ENDINGS AND TERMINATIONS

It is inevitable that most groups reach their termination points. Before the end of a group or of a single social conversation, the endings may be subliterally heralded by discussions about *death, funerals,* or *divorce,* or other topics that relate to endings and terminations. I began to recognize increasingly that I could predict a motion to adjourn in committee meetings, even though there had been no time limit set and despite the fact that the climate of the meeting did not suggest that it would come to an end shortly. For example, in a committee meeting discussing curriculum innovation, the topic shifted slightly to the topic of *"private schools that were closing down because of a lack of interest by students in their curricula."*

My prediction of adjournment was based in part on the following. First, the fact that the topic was about *termination.* Secondly, the topic was about private schools and the committee was at a private school. Third, the fact that a few minutes prior a member had excused himself from the meeting, which represents lack of interest? Then, I began to notice in other everyday situations that topics having to do with *termination,* such as *death* and *leaving on vacation,* were brought up during conversations just before the conversation ended.

As we saw in the previous section, not all discussions about death, however, herald the ending or termination of the group. Topics of death may be used to subliterally discuss feelings about losing a group member. The multiple ways that a given topic can subliterally *mean* different things points out the importance of understanding the context of the situation and of having a controlling method to validate the meaning of subliteral conversations.

CONCLUSION

All of the subliteral topics in this chapter are transformations of basic individual, interpersonal, collective feelings and concerns. (1) Individual feelings and concerns include topics of (a) identity, (b) being analyzed, (c) secret records, and (d) being bored. (2) Interpersonal feelings and concerns included topics of (a) equality, (b) double standards, (c) competition and rivalry, (d) currying favor, and (e) interpersonal personal politics. (3) Collective or group feelings and concerns included the topics of (a) rules, (b) social etiquette, (c) problems of sharing, (d) separation and loss, and (e) endings and terminations. Each of these different topics is a permutation or variation revolving around a single complex of emotional concerns: human relationships.

We also saw that these subliteral transformations were carried out by using various cognitive and linguistic operations. We saw (1) that topics were cognitively constrained by a Selection-Response Field; (2) that proper names are used to express feelings and concerns subliterally; (3) that initials are used to identify a person; that (5) pun-like sounds, (6) portmanteau constructions, and (7) numbers are used to express subliteral cognitions; (8) memorial or strategic misremembering; and (9) the unconscious use of hand and body gestures.

Finally, we saw that much valuable information can be learned about interpersonal and social dynamics from listening subliterally that we might otherwise not know about. In addition, we saw that what often might appear to be a conscious meaning is in fact unconscious. It's now time to look much closer at one of the operations used in these subliteral narratives, numbers.

CHAPTER 5

FIGURES OF SPEECH

NUMBERS IN THE MIND

This is one of the more important and intriguing chapters in this book. At least I think it is. Nevertheless, I approach this chapter with fear and trepidation because to suggest that numbers used in conversations have unconscious meaning is, at best, to be aligned with the wildest of psychoanalytic interpretations and, at worse—and more likely—with ancient and New Age numerology. Indeed, to suggest that numbers in conversations may have unconscious meaning conjures up suspicions of a kind of psychological alchemy. Given the history of psychoanalysis and of occult numerology (see below), my fear and trepidation is perhaps understandable. Nevertheless, I have found that numbers mentioned in conversations can function as subliteral "figures" of speech. [1]

How do you explain, for example, the repeated occurrence of the number 5 in a conversation where only 5 people are active in the discussion? Or how do you explain the repeated occurrence of the number 14 in a seemingly casual conversation when the conversation is composed of exactly 14 people, only to have the number 14 in the literal stories change to the number 13 after one person excuses himself to leave early? Further, what does it mean and how do you explain the repeated occurrence of other numbers that "just happen" to come up in the course of stories or ostensibly unrelated conversations that correspond exactly to the various subgroups or factions in the conversation?

In this chapter I show that conscious and literally intended numbers contained in stories and topics during conversations are often unconsciously selected for the conversations because they express people's concerns with the various factions in a social conversation. Accordingly, the number 5 (indicated previously) appeared in a conversation as a consequence of the concern of some members that 5 people were dominating the conversation. Just as words and topics function subliterally, then, so do numbers. And just as with subliteral language, people are not conscious of the subliteral meaning of the numbers that they "just happen" to use in their conversations.

In some ways, understanding the subliteral function of numbers in conversations is more important than recognizing the subliteral meaning of words, phrases, and stories. I say this because words are notoriously vague, and always leave room to have different meanings attributed to them. In the opening paragraph, I said that this was one of the most important chapters in this book. It is, however, one of the shorter ones because, unlike words, numbers are quite precise and concrete. They have nice, clear boundaries. Accordingly, their subliteral analysis is much less problematic.

The importance of subliteral numbers isn't just their unconscious meaning. They have another very significant function: They provide a structure, a concrete framework for cross-checking and validating the analysis of subliteral language. Subliteral numbers function as a cognitive map, a kind of grid system within which to navigate the subliteral meaning in the words, phrases, and stories that are told. They provide a kind of cognitive longitudinal and latitudinal grid system for finding our way around the sea of subliteral word meanings.

But before we see what numbers subliterally "mean," it's useful and, I think, quite interesting to look at how various groups throughout history thought that numbers express symbolic meaning. I'll keep this brief because the history of numbers itself is a short history, at least as it relates to my purposes here. My main purpose for briefly looking at this history is to separate my subliteral analysis of the meaning of numbers clearly from any hint of ancient and New Age numerology or the often fast-and-loose psychoanalytic interpretation of numbers.

BRIEF HISTORY OF NUMBERS AS SYMBOLIC

Neither the field of psycholinguistics nor the broader fields of the psychology of language and cognition have recognized that numbers carry meaning outside of the literal referent that they refer to in the literal conversation or topic of which they are a part: five apples, simply means five apples, no more, no less. I categorize the scant literature on the psychological meaning of numbers into five basic areas, four of which, because of their occult and quasi-occult character have been responsible for the scientific neglect of numbers as valid cognitive data. Because of the occult-like nature of past approaches to the meaning of numbers and the lack of an appropriate controlling method with which to analyze and validate them systematically, understandably no "respectable" cognitive scientist has or would consider conducting research on the unconscious meaning of numbers—until now. The use of numbers in history can be divided into two broad areas, the mystical and the psychological. These areas are not always mutually exclusive, however.

MYSTICAL MEANING OF NUMBERS

The first area concerned with the meaning of numbers is what I will call the mystical or cosmological. This includes the ancient belief in the mystical and secret meaning of numbers. This belief was propounded by Pythagoras (582–507 B.C.), the pre-Socratic Greek philosopher and mathematician, who applied mathematics to the study of musical harmony and geometry, both of which he thought reflected the structure of the universe (remember from grade school, the Pythagorean theorem: the sum of the squares of the lengths of the sides of right triangles is equal to the square of the length of their hypotenuse?). He is generally considered the first mathematician. The school that he founded became a secret mystical order. His followers believed in the transmigration of souls and discovered the numerical relationships between musical tones and numbers. They also believed that the essence of all things involved numbers and that all relationships, including abstract concepts like justice, could be expressed with numbers.[2]

With all due respect to Pythagoras—and to more knowledgeable historians than I—out of this early belief in the mystical quality of numbers evolved both medieval and contemporary occult groups who believe that numbers possess mystical and cosmic meanings. This is known as numerology. Numerology believes that each number has a cosmic meaning. From ancient to modern times, numbers have been assigned to each letter of the alphabet, to names, to birth dates, and so on. It is even thought that each person's "soul" has a number. Another area is what might be termed the *mythical*, which includes the meaning of numbers used in primitive myths and folklore where they are believed to possess both universal and concrete significance.[3]

PSYCHOLOGICAL MEANING OF NUMBERS

In addition to mystical and cosmic meaning, it is thought that numbers also have psychological meaning. One area is what may be termed the *pathological*, which includes schizophrenic thought processes where it is often believed that numbers possess both personal and cosmic significance.[4] Another area is a general *psychoanalytic* view of the meaning of numbers. This includes numbers as they function in dreams and in other psychoanalytic interpretations. Historically, that numbers may possess psychological meaning has largely been the purview of psychoanalytic theory. In addition to Freud, other psychoanalysts have noted instances of numbers possessing symbolic meaning.[5] By and large, their interpretations were that numbers held *universal* symbolic meaning. For example, the number 5 has been said to represent psychological integration. Examples from this approach, however, are few in number and also are analyzed by the loosest of free associations. The rules for their combination, transformation, selection, addition, multiplication, and subtraction are left to the intuitive discretion of the analyst. For example, the psychoanalyst, Emil Gutheil,[6] says that the number "3" equates to male genitalia, or they may have meaning based on similarity of sounds, where the number "50" equates to "filthy."

Outside of occult numerology, it was Freud's discovery set forth in his *The Interpretation of Dreams*[7] that numbers have psychological meaning. His aim was principally therapeutic. However, he does not seem to have been overly concerned that numbers have much real cognitive significance outside of representing dream thoughts. Consequently, he discovered only a small group of examples. Because his aim was therapeutic, it is perhaps all the more to his credit that he formulated any theory at all regarding the cognitive function of numbers. Because of serious methodological shortcomings, and a small number of instances, Freud's findings are limited with regard to the method of recognizing their unconscious meaning and their scope. The procedure he used for validating the unconscious meaning of numbers was by a very loose method of free association. As we saw before, long before Freud, it was widely believed that numbers possessed religious or cosmic meaning, and Freud's attempt to analyze them from a psychological perspective was seminal.

A more modern and cognitive area is what may be termed the *associative selection* area. It includes a few scientific statistical association studies.[8] No psychological meaning, however, is attributed to numbers. Finally, my findings suggest that numbers have unconscious meanings reflecting here-and-now concerns in social conversations and they also use fairly sophisticated *cognitive operations*. With this brief history, I can begin to present what I have found in my research.

NUMBERS IN MIND

Rather than present multiple subliteral stories from different conversations that have numbers in them, instead I present numbers from a single ongoing conversation. Presenting multiple examples from within a single conversation allows me to show how numbers are integrally and structurally related to other subliteral aspects of a single conversation. It also allows me to demonstrate more fully my method of validating them. In addition, it allows me to show how subliteral numbers can help to validate my analyses of subliteral words, phrases, and sentences. In any case, many of the narratives throughout this book provide a variety of other examples of the subliteral use of numbers. I should mention that sometimes the analysis of numbers is a little tricky. But bear with me. It's worth it.

THE THREE LEADERS THEME AND ITS VARIATIONS

The following analysis of numbers is about a subgroup faction in a session from one of my T-groups. Before presenting each subtopic, which is characterized by the repeated use of the number 3, it is helpful to present them first as a composite. This approach provides a general overview and an initial feeling for the way each topic relates to the others. It also shows how each literal topic that's characterized by the number 3 is in fact one unconscious topic, generated by a single emotional concern about 3 dominant leaders in the group. I refer to the three dominant members as the *triadic* leadership structure within the conversation.

The group membership included myself and 15 members, of whom 12 were present during this session. Broken down, the membership included 1 very active male; 11 females, of whom 1 was an older, quite active woman; 10 females about 18–20 years of age, of whom 5 were active, making a total of 6 active females. Seven members were active, 8 counting me. There were 2 males counting me, 2 dominant leaders, the male and the older female, 3 counting me. Within this group discussion, there were 3 very dominant members. The session is dominated by the themes of bars, drinking, and of being drunk.

The general overview of the discussion shows thirteen references to the number "3," and other numbers integrally related to it. I present them in the order in which they appeared. All thirteen topics are subliteral references to

3 members who dominate the conversation. It's important I note that these "numerical topics" are from a transcribed tape recording of the entire session, so it was possible for me to account systematically for each and every time that any number was used in the conversation during that session. This is important because it eliminates bias in selecting only certain numbers which to attribute meaning.

In addition, other numbers were used in the session. Along with the number "3," these other numbers make up a very complex matrix of integrally connected semantic and numerical topics. I limit this chapter primarily to the number "3," however, because including the others would be tedious and require too much space, though I must note a few of the other integrally related numbers. To detail more of these related numbers would probably tax your mind far beyond what is necessary to illustrate their subliteral meaning. I know that tracing the extensive matrix of subliteral numbers still taxes my mind, even after all these years of analyzing them. With this said, let me now summarize the thirteen *triadic* themes.

1. "We Narrowed Them All Down to 3 Different Options."
2. "About 3 Weeks Ago . . . They Were All down behind Pantry Pride."
3. "Being under 21."
4. "The 3rd Stream Was Playing."
5. The "3 Lucky Spots."
6. "LCB Men Were Coming, Like in 2 or 3 Weeks."
7. "3 of the 10 People (Who Came into the Bar) Were Really Drunk."
8. "The Bartender Can Refuse If He's Served You, for Instance, 3 Drinks."
9. "3 Seniors Were Drunk on an Airplane during Their High School Class Trip."
10. "This 1 Girl who Was with These 2 Guys."
11. "It Started Snowing 3 Hours Before . . ."
12. "The 3rd Day They Said, 'Well, We're Just Gonna Bus All of You.'"
13. "3 Old Greyhound Buses that Took People from the Airport."

Together these narrative variations on the number "3" reflect a primary emotional concern that the nondominant members in the discussion had about the triadic leadership structure of the group, which reflected peer jealousy and rivalry. In addition, each topic provides an access point into the subliteral matrix of meaning of the entire discussion (see Figure 3). We must now understand each of these topics in more detail.

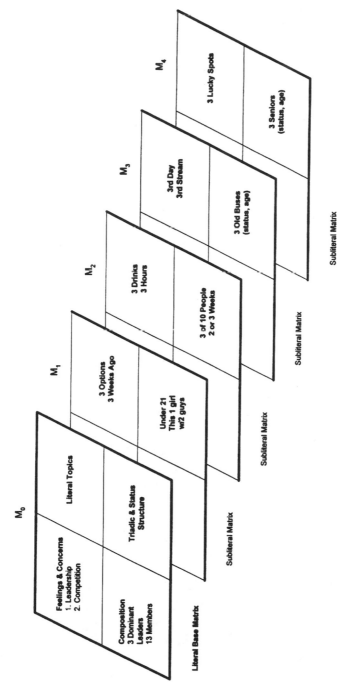

FIGURE 3. Composite transformational matrices (numbers).

PARSING THE TRIADIC LEADERSHIP THEME

In this section, I subliterally parse the thirteen literal phrases separately and then show how they are all integrally connected. I should give you advanced warning again, that even this relatively straightforward analysis of the subliteral meaning of numbers may prove to be a rough trip, so hold on tight to your mental stability (you may end up thinking I've lost mine).

TOPIC ONE: "WE NARROWED THEM ALL DOWN TO 3 DIFFERENT OPTIONS."

During this session a male member told a story about another teacher, saying, "she took and just threw stuff down on the board that were suggestions from students and then once they got all down on the board, *we narrowed them all down to three different options*." The literal topic of "we narrowed them all down to 3 different options" subliterally refers to the emergence of the triadic leadership structure in the group, i.e., it was narrowed to three leaders.

It's important to note that the member who is telling this story is part of the triadic structure.

Psycholinguistically, it's appropriate that the member who is telling the story is part of the triadic structure because, subliterally, as the story line notes, *"we"* (means the 3 leaders) narrowed them (means the total group membership) down to three options" (means the 3 leaders). For members who were not part of the triadic structure, this wording would not have been expected (these kinds of observations provide fertile ground for creating hypotheses which then can be tested), because they didn't control the topics being discussed in the group and couldn't narrow the leadership to 3 people. The 3 emerging leaders did that.

TOPIC TWO: "ABOUT 3 WEEKS AGO . . . THEY WERE ALL DOWN BEHIND PANTRY PRIDE."

The phrase "about 3 weeks ago," again, subliterally references the three dominant leaders. The semantically connected phrase, "down behind Pantry Pride," subliterally references the older woman who is a part of the triadic leadership structure. In terms of verification, this is indicated in part by the phrase "Pantry Pride," that was associated in a previous session when the older woman said she was "proud" (equals pride) to be a homemaker (equals pantry). In the city in which this session occurred, Pantry Pride is a statewide supermarket chain. Verification is also indicated by the dimensional vector "down behind." The phrase, "they were all down behind," means the larger group membership that was *under* (see topic three later) the leadership of the 3 leaders, one of whom was the older woman. In terms of verification, invariably, high status, i.e., being a leader is associated with the dimensional vector "up," and low status, i.e., being a follower, with "down." (see Appendix, 4.2. Dimensional Evaluative Vector Operations; 4.3. Dimensional Vector Equivalence Operations; 9.7. Dimensional Tracking of Deductive Subset Invariance; and 9.8. Dimensional Tracking of Permutation Invariance).

TOPIC THREE: "BEING UNDER 21."

Just as topic two above is a subliteral reference to the 3 leaders, so does the phrase, "being under 21" subliterally reference the 3 leaders. But more than this, it breaks the triad down into its appropriate parts. The number 21, subliterally breaks down into $2 + 1 = 3$. The "2" subliterally represents the two males, and the "1" subliterally represents the one older woman. Thus the "21" represents, $2 + 1 = 3$. In addition, the preposition *under* in the phrase "being *under* 21" is dimensionally or spatially consistent with the previous reference to being "*down behind* Pantry Pride" (See Appendix, 8.4. Single-Number Operations; 8.5. Addition Operations). On another level, the "being *under* 21" subliterally references the remaining members of the group who were all younger than the 3 leaders. They were in fact *under 21* years old. As partial verification of this last interpretation, almost immediately connected to this phrase was the statement "Over half of them were *under*age. The younger female members, who continued this topic about people in a bar being underage, were themselves underage.

TOPIC FOUR: "THE THIRD STREAM WAS PLAYING."

A further subtopic referencing the triadic leadership structure was the brief mention of a Rock group, *The Third Stream*. This may reference the slightly older male who talked almost incessantly, i.e., in common vernacular, he talked a "steady stream." This is possibly indicated by an immediate association to a male directly connected to the "Third Stream" topic. Nevertheless, that this is a specific reference to the male is on a little more shaky ground than the meaning of the number "3" itself referring to the three dominant leaders.

TOPIC FIVE: THE "3 LUCKY SPOTS"

The "3 Lucky Spots" is a local bar. Again, the number "3" corresponds to the actual triadic leadership structure of the conversation. The reference to "lucky spots" in the name of the bar is an additional *semantic association* corresponding to the significant status of the 3 active members who were the leaders. The phrase "lucky spots" has linguistic legitimacy because it's a phrase commonly used in one variation or another to refer to desirable status positions. The concern of members is that they are being evaluated on their leadership, interpersonal, and communication skills. Thus in this situation, there are in fact "3 lucky spots" or 3 lucky people who, because they have been active leaders, are perceived as the recipients of excellent evaluations or grades.

It is also significant that the "3 Lucky Spots" is a bar. Logically, the topic simultaneously relates to both a part of and the whole group. In other words, the number "3" is not just an isolated number. It's associated with a group, a bar, just as the 3 leaders are part of a whole *group*. Occasionally, members dream about the T-group sessions. Typically, groups are represented in the dream by a whole with various parts, for example, a station wagon full of children or people in a bathtub or swimming pool (see chapter 11).

In terms of psychosociometric validity (see Appendix, 3.1. Resonance Operations; 3.2. Sociometric Operations), this topic, unlike others, is neutral in terms of the significance of who brought the topic up for discussion. The three lucky spots can be seen as equally poignant for either the three leaders or other group members.

TOPIC SIX: "LCB MEN WERE COMING, LIKE IN 2 OR 3 WEEKS."

Connected to the previous topics, this sentence also reflects the triadic leadership structure of the group. It even breaks the triadic structure down into its components again like the "being under 21" topic, only with a variation. The "2" represents the two males, and the 3 represents the entire triadic structure, including the female. It's possible, too, that the three letter acronym LCB referencing the liquor control board men also reflected the triadic structure because liquor control board men are authorities. But I won't push this last point too hard.

TOPIC SEVEN: "3 OF THE 10 PEOPLE (WHO CAME INTO THE BAR) WERE REALLY DRUNK . . . AND THEY WOULDN'T SERVE ANY OF THEM."

Because the group members continued their stories about bars, again, the numerical structure of this seemingly literal topic, containing the numbers "3" and "10" corresponds to the physical group composition, the 3 leaders and the remaining 10 young female members. As in the first topic, the number "3" gains additional validity by being directly a part of a phrase that included another significant number, the number "10." Combined, the 3 + 10 totals to 13. The significance of the number 13 is that it corresponds to the exact number of people in the group that day, including me.

On the literal level, the number "3" is included within a total number of "10" (i.e., 3 *of* 10 people), but in subliteral thinking they are separate, thus adding to 13. The literal arithmetic structure of the number 3 being included as part of the number 10 would not have fit the subliteral reality of the total group membership. In other words to have said something like "3 people came in and sat down with the other seven people at the bar, which made a total of 10 people," would have precluded the adding of 3 and 10, to total the 13 members (see Appendix, Mathematical Computation Operations, 8.1, 8.5, 9.5). The "10" probably also references the 10 young females in the group.

In terms of associative connections, the phrase, "and they wouldn't serve any of them," subliterally references the fact that the rest of the group would not accept the leadership of the 3 leaders, that is, they would not *serve* as followers.

TOPIC EIGHT: "THE BARTENDER CAN REFUSE IF HE'S SERVED YOU, FOR INSTANCE, 3 DRINKS."

Another brief story connected to the same general topic of bars and drinking was about bartenders being able to refuse serving drinks to someone if someone has had too many, "for instance, 3 drinks." It's interesting here to ask why the member making this statement would specifically select "3" drinks as indicating too many? This would certainly not be a typical number of drinks that would be considered too many, especially by young people. This particular number selected for indicating too many drinks is not normative and is so extreme that it functions as a clue that something subliteral is happening. Again, the number was selected because it subliterally fit the unconscious concern of the person making the statement, i.e., the 3 leaders. The T-group situation is often experienced and subliterally referenced as being crazy or drunken, as the next topic shows.

TOPIC NINE: "3 SENIORS WERE DRUNK ON AN AIRPLANE DURING THEIR HIGH SCHOOL CLASS TRIP."

Once again, the number "3" in this topic corresponds to the actual group leadership composition, and again the number 3 is part of a larger group (total). The literal term *"seniors"* also subliterally corresponds to the age differential of the 3 leaders in the group, composed of myself, an older woman, and a male who is slightly older than the remaining female members, i.e., *seniors*. And once again, too, there is a semantic or metaphorical association to the 3 leaders being *drunk*, i.e., acting absurdly as they perceive it. The story also reflects an association with school-related activity. I'll refrain from suggesting the possible subliteral meaning of selecting a *high* school class trip as an association with being "high," as in drugged or drunk.

Moreover, like the 3 people in the bar, the "3 seniors" were a disrupting influence and removed. Affectively, the rest of the group would like to remove the 3 threatening leaders. Once again, psychosociometrically, the member telling this story was not a member of the triadic leadership structure which is subliterally being criticized.

TOPIC TEN: "THIS 1 GIRL WHO WAS WITH THESE 2 GUYS."

This topic is yet another specific subliteral reference to the 3 leaders, as indicated by the 1 girl with 2 guys = 3. Now, this specific topic is most revealing in terms of showing how subliteral meaning is created, analyzed, and verified. First, the gender composition of the people in the literal topic is isomorphic or identical with the gender composition of the three leaders. The "1 girl" represents the older woman, and the "2 guys" represents the two males. Second, the particular phrasing of this topic is equally as revealing. In the phrasing, "This 1 Girl Who Was with These 2 Guys," note the use of pronouns. The use of the pronouns "this" and "these" were used, as if the people being talked about were present, instead of the more appropriate "that" 1 girl and "those" 2 guys. This *tense shift*, psychologically and linguistically links the story with the here-

and-now conversational situation. Any number of phrasings could have been used. For example, it could have been said, that *"there* was a girl who was with two guys," etc. (See Appendix, 6.5. Temporal Shift Operations).

TOPIC ELEVEN: "IT STARTED SNOWING 3 HOURS BEFORE . . ."

Once again, we see the number "3." For the statement, "it started snowing three hours before the plane arrived at the airport," we might ask again, why both the subtopic of "snow" and the number 3 were selected into the conversation? In terms of contextual information adding to the validity of this interpretation is the fact that in the first meeting during my one and only lecture, I had overloaded them with a sort of crash course on group dynamics, that is, in common vernacular, I "snowed" them with my initial lecture. So this particular subtopic about snow is probably a specific subliteral reference to me and/or to the fact that the group situation is confusing. Other associated references were a part of this conversation. For example, it was said that the snow caused "air traffic problems" so that they were "flying around in circles" waiting to land. The air traffic problems subliterally refers to communication problems in the here-and-now group. For example, not all members had equal "air time," and the rules still were not established. The reference to flying around in circles has two subliteral meanings. First, it refers to the standard T-group seating arrangement of sitting in a circle, and second, the conversation was not going anywhere, that is, in common vernacular, it was just going in circles.

TOPIC TWELVE: "THE 3RD DAY THEY SAID, 'WELL, WE'RE JUST GONNA BUS ALL OF YOU.'"

This statement "The 3rd day," is still another reference to the triadic leadership structure which includes (as in most of the topics above) a larger unit, a "bus," which represents the rest of the group.

TOPIC THIRTEEN: "3 OLD GREYHOUND BUSES THAT TOOK PEOPLE FROM THE AIRPORT."

Finally, like the other topics reflecting the triadic leadership structure of the group, this "3 old Greyhound buses" story corresponds to the triadic leadership structure and also to the number 3 logically included as part of a larger whole, i.e., 3 buses that were part of the airport system. In addition, that the buses were "old," corresponds to the 3 leaders who are older than the rest of the group, as in the *3 seniors* example above. But there is still more to this story.

SUM OF THE NUMBERS IN MIND

At this point, if your mind isn't the consistency of oatmeal, consider this. There are a number of additional interesting observations to make regarding these thirteen subliteral references to the triadic leadership structure of the previous conversations. First, the total number of topics, 13, equals the total number of people in the group that day (including me). Second, except for Topics One and Five (which were initiated by the male member), the remaining 11 topics (all initiated by the young females) are equal to the total number of females in the group. The question is, is it just coincidence that the total number of topics, 13, equals the total number of people in the group and that the 11 topics—all initiated by the young females—equals the exact number of females in the group? Perhaps. In any event, lacking data on further such examples from other groups, at this point I am willing to concede that perhaps this particular analysis is coincidental. Though given the highly structured nature of my subliteral findings, it's reasonable to hypothesize that these two findings may not be coincidental.

As for the topics themselves all of which are about the number 3, being coincidental—well, this is another matter all together. Would you seriously contend that the thirteen statements with the number 3 are not subliteral for the triadic leadership structure of the group, and that they, too, are coincidental? I think not. At least I think it wouldn't be reasonable to hold such a position, given the verification procedures, which I summarize at this point.

I divide my summary into three areas: (1) structural, (2) associative and (3) linguistic consistencies. I should point out that these areas are not always mutually exclusive. The same topic may illustrate more than one set of subliteral operations. I list them one by one so that you can get the full flavor of the systematic nature by which subliteral meaning may be considered verified, true, or factual.

In terms of verification, it's also important to note that the numbers in the topics that subliterally refer to the membership change systematically when the membership of the group changes because of absences. I have found this consistently across many different group conversations.

STRUCTURAL CONSISTENCIES

The structural aspects of the subliteral topics refer to the isomorphic or structural identity of features of the literal topics with the actual membership structure of the conversation.

One, there were 3 members who where dominating the group.

Two, all 13 stories contain the number 3.

Three, all stories methodologically correspond to the triadic leadership structure.

Four, except for Topics One and Five, which were explained contextually, the remaining 11 topics were generated by members who had emotional concerns about the triadic leadership structure.

Five, the triadic structure was generally broken down into its components, in Topic Six, the reference to the liquor control board men who were coming "Like in *2 or 3* Weeks," where the "2" referred to the two males and the "3" referred to the total triadic structure, as perhaps did the acronym LCB.

Six, the triadic structure was correctly delineated from the rest of the 10 young females in Topic Seven, about "3 of the 10 People (Who Came into the Bar), and which

Seven, combined (3 + 10) totaling 13, the exact number of people in the group that day.

Eight, the triadic structure was specifically broken down into its components of 2 + 1 in Topic Three of "being under 21 and Topic Ten about "this one girl who was with these two guys."[9]

Nine, the triadic structure was broken down into its components by the correct gender composition, as seen in Topic Ten about "This *1 Girl* Who Was With These *2 Guys.*"

Ten, the composition of the triadic structure was correctly differentiated by age from the rest of the group by the term *seniors* in Topic Nine and by the term old associated with the 3 Greyhound buses in Topic Thirteen.

Eleven, the rest of the group was correctly differentiated from the triadic structure by the statement "Over half of them were under age."

ASSOCIATIVE CONSISTENCIES

Associative aspects of the subliteral topics refers to the related aspects of each individual topic and that the topics collectively are logically and contextually consistent with each other.

> *Twelve,* most of the "3's" are not just isolated "3's." They are associated with a larger group-like unit, as in rock groups, bars, airplanes, and buses.

> *Thirteen,* semantic associations correspond to the significant status of the 3 active members, as in the phrase "3 *lucky spots*" found in Topic Five.

> *Fourteen,* that members not belonging to the triad were subordinate to the triad is associatively reflected in the aspect of Topic Two that refers to a large group of people who ". . . were all *down behind*" the food market called Pantry Pride which was associated in another session with the older woman (who was part of the triad saying she was "proud" (equals pride) to be a homemaker represented by "Pantry." In other words they were subordinate to the older woman.

> *Fifteen,* that the Topic Four phrase, *"The 3rd Stream,"* refers to the slightly older very verbal male is an association with the common vernacular of someone talking a "steady stream."

> *Sixteen,* The statement, "It *Started* Snowing 3 Hours Before . . ." in Topic Eleven, is associatively connected by the fact that *3 sessions before,* the trainer had "snowed" the members with an extensive lecture on small group functioning.

> *Seventeen,* in Topic Eight about bartenders having the right not to serve a person who has had too many drinks, which was given as "for instance, 3 drinks," it's likely that it was selected—out of all possible numbers that could have been selected—by association with non-triadic members' concern about the triadic leadership structure.

LINGUISTIC CONSISTENCIES

Linguistic aspects of the subliteral topics refers to the specific use of semantics, phonology, and syntax that each individual topic and the topics collectively consistently exhibit.

> *Eighteen,* Consistent conjugations of pronouns are used subliterally to connect a literal topic with its subliteral meaning. This is done by

tense shifts. For example, the pronouns "this" and "these" as in the statement "/ *This*/ 1 Girl Who Was With /*These*/ 2 Guys," instead of saying "*there* was 1 girl who was with 2 guys," to link the story to the here-and-now situation.

Nineteen, Consistent conjugations of pronouns are used to link literal stories subliterally to the here-and-now situation. For example, in telling a story it was said, "/*We*/ narrowed them down to 3 options," instead of saying "the options were narrowed down to 3," or some similar phrasing.

Twenty, Nouns are consistently used as adjectives and adverbs to link stories subliterally to the here-and now situation. For example, the statement, "The 3 *seniors*" literally used as a noun phrase (to refer to high school seniors) was subliterally used as both a noun and an adjective to describe subliterally the *older* members of the triadic leadership structure.

Twenty One, the prepositions are consistently shifted to their adjectival form to link stories subliterally to the here-and-now situation,[10] as in the statement "being /*under*/ 21," referring to being less than twenty one years old and to being under the authority of the triadic leadership structure, or as in the statement that "/ *Over*/ half of them were under age."

The famous German philosopher, Martin Heidegger (1889–1976) once said that every poet poetizes out of a single poem.[11] The work of any poet, painter, sculptor, or novelist then, can be said to spring from the depths of his being, and the artist's complete works are a working out of or variations on a fundamental theme (i.e., feeling), just as a group "poetizes" out of a single concern. (Exactly what "poem" this book originates from I can't say.)

In addition to illustrating some rather specific and strange cognitive and linguistic operations underlying them, there is an even more sophisticated set of higher order mental operations occurring. After all of this, if your mind is still working, further consider the fact that for this series of subliteral numbers to occur, each numerical representation and its other consistently associated aspects must somehow be mapped, tracked, and stacked systemically throughout multiple levels of meaning and through the various story permutations and must remain invariant with respect to the specific set characteristics (e.g., age, gender, spatial dimension) and meanings. In addition, there must exist a set of underlying operations that function as if there were a set of transformational rules that create this invariance of feeling and meaning (see the chapter on the Subliteral Mind).

Now, if you are still somewhat incredulous, I don't blame you. I am, too. It's deep. Even after all these years of working with this material, I sometimes look at the complex cognitive operations that I've consistently found and say to myself, "What!—Give me a break." The fact is, however, I have to believe what the evidence suggests from the systematic method of verification that I've specifically developed and also from similar corroborating cognitive and linguistic operations found in dreams, primitive myth narratives, and in the works of the great poets.

POSTSCRIPT ON METHOD

Although the internal order of the above numbers that I've developed is crucial and necessary for analyzing and validating the illustrations presented here, it's not sufficient. As I lamented in chapter 2, is it possible that, like the Ptolemaic model of the solar system or a complex mathematical equation or theory that's internally consistent, I've simply but cleverly created an internally reliable and logically coherent system? In mathematics the "proof" of an equation or theorem is established by its internal consistency and deductive properties. Proof has nothing to do with external reality. The pragmatic "proof" of an equation or theorem, however, depends on whether it describes something real in terms of the external world (with all due deference to mathematicians). This kind of proof relies on its correspondence to real things in the world. This is what philosophers call a correspondence theory of truth. For example, $1 + 1 = 2$ can be proven by its applied correspondence to 1 egg, and 1 other egg = 2 eggs. Or take the exponential law that's illustrated by compounding of interest in a bank account. The formula also corresponds to the growth of populations and a host of other real things in the world.

Without external correspondence, the mathematical proof-like internal order of my findings might be interesting but they would not refer to any empirically valid reality, just as the Ptolemaic model of the solar system was reliable but not empirically valid. But they in fact do correspond to the reality outside their own order. The "proof" of the method I have developed lies in two factors. It is a systematic and internally consistent set of cognitive and linguistic operations that, by way of a mapping process, includes their *correspondence* to the external reality of the actual conversational situation, and it is *corroborated* by other data and theories (see Appendix, 12.1. Internal Order Structure; 12.2. External Order Operation). In addition to abstract concepts corresponding to things in the world, it's also important that they be related to other known theories. We might call this a corroborative theory of truth. In other words, are my findings supported by other known facts or theories? I address this issue in chapters 6, 7, and 8.

PART II

How Subliteral Meaning Is Made

CHAPTER 6

FEELING AND EMOTION
MISSING LINKS IN A GREAT PSYCHOLOGICAL DIVIDE

If we are to believe the rather deviant and often bizarre examples of language presented in this book, reasonable people should demand to be given some idea how such seemingly improbable meanings and cognitive operations are psychologically and linguistically possible. What is the inner psychological source for such material? In other words, are the illustrations of subliteral language in this book based on any known data or theories that could corroborate or provide a reasonable basis of initial support? Aside from scientists wanting to know these things, just out of plain curiosity it's a fascinating excursion by itself. But more importantly, showing how subliteral meaning is possible is necessary to really understand how it all works and to recognize it in everyday conversations. This chapter, then, presents preliminary theoretical—but concrete, and of necessity, brief—evidence that begins to explain how the subliteral narratives presented are possible.

Up to this point, I have (1) put forth much of my extensive methodology which I have applied in analyzing literal linguistic and numerical narratives, (2) shown how literal stories in conversations correspond in multiple ways to the composition and events that occur in the conversations, and (3) briefly touched on aspects of structural linguistics that are congruent with my analyses of subliteral meaning. In this and the following chapters, I present further supporting evidence and illustrations.

FEELING, EXPERIENCING, AND MEANING

A major point of theoretical significance to the subliteral mind is the role of emotions in shaping our thinking and everyday use of language. The subliteral findings presented so far show that feelings and emotions are integral to cognition and language, that the origins of subliteral talk are deeply rooted in *experiencing* and *feeling*. I have already alluded to the fact that neither cognitive science nor the field of linguistics have addressed the issue of feeling and emotion. The structural linguistics of Noam Chomsky doesn't deal with the role of emotions or with meaning, especially with "metaphorical" kinds of meaning. In fact Chomsky doesn't deal with meaning at all (see chapter 1). Although he suggests that language has a deep cognitive structure, his theory of syntax or grammar is an empty formal calculus, like the arithmetic $1 + 1 = 2$, without saying to what $1 + 1 = 2$ refers. With few exceptions, mainstream cognitive science has, historically, maintained that feeling or emotion is not integrally involved in cognition—or if it is, it's not important. Emotion (psychologists call it affect) in mainstream cognitive science has a long and controversial history. Moreover, mainstream cognitive psychology has adopted a computer-information processing model to explain thinking—and, I might add, with considerable applied success in certain areas. But when it comes to the role of emotion, the computer model has failed.

Current models of cognition based on a computer analogy applied to the mind cannot explain subliteral-type linguistic phenomena, and they don't deal with feeling, either. Neither do the computer models consider the person as a source of meaning. Computational models of the mind are deterministic models that leave little to no room for human intention and volition. This scandalous omission, however, is increasingly recognized by some researchers, but in only a general way. I don't use the word scandalous lightly. What could be more scandalous than something as humanly universal and of such everyday importance as feelings and emotions and their obvious relationship to how the mind works not to be primary subjects of research for cognitive science? I'll address this more in the closing paragraphs of this chapter.

So, how am I to explain, for example, the comment in chapter 3, about "pierced ears," which I noted (a) came on the heels of my making an intervention that (b) members often experience as criticism? Although noting that these two contextual items constitute one level of explanation, other levels are not being explained. For example, why was the particular adjective "pierced" selected to describe the noun "ears?" Another level of explanation is that the literal topic of "pierced ears," was used subliterally as "metaphor," as in cutting, stinging, or biting sarcasm. In other words, my intervention was *felt* emotionally as piercing. This explanation is all well and good, too, but it still leaves something unexplained. How are these so-called "metaphorical" connections made?

One explanation for the metaphor of feeling "pierced" is what I discussed in chapter 3 as a holophrastic transformation. This occurs when an insult is commonly expressed as "It felt like they just slapped me in the face." This explanation of the "pierced ears comment applies to a whole class of such narratives presented in this book. For example, the reference to "speakeasies," that came after an incident with a tape recorded conversation, the narrative of store owners "ripping off the public," which followed my unannounced absence for a couple of sessions, the references to the booklet title "Help Kill Dandelions" *and to* "Rh negative blood," which were responses to my analyzing the group, and the reference to the movie "*Star Wars* that was a subliteral reference to members who were in conflict over leadership, were all holophrastic transformations. Somehow, unconsciously experienced feelings are transformed integrally and are specifically involved in constructing language.

Although this explanation, too, may help, it still leaves something to be desired. So, the question still remains. How exactly does this transformation of feelings into language take place and where does it come from? The short answer is, we don't really know. This brings me to yet another question. Why don't we know? Answering this last question requires a somewhat longer answer about how we look at feeling in relation to thinking. As an introduction to answering these questions, I need to explain briefly two important divisions or divides in the history of philosophy and psychology. The first involves the relationship between the body and mind, and the second between emotion and feeling.

Understanding these divisions is not just a semantic quibble or an academic exercise. These divisions lay at the very core of the reason that psychologists and philosophers have been uncomfortable in incorporating emotions and feelings into their theories and models about the way the mind works. The divisions also lay at the core of understanding the subliteral mind. Moreover, they are equally important for understanding why the subliteral mind has not been recognized in psychology. In briefly tracing these divisions, it will become clear that philosophical ideas and theoretical notions are not just academic exercises but have everyday consequences.

THE GREAT PHILOSOPHICAL DIVIDE

Sometimes in science (and in the culture at large) ideas get lost, misplaced, or simply ignored. As I noted in chapter 2, science is often not the rational process that textbooks describe, where it progresses, step by step sequentially, continuously and progressively adding stone upon stone to build a grand edifice of knowledge. Although sometimes science approximates this rational progression, it often doesn't. In any case, the physical and biological sciences approximate this image of science more than psychology. In science, as in the larger culture, ideas are often ignored because they don't fit a current zeitgeist. I think this has been the case with the mind/body and the emotion/thinking split. It has been these divides that have led most all of Western philosophy and psychology to ignore the data which could have been recognized as initial support for the reality of subliteral kinds of language and thus long before now could have provided the basis for research into subliteral meaning.

THINKING AND FEELING

It's generally accepted that the main divide in Western philosophy began in the year 1637 with the publication of Rene Descartes's *Discourse on Method*. René Descartes (1596–1650) was a French philosopher, mathematician, and scientist who is considered by some to be the father of modern philosophy. He is perhaps best known for his famous dictum, *"Cogito, ergo sum,"* which translated says, "I think, therefore I am." You will note that he didn't say, "I *feel,* therefore, I am." This is a most important point.

Descartes is usually blamed (or credited, depending on the point of view) for what has become known as "mind-body dualism," where the body is seen as separate from the mind. Now, this is no ivory tower academic theorizing. His dictum has had profound effects on everyday thinking. In Western culture, most people consider their minds separate from their bodies. In medicine, we've even had to create a new approach to compensate for this split, called holistic medicine. In holistic medicine, it's recognized that the mind has direct effects on the state of our bodies. A precursor to the new holistic medical orientation to healing was developed in clinical psychology and psychiatry. It was called psychosomatics, which recognized that the mind (psyche) affects the body (soma). Psychosomatic and holistic medicine, then, are attempts to bring together what Descartes put asunder.

Somewhere along the line, religion also played a role in Descartes' philosophy of splitting the mind and body. At the time he wrote, Christian religious doctrine was extremely influential in Europe. During this period Galileo (1564–1642), the Italian astronomer, mathematician, and physicist was put on trial by the Catholic Inquisition for agreeing with the Copernican theory that the sun, not the earth, is the center of the solar system. It's no secret that in Christian doctrine the body is seen as weak, harbors sinful *feelings* of the flesh, and should be purged of these feelings if one is to be pure in body and soul. It's somewhat of an irony, I think, that strong religious *feelings* led to the *thinking* that these so-called bodily emotions should be purged. From this "purity" of religious thought, separating the mind from the body, it's only a short step to the "purity" of philosophical thought, purged of all feelings.

Descartes solidified the legacy of ancient Greek philosophy, too. Although Greek philosophy had many currents, it's main emphasis, *a la* Aristotle was one of rationality. In any event, since Descartes, the split between intellectual and emotional processes has been adopted in linguistics and cognitive science. Indeed both linguistics and cognitive science have followed in the footsteps of a philosophy that was a logical extension of Descartes's mind-body split, called logical positivism. In the 1920s a group of philosophers, who formed what was called the Vienna Circle, attempted to apply the methodology and precision of mathematics to the study of philosophy and language. Logical positivists tried to assess truth by direct observation and by carefully analyzing language. The goal of logical positivism was to eliminate all emotion from linguistic statements; to purge all subjective meaning from philosophical language.

EMOTION AND FEELING

The second division we need to understand is between what is called *emotion,* on the one hand, and *feeling* on the other. Actually this division, too, follows from Descartes's great divide. Emotions have been generally considered irrational, illogical, and belonging to the body, not the mind. Remember Mr. Spock from Star Trek who was a Vulcan, a race that had managed to purge all feelings, and could thus be purely logical? Such has been the Western legacy of Descartes and the logical positivists. The legacy has not been void of terrible conflict, however. After all, like Mr. Spock who was half-human, we have not been able to purge our feelings. With the possible exception of poets, it has not generally occurred to anyone that emotions could be "logical."[1]

There has been growing uneasiness with the view that emotions are— by definition—irrational. But this uneasiness has been the concern of only a few philosophers, who are interested in how language works, and by those who have an interest in poetry. One of these philosophers of language, Paul Ricoeur (1913–), has suggested that we should distinguish emotion from feeling. According to Ricoeur, emotion is a first-order experience, it's raw material, so to speak. Presumably it's "noncognitive;" and is what we usually think of when we think of being irrational or very angry. Emotion is more or less a physiological event. Feeling, on the other hand, he views as a second-order experience with cognition involved, a precursor or forerunner to conscious thought.[2]

An analogous distinction is made in cognitive science between sensation and perception. Sensation is the raw material and perception is the interpretation of the sensory stimuli. For example, in experiments where subjects are injected with adrenalin (but are not aware of what they are being injected with), they begin to experience the effects of the hormone. What they think they are experiencing depends on the context surrounding the injection. If they are watching a horror movie, they are likely to interpret what they are feeling as fear. If they are watching comedy, they are likely to interpret what they are feeling as elation, etc. Similarly, then, feelings come from interpreting our emotional experience. The analogy to sensation and perception is not exact, however, because feelings for Ricoeur are not just interpretations of emotions, they are "intentional structures."[3] This means that what we call feelings are internal organizing processes. They are a kind of proto or "primitive" thinking process. I have called this affective organizing process deep cognition.[4]

Deep cognition is an affective organizing, constructive form of thinking that operates below the level of normal awareness and issues from a cognitive sensory matrix. Others have theorized about this connection of feeling with thinking. Jean Piaget recognized that one of the most significant tasks of the social and behavioral sciences is "trying to characterize affective life in relation to cognitive functions." He was also, I believe, the first to introduce the concept of an "affective unconscious," thus suggesting that unconscious feelings are a form of thinking.[5] Because Descartes's legacy of the mind/body split has become like the air we breathe, the idea that feeling is thinking may immediately strike us as a kind of Orwellian newspeak (where good means bad, and up means down) or a kind of oxymoron, where incongruous or contradictory terms are placed together. In short, it seems to make no sense. This is why cognitive scientists and linguists have had such a problem with unconscious meaning and why the subliteral meaning and operations that I've presented have not been considered possible. Given the importance of feelings in subliteral conversations, we need to look further at what some other lone voices have been saying about the idea that feeling is a form of thinking.

FEELING AND FORM

The idea of an inner sensory apparatus is not entirely novel outside of psychology. Poets and philosophers have alluded to such an inner sensory source for years but have not articulated its workings in any concrete or empirical form. Students of art and language have told us for sometime, as did the philosopher Suzanne Langer (1895–1985) in her now classic book, *Feeling and Form*,[6] that externalized forms of experience like art and language spring from deeper layers of emotional and sensory experience. The symbolist poets,[7] too, maintained a similar idea, as do some philosophers of language like Paul Ricoeur whom I mentioned before. The philosopher Hans-Georg Gadamer (1900–   ), for example, maintains[8] that an inner linguistic form exists that's based on feelings, which he calls "linguisticality." The great German writer and scientist, Wolfgang von Goethe (1749–1832), also believed that there exists what he called an "exact sensory imagination."[9] Poets and philosophers, then, have been pointing to a deep form of thinking that's based on feelings (see chapter 8, the section of the Genesis Matrix).

Although the thoughts of poets and philosophers are not exactly scientific evidence, their thinking is at least based on a systematic observation of everyday empirical data. This kind of observation may not be grounds for considering their thoughts equivalent to scientific hypotheses, but we need to recall that the existence of a gene was hypothesized before the science of genetics demonstrated it. This was done on the basis of systematic observation of the results of both natural and artificial breeding of animals and the crossing of plants—long before the science of genetics came into being, very long before James Watson and Francis Crick discovered DNA,[10] the basic genetic stuff of life, and very long before electron microscopes allowed us to see that genetic stuff. The early reasoning about the existence of a gene was that given certain systematic observations about animal offspring and plant hybrids, some internal mechanism must exist that produces the systematic effects, some kind of internal organizer.

If I can be permitted a slight but pertinent digression, here, I must confess that the distinction between philosophy and psychology often escapes me. There is some psychology that is "philosophical," for example, existential and humanistic psychology, neither of which is subjected to testing. By the same token, there is some philosophy that's psychological, for example, Suzanne Langer's work. If we mean by psychology "empirical research," certainly much of philosophy is empirical, too, because it's based on systematic observations. If, however, by psychology we mean "experimental research," then perhaps most philosophy is excluded, but so too is much of psychology. The question is raised, then, when psychologists are theorizing, are they being philosophers, and when philosophers use empirical data on human behavior, are they being psychologists?

A close kinship has always existed between psychology and philosophy. In fact, psychology evolved out of philosophy. As Howard Gardner points out in his book, *The Mind's New Science: A History of the Cognitive Revolution*,[11] philosophy has provided psychology with much of its past and current agenda. Descartes's agenda has been a major one. Psychology and cognitive science, however, have systematically overlooked what some philosophers—and poets, who wax philosophical about the workings of their poetic processes—have been hypothesizing about connections between feeling, language, and thinking.

(I can't resist a short commercial break, here, for my philosopher colleagues. In our increasingly technological, pragmatic, and vocationally oriented society, philosophy, as an academic major and as a general education requirement, has been declining for the past few decades in university curricula. Philosophy isn't considered practical enough. This is a great loss for our culture. It's a loss, because the great contribution of a philosophical education is that it teaches one how to think—sharply and profoundly.[12] With this slight digression, let me now return to the idea of an inner sensory matrix.)

In his monumental work, *The Philosophy of Symbolic Forms*, Ernst Cassirer (1874–1945) formulated and hypothesized an "inner sensory form," that generates metaphorical meanings and also the symbolic forms of religion, myth, art, language, and science.[13] For Cassirer, all derive from a common source, an inner sensory matrix, which does not function rationalistically (as the term is normally understood). I might note that Cassirer was an empirical philosopher. By that I mean he didn't just sit in his armchair and think up these ideas in his head. He analyzed the considerable data on religion, myths, language, and science. Thus, he could be considered a "theoretical psychologist," and his ideas as scientific hypotheses. Suzanne Langer was greatly influenced by Cassirer, and Cassirer was greatly influenced by the Italian philosopher, Giambattista Vico, whom I mentioned in chapter 2.

THE GREAT DIVIDE THAT WASN'T

Vico's (1668–1744) book, *The New Science*,[14] constituted a great divide in philosophy that didn't happen. His book was a watershed philosophical work that marked a critical point in the history of Western philosophy.

Unfortunately, it's a book that's still not widely appreciated by philosophers in our highly technological society. Vico's ideas are important for understanding the subliteral mind. His book was a watershed because Vico had to overcome much of the rationalistic legacy of Aristotle, and he also had to overcome Descartes's widely accepted mind/body split and the death blow it delivered to all things emotional in the thought process, as well as the views of Francis Bacon (1561–1626), the renowned English philosopher who advocated a theory of scientific knowledge based on observation and experimentation. Until recent decades, with notable exceptions like Cassirer and a few other philosophers and literary authors who understood Vico's significance, his work remained largely unexamined. Even now, despite a small renaissance on Vico's work launched by a small cadre of scholars, it is not widely known. History passed him by. But the future won't.

Vico's philosophy was a counter to the abstract rationality of his day (and today). Vico, too, was what can be called an empirical philosopher. But his data and assumptions about how the mind worked are extraordinarily singular. His data were the ancient fables, myths, and the epic poetry of the ancient Greeks, including the epic poet, Homer (850 B.C.?) who is credited with writing the *Iliad* and the *Odyssey*. Vico's method was the linguistic analysis of those fables, myths, and poetry—all written in different historical times. He discovered a series of cognitive, structural, and linguistic transformations that changed throughout the different periods in which they were written, indicating that the changes he observed in the surface language of those fables, myths, and poetry reflected changing developmental cognitive and linguistic processes. As I suggested in a book chapter entitled, "Giambattista Vico and the Discovery of Metaphoric Cognition," whatever else Vico may have been—philosopher or social theorist—he was, in effect, the first cognitive psychologist.[15]

Moreover, Vico developed a method based on his principle that "doctrines must take their beginnings from that of the matters of which they treat."[16] By this he meant that our method of investigating a subject should be based on the nature of that subject. Vico's principle brings to mind Alfred North Whitehead's (1861–1947) dictum that every science must create its own methods.[17] In other words, logic isn't the most appropriate method for understanding a poem. Accordingly, the experimental method isn't the only appropriate primary method for investigating subliteral meanings. In broad outline, Vico's method was not too different from many contemporary approaches to studying the mind by analyzing ancient myths and fables. In anthropology, for example, Claude Levi-Strauss,[18] based his "cognitive anthropology" on analyzing the structure of cultural myths around the world. The scholar Joseph Campbell (1904–1987) is also well-known for his study of mythology for what it may tell us about the mind.[19] Vico's method is also similar to the psychologist Julian Jaynes (see chapter 2 and later).[20] Because myths are a kind of narrative, Vico's method bears some similarity to my use of group and social conversations to study the mind.

In section two of his book, tellingly entitled, "Poetic Wisdom," Vico delivers his own tour de force against Descartes and the rational view of the mind and advances his own unique cognitive theory of the way the mind works. To develop his theory of the mind, he had to perform a virtual autopsy on an entire philosophical body of knowledge from Aristotle and Descartes. What he found was that cognitive rigor mortis had set in.

Vico based his theory of the mind on what we call metaphorical reasoning. For Vico, what we call metaphor, however, was not a mere linguistic figure of speech. It was a primary process of cognition responsible for creating our entire edifice of language and thought. Vico developed and founded his entire theory of the mind (and also his theory of culture) on metaphorical reasoning. In Vico's time (and beyond, for that matter), metaphor was considered simply a figure of speech. The ancient Greek philosopher Aristotle, (384–322 B.C.) wrote about metaphor as simply a figure of speech. And, Vico's near contemporary, Descartes, held that clear, distinct, and logically precise ideas and categories are the only methods of assessing what is real and rational, not logically messy metaphors. Vico believed that he demonstrated, however, that our clear, distinct, logically precise ideas and categories are merely the end result of an older more primary metaphorical or "poetic" process, what I call deep cognition (see chapter 8). Vico's work is complex, intricate, and written in a style that demonstrates his theory of the mind. In many ways, it's closer to poetry than to prose. This is likely the reason that Vico's philosophical turn was not taken. We've been lost ever since.

Consequently, I will give only its headlines, so to speak, as they relate to the origin of subliteral meaning. To begin again, according to Vico, primitive humans could speak only in what he called "poetic sentences," which are generated from a feeling and sensory base, or in what he called "sensory topics" leading to "poetic sentences" which were *felt* more than thought. He says, "It is equally beyond our power to enter into the vast imagination of those first men, who minds were not in the least abstract, refined, or spiritualized because they were entirely immersed in the senses, buffeted by the passions, buried in the body."[21] The first humans, he says were "Almost all body and almost no reflection,"[22] and "The many abstract terms in which language now abounds . . . came to it from the body."[23] In gross shorthand by way of illustration, we use the metaphorical phrases, "coming to a *head* . . . . on the one *hand* . . . . I *see* your point," etc. After Descartes surgically removed the mind from the body, Vico transplanted it back into the body—from whence, according to him, it came.

His theory of metaphor and especially his theory of feeling/emotions involve what he called *sensory topics*. It is from these sensory topics that poetic sentences are made. In Vico's logic, this *sensory imagination* connects phenomena in a prerationalistic manner. Prerational, however, doesn't mean unlawful. It asserts inner sensory identities, not simple similarities. What this means is that particulars are perceived in the primitive mind as universals, where each individual person is every person. For Vico, sensation is a form of thinking.

According to Vico, poetic or figurative language developed first, and literal or propositional language appeared later, not the other way around as many currently conceive it. For Vico, "the first men were poets"; and the first spoken language was "metaphorical" just as it is with children. Indeed, Vico maintained that the origins of modern logic are to be found "hidden in the fables."[24] Most importantly, says Vico, these first ideas and categories were "felt and imagined."[25] Only "later as this imagination shrank and the powers of abstraction grew, these vast imaginations were reduced to diminutive signs,"[26] that is, to language, logic and abstract ideas.

So how did these sensory topics begin? Vico had a kind of big bang theory of metaphor and language. Through an analysis of the language of fables, myths, and epic poetry, Vico imaginatively enters into the mind of what he metaphorically called the "first men," to a time before the dawning of conscious rationalism. This protoexemplar or model was used by Vico to illustrate the origin of this transmutational process from something that was only "felt and imagined" to something that became "clear and distinct." The origin was the response of primitive men to the natural sound of thunder. In some far distant and very dim past, says Vico, groups of men huddled together and identified a sudden and loud clap of thunder as *anger*. In effect, thunder was experienced as the first word.

This process of sensory metaphor is not too different from young children believing that there's "someone" up there in the sky who is causing thunder. According to Vico, on the basis of tone, volume, and power of the sudden clap of thunder, these first men identifying thunder with the human emotion, anger, illustrates the primal transformation of sensory experience into the abstraction of imagery and language. Thus was created what we now might call synaesthetic or sensory metaphor. What better description of the emotional basis of subliteral narratives?

OTHER VOICES

There have been other more "scientific" voices, too, suggesting that feelings and emotions powerfully affect our use of language. Some of these voices, like Vico and Cassirer, have seen that deep sensory cognition affects what we have come to call metaphors in language and is also responsible for the origin of the entire corpus of language itself. Other, ostensibly more scientific voices, add harmony to the small chorus of people who, in effect, have seen that Descartes's great divide led to a terribly wrong turn.

VOICES IN THE BICAMERAL MIND

One of the voices that I mentioned in chapter 2 comes from the psychologist Julian Jaynes's controversial book, *The Origin Of Consciousness in the Breakdown of the Bicameral Mind.*[27] His interest was how consciousness developed. Like Vico, Jaynes developed his theory, in part, by a historical analysis of ancient Greek texts, myths, and epic poetry, such as the *Iliad* of Homer. In researching consciousness, he said "I traced it back until it disappeared in some of the works ascribed to Aristotle, and then in some of the pre-Socratics, and then it vanished in the *Iliad.*"[28] This perhaps sounds like terribly esoteric stuff, with all this talk about Greek myths, but it's not. It's simply going back in time to recover lost knowledge. Jaynes, like Vico and some other classical scholars, maintained that the Gods mentioned in the *Iliad* and the *Odyssey* were not mere poetic devices as traditionally believed. He viewed the *Iliad* as a literal historical document. Says Jaynes, "We may regard the *Iliad* as standing at the great turning of the times, and a window back into those unsubjective times" before our modern consciousness.[29] Indeed, Jaynes proposed that the *Iliad* be regarded, "as a psychological document of immense importance."[30] This is a profound claim. What Jaynes is saying is that what we thought was just ancient poetry is in fact factual. But more than this, he is saying that we can learn a great deal from this ancient narrative about the way the human mind evolved and the way it works. In the same way, I am suggesting that what appear to be simple everyday conversations are of immense psychological and linguistic importance.

Jaynes said that human beings were not always conscious. Prior to be-coming conscious as we understand it, the "mind" was bicameral, i.e., anal-ogous to the term used in political science, divided into two "houses"or parts. Jaynes, too, maintained that consciousness was fundamentally formed by language, particularly by metaphor and analogy. For Jaynes, "metaphor is not a mere extra trick of language . . . it is the very constructive ground of language."[31] More than this, like Vico, Jaynes maintains, "Consciousness is the work of lexical metaphor."[32] Further, "In early times," says Jaynes, "lan-guage and its referents climbed up from the concrete to the abstract on the steps of metaphors, even, we may say, created the abstract on the bases of metaphors."[33] Like Vico, Jaynes maintains that figurative or poetic language evolved first. Metaphor for Vico and Jaynes, then, was a cognitive operation before it was a linguistic device.

Moreover, Jaynes recognized that feelings and the body are integrally involved in the mind. He says, "The conscious psyche is imprisoned in the body as in a tomb."[34] In this time before modern consciousness, in what Jaynes calls the bicameral stage, humans hallucinated voices in their minds, which they took to be the voices of gods. These voices (as in some schizo-phrenics) became their volition, what we would call their unconscious thoughts and feelings. Jaynes supports his theory with considerable data from neurology and other psychological research.

LANGUAGE AND THE EXPRESSION OF THOUGHT

Two other voices that traverse Descartes's great divide are the psychol-ogists Heinz Werner and Bernard Kaplan. Their book, *Symbol Formation: An Organismic Developmental Approach to Language and the Expression of Thought*,[35] is seminal in terms of research that systematically demonstrates concretely the operations involved in what I refer to as a cognitive sensory matrix. Thus, their book is significant for a subliteral theory of the mind (see chap-ter 8). Only recently has their work attracted metaphor researchers sys-tematically. Werner and Kaplan believe that they have demonstrated a "primordial unity of the senses." This primordial unity is characterized by an integral interaction and coordination of inner sensations, feelings, mo-tor-muscular, and gestural schemas. A schema is an internal (presumably neurological) pattern that organizes the complexity of stimuli coming in to our nervous system into a manageable form. Then, this form acts as an in-termediary to guide future inputs and behavior. In my view, schemas are outgrowths of a deep cognitive sensory matrix.

The cognitive sensory matrix generates the phenomenon called synesthesia in which the different sensory connections become crossed. In its extreme form, for example, some people can *feel* colors, or a particular sound can create the visualization of a particular color (see Marks later). Werner and Kaplan consider synesthesia and phonetic symbolism evidence of a primordial unity of the senses and of the process of what they call physiognomized language.

Physiognomized language has three basic characteristics. Words have a (1) quasi-substantial thing-like character; (2) a pictorial dynamic character; and (3) an embeddedness in and development out of postural-affective motor schemas or patterns. As words lose these connections to a deep cognition, they become literal and technical language, having lost their figurative/metaphorical basis. For Werner and Kaplan, then, like Vico and Cassirer, cognitive development evolves from a primitive sensory matrix into abstract symbols of language and mathematics.

From their study of infants, Werner and Kaplan describe the dynamic nature of early physiognomic transfer or transformations. In response to a researcher opening and closing his eyes, for example, a child may open and close its mouth. In response to an experimenter extruding and wiggling his tongue, a child may raise and move its forefinger rhythmically. In other words, it's the *felt* and deep structure of the action that's perceived and "transferred" to another modality.

In young infants, an extruding appendage, for example, a tongue, is not as yet differentiated into its specificity of tongue versus nontongue-ness. Thus, in response to a moving tongue, an infant equates the movement of its forefinger, its arm, or its leg as the "same thing." Accordingly, the child's movement of a finger as imitation of the movement of a researcher's tongue is a sensory-motor metaphor. Developmentally, these deep transformations lose their generality and become specific and particular. On the level of language, words are increasingly detached from their deep sensory-imaginal substrate and on the "conscious" level become the abstract, rational, symbols of literal language. Synesthesia is also a part of Vico's inner sensory logic.

PREVERBAL LOGIC

More recently, the hypothesis of an inner sensory matrix was advanced by Brenda Beck, an anthropologist.[36] Based in part on anthropological studies of metaphor in preliterate societies, Beck suggests a "preverbal sensory logic" to explain metaphor. Anthropological research, says Beck "leads us to think of conscious sense perceptions as resting in a mesh of associations at the motor and emotional level that builds up with experience over time," and that "cluster around body-based imagery."[37] Similar to Vico's notion of imagination as memory, Beck suggests that "metaphors deal not with immediate experience, but with sense images remembered (and recombined) in the mind's eye."[38]

In Beck's view, sensory logic does not deal with clear and distinct ideas but with analogical reasoning in a dense associational network within a multidimensional space in our brain/minds. The transferring of categories or the crossing over of categories as in synesthesia occurs not from a "distinct category-to-category transfer" but "along clines and gradients,"[39] by which she means gradual changes based on probabilities, not strictly logical categories. She insightfully observes that there are so many dimensions and relationships in sensory space that even a sophisticated poet can only crudely describe the process. Further, as Beck correctly infers, passing a sensory level of experience over to a semantic level involves including affective and perceptual qualities that bridge the logical gaps which separate the categories at the more abstract level. The experienced wholeness of a metaphor is explained by the fact that a given experience is recoded in several different ways within the sensory matrix.

Similar to Werner and Kaplan, Beck bases the hypothesis of a preverbal sensory logic in large measure on the empirical findings of the synesthesia phenomenon. Based on work in the sensory structure of synesthesia, Beck argues that synthaesthesia does not rest on mere verbal and affective transfer and therefore not simply on metaphor (as linguistically understood) but rather on a "protosynthesis of sensations at a . . . primary level of motor and emotional consciousness."[40] This is deep stuff.

UNITY OF THE SENSES

In addition to Vico, Cassirer, Werner, and Kaplan, Beck and other writers have made significant note of the relationship between metaphor and the sensory phenomenon of synesthesia. More recently, the psychologist, Lawrence Marks's book, *The Unity of the Senses*,[41] thoroughly traced and documented the phenomenon of synesthesia and its relationship to metaphor.

Using his own experimental research in sensory processes and the research of others in psychophysics, Marks offers data that clearly indicate a level of sensory processing where the senses form a unity. The concept of a *Sensus Communis*, as Marks reminds us, goes back at least to the fifth century

B.C. to the ancient Greek philosopher Democritus and extends to Aristotle. Marks, like Vico, Cassirer, Werner, Kaplan, and Beck, finds synesthesia essential to understanding metaphor. Marks in fact suggests synesthesia as an explanatory model for much of what is called metaphor.

Synesthesia, of course, is the transposition or transfer of sensory experience from one sense modality to another, as in perceiving a high note of music to be "bright," "sharp," or "tinny." The synesthetic process is what Marks refers to as cross-modal transfer. There are two basic types of synesthesia: (1) the "normal" synesthesia in which we metaphorically experience a high note in music as "thin"; (2) true synesthesia in which people who "see" sounds, experience a high note as a light color, or conversely a low note as a dark color (ostensibly these people comprise about 10% of the population). True synesthetes are neurologically "wired" differently from most people. Synesthetes are not "freaks." What synesthesia exhibits is the evolutionary origin of the unity of the senses, the *sensus communis*. According to Marks, much of what is perceived as "similarity" and therefore analogy and/or metaphor has its origin in the structure of cross-modal sensory processing. As these sensory interrelationships become detached through increasingly higher levels of neurophysiological and psycholinguistic processing, there remain in our perception only the abstract "features" of similarities.

In the opening of this chapter I noted that so-called mainstream cognitive science does not include emotion in its explanations of the way the mind works. This statement is somewhat of a generalization. There has always been a parallel universe of researchers—I hesitate to call them a cognitive science underground—that has pushed to include emotion in cognition. The history of emotion's role in the mind has been controversial.[42] Even when it has been recognized, it has generally been considered—à la Descartes—that it distorts our mental processes or influences our attitudes. This has especially been the view of intense or strong emotions or what has been labeled "hot cognition."[43]

More recently, there is a resurgence in recognizing the importance of including emotion in the study of mind. Daniel Goleman, a behavioral science writer for the New York Times, published a book called *Emotional Intelligence,* that has had quite an impact on our understanding of the significance of emotion in our everyday life.[44] Neuroscientists, too, have renewed interest in the role of emotion in the brain and mind.[45] One of these is Joseph LeDoux. In his book, *The Emotional Brain,* on the basis of his review of the physical brain he concludes that, "The mammalian system is clearly constructed as an emotional system."[46] He goes on to suggest that "By treating emotions as unconscious processes that can sometimes give rise to conscious content, we lift the burden of the mind-body problem from the shoulders of emotion researchers and allow them to get on with the problem of figuring out how the brain does its unconscious emotional business."[47] Under the best intentions of including emotion in cognition, however, there is never the suggestion that emotion is integrally involved in selecting specific words, phrases, and sentence order in creating subliteral meaning.

CONCLUSION

In this chapter we have seen that Rene Descartes's great divide in philosophy, which severed the head of rationality from the emotional body, has led to ignoring evidence about feelings and emotions to explain how language and mind work. On one side of this great divide has been most of Western philosophy and cognitive science and their disembodied theories of mind. On the other, have been a few lone voices. As we have seen, these voices, many of which have not heard each other, nevertheless, have spoken an amazingly similar language in explaining how feelings are integrally involved in constructing language and mind.

The philosopher of language, Paul Ricoeur, spoke about an inner linguistic process based on feelings that is characterized by unconscious "intentional structures." The great German writer and scientist, Wolfgang von Goethe, believed there exists what he called an "exact sensory imagination." We saw that Hans-Georg Gadamer spoke about a "linguisticality" based on feelings. We also saw that Suzanne Langer spoke about the relationship between feeling and form and Ernst Cassirer hypothesized an "inner sensory form," based on feeling, which does not function rationalistically.

Then, of course, Giambattista Vico believed that he demonstrated that underlying modern language and mind were primitive "sensory topics" generated from a feeling and sensory base or what he called leading to "poetic sentences" which are *felt* more than thought. Then we saw that the psychologists Heinz Werner and Bernard Kaplan, and Lawrence Marks, Julian Jaynes, and the anthropologist Brenda Beck, in one way or another, all spoke of a "primordial unity of the senses" and a "preverbal sensory logic," a "bicameral mind," a "unity of the senses," and a *"sensus communis,"* all similar to the "inner linguistic process," the "exact sensory imagination," a "linguisticality," an "inner linguistic form" an "inner sensory form," and the "sensory topics" of Ricoeur, Goethe, Gadamer, Langer, Cassirer, and Vico.

We saw, too, that these authors considered that what we call metaphor is a fundamental cognitive process responsible for creating both language and mind. Finally, we saw that common to all these deep sensory and cognitive structures, either implied or directly stated, was perhaps the process of synesthesia, which Vico demonstrated by his description of early mankind experiencing a clap of thunder as anger and Werner and Kaplan demonstrate in describing the nature of physiognomic transfer, where in response to a researcher opening and closing his eyes, an infant opens and closes its mouth. In response to an experimenter extruding and wiggling his tongue, an infant raises and moves its forefinger rhythmically.

There have been others who have theorized similarly about the unity of the mind and body. Most of them are philosophers and poets, not psychologists and cognitive scientists. However, it would take us too far afield to give adequate time to them. It can be seen that subliteral narratives originated out of these "primitive" processes described previously. As I mentioned in the opening of this chapter, anyone in science who advances a novel theory had better be able to back up the theory beyond what is normally required. This chapter has been the first installment in this requirement, and it has also laid the groundwork for chapter 8 where, in outlining the subliteral mind, I describe a cognitive sensory matrix based on feelings and emotions, out of which subliteral narratives and meaning are born. As I hope to show, if the omission of the role of feeling in linguistics and cognitive science has been their Achilles' heel, limiting their explanatory power, then subliteral meanings may be their Trojan horse.[48]

Finally, until relatively recently, nowhere—with rare exception—has it been suggested that emotion is involved in the physiognomic[49] and synaesthetic sensory integrations that I have shown in subliteral narratives. And nowhere—again, with rare exception—has it been suggested that emotion is integral to creating words, phrases, sentences, entire narratives, and to the very creation of syntax that I presented in this book.[50] What a colossal mistake it has been to divide emotion from mind and the mind from the body. Ideas have consequences, it seems.

POSTSCRIPT

This chapter has been about the long, controversial relationship between feeling and thinking. In looking at this relationship, we saw that they have been separated by Descartes's great philosophical divide, that this great divide is largely responsible for ignoring the role of feeling and emotion in cognition and language, and that this split kept us from discovering the subliteral mind and meaning where feeling shapes our use of language.

You will recall I pointed out that Descartes said, "I think, therefore, I am," not "I *feel*, therefore, I am." His separation of thought from feeling, then, was a radical disconnect from which we have yet to recover. We have been half out of our minds ever since. I said part of the reason for this disconnect was the Christian religious belief that bodily feelings were weak and sinful. But another more basic reason is that we have a natural disconnect between our conscious and unconscious minds. This disconnect leads us to believe that the very essence of who we are emanates from our sense of consciousness. By definition, we are unaware of our unconscious selves. Thus, it *appears* that we *are* only our conscious selves because of what is called a phenomenological analysis of the world around us. The term phenomenological simply means describing things as they *appear* or consciously *feel* to us. In the Introduction, I used the example of the sun *appearing* to rise in the East in the morning and setting in the West in the evening. It doesn't, of course. It just appears to. Similarly, our everyday experience tells us that we are our conscious selves. We're not, but we just appear to be (see chapter 8 for more). It was Descartes's phenomenological analysis of his "self," as it appeared to him, that created his philosophical disconnect.

We see this radical disconnect between our conscious and unconscious selves in subliteral narratives. An interesting aspect of subliteral narratives is that, despite conscious knowledge about a situation, our unconscious doesn't seem to get the message. For example, in chapter 3 we saw that although people were consciously aware of the tape recorder, the reasons for it, and that the tapes were available to them, subliterally, we saw that it was as if their unconscious acted as though they only had a suspicion that they were being recorded. There was a radical disconnect between their conscious knowledge and their unconscious feelings. It's out of this great divide, this radical disconnect, that subliteral meaning emerges.

CHAPTER 7

THE SOUNDS OF REASON
THE PUNS AND POETICS OF EVERYDAY CONVERSATION

On one weekend, my wife was leaving for the week to attend law school in a neighboring state. Our young daughter, Melyssa, lived with me then in Maine. Melyssa was a little upset because her mother was leaving, and of course it wasn't my first preference to be left alone to parent my daughter. In making preparations to leave, my wife had just made a batch of chocolate chip cookies, which she was taking with her. Chocolate chip cookies were my favorite. As she was about to leave, I jokingly said, "So, you are deserting us." This didn't simply refer to the fact that she was leaving for the week. Not only was she leaving or *deserting* us, but by taking my favorite *dessert* with her, she was in fact also *desserting* us. This is no simple pun or a verbal slight of tongue. This is a window into the workings of the subliteral mind.

To understand how subliteral conversation is possible and why it has generally been considered impossible, in this chapter, as in the last one, we go on a journey back into time to find knowledge that's been ignored, misplaced, and lost. It will take us into a mental space where sounds of oral speech transmit and create meaning. I show how this lost knowledge may be reasserting itself in a disguised, modern form and how sounds of speech are crucial for understanding subliteral meaning.

INTRODUCTION

Just as there is more than what meets the eye of the beholder, there is more than what meets the ear of the listener (see Appendix, 6.2. Phonetic Operations). Historically, the pun has been seen as a low form of wit or humor or considered a cheap joke. But there is nothing cheap about the cognitive processes underlying the pun. These processes are the cognitive coal deposits from which the diamonds of meaning are formed. They involve the very sounds of reason. As I briefly mentioned in chapter 1, puns have been given a bad rap. The hard fact, however, is that they provide a window into the complex workings of our minds, as many of the examples of subliteral conversations in this book have already shown. In fact these processes constitute sound reasoning. Poets have always understood this. Scientists haven't.

Understanding the way the mind uses sounds is important in uncovering hidden meaning in conversations. In this chapter, I explain the use of pun-like language that our mind uses to create subliteral meaning. Let me begin by revisiting some of the briefer examples presented throughout this book so far. Then, I will extend the analysis of others that I've only briefly presented. Recall the following. There was the example of the person whose last name was *Heapes* who was about to trade in his old car because he said he was tried of driving old *heaps*, meaning old dilapidated cars. Then there is the advertisement for the product Reynolds Wrap for wrapping food, that said it was the "best wrap around," literally meaning not only that it was the best product around, but subliterally that the advertising pitch was the best rap i.e., talk, or words around (see chapter 10). The use of sound can also be clearly seen in the reference to crystal *balls*, when the psychologist William Schutz shaved himself *bald*, and in the subliteral use of names, as in the example of using the name of movie director Stanley *Kubrick*, who was known for his special effects to reference subliterally a person whose last name was *Kulick* and who was constantly using interpersonal *techniques*. Or the use of sound in the example of my wife subliterally commenting on my speaking in a broken manner by calling attention to a fence with a *broken spoke*, when I was stumbling over words, mispronouncing them, repeating syllables, and otherwise talking in broken sentences. It's clear that the pun-like use of sound creates meanings. The pun, then, is a sound concept.

Some pun-like processes are completely internal and thus not directly recognized by the spoken word. We saw this in chapter 4 in a conversation about not placing plants in *direct sunlight*. Recall that the word *sunlight* was constructed out of two members' names, one of whom was much older than the other females. Her name was *Firestone* (which represents sun; i.e., a big stone of fire), and a young male who was young enough to be her son (represents sun), had the name *Wright* (i.e., phonetically or by rhyme equals light). Hence, *Firestone* + *Wright* equals *sunlight*. Although all these examples certainly involve a play on words, they are certainly not merely playing with words. And, unlike what common wisdom would have us believe, playing with words is serious business. Now, let me extend some examples further that I've only briefly presented in previous chapters.

In chapter 1, I presented the example of a slip of the tongue by a co-host of the CNN program, *Burden of Proof*.[1] Let's look a little more closely at this example. Roger Cossack made a so-called speech error. In announcing that President Clinton was being required to testify before a grand jury, he meant to say that it was "unprecedented," but he slipped and clearly began to say, "unPresidented."

The linguistic explanation of this slip is that it was simply caused by the similar sound and spelling of the two words which were confused and interfered with each other, indicating no hidden meaning. Looking closely at the spelling of "unprecedented," and "unPresidented," they both begin with "unpre......", followed by either the consonant "s" or "c" which can be pronounced similarly. Then, these letters are followed by the two vowels, "i" and "e" which also can be pronounced similarly. Finally, they end identically with "......dented." But this is not a meaningless speech error caused by the similar sound of the two words. The slip has meaning. An analysis of the linguistic mechanisms involved may explain the *how*, but it doesn't explain the *why* of the slip. To understand the *why* we have to understand the context of the slip.

The context of the CNN program and previous programs was about the possible impeachment of Clinton because of charges of perjury. The slip "unPresidented" in this case refers to being removed from his office or impeached, that is, un-Presidented, as in becoming "unseated" or coming "unhinged." The slip may reflect Cossack's feeling that Clinton's appearance before a grand jury is unprecedented, as in the adjectival form and also "unprecedential." In other words not only is a President being called before the grand jury *unprecedential*, but so are the sexual charges being investigated *unprecedential*. Clinton's behavior in the workplace, if true, are thus both unprecedential and unpresidential.

Without access to the personal views of Roger Cossack, however, there is no way of responsibly assessing the deeper subliteral motivations of this slip, i.e., whether Mr. Cossack presumably believes that Clinton should be impeached because of the scandal or whether the slip means that he thinks Clinton will or might be impeached.* Playing around with sounds and words

*As this book goes to press, it has become evident to me that my subliteral analysis of Roger Cossack's position on Clinton's impeachment seems to be appropriate. When *Burden of Proof* first began reporting on the Clinton/Lewinsky affair, both co-hosts Greta Van Susteren and Roger Cossack seemed to be reporting in a "neutral" manner. Recently, it seems to me that Van Susteren has clearly become pro-Clinton on the CNN program—as well as from listening to her on the *Larry King* show—while Cossack clearly seems to be leaning toward the anti-Clinton side (Note: While Cossack's position could be the result of conscious programming on the part of is not just "playing with words." It's exploring the depths of language in all of its linguistic complexity. Indeed, it's creating language and meaning.

PLAYING SERIOUSLY WITH WORDS: A BRIEF HISTORY

The negative view of puns and playing with words can be traced to early Greek philosophy from which Western philosophy inherited much of its tradition. As Hans Gadamer[2] and others have noted, Greek philosophy began, more or less, with the insight that a word is only a name, i.e., that the word has no inherent connection to the thing it represents (except onomatopoeic words, see later). The Greek Heraclitus and other Sophists (fifth-century B.C. Greek philosophers who were known for their skill in argumentation) were characterized by their audacious plays on the ambiguity of words. But, for Heraclitus, "playing with words" was not a simple stylistic device. He recognized that playing with words is the necessary expression of thought itself.

In his book the *Republic,* the Greek philosopher Plato,[3] who is generally considered the father of the Western philosophical tradition, attacks sophists and also poets and poetry. Indeed, in Plato's Republic, the poet has lowly status (though Plato himself is fond of playing with words). Plato's teacher Socrates also considered poetics a lowly art. But on his deathbed in prison, we are told that he began to extol the virtue of poetics. Such was the early status of playing with words. Plato's rational view came to a head during the Renaissance (roughly from the fourteenth to the seventeenth century) and the subsequent period of the Enlightenment (seventeenth and eighteenth century) often called the Age of Reason. This "Rationalism" led to a kind of prelogical positivist view of language. Subjective, imaginative, and figurative language was banished from rational thought and was considered only stylistic or literary.

Then, in the twentieth century, the logical culmination of this view of language was expressed by a group of philosophers who formed a group called The Vienna Circle and became known as Logical Positivists. As I mentioned in the last chapter, they thought that truth could be assessed only by direct observation and by the use of a philosophical language that had been purged of all subjective, emotional, and imaginative content. For the view of

---

the producers of the program, this does not necessarily undermine my subliteral analysis of his slips, as he would have this anti-Clinton position on his mind while apparently trying to appear objective).

language as a repository and rich corpus of connected sounds and meanings and as a vehicle for the discovery process, the Vienna Circle was the
Last Supper (at least in philosophy and science). Is it any wonder, then, that
playing with words has received such bad press? Although playing with
words was basically banished, it didn't die.

Some well-known philosophers and scientists have had a penchant for
playing with words in their writing, sometimes quite seriously. Giambattista
Vico often played with the sound of words. In the modern age, Freud first
brought to light the importance that "playing with words" has for thinking
in general. In his *The Interpretation of Dreams*,[4] Freud points out that ancient
"Oriental" books on dream interpretation based a greater number of their
interpretations on tracing similarities of sound and resemblance between
words, a fact that was not lost on Freud. Extraordinary importance is placed
on punning in the ancient civilization of the East (just as with the Sophists
of ancient Greece). Freud pointed out that Western books on dream interpretation, which were largely translations of those ancient Asian dream
books, omitted the similarities of sound and resemblances between words.
According to Freud's research, puns and "turns of speech" also occur frequently in old Norse sagas and scarcely a dream is to be found in which
puns do not play a large role.[5]

Freud learned his lessons well from his research. In his analyses of
dreams, jokes, and parapraxes, or slips of the tongue, he made important
use of what he learned about playing with the meaning and sounds of words,
though even Freud primarily relegated such processes to secondary importance. Psychoanalysis has connected such playing with words to what they
called primary process thinking, a primitive unconscious process. Schizophrenics often exhibit this kind of archaic thought. Salvvano Arieti,[6] the psychiatrist (and others) have pointed out the similarity of playing with words to
schizophrenic language and logic, what he calls "paleologic" or "archaic
logic," which is considered a form of archaic or primitive rationality. As the
progeny of this long philosophical tradition, modern linguistics and cognitive science still consider such playing with words and slips of the tongue
mere mistakes or errors. Other notable exceptions to the Western bias
against playing with words are the anthropologist Claude Levi-Strauss[7] and
the rogue psychoanalyst Jacques Lacan.[8] As might be expected, Levi-Strauss
is charged by many of his colleagues with what one critic has specifically
called his "mental gymnastics" and "playing tricks with language."[9] This is
very telling criticism—but about the critic, not the work being criticized.

In the last chapter, I noted that sometimes ideas in science and in culture become lost, misplaced, or simply ignored. In that chapter, I showed

that the fundamental importance of feelings and emotion in the origin and production of language was lost. Now, we have been witness to another lost part of our minds, the poetic and linguistic sound connections between words. Beginning with the rational Greek philosophy of Socrates, Plato, and Aristotle, from Descartes's great divide, up through the Renaissance and the Enlightenment's Age of Reason, to the Logical Positivists, and down to contemporary times, the pun and playing with words has, like the role of feelings, been considered, at best, the province of the poets, a defective speech process, or worse still, the workings of otherwise demented minds.

To understand this negative view of puns and playing with words, we need to understand that we lost something else as we went along our historical way to the modernization of our mind: the oral tradition. Understanding this oral tradition is likewise crucial for understanding subliteral meaning.

SUBLITERAL MEANING AND THE ORAL TRADITION

There were two major historical events that deeply affected the development of our modern mind. It's generally considered that the first, the invention of writing, occurred about 8,000 years ago. The second major event in the modernization of our minds, the invention of moveable type and the printing press, occurred in the fifteenth century. We have no idea who invented writing. The inventions of movable type and the printing press are generally attributed to Johann Gutenberg (1397–1468). We shall see why these two major historical events were so momentous for understanding how the subliteral mind works. Before the invention of writing, early societies relied exclusively on the spoken word to pass on traditions and knowledge from one person or generation to another. This was primarily done by telling stories or great narratives, often by traveling story tellers—the ancient equivalent of the evening news.

THE GUTENBERG TONGUE

With the invention of writing, exclusive reliance on the spoken word was somewhat reduced. But not until the invention of the printing press and the mass production of the written word did oral histories became antiquated, at least in modernized Western society. Before Gutenberg, there were "books." These were the handwritten manuscripts of scribes who wrote down oral stories and histories, but these "books" were used only by scholars and the elite.

There has since developed a bias to understanding oral discourse as if it were written or printed language that's simply spoken. I should point out that this bias is not universal. It's generally true of Western/European culture, the highly educated, and certainly of academics and scientists. With the advent of the printed word, we lost the oral tradition and some very important knowledge that went with it. This is why. Understanding and analyzing the spoken word is quite different from understanding and analyzing the printed word. The distinction between oral "speech," on the one hand, and "written" language is basic. The field of linguistics has made a similar distinction between competence and performance. Competence refers to a speaker knowing—mostly unconsciously—the correct rules underlying language. Performance is the way a speaker actually uses language in speaking. Speech is considered a more individualized, creative, and psychological process, in which the speaker produces personal variations within the ostensibly inherent limiting structure of the language being spoken. But oral "speech," as understood by some philosophers of language and those who study ancient oral traditions,[10] recognizes the unique characteristics of oral speech that go far beyond the modern linguistic distinction of competence and performance.

Now, the concept of oral history has modern and ancient meanings. Some anthropologists, historians, sociologist, psychologists, and other researchers use personal interviews to obtain information, which they have transcribed. Then, they are analyzed—albeit unknowingly— as if they were printed language. Similarly, even though conversation in general and small group narratives are an oral mode, research on social and small group conversation has been analyzed as if it were "written" language, that is, as if it were regulated by the "correct" rules of traditional grammar and rational discourse. In analyzing oral speech as if it were written communication, we ignore crucial information.

What was lost in the "advancement" from the oral tradition to the modernized written and print tradition was our roots in the psychological and emotional origins of speech. For example, in oral speech, punctuation was originally a natural psychological and bodily process. In historical terms, written punctuation is a fairly new way of marking a string of words. A "period," for instance, which marks the end of a "sentence" (itself a relatively new invention) in the ancient oral tradition was the natural stop at the end of a length of breath. Other punctuation was marked by pauses, tones, and pitches of voice. Still others emanated from one's subjective psychological state. In English print, we use the comma now to separate words or phrases, the colon is used to introduce material that elaborates on what has already been said, and the semicolon marks the separation between elements in a series of related phrases. Other intonations are shown by the exclamation point, the question mark, parentheses, and quotation marks. We also have brackets, parenthesis, ellipses, the dash, the apostrophe, and the hyphen. By its nature, oral speech is aural and surrounds us, whereas print is graphic and directional. We err when we listen to oral speech as if it were printed language spoken out loud.

INNER SPEECH AND THE CADENCE OF SPOKEN LANGUAGE

Unlike written language (again, even written language that's spoken), oral speech emanates and resonates from a deep unconscious cognitive and linguistic reservoir. Oral speech is characterized by what is called prosody, a metrical structure. Oral speech is closer to singing than is the written word that's spoken. In fact some classical scholars, who study ancient literature, believe that spoken language was originally executed in a melodious song-like cadence.[11] Vico's research also led him to believe that early humans "formed their first languages by singing."[12] Jaynes, too, suggests that ancient poetry, "was much closer to song."[13] Anyone who has attended a Catholic High Mass spoken in Latin has a sense of what this "first speech" sounded like. The implications of the origin of speech as a poetic and song-like vocalization are important for understanding the role of sound and puns in subliteral meaning. In some theories of early language development, it's thought that poetic type language and playing with sound is fundamental. For example, it's thought that onomatopoeia played a significant role. Onomatopoeia is the creating of words that sound like what they represent, e.g., many children use the sound "bow-wow" first to refer to a dog. The term comes from the Greek, *onomatopoiia*, from *onomatopoios*, or coiner of names. Roger Brown, the psychologist, refers to the role of onomatopoeia in the origin of language as the "bow-wow" theory in his classic book, *Words and Things: An Introduction to Language.*

Both Levi-Strauss and Lacan understand the nature of oral speech, as I have suggested elsewhere.[14] This is the reason that they both play with words in their writing. In playing with words, they are attempting to reproduce, to return to, and to demonstrate an oral tradition by way of the written word. They do this because their very theories are based on the ancient notion of speech and all that it implies. Readers who are not familiar with the oral tradition, simply think that Levi-Strauss and Lacan are just playing around with words. They're not. They're seriously playing and demonstrating the workings of language and the mind.

In any event, the origins of speech, however shrouded in the blank spaces of early history, are anchored in our inner sensuous and rhythmical spaces of sound and meaning. Those interested in uncovering subliteral language and meaning, then, must tune not their eyes but their ears, for it's in these early sensuous, bodily, emotional, lyrical, metrical, homophonous (as in good night, good knight), and playful auditory spaces of language that the cognitive operations which create subliteral language and meaning will often be found—and understood. Entering this space is not an easy job (unless one is poetically inclined). As Vico warned us, it is "beyond our power to enter into the vast imagination of those first men, whose minds were not in the least abstract, refined, or spiritualized, because they were entirely immersed in the senses, buffeted by the passions, buried in the body."[15] Upon first entering this kind of non-Euclidian or curved cognitive space, it may not make any sense. Because it is considered that early speech has an affinity to music, perhaps an analogy to music is appropriate here.

A number of years ago, I went to hear a new musical group called *Do'A* (pronounced like door). They played ancient and strange instruments—mostly percussion instruments—from various cultures around the world. The instrumental sounds and the rhythms were so foreign to my Western ears that at first it didn't sound like music at all, just a collection of noises. Then as I listened more carefully, I began to barely hear what I considered music. At that point, I had a kind of epiphany, a revelation that what I was hearing was probably what music sounded like in the very beginning of its creation. This insight made a great impression on me. The analogy here is with what it may have been like to enter the mind of Vico's "first men" when the sounds we call language were first combined into a complex utterance.

In many ways language, especially spoken language, and music are similar. Both, of course, are made up of sounds. But more than this, music, like language, has a syntax or grammar. Both arrange sounds in time, creating a continuous composition. Both have a rhythm, and both can be improvisational. And, of course, both play with sound. In addition, contrary to the printed word, oral speech is expressed and experienced as more emotional and participatory. Consequently, in listening to speech it accesses our memory differently than either speaking or reading the printed word. But more than this, both speech and music create a shared or communal collective emotional consciousness. Unlike most of Western societies, oral cultures are more communal than cultures based on the printed word.

Certain subcultures in our society may, however, be returning to a kind of oral tradition. Perhaps beginning with the first TV generation of youth, we are seeing the effects of a neo-oral tradition of sorts. These youths are weaned on thousands of hours of visual and oral material, not to mention teenage music whose meaning is orally delivered in lyrics that resemble oral-tradition poetry. This seems particularly true of Rap music.

BACK TO THE FUTURE: RAP MUSIC AND THE ORAL TRADITION

In the mid 1970s, African-American and Hispanic youths created a new form of music. Rap is characterized by a repetitive, syncopated rhythm, whose rhymed lyrics play with sounds. Like speech, it's improvisational. This street poetry is accompanied by a disco or funk musical instrumentation. Its improvisational poetry resembles a jazz-like verbal jam session. Moreover, its tonal qualities are often described as similar to chants. It could also be described as what classical scholars maintain that early spoken language sounded like—having a melodious song-like cadence. Was early language the first Rap music?

Yet another difference between speech and the printed (and to a lesser extent, the printed word that's read out loud), is that improvisational speech, like sound in general, is not experienced as linear, going from point A to point B, step-by-step. Sound is experienced as more simultaneous. The printed word is right before our eyes. Speech, on the other hand, is wrapped around us.

Modern youth culture is increasingly communal, and also it seems less linear in its thinking and feeling. The TV image and youth music make youths, who are a part of this culture, more psychologically tribal. Marshall McLuhan noted this in the early 1960s in his now classic book, *Understanding Media*.[16] As an oral culture and TV culture, the youth seem more attuned to sound and the instantaneously grasped image than to the linear printed word. Indeed, increasing numbers of youths find reading the printed word difficult and disagreeable.[17]

It is interesting to note here that McLuhan was quite familiar with Giambattista Vico's work. McLuhan was also a well-known scholar on the writer James Joyce, who was more than familiar with Vico's work. Indeed, his famous novel, *Finnegans Wake*,[18] which took him seventeen years to write, was heavily influenced by Vico. The novel is nearly unreadable except by a small cadre of literary scholars, however, because it's written using multiple levels of meaning created by a masterful use of an incredibly complex network of pun-like sounds and plays on words.

THE SOUND OF MEANING

At this point, let's look more closely at an example I briefly presented in chapter 1 to see how sound and meaning are integral with each other. The example was about my fiancee's mother who had recently visited her podiatrist to have her feet worked on. As she lay on his couch having her feet massaged and talked to fill an otherwise silent activity, the podiatrist said that clients often told him very personal things about themselves. She replied that lying on a couch while having one's feet massaged is very relaxing and soothing. She said it was like being in a psychologist's office having therapy, so people would have a natural tendency to "bare their souls" to you. When she said this, she immediately became conscious of the double meaning. They bare their souls is equivalent to they bare the soles of their feet to him. This is not just a simple pun or play on words.

Think about it for a moment. We must first ask (a) why the particular subject was selected and (b) why these particular words were combined into this particular phrase. There were many other words and phrases that could have been used (i.e., selected) to express the meaning she was expressing, that his patients tell him lots of personal things about themselves. For example, she could have replied to her podiatrist that his patient's would "pour their hearts out" to him (maybe this would have been more appropriate for a cardiologist's office). She could have replied, they would "spill their guts out to you" (maybe this would have been more appropriate for a gastroenterologist's office). Or she simply could have replied, "Yes, I guess they tell you their life stories." But she didn't. She specifically said they "bare their souls" to him. Again, the question is, why did she use the particular phrase and not any of the ones I just mentioned, or the myriad of others from our common stock of clichéd sayings?

The first reason she didn't use any of the other possible phrases—and the most obvious—is that the homophones, *bear* and *bare,* and *souls* and *soles* are semantically appropriate for a podiatrist. *Bear* has the meanings to carry in the mind and to harbor, and of course the meanings of *bare* are to expose, and to become naked. Secondly, the soles of her naked feet exposed to view are semantically equivalent to baring/bearing one's *souls,* to revealing deep personal aspects of oneself. Third, the other possible phrases that could have been used with the words "hearts" and "guts" would not have been phonetically and thus semantically congruent with the parallel to a psychologist's office as the word "soul" (psychology often being defined as the study of the soul). Fourth, the other phrases would not have been as semantically congruent with the stereotypical association of the "Freudian couch" with the couch she was actually lying on in the podiatrist's office.

This narrative also exemplifies another aspect of creating subliteral meaning. Often physical objects and events in the persons environment either precipitate or are involved in creating subliteral meaning. In this case, the two objects are my mother-in-law's (1) bare (soles of her) feet and (2) the couch she is lying on. This precipitating and incorporating of objects and events in the environment into a narrative is similar to dreams being precipitated by or incorporating events that occurred during the day (Freud called these physical events "day residue") or something that occurs while the person is dreaming, like the sound of a telephone ringing incorporated into the dream.

It was thought that these kinds of dreams were simply about these external objects and events. It's generally accepted, however—at least among those who believe that some dreams have meaning—that these events are cognitively used in constructing the deeper meaning of the dream, not simply reflected in the dream.[19] So, too, it's the case with puns in subliteral meaning. The similar sounds used in my mother-in-law's narrative, then, are not simply puns. As I have shown so far, punning is often the sound of meaning.

Steven Pinker of the Massachusetts Institute of Technology (MIT), describes the linguistic complexities involved in how we hear the many phonological sounds of our spoken language in his wonderfully readable, yet seriously important book, *The Language Instinct: How the Mind Creates Language*.[20] Although I won't go into the intricacies here, suffice it to say that reading his account of this process clearly applies to and points out the incredible difference and significance of the oral and the print traditions. I call this vast array of sounds a psychoacoustic matrix.

THE PSYCHOACOUSTIC MATRIX OF MIND

It is, of course, no great revelation that the mind uses sound in creating spoken language. That the mind uses sound in the way I have described here is not quite so uncontroversial. As I have shown, however, subliteral meaning often revolves around phonetics and sound symbolism. The primitive source for making meaning with sound is what I call the psychoacoustic matrix.[21] A matrix is generally considered a source out of which something originates, a womb in which something develops. In mathematics a matrix is an orderly arrangement of elements or numbers into rows and columns which are subject to mathematical operations. The psychoacoustic matrix, then, is to be understood as (1) the primitive source of sounds, (2) where operations and transformations are performed to (3) create subliteral meanings.

In this section I briefly outline this wonderland of sound from which many of the subliteral illustrations in this book have been born. My description of this psychoacoustic matrix is a part of the Genesis Matrix that I explain in the next chapter on the subliteral mind. But it's more appropriate to outline the workings of this matrix in this chapter on sound and playing with words.

Like playing with words, the concept of phonetic or sound symbolism has a long, venerable, and controversial history that goes back at least as far as Plato's *Cratylus*. Onomatopoeic words, words that sound like what they refer to, are probably the most well-known sound symbolisms, but they are only a subset of the more general concept of sound symbolism. The notion that the sounds of words are arbitrary and have no inherent relationship to their meaning has been controversial and remains so especially to those who consider words as arbitrary conditioned responses. Historically, sound symbolism has been the subject of extensive theory and research in literary circles.[22] Creative writers, poets, and others have talked about the importance of sound to making sense and meaning.[23] In the last chapter on feelings, I outlined the ideas of Giambattista Vico, Ernst Cassirer, Heinz Werner, Bernard Kaplan, Lawrence Marks, and others. Werner and Kaplan refer to sound symbolism as physiognomic sound. Cassirer and others refer to sound or phonetic symbolism as phonetic metaphor, a form of metaphor that most of those who identify metaphor as a rhetorical or lexical phenomenon would deny that it's metaphor at all.

Sound is transmitted in a vibrational or frequency waveform. When an acoustical wave form is received as a speech sound, it's processed and broken down into its discrete phonological units. Then, these units are related across the various sensory modalities, giving rise to what may be termed micro- and macromeaning equivalents (i.e., phonetic metaphors). Microlevel high-pitched phonetic sounds, such as the vowels /e/ and /i/, are usually cross-modally equivalent to "brightness" and "light colors." Low-pitched vowels, such as /o/ and /u/, synesthetically mean "darkness" and "heavy." When we leave true synesthesia, then we are concerned with acoustical cognition, that is, the transformation of acoustical waveforms into "semantically" meaningful complexes. For it is here that we leave (to some degree) the "intrinsic" neurophysiologically "wired" patterns and correspondences and enter the realm of cognitive patterns and transformational processes. As simple frequency vibrations, words are simply an arbitrary string of sounds, sequences of noises in search of meaning. Through constant and consistent association and social agreement, however, these arbitrary sounds take on individual and consensual meaning. On a macrolevel, phonetic metaphor gives rise to the pun and play on words. Some of these equivalences, says Marks, reflect "invariant aspects of the primary physiological responses to stimulation in different modalities,"[24] i.e., our various senses. Others, however, reflect cultural and other mediational processes.

THE SOUND AND SYNTAX OF MEANING

An incredibly large store of similar sounds, similar words, and similar meanings are in this matrix for the mind to work with. There is, for example, an entire lexicon of words that have similar sounds, like feet/feat, pair/pare, breach/breech, dear/deer, and to/two.[25] There are hundreds of homonyms, words that have the same sound and may be spelled the same but have different meanings. There are homophones, words that are pronounced alike but have different meanings or spelling (such as to/too/two). There are homographs, words that are spelled alike but have different meanings or pronunciations (such as bow, as in the bow of a ship, and bow as in a bow and arrow). There are synonyms, words that have nearly the same meaning as other words, and paronymns, words that derive from the same root or stem like meanie, and meaning.[26] Then there are portmanteau words that are formed by merging the sounds and meanings of two different words like slithy which is made from lithe and slimy.[27]

Finally there is a whole class of sounds called oronyms. These are strings of sounds that can be heard in two different ways in terms of meaning. For example, pay particular attention to the sounds as you quickly read out loud the following two sentences from Steven Pinker's book:

The good can decay in many ways.
The good candy came anyways.

Or try

> *The stuffy nose.*
> *The stuff he knows.*[28]

This phonological or acoustic matrix of similar sounds, spellings, and meanings, which are linked to the semantics and syntax of language, provide an incredible matrix of possible permutations of subliteral narratives by superimposing, fusing, and otherwise combining sound, linguistic structure (syntax), and meaning. This matrix also provides fertile ground for what we normally call slips of the tongue. Let's see how this psychoacoustic matrix in our minds works.

In chapter 4, I presented examples of the ways that our unconscious mind communicates with names and initials to create subliteral meaning. I extend those examples here to illustrate how sound, linked to linguistic structure, creates meaning. Sometimes a single name subliterally refers not to one person, but simultaneously to two people. This is illustrated by a group which was concerned that I was writing notes about them. Hence the topic of journalism was unconsciously selected for its subliteral meaning. So, to select the name of some particular journalist for such a discussion was nearly inevitable. A journalist, whose name was Harry Harris, was selected for the discussion. It was said that he was a well-known journalist and columnist. The question is, out of all possible names of journalists, why was the name Harry Harris selected? This is the answer.

The single name, Harry Harris, served as a double referent within what can be termed a matrix of the semantics of sound. The first name, Harry, by way of a phonological transformation, was a semantic and subliteral transformation of the word *"hairy"* and is a reference to me because I had a beard, i.e., I was *hairy.* Therefore, it functioned subliterally as a homophone, just as the words *night* and *knight,* which, although pronounced identically, differ in meaning. Here we can see that a literal noun functioned subliterally as an adjective. Similarly, the last name of the journalist, Harris, by way of a phonetic transformation, was a semantic and subliteral transformation of the adjective *"hairless,"* a corresponding reference to my colleague who was a cotrainer in the group—and who was unbearded, i.e., *hairless.*

Although at first glance this may surely appear as sheer reckless punning and a mere play on words, I can assure you that it's not. There was more than sound at work here. *First,* the initial letter of each part of the name, *H*arry *H*arris, constitutes double H's, the same as the initial letter of my last name and the last name of the colleague I was training, *H*askell and *H*eapes. *Secondly,* integral with the phonological transformations, there is an additional subliteral relationship of order or syntax that provides further support for this analysis of subliteral meaning. The apparently literal name, Harry Harris, which subliterally translates into *hairy* and *hairless,* reflects the status order of me and my colleague, that is, I am the senior trainer, and therefore mentioned first (i.e., Harry/*hairy*), and my colleague is the junior trainer, therefore mentioned second (i.e., Harris/*hairless*). In other words, the *hairless* beardless junior trainer was not subliterally mentioned first but second, and the *hairy* senior trainer was not mentioned second, but first (see Figure 4). Now, if you think this is deep, it gets even deeper.

Again, it could be argued that both the phonological and the syntactic order reflected in the name Harry Harris surely must be coincidental. But consider these two further aspects. First, there was a host of possible journalists' names that could have been selected, but they weren't. Why? The answer is that other names would not have subliterally expressed what the speaker wanted to express. Only the name Harry Harris did that. Second— and this is the fatal coup de grâce to the coincidental argument—the name Harry Harris was not in fact the correct name of the journalist being discussed. It wasn't even the name of any known journalist. It was a misremembered name, a "mistake."

To verify this misremembering, I asked the member if she could find his column for me. The next day she brought in the column. She was embarrassed and apologized, noting that the journalist was actually the well-known columnist, Sidney Harris. The correct name of Sidney Harris, however, would not have worked to express her perceptions subliterally. Further, given that it was an unconsciously made-up name, any name could have been unconsciously made up and selected for the conversation. But again it wasn't. Harry Harris was selected.

A real hard-nosed critic, might still maintain that, as wild as it may sound, all the above could still be a gigantic coincidence. But if we believe this, how do we explain other similar subliteral sound transformations like *hairy* for Harry? For example, in another conversation about journalists where I was the only trainer in the group, the journalist Harry Reasoner was selected for the conversation. Just in case you haven't acquired the knack for interpreting subliteral meaning yet, being a bearded academic, Harry Reasoner subliterally meant that I was a *hairy reasoner.*

Further, as for the argument that misremembering the name Harry Harris was also coincidental, is it coincidental that other examples also

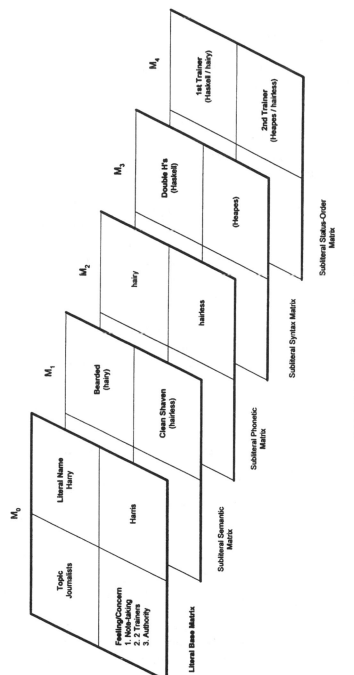

FIGURE 4. Transformational matrices.

demonstrate strategic or unconscious misremembering to express unconscious meaning? Recall from chapter 4 the example of misremembering the childrens TV program, Mr. Rogers as Mr. Roberts, so it would subliterally reference me correctly. All coincidence? I think not.

So this, in brief, is how the psychoacoustic matrix works. Why the mind creates this kind of matrix is not known, but one theory might be that it's for efficiency of information storage in our brain. In talking about the mechanics of double meanings involving compression and condensations, Freud quotes Shakespeare's *Hamlet:* "Thrift, thrift, Horatio."[29] It was, however, perhaps the French philosopher Henri Bergson (1859–1941)[30] who first introduced the idea of the mind as a reducing value (in modern terminology, the mind is equivalent to the nervous system). Now, the idea that the brain filters out and compresses information is commonplace in psychology. We constantly filter out stimuli at various levels of neurological processing. Because of an evolutionary decrease in genetic programming in the human species and the subsequent need to cope with an increasing amount of information from the environment, our brain must have evolved a mechanism to reduce and compress this wealth of information to a manageable proportion. One of the primary ways it does this is to reduce difference to similarity. It does this by invariance transformations (see next chapter) that reduce differences to similarities. In using sounds conceptually to create meaning, the traditional rules of grammar are often changed, but—and this is important—they are changed in consistent ways.

SLIPS OF THE TONGUE AND SPEECH ERRORS REVISITED

Now, it's time to address the issue of slips of the tongue. Modern linguistics and cognitive science see slips of the tongue as just that, slips and errors. They see them as errors that have no underlying meaning.[31] Freud's well-known explanation that slips of the tongue reveal unconscious meaning is considered just unproven excess baggage in explaining slips and errors of language. The issue of meaning in slips of the tongue is central to subliteral meaning. According to linguistics and cognitive science, slips are simply caused by mechanical problems, because one of the similar sounds in the psychoacoustic matrix is confused with an intended sound. Essentially this view maintains that errors often occur because the muscles used to vocalize the intended sound are the same as those used to vocalize an unintended sound. These mechanical mistakes are often called spoonerisms, so named after the British cleric and scholar William Archibald Spooner (1844–1930). For example, a person might mean, "allow me to *show* you to your *seat*," but actually say, "Allow me to *sew* you to your *sheet*," where *show* and *sew* and *sheet* and *seat* are misvocalized. Certainly, some slips are simply mistakes like this particular spoonerism and can be explained linguistically in terms of mechanical error. Sometimes a slip of the tongue may even be psychological, but still be an error, and the error is caused by a mistake in associating one sound (or phoneme) or meaning with another.

THE MECHANICS OF MEANING

Because some slips are errors and because some slips (perhaps even most) can be explained as mechanical or linguistics mistakes in executing the phonological system, it doesn't follow that all slips are errors and have no meaning. This non sequitur is a fundamental logical mistake of momentous importance, and the implications are equally profound. It's of importance for subliteral meaning and also for psychological and linguistic explanation of everyday language. The non sequitur—because some slips and errors can be explained as mechanical or linguistics mistakes, then all slips have no meaning—results from a number of assumptions by those who hold to a mechanical explanation for slips of the mind.

The first assumption is based on a kind of "as-if" philosophy. This view says that researchers must act "as if" slips were simply mechanical. In this view, the idea is that to assume that they are unconsciously motivated leads to a very messy and hard to control set of factors. This position is adopted simply for research convenience. Although there is some justification for this position for certain purposes, it's a little bit like the story of the intoxicated man looking for his lost keys under a streetlight on an otherwise dark street. When asked if he lost his keys somewhere around the light, he answers "No." When asked why he's looking under the streetlight, he replies, "Because this is where the light is."

The second assumption is that because many slips can be explained as mechanical errors, then all slips can be explained as errors. This is clearly an unwarranted inference, especially when possibly meaningful slips are not typically selected for analysis: only certain classes of slips are subjected to analysis. Slips of the Freudian kind are generally ignored by laboratory researchers.[32] This practice, too, is like the drunk looking for his keys only under the street lamp because this is where the light is.

Neither of these two rationales enlightens us about the meaningfulness of slips of the mind.

The third assumption for maintaining the position that slips are explainable by mechanical errors is simply that linguistics and cognitive science have not been very friendly toward the idea of an unconscious mind, let alone one that thinks and reasons (see next chapter). The fourth, and by far the more widespread assumption, is based on the belief that because a lawful set of linguistic processes can be demonstrated (e.g., low-frequency words are "slipped" more often than are high-frequency words), this shows slips are determined and not intentional or motivated, that they have no psychological meaning. Before I explain why this is a most egregious logical error, let me say that I, too, have no doubt that lawful linguistic mechanisms are involved in *all* slips of the tongue and mind, whether or not they are simply mistakes or they derive from deep unconsciously motivated meaning. It doesn't logically follow, however, that because there are lawful linguistic mechanisms underlying slips and errors that unconscious meaning is ruled out. Let me explain why this is a most egregious mistake by using a couple of simple common sense examples. After they are explained, it makes one wonder how such an egregious rationale can be seriously maintained.

As the first example, let's take the behavior of a tennis player. Even though an analysis of the neuromuscular mechanisms explain how a tennis player returns a tennis serve, it doesn't explain the cognitive-motivational processes included in the act. In short, it explains the *how* but not the *why*. Surely, only a lunatic would deny that a tennis player functions solely as a neuromuscular automaton. Yet, this is exactly what view is taken to explain all slips of the tongue. The linguistic and cognitive science explanation, then, is a *how*, not a *why* explanation.

The second example is explaining language as a series of lawful neuromuscular mechanisms and grammatical rules—which speaking certainly is. As in the tennis player example, it would be equally lacking in reason to claim (for other than purposes of analytical convenience, as in the first assumption above), that the sentences spoken by a person have no meaning-motivated basis. Thus, by the same logic, just as it's crazy to claim that a tennis player and someone speaking are just being mechanically caused to play and speak in a certain way and that intention and motivation have no role in their behavior, so too it's inappropriate to say that because slips are explained mechanically that there is no intention or motivation underlying them (see also end note #27 in chapter 1). The entire argument assumes that because we discover that something is explained mechanically and that certain linguistic laws are obeyed that this precludes meaning. It doesn't. If you are asked to believe that it does, don't.

Now, I don't mean to imply that if we asked structural linguists or cognitive scientists if a tennis player was just an automaton and that the very sentences spoken in describing the action of the tennis player were neither intentional nor motivated, that they would agree. They're not crazy. What their answer shows, however, is the radical "disconnect" of their otherwise excellent theories from everyday life. It's no wonder that the public often becomes incredulous and disenchanted with "academic" theories. In chapter 11 I show how this "disconnect" applies to meaning in relation to dreams. In short, the mechanisms that linguists have discovered which create slips simply provide a vehicle for expressing the intentional and motivated meaning underlying them.

CONCLUSION

In this chapter, we have seen how "speech" as understood in the ancient oral tradition is quite different from the printed word and from the printed word that's spoken. We have also seen how various vocal sounds, puns, playing with words, and slip or errors in "speech" are involved in creating poetic language and subliteral meaning. I have hinted throughout this chapter and previous ones that there must be a robust primal code, a kind of psychological DNA of thought, underlying these sounds of language and the cognitive operations that transform the sounds into subliteral meaning. I am still in the process of trying to unravel this code.

POSTSCRIPT: DEEP BLUE

In the Introduction to this book, I mentioned that cognitive science and its view that the mind works like a computer was not friendly toward research into an "unconscious mind" or the study of subjective meaning. One of the fundamental reasons that a subliteral analysis of language continues to be avoided by cognitive science research is that it doesn't lend itself to the very concrete, computer-like, and highly formalized procedures used by these sciences. Because no investigatory method exists, it is believed that subliteral meaning does not exist. Again, we meet the drunk under the streetlight looking for his keys.

Artificial intelligence systems are well-known to be "brittle," that is, any minute change or difference cannot be tolerated by most of these systems. At this point in their evolution, artificial intelligence systems are quite dumb—fast at computations, but brittle and dumb, nevertheless. In 1997, Anatoly Karpov, who is considered by many the greatest chess player in history was beaten by Deep Blue, an RS-6000 SP supercomputer. But it wasn't because Deep Blue was smarter than Karpov (at least in human terms). It was because Deep Blue was faster at computing and calculating the information about chess moves (including strategies) fed into it's memory. Karpov can look at two moves per second, but Deep Blue looks at 200 million moves per second.

Some years ago at the suggestion of some researchers who had devised a computer program for analyzing and recognizing various dynamics in groups, I sent a transcription of an extensive subliteral narrative to see if the meanings could be recognized with their program. The program was apparently sensitive to conversational language. Because I never heard from them, I assume it didn't work on subliteral narratives. Not surprisingly, the computational-like models in cognitive science cannot handle subliteral meaning and the various operations discussed in this and previous chapters that undergird them. For example, despite so-called speech recognition programs (I can talk to my computer and tell it to open and close files, etc.), they in fact are not "speech" recognition programs in the oral tradition sense that I've explained in this chapter. These programs, too, are quite dumb. Any nuance or change throws them into a high-tech psychotic break.

I don't say all this out of any phobia of technology. I am no technophobe. I love computers and electronic gadgets. In fact, I think that someday computers (but of a very different species) will analyze subliteral types of phenomena. Until then, however, HAL, the computer in the movie 2001, is more than a couple of years away. The point of this postscript is this. We are inappropriately letting an inadequate technology drive our search for knowledge, like the drunk, looking only where technology allows us to look. This is the way knowledge becomes ignored, misplaced, or lost. Let's not forget, however, that each of us has a technology at our disposal that's been undergoing rigorous testing for millions of years. In the face of this, why are we so enamored by a fast calculating machine?

CHAPTER 8

THE SUBLITERAL MIND

THE UNCONSCIOUS AND THE GENESIS MATRIX

To understand how subliteral narratives work and how they are possible, we need to see more than just the cognitive and linguistic operations that create them. We need to understand the nature of the subliteral mind. This chapter lays out what the subliteral mind is made up of. I developed the concept of the subliteral mind to carve out an unconscious mind from the many nearly all-meaningful notions that currently exist, a more concrete and specific picture of how subliteral meaning is possible.

Whenever the term unconscious mind is mentioned to most people who are not psychologists, the almost reflex-like response is, "Oh, yes, Freud." Freudian ideas have permeated popular consciousness, and they have also nearly coopted all discussion of things unconscious. This reflex response is equally true for many of my colleagues in Departments of Humanities in universities across the country. Although this response is understandable due to the spread of pop psychology in our society by so-called psychological counselors and therapists who should know better, it drives cognitive psychologists nearly crazy. Reducing all talk of the unconscious to Freud drives me to the outer limits of my rationality. So, let me try to set the record straight before proceeding further.

First, I've indicated—and indeed, genuflected appropriately—in previous chapters, that we certainly owe a debt to Freud for his work on unconscious processes. The idea of an unconscious mind, however, was around long before Freud and has gone far beyond him in many ways.[1] Continuing to call all unconscious processes Freudian, is like calling all mathematics Pythagorean (or Arabic because the Arabs invented the zero). Although a general understanding of a Freudian unconscious may be useful in some ways, it has also led us astray into what John Kihlstrom has called a "hermeneutic wonderland"[2] of clinical interpretations, where nearly all meanings are possible. Thus, most cognitive scientists have been reluctant understandably to deviate from their tightly controlled experimental laboratory methods. As I suggested in a similar context, it evidently remains a fear that if the meticulous experimental door to the unconscious is opened to other methodologies, "all manner of Freudian specters will be let loose in the cognitive laboratories."[3] If psychoanalysis has been too open-ended, cognitive science has been too closed off. Enter the subliteral mind.

Before I describe what the subliteral mind is and how it works, I need to outline briefly the various ways in which the term unconscious is used. This will provide the background for understanding the subliteral unconscious mind.

WHAT DOES IT MEAN TO SAY THAT SOMETHING IS UNCONSCIOUS?

We often make up names for things that don't really exist, for example, the equator, that great imaginary line in our mind that circles around the earth's circumference, dividing the Northern from the Southern Hemisphere. The concept of the unconscious is like the equator. It, too, doesn't exist—at least as a single entity. We simply made up the single entity. Such schemes, like the equator and the unconscious mind, however, can be useful fictions to help us navigate, to act as a reference point to find our way around the mind. The problems is that once we have created a name, the named thing often takes on a reality of its own. Then we tend to acquire certain nearly unshakeable beliefs and stereotypes about it. I begin this chapter by profiling some of the many faces of what is commonly called the unconscious mind because it's important that we have a more nuanced view of it. In fact, cognitive and neurological research has shown for some time that there are many unconscious minds (more correctly there are many unconscious parts or processes to our mind).

Psychoanalysts have tended to believe in the unconscious mind, and many cognitive scientists have tended to believe in only certain narrowly defined unconscious parts of our minds. At this point, I should clarify what's called cognitive science and what's called psychoanalysis. First, they are not simple monolithic enterprises, so any characterizations I make about cognitive science or about psychoanalysis are generalizations. Both are comprised of a very disparate group of people. In the beginning of the modern investigation into the mind was cognitive psychology and its emphasis on experimental methodology. Later it adopted what's called a computational theory of the way the mind works. Simply put, a computational approach views the mind like a computer. It should come as no surprise, then, that the broader term, cognitive science, includes cognitive psychology, philosophy, neurology, and sometimes anthropology, but also the field of artificial intelligence, which is interested in creating computer programs that think and solve problems, e.g., programs for robots. I'll have more to say about this view of the mind later. The one thing that ties these cognitive sciences all together, however, is the insistence on a rigorous scientific approach to investigating how the mind works. As for who is a psychoanalyst and what ties them all together, I can't say (and neither can they, for that matter).

With this said, let me now describe the differences between the psychoanalytic and the cognitive unconscious. Then, I outline how both fields enter into understanding the subliteral mind. Before I can do this, however, we need to have a common understanding of what is meant by the term unconscious.

THE UNCONSCIOUS(ES): PSYCHOANALYTIC

To begin, in most of Freud's writings, the id belongs to the unconscious proper. That cauldron of primitive impulses and instincts seeks expression of primitive sexuality and aggression, etc. Things other than the primitive instinctual material can also find their way by repression into this deep unconscious. Some preconscious thoughts and feelings that we do not want to recognize are shunted down in to this deep unconscious mind. There is no direct access to the deep unconscious. The Freudian unconscious is the seat of all that's irrational in our psyches. Even within the classic Freudian framework, however, there is a distinction between unconscious and preconscious, and sometimes subconscious. The preconscious contains parts of unconscious contents which were once conscious and/or almost conscious. Under certain conditions we can access our preconscious mind. Freud, however, was primarily interested in a deep unconscious. I should point out here, that contrary to popular belief, a Freudian unconscious doesn't perceive reality and it doesn't think and reason. This latter point is crucially important for understanding the contribution of the subliteral mind. More on this later in chapter 12.

In addition to Freud's classic formulation of the unconscious mind, there have been other formulations by what are called neo-Freudians. These are psychoanalysts who have made relatively significant changes to orthodox psychoanalysis and its conception of the unconscious mind, including reducing the importance of the id/irrational aspects of the unconscious.

These many neo-Freudian formulations can't be detailed here. I will mention, however, one analyst who is the most widely known. Carl Gustav Jung (1875–1961), the Swiss psychoanalyst, was Freud's heir apparent, but he later split with Freud and founded his own school of psychoanalysis called analytical psychology. When he broke ranks with Freud, Jung formulated his own analytic theory, including a unique formulation of the unconscious. He postulated two dimensions of the unconscious. First, there's a personal unconscious containing repressed and forgotten content. Second is what he termed the collective unconscious. This contains behavior and mental patterns shared either by members of a culture or shared universally by all human beings. According to Jung, the contents of the collective unconscious are passed down genetically. Jung has become a kind of pop guru in our culture, nearly rivaling Freud.

THE UNCONSCIOUS(ES): COGNITIVE

As I have noted before, cognitive science has had a conflicted relationship with the idea of an unconscious mind, in large measure because of the Freudian image attached to it. Indeed, for a long time, cognitive science denied that anything remotely resembling an unconscious mind exists. Currently, however, cognitive science recognizes that an unconscious mind exists.[4] In fact, cognitive scientists recognize many unconscious minds—or more correctly stated—recognize many unconscious processes. But the cognitive unconscious is still far from a psychodynamic unconscious which thinks and reasons. From the perspective of cognitive science, there are many brain structures or sets of neurological circuits that have been identified with what we normally mean by the term unconscious.[5]

Perhaps the best initial example to illustrate unconscious processing is our everyday use of language. Recall from chapter 1 that most of the grammatical rules or syntax of language isn't in our awareness as we speak. More than this, how many of us ever consciously learned most of the thousands of grammatical rules of our language? The answer is virtually no one. Yet we use them correctly (or fairly much so) every day. In addition, like language, we perform most of our procedural knowledge (how-to knowledge, like driving a car) unconsciously. But more than this, brain research clearly shows that there are specific neurological circuits that make possible both our conscious and unconscious activities and that a great deal of mental processing occurs outside our conscious awareness. Certain neurological deficits make this very clear.

One of these deficits is the neurological disorder known as the "neglect syndrome." This disorder is the consequence of damage to certain neurological tissue involved in vision. People who have lesions on the left side of their brains consciously don't "see" objects on the right side of the room at which they are looking, or they see only the right half of a clock face. When asked to describe the contents of a room, such patients describe only the left side of the room, or, when shown the word "baseball," see only "base" and not "ball." But in fact these people are not completely blind. The information from the right side of the room is received and transmitted to their brains, but it just isn't conscious. It doesn't reach the circuits responsible for making us consciously aware of the material. How do we know they are "seeing on some level? We don't know it just by intuition. We know it because of some fascinating experiments. For example, when neglect syndrome patients are forced to select from an array of objects, some of which were located on the right half of the room, their "guesses" achieve statistically better than chance levels of choosing the correct objects. In short, they unconsciously "know" what is on the right side of the room.

Similar nonconscious visual neurological deficits have been observed in what is called blind sight. The blind sight research with patients who are "blind" on both left halves of their visual fields because of brain lesions demonstrates that these patients are, like the previously mentioned neglect syndrome patients, unconsciously receiving, transmitting, and processing information in their left visual fields. Again, when these patients are forced to describe or "guess" what was presented to their left visual field, subjects said they just had a "feeling' that the objects they chose were "there." Still other similar findings have been explained by what is called cortical blindness. This deficit is caused by damage to central visual pathways and renders the person "consciously" blind. In short, what this kind of data suggests is that, in vision at least, there are multiple neurological pathways that cognitively process information on multiple nonconscious levels which can be acted upon without consciously knowing or knowing why. Similar findings have also been demonstrated in other research.[6]

Findings from so-called split brain experiments are another example. It's well known that the cortex of our brain has two cerebral hemispheres, one on the left and one on the right side. Connecting the two hemispheres is a structure called the corpus callosum. The left hemisphere is the seat of our language functions (at least for about 95% of people). We are conscious only of information which goes to the linguistically developed left hemisphere. The right hemisphere doesn't have a well-developed active language function, so if information goes only to our right hemisphere, we are not conscious of that information. The corpus callosum allows each side to transmit information to the other side. Now, because of intractable epilepsy, some people have had their corpus callosum partially or totally severed (called a commissurotomy). The function of the brain's corpus callosum is to transfer information received by one cerebral hemisphere to the other hemisphere. When the corpus callosum is cut, new information in one hemisphere is not transferred to the other, so we have two separate brains (though not really). A great deal of the so-called "right brain/left brain" research demonstrates that, under certain conditions, our hemispheres may function relatively independently. Each hemisphere is sometimes unaware (not conscious) of the experiences of the other.

For example, in a now well-known experiment, a split-brain patient was shown pictures only to the left visual field, information from which was ostensibly going only to the right hemisphere.[7] One of the pictures was of a nude body. The patient giggled and blushed, but did not consciously have any idea why he giggled. The explanation is that, because the information went only to the right hemisphere, which does not have an active language function (at least for about 95% of people), the patient could not report it. Here, we have an example of felt—or intuitive—meaning, of nonconscious cognitive processing on a meaningful level but no conscious awareness of it. Like the cortically blind subjects mentioned before, split-brained patients can often "guess"—intuitively know—what was presented to the right hemisphere. Some researchers are speculating that many unconscious phenomena can be equated with our brain's right hemisphere. There are even some who believe that Freud's concept of the unconscious may be equated with the brain's right hemisphere.[8] Although I doubt that this is the case, certainly some unconscious processes are associated with the right hemisphere.

Yet another unconscious channel is called implicit memory. One form of this is illustrated by a classic example involving amnesia. An early clinical observation by Claparede was of a hospitalized Korsakoff syndrome patient. Korsakoff syndrome, discovered by Sergei S. Korsakoff, a Russian neurologist, is characterized by severe mental impairment, confusion, disorientation, and amnesia even for memory of recent events. Patients often attempt to compensate through confabulation. It seems a patient was reluctant to shake hands with the doctor (Claparede) who just a few minutes earlier had pricked the patient's hand while shaking hands with him with a pin hidden in his hand. When the patient was asked why he wouldn't shake hands, he said, "Sometimes pins are hidden in people's hands." The patient didn't understand (remember) that the reason he wouldn't shake hands was because of the incident a few minutes before.

I should point out that we often find this confabulation—or rationalizing—in other conditions where information is processed outside of our awareness. For example, when a person in hypnotic trance is given a posthypnotic suggestion to close a window when the hypnotist scratches his nose, the person professes to have closed the window because of the thought that it was getting chilly in the room (or some other such rationalization). We find this, too, with split brain patients, where a suggestion or request to engage in some behavior is transmitted to the right hemisphere. Because the request doesn't get to the left linguistic hemisphere, consciously the patient doesn't "know" or really understand why the behavior was initiated. Consequently, the left linguistic hemisphere rationalizes a reason or motive to explain the behavior. It seems that we must see a reason for our behavior, and when we lack a conscious understanding of the real cause, we make one up. There is still one more interesting unconscious module or channel.

Yet another area of research on cognitive unconscious processing is called implicit learning.[9] Essentially, this suggests that we learn unconsciously. In other words, we may know or learn something but not consciously know that we know it. This has been called *tacit knowledge* by the philosopher Michael Polanyi.[10] I'll talk more about this later.

A final and one of the most widely known examples of processing information outside of awareness is subliminal perception. This involves the presentation of information of which we are not consciously aware. Now, the phrase "not consciously aware of" can involve two different phenomena. First, it can mean information is presented at such a low or a rapid rate that we can't consciously perceive it. The second sense involves information that is presented at a level at which we could perceive it if we were paying attention. In this case, however, we may be focused on something else, so that we do not consciously perceive the information, but it nevertheless registers in our mind. An everyday example of this kind of selective attention is when we are intensely preoccupied with reading a book and don't consciously hear someone talking to us.

In addition to just nonconsciously perceiving information, there is the issue of that information affecting us. This is called subliminal activation. Subliminal activation is not just registering information outside of awareness, but the information elicits behavior from us and we are not aware why we are engaging in the behavior. The most widely known illustration of sub-liminal activation occurred in 1956 when it was reported that during a movie, the phrases "buy popcorn," and "drink Coca Cola," were superim-posed on the movie screen at a rate that the audience could not consciously perceive. Reportedly, sales of popcorn and Coca Cola increased.[11] It turned out to be a hoax. But the public imagination was stirred. Subsequent ex-periments have found little evidence for such subliminal effects.[12] In any event, it spurred continuing research by both psychologists and by those who design advertising. Some advertising is designed to elicit subliminal ac-tivation for buying the product.

From this brief excursion into the various unconscious aspects of the mind, it can be seen that the phrase "the unconscious mind" is a misnomer. There are multiple areas or levels of unconscious processing going on in our heads. In fact, we have many unconscious minds. For ease of expres-sion, however, I generally continue to use the phrase "unconscious mind" in the singular. Clearly, then, to see all unconscious processes as psychoana-lytic is not correct—not even close.

Both mainstream and not so mainstream researchers today generally accept the fact that the brain is made up of a multiplicity of neurological module-like circuits, each having evolved to carry out a specific task or set of functions. The term "module" is metaphorical for a set of circuits that are relatively separate (modules are not boxlike places in the brain). I might note, too, that the modular view of the mind is supported by evolutionary biology.[13] It follows from this modular view, then, that the so-called uncon-scious mind is in fact a number of unconscious minds (assuming that we want to equate *brain* with *mind,* at least for the moment). Even those who are more clinically and psychodynamically oriented recognize that under a condition known as dissociation the mind can functionally separate into module-like compartments or levels. The resulting classic examples are cer-tain hypnotic states, amnestic conditions, and—for those more serious be-lievers—multiple personalities. With this background, now we are ready to lay out the boundaries of the subliteral unconscious mind.

THE SUBLITERAL MIND

The subliteral mind is simply a set of unconscious processes. Many of these unconscious processes are only just beginning to be understood in terms of the way they are carried out within the neurological circuits of the brain. Therefore, in describing the subliteral mind, I limit my description to cognitive, emotional, and linguistic processes. I begin by looking at (1) mental maps, called schemas, (2) the genesis matrix, and (3) invariance transformations.

MENTAL MAPS: SCHEMAS

As information comes into our brain's various circuits, this input needs to be ordered in some way to make it manageable. Psychologists call this order or pattern a schema. Schemas act as intermediaries that organize future incoming information. There is a host of schemas on various neurological levels. There are linguistic schemas, emotional schemas, postural schemas, motor schemas, face recognition schemas, memory schemas, and many others (you can think of them as templates). These schemas come together on various levels, depending on the circumstances (see the Subliteral Unconscious section later). Schemas function as mediators or go-betweens that link our inner experience and input from the external world. They may also function as mediators or go-betweens in our internal worlds.

Abstract Schemas   In cognitive science, schemas are thought of as abstract representations of the world—like a very abstract painting. For example, often we don't remember the exact words of a story or an idea that someone told us, but we do remember the *gist* of the story or the general idea or meaning of it. This "gist" is the abstract structure or meaning of the story or idea. Richard Honeck of the University of Cincinnati and his colleagues,[14] use the proverb "Great weights hang on small wires" to illustrate the abstract structure of schemas. Although we may not remember the exact wording of the proverb, we often remember its "gist," which can be translated as "important events often depend on minor details." Again, an analogy that has a simple arithmetic operation will illustrate the abstract nature of a schema. The operation $1 + 1 = 2$ is an empty abstract form. Into this abstract form we can plug an infinite number of things, peaches, plums, humans, or Buicks. The operation renders all the differences among these things irrelevant. For counting purposes, they are all the same, all identical. The same is true for abstract schemas. They render different stimuli or experiences—given a certain goal, purpose, or set of criteria—the "same," or invariant (see later).

Sensuous Schemas   Some schemas involve sensuous elements. In chapter 6, I mentioned the work of Heinz Werner and Bernard Kaplan on what they call physiognomized language, where words are treated as quasi-substantial things (having a pictorial-like character, growing out of feelings, body postural, and muscular motor schemas). I gave the example an infant who equates sticking out a tongue and wiggling it with a wiggling a finger. On this level this is not a transfer of one modality onto another. On a basic physiological level, the movement of the tongue and the movement of the finger IS the same thing. This is called a physiognomic perception. (The term physiognomy comes form the Greek *phusiognomia,* variant of *phusiognomonia*: *phusio-,* physio- + gnomon, gnomon-, interpreter). Thus, physiognomized "transformations" are physiologically experienced or *felt* interpretations. Literally, it means a physiological interpreter.

Like all schemas, sensuous schemas function as mediators or go-betweens that link our inner experience to the external world. The genesis matrix (see later) contains most of our past emotional and abstract experience. Sensuous schemas are where the beginning of the relationship between feeling and form has its origins, where pure sensation meets feelings and where both are transformed into language and meaning.

Feeling Schemas   Though sensuous schemas involve emotion or feeling on some level, often involving muscular or physical sensation, it's useful to divide the two for ease of explanation. You will recall in chapter 6 that I distinguished between emotion and feeling. Emotion is considered a first-order sensation that's presumably "non cognitive," and feeling is a second-order experience that involves cognition. Although not strictly analogous or the same, feeling schemas can be relatively separate from sensuous schemas. Sensuous schemas arise when the feeling circuits link with physical, bodily or muscular schemas. Thus, feeling schemas can be relatively distinct from sensuous schemas. Feeling schemas are central to creating subliteral narratives, as I have shown throughout the examples in this book.

Deep Linguistic Schemas   In chapter 1, I introduced the basic components of language, semantics, phonology, and syntax. These components operate at a deep genesis level. Let me review these components. Semantics basically has to do with words and their meanings. We have a large store of words and their meanings in a kind of mental dictionary called a lexicon. From our mental dictionary we select the appropriate word to express a meaning. Most words have multiple meanings. This is called polysemy. Words have meaning by being connected or associated with past experience. Some words acquire meaning by comparing their meaning to other words that have similar meaning. These are often called metaphors. Other meanings are acquired or linked by their similarity of sound. This study of the elementary sounds that make up a language is called phonology.

Phonology studies the elementary sounds (like "ba" for the letter b) that make up a language and also the rules of their distribution and patterning that govern pronunciations. On a less elementary level, the sound of an entire word can be similar to a word that has a different meaning, like *knight* and *night*. Recall that these are known as homophones. How we put meaning (semantics) and sound (phonology) together involves syntax. Syntax is the study of the rules by which words or other elements of sentence structure are combined to form grammatically correct sentences (the term grammar is a broader term that includes the arrangement of words, the combination of their component parts, and sometimes pronunciation and meaning).

As I noted in chapter 1, in applying the linguistic concepts of semantics, phonology, and syntax to explaining how slips of the mind are created, I have extended the rather narrow and traditional meaning given to them by the field of linguistics. Although the concept of phonology deals with elementary sounds, it is thought that they carry no semantic meaning. I have raised the concept of phonology to a higher order or level, however, to include the sound of whole words as with homophones and the sounds involved in puns. Similarly, I have extended the concept of syntax to include what I have termed syntactic metaphor. This extension of their meaning is important to understand and explain how subliteral meaning is created.

An incredibly large store of similar sounds, similar words, and similar meanings are stored in this matrix. As I explained in chapter 7, there is an entire lexicon of words that have similar sounds, hundreds of *homonyms* or words that have the same sound and may be spelled the same but have different meanings, *homophones* or words that are pronounced alike but have different meaning or spelling (such as to/too/two), *homographs* or words that are spelled alike but have different meanings or pronunciations (such as *bow*, as in the *bow* of a ship, and *bow* as in a *bow* and *arrow*), *synonyms* or words that have nearly the same meaning as other words, and *paronymns* which are words that derive from the same root or stem like meanie and meaning. In addition, there are portmanteau words that are formed by merging the sounds and meanings of two different words like *slithy* which is made from *lithe* and *slimy*. Finally there is a whole class of sounds called *oronyms*. Recall that these are strings of sounds that can be heard in two different ways in terms of meaning (as in *The good can decay in many ways/The good candy came anyways*).

These similar sounds, spellings, and meanings provide an incredible matrix of possible permutations for subliteral narratives by superimposing, fusing, and combining these various sounds into multiple and parallel meanings. This matrix also provides fertile ground for what are normally called slips of the tongue and for the changes in language seen in this book that create subliteral meaning.

Depending on the particular set of conditions and context, all of these schemas, individually or collectively, influence semantics, phonology, and syntax to produce a particular subliteral word, phrase, sentence, or story.

THE GENESIS MATRIX

At the core of the subliteral mind lies what I call the genesis matrix. This matrix contains the basic stuff of meaning, and out of it flows the subliteral narratives presented in this book. All of these schemas operate in this matrix. The genesis matrix is the source of what the authors in the previous chapter variously referred to as an "inner sensory form," an "inner linguistic form," a "preverbal sensory logic," an "exact sensory imagination," and "sensory topics." It is the deep source of the so-called "primordial unity of the senses." At this point, I need to clarify a misconception.

The unity of the senses is not the primordial bedrock level of our mind that—as we have seen—some philosophers and other would have us believe. It's in fact at least a second-order level, perhaps third-order level of unity. All of the philosophical views in the last chapter about the primordial unity of the senses are not exactly correct, though they were important maps pointing in the general direction of a subliteral mind. The erroneous belief that our senses are originally united is a consequence of what is called a phenomenological analysis of the world around us. Recall from chapter 6 that the term phenomenological means describing things as they *appear* or *feel* to us. Recall, too, that in the Introduction, I used the example that the sun *appears* to rise in the East in the morning and set in the West in the evening. It doesn't, of course. It just appears to do so. Similarly, our everyday experience may often tell us that our senses are unified. They're not, They just appear to be so.

Neurologically, we know that the brain has specific and separate circuits for each kind of information entering. Then, there are other circuits and structures that integrate the information from these separate circuits. There are still other circuits and structures that integrate lower level integrations, etc. So when we refer to the "unity of the senses," we should ask, on what level of integration, i.e., unity, are we talking about. The genesis matrix is the set of massively parallel brain circuits that integrate the subliteral processes presented in this book. Within the genesis matrix, various linkages and transformations are carried out that fuse together or superimpose (i.e., unify) information from the various sensory circuits, for example, cross-modal processes. This is where information from the separate circuits fuses, and superimposes on each other to create primitive "meanings." One of these cross-modal linkages and transformations is what I described in chapter 6 as synesthesia, in which some people can *feel* colors or where particular sounds create an image of a particular color. In our conscious and rational cognitive universe, this cross-modal process creates "normal" synesthesia in which we metaphorically experience a high note in music as "thin," and a low note as "thick." The different sensory modes are crossed. This is what we typically call a figure of speech.

There are people, however, who "really" (not just metaphorically) "see" sounds, experience high notes as light colors, and conversely see low notes as dark colors. These true synesthetes, as they are called, are actually neurologically wired differently from normal people. Their various senses are cross-wired, so to speak. In addition to demonstrating the developmental process of certain normal metaphors, more importantly, true synesthesia demonstrates the workings within the deep origins of what we normally call metaphors.

When any of the schemas functions as a relatively coordinated set, it often creates the conscious or semiconscious experience of things "feeling right." Even abstract schemas can create this feeling. For example, in the highly abstract field of mathematics, it's well known that many gifted mathematicians, are often guided by nonconscious feeling schemata in constructing their highly abstract and symbolic work. These mathematicians often speak of an equation "feeling right" or that an equation is beautiful or elegant. On a deep genesis level, poetry and mathematics are made of the same stuff.[15]

Language processing is also a part of the genesis matrix. Semantics, phonology, and syntax intermix and mutually influence each other. Once again, it seems reasonably clear from neurological data that these three components are initially encoded in separate brain circuits, so that any unity, including the genesis matrix, is a derived process. Linguistically, the genesis matrix is a sound and sensory mixer in which the various concrete, experiential feelings and sensory schemas are fused and superimposed onto the more abstract semantic level and end up creating language and meaning. The genesis matrix is a very dense multidimensional set of neurological circuits and schemas where meaning is created and where the linguistic operations illustrated in the subliteral narratives throughout this book are created (see also entire Appendix).

Finally, within the genesis matrix is a set of functions that direct the integrations on the level of meaning. This means that it includes "intentional structures," which guide the creation of meaning. In other words, thinking and reasoning is going on just as in our conscious mind (see the Executive Function section later). It's the specific address where the inner beings of the great poets reside.

Within this genesis matrix the subliteral language and operations are constructed using the various cognitive operations already mentioned, many of which involve the syntactic, semantic, and phonological aspects of language and multiple affective and sensuous schemas. The exact microworkings of this matrix are not well understood. The incontrovertible fact, however, is that something resembling what I am describing as a genesis matrix must be going on. We know so little, that the process is difficult to describe in words. In fact the words we use to describe these deep processes are "metaphors," not the reality of what is really happening. It's probably ultimately beyond words, as the poets never tire of telling us scientists. We have to try to explain it as well as we can, however, to make some sense of out subliteral meaning. Every inroad to explain its workings increases our understanding of ways to investigate and conduct further research.

MAKING THINGS THE SAME: INVARIANCE TRANSFORMATIONS

Implied in the notions of schema, cross-modal transfer, synaesthetic metaphor, and physiognomic transformations is a mechanism for creating invariance, by which different "things" are made "identical," the "same as" or "like" some "thing" else. Otherwise, the pun couldn't have double meaning, and a literal story couldn't have subliteral meaning. I have termed this mechanism an invariance transformation (I should note that I use the term transformation in its mathematical sense where invariance or constancy is maintained, not from the field of linguistics where transformations generate difference).[16]

Invariance transformations are not just peculiar to creating subliteral meaning. They're also responsible for what we call transfer of learning where we can apply what we have learned in one situation to a situation that may appear quite different or as in seeing analogies. Invariance transformations enable us to recognize a musical composition though it's played in a different key. In short, because no two things are absolutely identical, invariance transformations enable us to say that something is the "same" as something else. This same invariance transformational process generates the multiple subliteral stories and permutations or variations on a single emotional concern.

After being reduced to their invariant similarities, the multiplicity of incoming data is probably stored in schemas as isomorphic structures. Isomorphism in biology refers to a similarity in form. Isomorphism in mathematics refers to a one-to-one correspondence between the elements or sets, so that the result of an operation on the elements of one set corresponds to the result of analogous operations on the other sets. In chemistry it refers, for example, to a close similarity in the crystalline structure of two or more substances which have similar chemical compositions. Now, it should be clear that the notion of invariance transformation is a significant mechanism for transforming the apparently different surface or literal meaning of a word, phrase, sentence, or story into a single subliteral meaning. It should also be clear that the psychological capacity to see "similarities" is also integrally involved. On a more phenomenological level, the ability to reason metaphorically and analogically and the transfer of learning are integrally involved in the subliteral mind. In fact the phenomenological level is based on the more basic and hardwired invariance transformations at a genesis matrix level.

INSIDE THE SUBLITERAL UNCONSCIOUS

In this section, I outline what I call the subliteral unconscious. Strictly speaking, the subliteral unconscious is part of the subliteral mind. In fact the subliteral mind is made up unconscious schemas and is therefore unconscious itself. In fact, the subliteral mind and the subliteral unconscious are one and the same. I have separated them here for convenience in explaining this new kind of unconscious mind. In effect, this section is a summary and extension of the ideas discussed so far.

As I explained in chapter 6, philosophers, poets, and others have alluded to such inner sensory processes but have not articulated the workings of these inner processes in any concretely empirical way that connects to everyday life. The subliteral unconscious, then, may be understood as a complex of widely distributed neurological circuits variously integrated into a multilevel series of networks all linked together by invariance transformations. These processes include the abstract, sensuous, feeling, and language schemas (along with many others) explained previously. The subliteral unconscious also includes unconscious perceptual and psychodynamic processes that create intentional or unconsciously motivated behavior (see later).

THE UNCONSCIOUS HYPERSPACE

The subliteral unconscious, then, is not a vague psychological black hole in our meaning universe—as much of the theorizing about the unconscious tends to be. Nevertheless, we have gone, and are going, where few have gone before. As a longtime trekkie, I can't resist the Star-Trek-like language. I think the language of astrophysics, however, is a good analogy for describing some of the characteristics of the subliteral unconscious mind. As we have seen so far, the unconscious abstract, sensuous, feeling, and language schemas "warp" our psychological sense of time and space, so that past situations and feelings are fused with present situations and meanings and are stacked upon each other resembling a cognitive hyperspace where the subliteral meaning of words, phrases, sentences, and whole stories exist in parallel universes. One of the defining characteristics of the subliteral unconscious—unlike the unconscious of cognitive science and classic psychoanalytic theory—is that it "thinks" and "reasons" just like our conscious mind. In other words, it's smart. Very smart.

How can it be so smart? Probably in the exact same way that our conscious mind is smart (I have more to say about this later). Any brain-based theory of mind should only have one theory of the way it works, not two theories—one for conscious and the other for unconscious processes (see chapter 11). Given that the subliteral unconscious is a complex of neurological circuits integrated in a multilevel series of networks all linked together, *it* is not in fact an "it." In fact, *it* doesn't exist as a permanent unitary thing in a particular space and time. Different circuits and networks are used at different times, depending on what is called for, like a changing kaleidoscopic pattern. Moreover, the subliteral unconscious slips and slides from a deep unconscious state which is inaccessible, to a nearly conscious state, to a partially conscious state. Throughout this book we have seen examples of being in a nearly conscious state, when people immediately become aware of a slip of the tongue they've just made.

What I mean by being partially conscious is that some part is completely conscious. This occurs when a person has conscious thoughts and feelings that they are withholding from public view because of fear, social etiquette, or other taboos. Under such conditions the other parts of the subliteral unconscious—the complex of neurological circuits and networks that create the cognitive and linguistic operations—are initiated in the same way as when feelings are unconscious. Some of the more classical terms for different levels of unconscious functioning like preconscious, subconscious, or co-conscious can be roughly equated to the various levels of subliteral unconscious functioning at various times. Thus, the subliteral mind is often a mixture of conscious and unconscious processing.

Somewhere in the subliteral unconscious an incubation period in the problem solving and creative process occurs. In effect, incubation refers to our unconsciously ruminating for a period of time over all of the information given about a problem. Because of invariance transformations, differences are reduced to being the "same." In this sense, there is no "time" in the subliteral unconscious. An event that happened in the past that's similar to an event that's happening in the here-and-now is emotionally experienced as the "same" event, just as an infant experiences the movement of a protruding tongue with the movement of a protruding finger. Feeling schemas exist outside of time.

UNCONSCIOUSLY MOTIVATED BEHAVIORS: PSYCHODYNAMICS

Two basic approaches need to be clearly distinguished in analyzing subliteral communications. The first is *how* unconscious thoughts and feeling are carried out. This entails the various subliteral cognitive operations presented throughout this book. The second is *why* they are carried out. This is the territory of psychodynamics. Psychodynamics refers to conflicting thoughts and feelings that occur on an unconscious level. But the term is also used to refer to the unconscious motives of a person. Everyone uses psychodynamic explanations every day. For example, you may say, "He did that because . . . ," All "because explanations"—whether they are about conscious or unconscious events—are in effect psychodynamic. Psychodynamics simply involves thoughts and feeling that we suspect (or hypothesize) are taking place on a preconscious or unconscious (however defined) level.

Therapists use psychodynamic explanations based on their various theories. Because subliteral analysis is concerned with inferring unconscious feelings and thoughts which influence subliteral meaning, it uses psychodynamic explanations, but it's not therapy, though therapeutic psychodynamics can be used in interpreting subliteral communication in therapy (see chapter 12). Unlike therapeutic psychodynamics, subliteral psychodynamics uses data that are tied much more closely to direct here-and-now observation and known scientific evidence.

Subliteral psychodynamics in social and group conversations are based on five different kinds of data: (1) knowledge of group or social dynamics in general, e.g., (a) group level dynamics and (b) leadership and authority dynamics; (2) data about the specific group or conversational situation, e.g., (a) subgrouping and coalition forming, (b) the composition of the group, (c) the stage of development achieved by the group, and (d) knowledge of the dynamics in past conversation; (3) knowledge from social psychological research, e.g., (a) expectations and beliefs that people have about social situations, (b) how they should function, (c) norms of acceptable social behavior, and (d) general knowledge about various tensions and conflicts in human relationships; (4) knowledge about demographics, the history, and stereotypes of specific groups of people, including (a) race and ethnicity, (b) gender, (c) sexual preference, and (d) age; and (5) knowledge about individual members in the social situation, e.g., (a) what each has consciously said and done in past sessions, (b) about thoughts and feelings that are not being expressed or that are unconscious. This knowledge base, along with knowledge of the subliteral cognitive operations, makes analyzing psychodynamics possible in conversational situations.

PLANNING AND TRACKING SUBLITERAL NARRATIVES

Now, we come to these questions. How are individual subliteral narratives mapped onto the here-and-now social situation in structure and meaning? Further, how are the multiple corresponding narratives or variations on an original emotional concern planned and tracked? And how are the various linguistic operations planned and coordinated in subliteral stories? Recall, for example, that we saw in chapter 5 the quite sophisticated composition, planning, coordinating, and stacking of the thirteen subliteral stories that involved the number three. We also saw that they were all variants of a single concern about the three dominant members of the conversation, where the "separate" narratives were consistently and correspondingly broken down by gender, status, etc. This doesn't just happen.

I mentioned before that the subliteral unconscious is "smart" and that like our conscious mind, it thinks and reasons. This planning and tracking process implies an internal unconscious supervisor that oversees the entire process. Indeed, this is precisely what is needed to explain the complex production of tracking subliteral narratives. At first glance, this may sound even more bizarre than the subliteral narratives themselves and harks back to the idea of a homunculus, a miniature, human being who, by adherents of the biological theory of preformation believed, was present in the sperm cells that simply grew into an adult person.

Let's be clear. I am not suggesting that some little person or subpersonality who organizes everything is inside our brain. Though there's no tiny homunculus in our heads, there has to be those planning and organizing functions that such a homunculus would perform if there were one in our heads. For years psychologists ignored the issue of a central planning or control function, fearing that it would imply a "will" or, indeed, a homunculus. Numerous other stopgap concepts have been created like habit hierarchies and subsystems that are selectively inhibited and disinhibited depending on stimulus strength. Central control systems of some kind are now generally accepted.[17] Since the beginning of cognitive psychology, most theories have postulated the functional equivalent of a homunculus, only it was called an executive function.[18] This executive function coordinates and integrates the various sensory and cognitive mechanisms in subliteral narratives.

Although the relatively simple executive functions of cognitive science are not sufficiently smart to produce subliteral narratives, the postulation of some kind of executive function at least provides theoretical support for some smart planning supervisor to produce and coordinate subliteral narratives. The subliteral executive function that I am about to describe, however, is not merely theoretical. It's based on the empirical findings of Ernest Hilgard. Hilgard is a well-respected psychologist, who for years headed a laboratory at Stanford University that experimentally studied hypnotic phenomena.[19] Both he and his wife Josephine are well known for their research into hypnosis. While engaged in a classroom demonstration of hypnosis, he accidentally discovered what he metaphorically termed a "hidden observer." Let me quote Hilgard:

> We found in some demonstrations and experiments within our laboratory that two kinds of information processing may go on at once within hypnosis; some aspects are available to the hypnotic consciousness within hypnosis as ordinarily

studied; other aspects are available only when special techniques have elicited the concealed information. When these techniques are used, the additional information is reported as though it had been observed in the usual manner. Because the observing part was hitherto not in awareness, we have come to use the metaphor of a "hidden observer" to characterize this cognitive system.[20]

Despite the personified metaphor of a "hidden observer," which makes it sound like a person, it's not a little homunculus or separate "personality" inside our brain.

In terms of narrative planning, Hilgard reviews both the scientific and the literary anecdotal evidence that suggests this kind of internal monitor. Many scientists, mathematicians, and novelists describe a similar process in their creative process of unconscious "thinking" and planning. Hilgard quotes English poet, A. E. Housman's description: ". . . there would flow into my mind, with sudden and unaccountable emotion, sometimes a line or two of verse, sometimes a whole stanza at once, accompanied, not preceded, by a vague notion of the poem which they were destined to become a part of."[21] Housman was describing the unconscious work being done before conscious recognition.

Novelists often describe their characters as "taking over" and the story plot automatically unfolding without conscious planning. In working with a subject who told very extensive, creative and coherent stories, Hilgard's technique,

revealed that there was a part of him doing the planning, more like a stage director providing the promptings for the hypnotized part, the actor. The hidden part knew, for example, that the cavern was to have a beautiful room and that there would be a garden beyond. The hypnotized part did not know their qualities until *seeing* them. As he put it, "The two parts worked together to form a story." The hidden part also planned and monitored the length of the story.[22]

Some part of our unconscious mind, then, acts as a smart planning and coordinating supervisor. Hilgard notes that his findings open up the possibility of parallel processing in other mental processes, including dichotic listening and subliminal perception. Hilgard also adds that these processes lie within the known facts of neurophysiology.

In cognitive science terminology, this kind of unconscious process is made possible by what's called parallel processing. Simply put, this involves many independent systems (neurological circuits in our terms) working in parallel. By contrast, it's thought that our conscious mind works serially, step-by-step with one thing at a time. Subliteral narratives assume a complex use of similarity relationships and invariance transforms to carry out corre-

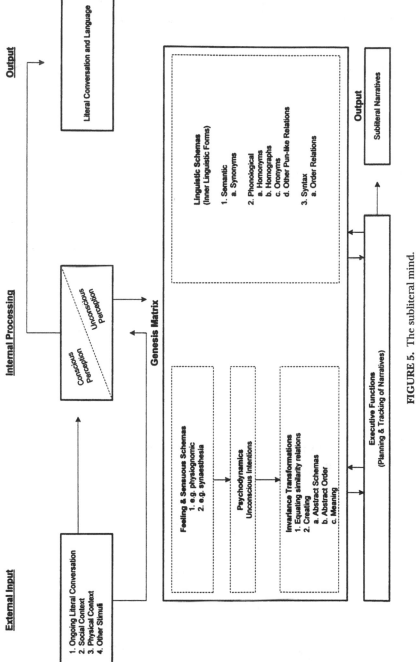

Output

Literal Conversation and Language

Internal Processing

Conscious Perception / Unconscious Perception

Genesis Matrix

External Input

1. Ongoing Literal Conversation
2. Social Context
3. Physical Context
4. Other Stimuli

Feeling & Sensuous Schemas
1. e.g. physiognomic
2. e.g. synaesthesia

Psychodynamics
Unconscious Intentions

Invariance Transformations
1. Equating similarity relations
2. Creating
   a. Abstract Schemas
   b. Abstract Order
   c. Meaning

Linguistic Schemas
(Inner Linguistic Forms)

1. Semantic
   a. Synonyms

2. Phonological
   a. Homonyms
   b. Homographs
   c. Oronyms
   d. Other Pun-like Relations

3. Syntax
   a. Order Relations

Executive Functions
(Planning & Tracking of Narratives)

Output

Subliteral Narratives

FIGURE 5. The subliteral mind.

sponding mapping of the various narrative permutations. These permutations involve a consistent and simultaneous parallel processing and tracking of conscious and nonconscious cognitions and parallel integration of affective, cognitive, and motor processes.

Although the "hidden observer" is a useful metaphor on the basis of empirical evidence and is congruent with other research on unconscious processing, like subliminal perception, it doesn't really completely answer the question, how is this unconscious thinking possible, and how can it be so smart? Again, the short answer is, probably in the exact same way that our conscious mind is smart. But, of course, we haven't explained how conscious thinking is possible, either, that is, how is it that we can think about ourselves thinking about ourselves thinking? A complete explanation would solve the very problem of how consciousness itself is possible. This would in turn solve the mind–body problem, that is, how does the physical brain turn into the psychological mind? Or more concretely, perhaps, how do neuronal firings in our physical brain lead to the experience of seeing something? Someday, some genius may solve this mind–body problem.

In the meantime, if there are still disbelievers in such a smart unconscious mind consider this. Though we can't explain how neuronal firings lead to our experience of "seeing" and though we can't explain how the physical brain turns into our psychological mind, we don't doubt for a moment that we do see and that we do have minds. By the same token, though we can't explain a smart unconscious, given the overwhelming evidence, why do we doubt that it exists? (See Figure 5.)

THE SUBLITERAL MIND AND THE NATURE OF THE CONSCIOUSNESS OF SELF

If all this talk about a very smart unconscious mind, which thinks and reasons, still seems somewhat unbelievable, it's because of a very important assumption that we make about the mind. The assumption is this: We assume the priority of our conscious mind over our unconscious mind; that our conscious mind is primary and our unconscious mind is, at best, secondary. "Yes, of course," you say, "this is the way it is—isn't it?" But, as usual, the answer is not that simple. Let me lead up to the finale of the consequences of assuming that the conscious mind is primary.

Arthur Reber,[23] a well-known and respected cognitive psychologist at Brooklyn College of the City University of New York, has made a most extraordinary suggestion that bears on this assumption. Reber suggests that the unconscious mind should be the "default" or primary mind. I can't go into all of the evidence he offers, including his own experimental research on what he calls implicit learning, which shows that unconscious learning is prerequisite to most conscious learning. But suffice it to say he thinks that the evidence leads to his conclusion that unconscious processing should be the default mode, not conscious processes. Now, this is a remarkable insight, and for a respected cognitive psychologist to make such a suggestion it's even more remarkable. I suggested before and as Reber also notes, the philosopher Michael Polanyi called such unconscious or implicit learning *tacit* knowledge. I should note here that though Reber's view is more restricted and holds that unconscious learning is primary, he is not likely to be very "friendly" to a subliteral unconscious mind. Nevertheless, I'll take supporting evidence wherever I can find it.

Now, the question is—and this question bears directly on the perceived credibility of the subliteral mind on which this book is based—why is there such resistance to Reber's insight on the primacy of unconscious learning (which he calls implicit learning) over conscious learning (which he calls explicit learning) and also to the idea of a smart unconscious that thinks and reasons, and especially to a subliteral unconscious? The answer is that our everyday experience and appearances verify this assumption (but, again, let's not forget that everyday experience "verifies" that the sun rises and sets, too).

In Western society, at least, we base our very identity only on the conscious aspects of ourselves of which we are or can be aware. Though most people are aware now that there are larger unconscious parts to our mind than what's in consciousness, our sense of self still remains welded to our conscious sense of self. For example, take dreaming. We experience a dream as happening to us, not as something that we created. It's perceived as ego alien, as something apart from our self. But, of course, who else created the dream but *us*, the dreamers. Consider further, that because most of what goes on in our mind is unconscious, most of who we are is based on parts of ourselves about which we know nothing.

Indeed, our Western legal systems are based on the premise that a person is defined by the conscious sense of self. If a court is convinced that a person was not aware of doing something with which the person is charged, the person is often excused or called mentally ill. After all, if the person's unconscious caused some illegal activity, then the person is not held responsible. Note that unconscious motivations are referred to as "impulses," not "reasons." Thus, they are considered irrational and beyond control. But what reasonable person would hold that you are responsible for your unconscious impulses? No one, right? Wrong, again.

The French philosopher and writer Jean Paul Sartre (1905–1980)— who declined the Nobel prize—held the view that it's untenable to maintain that human responsibility ends at the edge of consciousness.[24] According to Sartre, we are our unconscious mind, too. Our unconscious self makes decisions about our actions and behavior just as our conscious self does. To Sartre, we are a unity of "consciousness." What we call unconscious is just another level of consciousness. There are others, too, like the psychiatrist Thomas Szasz, who maintains that we are both our conscious and unconscious selves, and that we cannot disclaim this large area of learning, experience, and motivations that constitute our "self."[25]

Now I don't intend to take a position on this, but I do need to point out the problems with identifying our self with only the conscious part of our mind and the implications that this view has had—and continues to have— on convincing people that unconscious parts of our mind exist which think, reason, and make decisions. The assumption that consciousness is not only primary and that it alone thinks and reasons has retarded much needed research on a smart, cognitive, unconscious mind. Even more than this, the assumption that leads to the retort that all this stuff about the unconscious is just theory, itself flows from an assumption. As I've already noted, we don't have an adequate theory of the way consciousness works, either. It's just unthinkingly taken for granted. Our view of the way consciousness works is just theory, too.

Finally, the Western notion of the self centered only in the conscious part of the mind is equivalent to the pre-Copernican view that the earth is the center of the universe. To think otherwise affronts our sense of who we are. Now, perhaps we can understand the resistance to a smart unconscious mind, not to mention subliteral meaning. We need to reexamine seriously our view of the unconscious parts of our mind.

PART III

SPECIFIC APPLICATIONS

CHAPTER 9

RACE AND ETHNICITY

SUBLITERAL PREJUDICE IN BLACK AND WHITE

As we come into the twenty-first century, we live in an age in which the entire earth has been reduced to a global and incredibly diverse multicultural village. Ostensibly it's an age of enlightenment, an age in which education has supposedly replaced facts for superstition. But in social gatherings of mixed ethnic composition, prejudicial feelings, attitudes, and concerns are ever present in all peoples, regardless of skin color or ethnicity. As with our individual lives, so too our work and social lives become increasingly made up of different groups of peoples from around the world who not only look different from each other but who have different beliefs and cultural practices. It's important to understand and recognize negative behaviors and attitudes toward different peoples if we are to reduce the conflict in our individual, work, social, and political lives.[1] If we listen subliterally, we can hear current and vestigial remains of these feelings and stereotypes that cause much of our racial and ethnic conflict and misunderstandings. I have been listening to such subliteral racial and ethnic stories for years. In this chapter, I present many illustrations of subliteral racial conversations.[2]

In chapter 1, I noted that it's widely recognized that certain euphemisms such as you know how *"they* are," are consciously employed in everyday conversations to talk cryptically about ethnic out-group people. Similarly, certain phrases in a conversation may consciously be used to represent *black versus white* prejudices, stereotypes, and concerns, such as topics about *city versus rural*, or talk of *inner city* and *welfare*. This is called "coded speech," where everyone knows what's "really" being discussed. Similarly, racial topics are subliterally expressed.[3] In mixed racial groups of African-Americans and whites, the latter may select in literal topics about *watermelons*, or about people being *lazy*, but with no conscious awareness that these topics are stereotypic racial references to the minority members in the conversation. It's as if the very physical presence of an African-American acts as a stimulus that automatically evokes multiple layers of prejudices, stereotypes, and concerns.

Some of the stereotypes that the subliteral narratives in this chapter are based on may seem to exist no longer, as if they are from a time long past. Let me assure you that this is not the case.[4] Many of them are still operating on unconscious levels. I have found that this is especially true, though certainly not limited to, those without a great deal of formal education, those of lower socioeconomic class, and those who grew up before the 1960's.

Before I begin to illustrate these subliteral racial stories more fully, I need to sound a note of caution about interpreting conversations that seem to reflect prejudice. Although prejudicial and stereotypic attitudes can be revealed subliterally, I have found that often subliteral references to ethnic stereotypes may not necessarily mean that the person speaking is prejudiced in a negative sense. Such references may instead reflect cultural stereotypes that have been culturally ingrained in most of us and which may be automatically evoked. This caution applies to all subliteral references in conversations, and it especially applies also to racial topics (see Concluding Ethical Postscript at the end of this book).

CLARIFYING THE MEANING OF THE TERMS PREJUDICE AND RACE

The terms prejudice and race are widely misunderstood. Most people think that prejudice is negative because the everyday usage of the term in relation to racial and ethnic issues has overridden its psychological meaning.

PREJUDICE

Strictly speaking, prejudice means simply a prejudgment about something before looking at all of the relevant information. A related meaning is a preconceived preference, opinion, or idea. Other meanings include an adverse judgment or opinion that's not based on appropriate knowledge or examination of the facts. Finally—and this is the meaning generally attributed to the term prejudice—it's an irrational dislike or hatred of a particular group of people based on their ethnicity/race, gender, sexual orientation, or religion.

I use the term "prejudice" here not as a simple prejudgment but rather in two related senses. First, I use it in the typical sense of a negative or adverse prejudgment, i.e., as a prejudgment that negates or devalues an individual or group. This prejudgment is precipitated and organized by conscious and nonconscious belief systems made up of negative stereotypes and attitudes. In this sense of the term prejudice, a person is said to be racist, sexist, etc.

Second, I use the term nonprejudicial stereotype as a relatively benign "prejudice" based on attitudes created by, and reinforced on, a cultural level which nonconsciously influences our perceptions. People who subliterally generate nonprejudicial stereotypes are not typically racists or bigots, do not discriminate, and may in fact be involved in civil rights activities. Such subliteral references may simply denote a person's ignorance about a negative meaning or a buried stereotype that is automatically evoked. We may also think of this distinction as racial but not racist. I might note here that this distinction between prejudice and nonprejudicial stereotype is my own It comes uniquely out of my findings on subliteral talk and is an importar. distinction in terms of prejudice and in terms of our cognitive structure. I explain this more concretely at the end of this chapter. The term "race" is also problematic.

RACE

I use the term "race" as it's typically understood by th   , of the population, which apparently includes many scientists. Race is considered a significant biological and genetic distinction that defines a group of people who belong to an ideal "pure" genetic pool. I use it here only because it's the accepted medium of semantic exchange and therefore convenient in communicating the subject of this chapter. I consider the concept of "race" a myth, however, as does the anthropologist Ashly Montague in his book, *Man's Most Dangerous Myth*.[5] In my early career, I was giving a public talk on racism and included the Jewish people in my examples of groups discriminated against. Although I clearly understood that the term Jew does not—even in traditional biological terms—refer to a race, and indeed explained this, a Jewish person, nevertheless, became angry and walked out of my talk. I trust this won't be the case here.

Finally, as indicated by the title, all of the illustrations in this chapter reflect African-American and white relationships. This is not by design. The populations with which I have lived and worked have not been diverse enough to provide me with occasions for recognizing subliteral narratives about other minority groups. With this said, let me begin now to illustrate stereotypes, prejudices, and nonprejudicial stereotypes in subliteral references to race and ethnicity.

SUBLITERAL REFERENCES OF ETHNIC PREJUDICE
BY MEMBERS OF THE WHITE MAJORITY

In describing subliteral stories, I first begin by outlining the context of the story. Then, I present the literal conversation that occurred, followed by my subliteral analysis of the literal conversation. Finally, I briefly comment on the story. Some of the following subliteral racial stories reflect negative prejudice, and some nonprejudicial stereotypes. All of them, however, reflect long-standing stereotypical feelings and attitudes in our culture about African-Americans.

LYNCHING

While standing in line at a hardware store one day, a very well dressed black man in suit and tie was just ahead of me waiting to pay for his purchases. Among his purchases were some metal hooks which he had placed on the counter in front of him. They were rather big hooks, the kind used for hanging large objects in a shed or barn. In front of the black man was a working class white fellow dressed in work clothes who looked rather scruffy. The white fellow glanced behind him at the very well dressed black man. You could see a fleeting look of surprise on his face at seeing this well-dressed, coiffed, and manicured middle-class African-American male. It was one of those awkward social encounters when two strangers make eye contact that calls for some kind of social recognition. Having made the eye contact, the white man clearly felt socially compelled to say something, some little ritual verbal formula to acknowledge the other's existence, just as we ritually say "good morning" to a person when we first meet. Nervously, the white man looked at the black fellow and said, "Well, that looks like a man who's going to do some hanging."

On a literal level the statement meant that it looked like the black fellow was going to be hanging some things on a wall somewhere. Subliterally translated, however—if you haven't already guessed—the statement, "well, that looks like a man who's going to do some hanging," in my view clearly reflected the view or image that a black man who behaves as an equal with white men may find himself being lynched or hung, as was historically the case.

As with all subliteral conversations, it's methodologically important to understand that a large number of topics or phrasings are possible in any given conversation (see Appendix, 2.5. Selection Response Field). Out of a nearly infinite number of responses the white man may have made, why was the phrase "that looks like a man who's going to do some hanging" selected? Why were the "hooks" selectively perceived out of a number of articles on the counter? Further, out of a nearly infinite number of syntactic arrangements of words in which "hanging" could have been used, why this particular arrangement of words? Why not, for example, "What are you going to hang with all those hooks," or "Those hooks work well," or "That looks like a man who's going to hang some large garden implements," or some other similar phrase?

The phrase, "that looks like a man who's going to do some hanging," is an example of an ambiguous sentence whose surface structure has more than one underlying cognitive representation:

> *Surface Structure:* That looks like a man who's going to do some hanging.
> *Representation 1.* That looks like a man who is going to hang some objects.
> *Representation 2.* That looks like man is going to be lynched/hung.

Despite the compelling subliteral analysis, the statement may not be a "prejudiced" or a negative racist statement in the sense that it's generated from negative feelings toward black people, conscious or otherwise, though it probably was. Still having subliteral meaning, the statement may be meaningful on other psychological levels, as I suggested at the opening of this chapter.

The statement may be subliterally meaningful on at least three psychological levels. First, it may indeed reflect the fact that the man is racist and that the statement is a nonconscious "slip of the mind." Secondly, the statement may mean that the man is not consciously prejudiced in his everyday interaction and intentions but that the statement reflects an unconscious racism. Third, it may reflect a nonconscious expression of a stereotypical set of cultural associations or images that have been ingrained in most of our psyches. Such statements may be racial but not racist in the common sense of the term.[6]

Thus, to analyze any such statement, the level of meaning must be assessed carefully. The words themselves mean nothing. To assess a negative prejudice with any degree of certainty, we must know (1) about the person making the statement; (2) something about the context of the situation; and (3) if possible, weigh the remark against other instances or remarks that the person has made. Unfortunately, in everyday conversations, we often do not have all the information we need to verify a piece of subliteral talk.

RACIAL PURITY

One of the most enduring beliefs about many minority groups, especially African-Americans, is that they are genetically different in significant ways. Thus, when a person is perceived as being of mixed genetic heritage, this becomes important for some people. In a group where one of the members was perceived as being genetically, "half-black and half-white," the topic turned to talk of *animal pedigrees,* and a discussion ensued about *pure strains* versus *half-breeds.* Later in the same group conversation, there was mention of a brand of pipe tobacco called *Half and Half.* The ostensible literal topics of *animal pedigrees, pure strains* versus *half-breeds,* and of the pipe tobacco called *Half and Half* are subliteral references to the group member who is perceived as genetically "half-black and half-white."

It's no accident that these topics were selected for the conversation. Clearly, these topics are not on the same level of consciousness as the *city* versus *rural* or *inner city* and *welfare* examples of what is called coded speech, where everyone really knows what is meant. The use of the quantitative metaphor "half" is used, because historically—and I think even now—prejudicial thinking by some whites maintains that if a person has any African-American heritage, however small, that person is considered "black." (Actually, a light-skinned black person is almost never considered half black. In fact, a person who, it is thought, has any black heritage at all has generally been considered black). The use of the metaphor "half" is a strange unconscious math that rounds off any fraction into a whole number (see Appendix, 8. Mathematical Computational Operations).

BLACK BLOOD

As I've just mentioned, the very essence of most prejudice is the belief that many minorities are not just socially and genetically, but also biologically different. More specifically, still held (on some level of conscious/unconsciousness) by many whites is the notion that the blood flowing in the veins of African-Americans is significantly different from the blood of Caucasians.

One day while walking down a hallway behind a black female, a white female, and two white males, I overheard the black female say that she may need a blood transfusion and wondered if it was easy to get blood. One of the white males said that it was "usually" not a problem at all, stressing the word "usually." Then, he added in a changed tone of voice, "But if you have some kind of strange blood, it's more difficult." The white female said "I'd be afraid to give blood." The second male then responded "They wouldn't want your blood; look at you—you've got no color, no color at all." This is a most interesting piece of subliteral conversation that essentially said to the white female: Your blood is different from that of a black person.

This subliteral analysis is indicated by the following. The pronoun "they" in the phrase, "They wouldn't want your blood . . ." literally meant, any white person who needed a transfusion. However, it was actually equivalent to the black female who needed the transfusion but couldn't use the white person's blood. As I noted above, the pronoun, "they," is frequently used in conversation as coded speech to refer semicryptically to black people or other minorities, as in you know how *"they"* are. But this isn't just a case of consciously coded speech, it's subliteral. This is indicated by the phrase which immediately followed: "Look at you—you've got no *color,* no *color* at all." Literally, this apparently meant that she looked "anemic," so to speak, relative to the "colored" skin of the African-American female who needed the transfusion. But subliterally it meant that she was not black. The statement about "strange blood" literally meant that if someone was anemic or their blood had some other anomaly, that it wouldn't be acceptable. Subliterally, it meant that black people do not have "regular" blood like Caucasians. Similarly, the statement that the white female had *"no color at all"* was a subliteral reference to not having "black blood," just as the reference to "strange blood" was subliteral for "black blood" being different.

Subliteral references often involve pronoun shifts, as in the reference to "they" which is ambiguous in the previous conversation. The shift, indicated by the use of "they," linguistically links a literal topic to a current interaction (see Appendix, 6.6. Pronoun Operations). It's significant that the only part the black woman had in this conversation was initiating the topic by indicating that she may need a transfusion. Thus, the conversation in this mixed racial discussion was about deeply ingrained white stereotypes and inaccurate beliefs about blood transfusions between white people and black people. This story may also reflect that the white members of the conversation were not prejudiced in a negative sense—or at least on an overt level—but were reflecting nonprejudicial stereotypes. They were, after all, friends or acquaintances of the black female.

BLACK MALE SEXUAL STEREOTYPE

Perhaps one of the oldest racial stereotypes is that of the large black male being highly sexually potent and animalistic in nature (recall the topic of animal pedigrees). My closest friend and colleague, Dr. Aaron Gresson, who is an African-American male, and I were returning from a leisurely talk on a wharf overlooking an expanse of ocean near my cottage in Maine. At the time, a black person in the area was a rare event (relatively speaking, it still is). We passed a neighbor's house where a family was playing a game of lawn tennis. The males in the family were playing against the females. As we approached, the game was nearing its end. While walking slowly past the players, they briefly and quietly responded to our friendly "hello," with stares of obvious surprise at seeing a black man.

While still trying to play tennis, the players were straining to look at my black friend. Just as Aaron and I walked past, the game ended. The male team of the family had lost. It was clear from a flurry of brief comments that they had wagered money on the game. The patriarch of the family turned, looking at me and my friend, and loudly exclaimed, "There goes that buck." Literally this statement meant he had lost a dollar bet on the game or whatever the real amount as represented by the dollar.

Subliterally, the statement "There goes that buck," was, likely, a nonconscious expression of a racial stereotype. It's well known that large male animals are seen as sexually potent and are often referred to as "bucks," as are male deer. Indeed, native American males were sometimes historically referred to as "bucks." Similarly, it's well known that black males—who were stereotyped as sexually potent—were historically often referred to as "bucks" in the animalistic sense. Thus the literal phrase, "There goes that buck," subliterally referred to my black friend, Dr. Gresson.

Certainly I don't mean to imply that these people knew their racist history in any formal sense. The derogatory term, though not in general usage today, nevertheless, is extant in some subcultures and individuals' unconscious store of cultural folklore, as learned in movies and literature. The people playing lawn tennis were older, uneducated, "old Mainers," as we would say, unsophisticated outside their local world.

Specific phrasings often provide cues to the subliteral intent. In the above phrase, "There goes that buck," any number of topics, words, or phrases were possible to describe losing a dollar. The man could have said, for example, "There goes that dollar," or "Well, we lost that bet," etc. Why this specific phrasing? In linguistic terms some "deep structure" or "internal representation" or cognitive schema functioned as a selection mechanism for generating the specific syntax and semantics of the statement.

AFRICAN-AMERICANS AS EARTHY AND NATURAL

A stereotype frequently applied to African-Americans, which is a corollary of the association of African-Americans with nature is that they are, more "natural." This stereotype often lingers, even in the most, otherwise, sophisticated minds. My friend Aaron, a white colleague, and I were making small talk on various topics. The conversation went back and forth between abstract ideas, food, and other more mundane topics. My white colleague, a philosopher of some international repute, seemed uncomfortable when I questioned him about some of his abstract and philosophical ideas. My friend Aaron had been talking to the philosopher about more personal, or "natural," everyday things. Unlike myself, Aaron has learned through the years not to threaten white folk (though he's certainly no "Uncle Tom").

During the rapid switching of topics, as often occurs in casual conversations, the philosopher turned his back to me and began talking exclusively to Aaron. The philosopher picked up the topic of food once again and "just happened" to say that he thought *"brown bread is much more natural than white bread."*

In addition to being a subliteral expression of the difference between the content of the topics introduced by me and Aaron, the phrase that "brown bread is much more natural than white bread," is a subliteral reference that black people are closer to nature, and that brown bread is not made of finely processed white flour and therefore is closer to being natural. "Brown bread" was thus a subliteral referent to Aaron, and "white bread" was a subliteral reference to me. It was clear to me that the philosopher felt that my abstract conversation (referred to as white bread) was not as comfortable as talking to my friend about everyday issues (referred to as brown bread).

CHOCOLATE AND VANILLA

Again, my friend Aaron and I were standing outside smoking our pipes. A white woman who was also standing there, said, "I love the smell of pipe smoke, it smells so good." Then, she turned, looked at Aaron and said of his tobacco, "It smells like there's vanilla in it." The likely subliteral meaning is that my black friend is part white, at least in his socializing. Outside the sports and entertainment world, it's still relatively unusual to see a white male and a black male chumming around together. In addition, most whites do not have the stereotype of African-American males smoking pipes. So the statement "It smells like there's vanilla in it," may mean that Aaron was engaging in a white man's activity. It also likely contained subliteral references to Aaron's light brown skin being the result of having "white genes" in his heritage. It may also have been a subliteral reference to Aaron being an "Oreo," the phrase used to describe a black person who is culturally white, like a chocolate Oreo cookie that has white frosting inside.

SOCIAL DEPRIVATION AS CAUSING LOW AFRICAN-AMERICAN I.Q.

It's certainly no secret in our society that many whites believe that African-Americans as a group have a lower intelligence level than do whites. The recurrent and recent controversy over the book, *The Bell Curve,*[7] is testament to this continuing belief.

During a discussion of mental retardation in a group that was of mixed racial composition, a white female member introduced the subject of childhood deprivation. She explained that the first "5 years of life is crucial" for establishing I.Q. level later in life. Then, she talked about homes in which children were deprived, nutritionally and socially.

The statement, that the first "5 years of life is crucial" was likely a subliteral expression of the stereotype of the negative effects on black children growing up in the lower socioeconomic class environment of most black families and that such environments can lead to psychological and emotional deprivation which can result in lower I.Q. levels. In terms of here-and-now relevance to the conversation, the subliteral talk was a reference to the perceived lower level of functioning in the group by black members. That the topic of childhood deprivation was in fact a subliteral reference to the black group members is supported by the fact that the number "5" was the exact number of black members in the group. Indeed, throughout the group discussions, the number "5" was always linked or associated with negative topics.

RETARDED BLACK LABRADOR RETRIEVER

In a different group, the same stereotype about black childhood deprivation as the cause of the perceived lower African-American I.Q. level and functioning arose in the conversation. An older black female member in the group was having difficulty understanding and analyzing the group interaction. The topic initiated by a white member was about "dogs that were not too smart." An older "racially liberal" white woman, who in past sessions was extremely kind and friendly to the black woman, selected a story about a dog she once had who was "*gorgeous* but who had been deprived as a pup and couldn't learn well as an adult." Then, she emphasized that the dog was a "*black* Labrador *retriever.*"

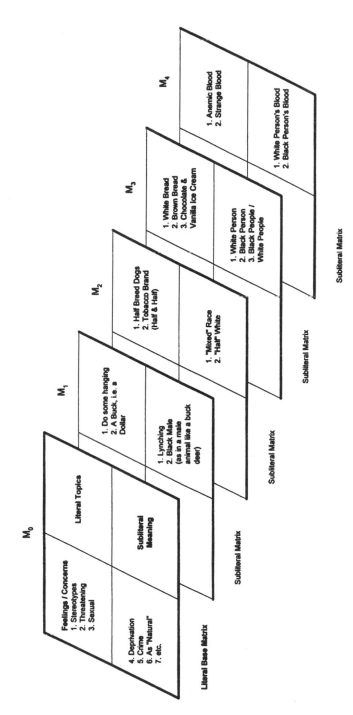

FIGURE 6. Partial composite racial/ethnic transformational matrices.

The topic of dogs who were deprived and who later in their life were slow learners (again, based on a stereotype of culturally deprived black people) was a subliteral reference to the older black female in the group who was having trouble understanding the group dynamics. The linguistic linkages here seem clear: it was a *"black"* dog; moreover it was a *"retriever,"* and therefore by association, meant slave behavior, as in being a servant.

In addition, the white female explained it was a *"gorgeous"* dog, indicating a further methodological linguistic linkage. Earlier in the session the black female had given the white female an ashtray she had made for her. The white female accepted it, exclaiming it was *"gorgeous"* (and thanked her as one would thank a small child). In addition, the black female had previously said that she was originally from *"Georgia."* The two words "gorgeous" and "Georgia" are linguistically significant in further subliterally linking the topic of deprivation and black dogs to the black female. I consider the use of *Georgia* and *gorgeous* a kind of subliteral paronymic connection. Paronymic words are those that derive from the same root or stem. Although strictly speaking these two words do not derive from the exact same stem, psychologically they are linked by their close similarity in spelling.

Similar repeated examples support the validity of the subliteral meaning of such talk. There had been white members of the group, too, who were having trouble understanding the group interaction, but there was no talk of childhood deprivation or similar topics that could be interpreted subliterally as pertaining to white members who were also having trouble understanding the group process (See Figure 6).

THEY SURE GOT RHYTHM, AND ALL THAT JAZZ

Another stereotype of African-Americans is that they have a genetically built-in sense of rhythm (a belief that presumably comes from a mistaken notion about Darwinian evolution and also from a cultural stereotype of a drum-beating African culture). This example is from a group that was composed of white members, except for 1 older black female. A white member talked about a night club and a white jazz group that played there.

The member related that the jazz group was named the "4 Daughters." The member further said that a "good old black person from Baltimore," who, although not registered to work in the club, occasionally joined in with the jazz group when the musicians invited him.

The "4 Daughters" jazz group stands for the 4 active white females in the group. The old black *person* from Baltimore refers to the older black woman.

This analysis is indicated in part by the fact that her last name was *Baltimore*. The "not registered to work there" refers to her relative lack of participation in the conversation until the other females actively engaged her, i.e., *invited* her, just as the "old black person" was invited to join the jazz group.

The conversation reflects a number of associations and stereotypes. That a musical topic was selected is associatively connected to the stereotype that blacks are innately musical; that the musical form of jazz evolved from black culture; and (as is well known) that the city of Baltimore has a large black population. There had been talk in the session about farm animals and in previous sessions about dog shows and that the dogs were registered breeds. Thus, the talk about the old black man who was not "registered" in the club is also a likely subliteral linkage to the black woman not being an acceptable, i.e., "registered" white person.

Methodologically, this episode demonstrates other validating methodological procedures. First, that a "club" is a group gathering; Secondly, that it's an older *person* who is mentioned; Third, that the older person was black (though not female. My notes do not indicate if the 4 Daughters jazz group was female); and finally, that the city, Baltimore, is the same as the last name of the black female. It's linguistically significant, too, that in talking about the old black man who was invited to play in the jazz group, he was initially referred to as a "good old black *person* . . ." The gender neutral term *person* was a *noun shift* (see Appendix, 6.7. Noun Shift Operations), so that the subliteral reference could include the black female.

BLACK HOLES IN WHITE UNIVERSES

In social situations where there is only one member of an ethnic minority, there are often concerns and questions about them. What are they thinking? What are they feeling? What are they going to say? In short, to someone with little experience with minorities, they are often a kind of psychological hole in a white person's universe (And, yes, there are still places where ethnic minorities are not a part of a nonminority's everyday experience. Come to Maine, sometime).

One particular group, I recall, had only one black person in it, a male. He was relatively quiet and thus was perceived as psychologically threatening to the white members. Quiet or silent members in a conversation are typically a concern because no one knows what they are thinking. Add race to this concern, and the concern about what the quiet person is thinking becomes even more threatening.

Not related to any topic in the group, the white male began to tell of a recent experience of his by saying, "I was watching TV . . . about the black hole in the universe . . . about this huge unknown void that exists somewhere far out in space. It's kind of frightening to think about it." The black male in the group was subliterally the "black hole" in the otherwise white membership of the group and thus was threatening and frightening to think about.

Historically, black males have always been perceived as more of a threat than black females. Given that there was only one black member in the discussion, it's also pertinent that black holes was mentioned in the singular, when in most conversations about black holes (just as I am now using the term) they are mentioned in the plural (see Appendix, 6.8. Plural Shift Operations).

DEATH PENALTY AND MINORITIES

As I mentioned before, we are all familiar with the euphemistic use of the pronoun "they" as in, you know how *they* are. Sometimes we are aware of the way this pronoun is used as a conscious indirect reference, and sometimes we aren't.

An ethnically mixed group was discussing the pros and cons of the death penalty. Most members were probably aware that the topic was a euphemism or an indirect way of discussing race. They were not aware, however, that the topic subliterally referred to the black members of the group. In this discussion, the white members of the group continually selected for the death penalty discussion the number "6." One white member, for example, suggested that "you could put *them* in jail for say, oh, 60 years."

Again, the term "them" of course referred to criminals on a literal level, but on a euphemistic level it referred to African-Americans, and members seemed to be aware of both levels of meaning. The reference to the number "6," however, was a nonconscious or subliteral reference to the six black members. Methodologically, the zero in the "60" gets canceled out. As is usually the case, zeros are "nothing," they don't count (see Appendix, 8.2. Cipher Operations; 8.3. Cancellation Operations).

The six specific black members in the group were what I have termed a cognitive equivalent in that to white members they cognitively represented blacks in general.[8] That is, the whites were obviously not suggesting that the specific black members of the group should be put to death or incarcerated, but rather they stood as a cognitive equivalent, a vehicle for discussing stereotypical perceptions about African-Americans in our society whom the members thought should be punished. Therefore, the topic represented the black members of the group as a cognitive equivalent.

Although these above beliefs about African-Americans are still consciously held by a segment of the white population, for many others the beliefs are unconsciously ingrained by years of cultural programing. The beliefs therefore often function mythically, just as we dream about ideas and doing things we wouldn't consciously think about or do. All too frequently, our nonconscious schemas are radically dissociated or disconnected from our conscious, intellectual, belief systems.

ETHNIC MINORITY SUBLITERAL REFERENCES

In most groups, being a minority in some socially significant dimension, such as age, gender, religion, or in this case, race, often generates concerns on the part of the minority members. It would be expected, then, that just as concerns by whites lead to subliteral conversations, the same hold true for African-Americans.

NORTHERN AND SOUTHERN PREJUDICE

Like all of the examples from my T-groups, this group occurred in a North Atlantic state. In a group that had been openly discussing the issue of race relations, the topic was suddenly switched by an older black male who had been quite vocal and who had grown up in the South.

The older black man said that he liked to hunt. During the discussion about hunting he said that he didn't like hunting "down South" because the terrain was so flat in the South that you couldn't hunt with a high-powered rifle. But "up North" hunting with a high-powered rifle is O.K. because of the mountainous terrain. Subliterally, this discussion translates into the black man's experience that one has to be careful in the South about discussing racial issues directly. The high-powered rifle subliterally means talking forcefully and *directly* (represented by the *rifle*), as opposed to *indirectly* and/or around a point (represented by the low-power shotgun). Further, the "flat terrain" in the South expresses the social clarity of one's status as an African-American man in the South, whereas up North one's status is more ambiguous, and just as in mountainous (social) terrain one's real status may be socially hidden, blacks can ostensibly speak more powerfully and directly.

Many African-Americans have noted this difference between acceptable and/or possible behavior by African-Americans in the South as opposed to the North. Either way, in the North or the South, black/white relations are often viewed unconsciously as a deadly game.

MINORITY CONCERN ABOUT BEING A MINORITY PERSON

In a discussion, where a black woman was the only minority person, she selected the topic of her work at a local mental hospital. She stressed that both male and female patients were in the same ward. She explained that in a "mixed ward no one should have to work alone like I do." Contextually, and methodologically, it's important to point out that this ostensibly literal topic was subliterally about her immediate concerns about being the only black person in the group. The literal topic of a "mixed ward" of males and females, subliterally meant the here-and-now group that was racially mixed, being the only minority person in the group, just as she was the only female worker on the mixed ward where she worked. The phrase "mixed ward" was a linguistic linkage between the literal story about her working in a mixed ward in terms of gender, and her immediate here-and-now situation which was racially mixed. Once again, as in most conversations, the issue could have been phrased many other ways. But it wasn't. And this is subliterally important.

MARTIN LUTHER (KING) AND REVOLUTION

A group of mixed racial composition had been discussing the effects of prejudice in society. There was a brief silence. Then the group began to topic hop. Within a short time, the topic of democracy was selected into the conversation.

The general political problem of "majority rule" and the issue of what happens to a "minority which is outvoted" became the topic of discussion. After a silence, a black member began talking about religion. Eventually the member mentioned the Protestant theologian "Martin Luther who rebelled" from Catholicism and started his own church because "he wouldn't conform" to the teachings of the Catholic church.

The topic of democratic functioning and the problem of the political minority often comes up in T-groups, so the general topic of democracy was not the subliteral issue. The subliteral issue was the specific concern of ethnic minorities in the group environment of a dominant majority.

It was clear that the literal topic of "majority rule" represented the white majority which was determining the direction of the group, and the "minority" topic represented by black members of the group who were a numerical minority representing the racial minority "which is outvoted." In short, the feelings by the black minority in the group were that they may have to rebel and go their own way, i.e., not "conform" to the majority white members. On a subliteral level, "Martin Luther" represents Martin Luther King, Jr., who like Martin Luther became the leader of the (reformist) 1960s civil rights movement. The reference to the Catholic church also probably referred to the group which was a formal (institutionalized) course. By subliteral implication, this made me the Pope, of course.

OUT-GROUP RELATIONSHIPS AND EQUALITY

Within any group or subgroup there is usually a pressure for members to be equal, to be the "same." A black female in the group was different from the rest of the black members in "genetics" and socioeconomic class and because she was the most studious member of the entire group, including the white members. A black male selected a literal topic about a girl he knew in "grade K-5" who was very bright. He said this girl should not have been in that grade because she was "in a class by herself" and that the school district was in effect holding her back by keeping her in that grade.

This statement was a subliteral recognition by the black male that the black female wasn't like the rest of the black members in the group. Thus, she was like the bright girl in K-5. More generally, she was in a "class by herself," because she was even different from most of the white group members.

Again, it is methodologically significant to note that the specific number in the topic of grade "K-5" was the same as total number of black members in the group (i.e., 5), counting the black female who was considered "half-black/white." In addition, the story was about a young girl and thus was parallel in gender with the actual or literal referent to whom it subliterally referred (see Appendix, 3.2. Sociometric Operations; 3.3. Gender Operations).

IDENTIFICATION AND DISIDENTIFICATION

In any group or situation, members differentially identify with each other along various dimensions, such as age, gender, and ethnicity. The minority composition of this group was two black males and three black females. With the exception of the third black female, who was light-skinned, middle-class, and considered by the other black members as "half-black," the other black members were of lower socioeconomic class, "militant," and did not conform to what she and the other white members perceived as my expectations for the course.

In a discussion about family, the third black female, who was perceived as being "half-black," emphasized that she had "no brothers or sisters" but that she did have "two sets of cousins." She said that in one set of cousins' family, both parents had to work, whereas in the other set only one parent worked. She said this made a difference in the way the children acted in school. One set always "sassed" the teacher, she said, whereas the other set behaved well.

The literal statement of having "no brothers or sisters" was a subliteral expression of disidentification with the "militant" black members in the group. The literal and biological kinship meaning of brothers and sisters was a nonconscious or subliteral meaning for the contemporary linguistic usage of the term, meaning that, socially, all blacks are brothers and sisters to each other. The linguistic expression of having "two sets or cousins" is a subliteral expression that indicates the extent of her distant relationship and/or disidentification with the other black members in the group and with white members in behavior, socioeconomic class, and skin color. The "fact" that she was "half-black" or conversely "half-white" made her differentially related to both the black and the white members in the same differential manner that siblings and cousins are related in terms of kinship. Having no sisters or brothers, also subliterally meant that she didn't have any completely genetic ethnic sisters and brothers, because she was perceived as biologically different from the rest of the black members.

The "two sets of cousins" statement was further refined subliterally by indicating that in one set of cousins' family, both parents had to work, whereas in the family of the other set only one parent worked. She further suggested that this difference in the two families made a difference in the way the children acted in school. One set whose parents both worked always "sassed" the teacher, whereas the other set, where only one parent worked, behaved well. The misbehaving set subliterally referred to the lower-socioeconomic class and militant black members in the group, and the well-behaving set of cousins subliterally referred to the white members of the group. The dominant nonconscious stereotype equates the white members with being in a socioeconomic class higher than black members and therefore with the latter set of cousins having parents who both have to work.

According to the anthropologist Claude Lévi-Strauss, one of the functions of myths is to comment on kinship structures. Frequently, like cultural myths, the literal group talk subliterally reflects the group as family. The discourse may be about parents and children or brothers and sisters so as to be identical to the group situation. One of the characteristics of myth, according to Lévi-Strauss, is that the whole reflects the parts and each part signifies the whole. Thus, the two sets of cousins topic viewed as a kind of "myth" reflected both the whole of the group and its parts simultaneously,[9] the two splits in the group as a whole (racial and male/female) and in one of its parts (among the African-Americans). Finally, it reflected the psychological split within the black female speaker herself.

LITTLE WHITE CHILD

This group had been involved in an open discussion of racial issues. Though I am white, I had never been openly identified as separate from the racial issue in the group, though I wasn't naive enough to believe that the black members considered me a neutral party. Finally, the group went on to other topics. They began discussing children and how they should behave. At one point in the discussion, a white female member suddenly arose from her seat and left the group, ostensibly to go to the bathroom. As most people have experienced, when someone in a meeting suddenly leaves without an explanation, members often imagine all manner of reasons: was the person, angry, ill, etc?

Almost immediately the subject of children running around in school came up as a topic. More specifically, as a part of a literal story about how children in school should behave, a black member of the group said, "Your child should not be running around in here." The sentence subliterally told me, You shouldn't let that girl who is a member of your race just get up and leave anytime she wants to.

This sentence was meant in a literal sense, with the pronoun "your" being used as a general "you." Likewise, the "here" was not literally meant as a reference to the here-and-now situation but to the general topic of children in school. Subliterally, however, the pronoun "your" referred to me and "child" referred to the white girl who got up and left the group. In the same way the adjective "here" subliterally referred to the here-and-now group situation. Of equal importance, methodologically, is the fact the plural noun "children" turned into using the singular form, "child," immediately after the white female got up and left the group. This discussion was equally a general, nonracial, subliteral statement meaning that a teacher shouldn't let students leave class without permission.

NONPREJUDICIAL SUBLITERAL RECOGNITION OF ETHNIC DIFFERENCES

In the opening of this chapter, I explained that although all nonconscious associations with race and the recognition of difference are, by definition, racial, not all nonconscious recognition of racial differences is negatively prejudicial or racist. Prejudicial associations are organized around negative feelings toward the minority. Nonprejudicial stereotypes are the consequence of years of cultural conditioning to recognition of racial difference. The fact that the recognition of difference (in this case color of skin) is by definition racial and the fact that this recognition of difference is manifested in various linguistic forms is not, I believe, tantamount to negative prejudice. Nonconscious subliteral expressions of racial stereotypes, then, don't always merit the assumption of negative prejudice when the racial context is not congruent with such an analysis. Let's see how this works.

RACE TO THE STARS

This example occurred years ago on the *Merv Griffin Show.*[10] Merv is interviewing LaWanda Page, the black actress who had starred on the TV program *Sanford and Son,* a show about a black family, and who was currently starring in a spin-off show called *Sanford Arms,* where she played the manager of a large apartment building.

During the interview, Merv was talking to her about show business. Ms. Page said how much she loves it, and Merv replies, "Yes, it gets in your blood." As the discussion continues, Ms. Page tells Merv about her agent and how he is like a mother to her. Then, Merv quickly says, "Yeah, some of those agents are . . . mothers!" pronouncing and intoning the word "mother." Ms. Page said that she had not moved out of the neighborhood or her house that she lived in before becoming a TV star. Then, Merv asked, "Do you have the same boyfriend?" She replied that she did. Following this interaction, Merv asked her what her ideal man looked like, and she said, "tall and handsome . . ." At that point, Merv introduced another guest, Virginia Graham, who jokingly said that she was the "token white person" on LaWanda's new program *Sanford Arms*. Talk ensued of "chocolate ice cream," the New York electrical "blackout" and "black eyes." The two women continued to interact. Then, Virginia said something and LaWanda extended her (brown) arm to shake Virginia's hand. There was a momentary pause, and Virginia started talking about *Sanford Arms* as if it had been in the current conversation all along, when it hadn't been. Merv, taken aback, exclaimed, "How did that get into the conversation?" Virginia replied, "I don't know" What does all this mean?

First, Merv saying, "Yes, it gets in your blood," is likely an association to the belief that African-Americans have different blood. Second, his response to LaWanda's statement about her agent, "Yeah, some of those agents are . . . mothers!" was said emphasizing the word "mother" with a tone and inflection suggestive of what has come to be identified as the black expression, "mother fucker," with it's shortened version, as in "you, *mother.*" Third, Merv asking La Wanda, "Do you have the same boyfriend?" is probably a subliteral association to the stereotype of unmarried, black, female, welfare recipients keeping boyfriends in the house. On some level, Ms. Page must have caught this subliteral racial slur because she went on to say that her boyfriend takes her *out* to dinner, etc. Her response was subtle, but clear. She did not have a live-in boyfriend. Fourth, the talk of "chocolate ice cream," the New York electrical "blackout" and "black eyes" were also subliteral associations with the recognition that racial issues were being expressed.

LaWanda's reply that her boyfriend was "tall and handsome . . ." with the usual descriptive "dark," (as in: "tall, dark, and handsome") omitted, was likely consciously omitted. Virginia Graham, who jokingly said that she was the "token white" on LaWanda's new program *Sanford Arms,* set the framework for the discussion. LaWanda's extending her (brown) *arm* to shake Virginia's hand, when after a momentary pause in the conversation, Virginia started talking about *Sanford Arms* as if it had been in the previous conversation all along, indicates a further cue that subliteral recognition of racial difference was extant in the conversation. This is further indicated by Merv, being taken aback at this apparent discontinuity, saying "How did that get into the conversation?" To which, Virginia replied, "I don't know."

Although some African-Americans would, understandably, consider all such references as evidence of racism, I do not think it makes cognitive sense to so interpret such talk. To do so is tantamount to considering all recognition of difference reflective of negative prejudice. Some negative associations may have become functionally autonomous (to resurrect an old psychological term), i.e., the original meaning is completely disconnected from current usage and therefore possess no prejudicial meaning. Whether these examples are racist may be arguable, but I believe the following subliteral illustrations from my family are not.

MY NUTTY BUDDY

When my daughter, Melyssa, was about four years old, my friend Aaron was playing with her in a very active and playful way, saying "foolish" things, as adults will do with children, picking her up and flinging her over his shoulder, and generally acting "crazy." At that point, with no other apparent reason or external stimulus transition, Melyssa asked "can I have a Nutty Buddy?" By this she meant a special ice cream bar that's chocolate, i.e., *brown* with *nuts* sprinkled on it.

The subliteral associations with Aaron were to (1) his actions represented by *nutty*, i.e., acting "crazy," (2) his being her friend i.e., *buddy* because he always talked and played with her, and (3) his color represented by chocolate, like the color of the ice cream bar. Thus Melyssa was subliterally saying that Aaron was her Nutty Buddy.

It would be stretching the meaning of the term to consider this illustration an example of racial prejudice. Not only had my daughter been attending a preschool where many of the students and her playmates were black, more importantly, she had known Aaron nearly since her birth, and Aaron was literally a part of the family.[11] If Aaron had been white and had big ears and if there had been an ice cream bar called Dumbo's Nutty Buddy, that is what she probably would have asked for. Although the illustration subliterally has racial content, it was not prejudicial but rather recognition of difference. A further example of recognizing racial difference without prejudice is the following.

WATS LINE

My former wife, Claudette, and I were talking with Aaron, and he was telling of his black friends around the country and of his telephoning them, especially his friends in California. In previous years, Claudette and I had lived in San Francisco and often talked about California. At that point my wife interjected, "Oh, you must use a WATS line" (the wide-area telecommunications service that charges less for phone calls). Thus, subliterally, by way of the spoken phonetic transformation of "WATS" and "Watts", what Aaron was seen to have had was a "Watts" line, i.e., a black telephone line, a subliteral reference to Watts, the well-known black community in California. Once again, there is a racial association and recognition of difference but no prejudice.

OLD BLACK JO(E)L

A final example of a racial association without prejudice. One evening, I was explaining to my former wife the racial meaning of a piece of subliteral conversation which had taken place in one of my T-groups that day. This was when I was first beginning to discover subliteral talk. She just looked at me and laughed half in disbelief. I was a little upset that she did not believe what I thought was a simple straightforward example of subliteral meaning.

I looked at her for a moment and said, "You ain't heard nothin' yet!" literally meaning that there was more to come. The subliteral association of the phrase was with one of my favorite old-time singers, Al Jolson. Al Jolson was famous for his singing in minstrels where he would charcoal his face imitating a black man (African-Americans were not allowed then to act in minstrels. White charcoaling their face to portray black people was called blackface). He is perhaps best known for his song about a black nursemaid, entitled, "Mammy," which he sang in the movie, *The Jazz Singer* (1927), the first major movie that had sound. During his stage performances, one of his favorite lines to the audience of fans was "You ain't heard nothin' yet, folks." Again, while my selection of this phrase is clearly a racial association, it's not racist.

In the previous subliteral illustrations, it's interesting, though not surprising, that African-Americans were more concerned with discrimination, whereas whites were more concerned with stereotypes of what blacks are like. It is interesting to note, too, that at least in the set of illustrations I have gathered from my small group laboratory (which is not a random sample), there is almost no physical violence or aggression expressed on the part of blacks or whites toward each other, except for the discussion of the death penalty. Why the particular examples reflected so little aggression is open to speculation. For subliteral references gathered from everyday conversations, the situation is not so clear as was seen in the "hanging" illustration.

CONCLUSION

All of these subliteral topics were transformations of basic concerns about racial differences and stereotypes, and each apparently different topic was a permutation or variation that revolved around the single complex of emotional concerns by both whites and African-Americans. With whites we saw numerous old stereotypes and images of African- Americans who don't "know their place," being (1) lynched, (2) having different blood, (3) being half-breeds, (4) being closer to nature like animals, (5) having lower I.Q. levels, (6) being inherently musical, (7) making whites feel uncomfortable, and (8) engaging more in criminal activities. With African-Americans, we saw (1) concerns about prejudice, (2) concerns about being in the minority, and (3) conflicts with identification in ethnically mixed conversations. We also saw the subliteral recognition of "difference" without prejudice.

We saw that these subliteral transformations were carried out by using various cognitive and linguistic operations. We saw (1) an increase in references to color, including (a) blackouts, (b) black eyes, (c) chocolate ice cream, (d) vanilla flavoring, (e) brown bread versus white bread, or (f) not having any color at all; (2) the use of names of things or people to communicate specific concerns or issues subliterally, like (a) the tobacco, *Half and Half* to reference someone who was considered to be of mixed racial heritage, (b) black dogs, (c) black holes, (d) the special phone line WATS, to refer subliterally to the black community Watts, California, and (e) the name of the Protestant theologian Martin Luther, to refer subliterally to the African-American civil rights leader, Martin Luther King, Jr. (1929–1968); (3) old stereotypes about mixed racial genetics with literal talk about (a) pure strains of dogs, (b) half-breeds, and (c) having strange blood; and (4) other negative attributions to African-Americans, like (a) hanging or lynching, (b) as a "buck" animal, (c) black welfare mothers, (d) with live-in boyfriends, and (e) slang that's perceived to have originated in the black community, like using the phrase "mother" with an intonation that implies the slang word, motherfucker; (5) the use of words that literally mean one thing to convey subliteral meaning as in (a) using the term retriever (see previous black Labrador retriever example) and its associations with slave behavior, which indicates a link to racial issues; (6) the use of subliterally paronymic words like *Georgia* and *gorgeous* to link racial meaning; (7) the shifting of nouns, pronouns, and tenses to transform literal topics to subliteral meaning; (8) the specific use of a kind of quasi-mathematical theory of "groups or sets," to communicate meaning subliterally (as in the "2 sets of cousins" illustration above); and (9) the use of specific numbers to indicate subliteral racial meaning.

And finally, once again, we saw that much can be unobtrusively learned about existing racial feelings, stereotypes, and issues by listening subliterally that might otherwise go unnoticed.

POSTSCRIPT

Many white people may find it hard to accept that such racial stereotypes are still operating today. To most older African-Americans, however, that these stereotypes are still operating is no surprise. Let me offer just a plain literal and personal story to support this. About 1992, my friend Aaron and I were traveling down to Key West in the Florida Keys. We were traveling in Aaron's big silver Mercedes Benz, which he was driving. We stopped to get some gas. The attendant came to my side of the car to ask how much gas we wanted. Then when he was through pumping the gas, he again came to my side to be paid. The most reasonable explanation for this unusual behavior was that he thought Aaron was my chauffeur. I guess he thought why would two middle-aged men in a Mercedes Benz, one black and one white, be traveling together, unless the black man was the the white man's chauffeur.

Related to this story, when we reached Key West, Aaron and I, being social psychologists, observed that people were looking at us. Again, this was because we were two middle-aged males, one black, one white. But more than this, knowing that Key West had a sizable gay population, we hypothesized that people assumed we were gay. Of course, Key West isn't all gay. Again, like the gas station attendant who must have thought that the only reason two middle-aged men, one black and one While would be traveling together was if one was the other's chauffeur, so too, many people in Key West probably thought why would two middle-aged men, one black and one white be traveling to Key West unless they were gay.

We decided to test our hypothesis. We asked a couple of waitresses point blank if they thought we were gay. Their immediate replies were "Yes, of course." We explained that we were social psychologists and were professionally curious. In fact, we couldn't convince them otherwise (As for their believing that we were social psychologists, it was analogous to patients in a mental ward saying that they are psychiatrists). Indeed, on the way down to Key West, a motel clerk asked us—somewhat shyly, with his head and eyes looking down at the counter—if we wanted a room *with one bed or two*.[12] What more can I say about racial stereotypes.

CHAPTER 10

SEX, GENDER, AND THE SUBLITERAL MIND
DOMINANCE, STEREOTYPE, AND SEDUCTION

It's no secret that one of the most enduring human concerns in interpersonal relationships revolves around sexual tensions. These concerns are present whenever men and women are gathered together. We certainly didn't need Freud to tell us that where males and females are, there is sexual tension. Contrary to popular conception, at their base these concerns have less to do with things Freudian than they do with things Darwinian. As Charles Darwin clearly showed us, the role of sex is cardinal to our survival as a species. Although this is obvious enough now, I don't think we really understand the emotional depths to which these concerns are ever-present.

In most social situations strong taboos prohibit the direct expression of these sexual feelings. On top of these taboos are also constraints based on the intricate biological and social rules of the "mating game." Given these primal and social forces, it should come as no surprise that the unconscious feelings and attitudes about sex are some of the stronger forces that generate subliteral comments. Some of these sexual feelings are unconscious, some are not, some are simply hidden from view, some are realistic, and some are stereotypical. Listening subliterally, we can often tune in on these otherwise hidden sexual tensions, concerns, and perceptions. Just as in understanding the subliteral meaning of all stories in conversations, these stories about sex and gender can be valuable in recognizing underlying dynamics that might not otherwise be evident. Let me begin with some illustrations from TV news programs, talk shows, and commercials.

SLIPS OF THE MIND IN TV NEWS, TALK SHOWS, AND COMMERCIALS

News reporters generally try to be objective and not let their own personal views influence their reports. But being human, this is difficult, if not impossible. Listening subliterally may tell us what the reporter's or host's real views are.

COME CLEAN, MR. PRESIDENT

A simple, but no less poignant, example of a slip of the mind is the following from a CNN news program.[1] CNN's correspondent, Wolf Blitzer, was reviewing and reporting the latest news on President Clinton's alleged affair with the young White House intern, Monica Lewinsky, and a dress that she kept which has the President's semen stain on it. After talking about Clinton being charged with lying about the affair and Clinton having to give a sample of his DNA to compare with the stain on the dress, he ended by saying the President should just *"come clean."* I don't believe that this is a simple pun on male ejaculate. On a conscious level, of course, Wolf's remark means that he thinks Clinton should stop lying about his affair. But on a subliteral level, it probably reveals either that Wolf (1) hoped that Clinton's DNA doesn't match the stain or (2) that Clinton should not be *staining* dresses with his semen, i.e., he should "come clean."

Because this is an everyday example, I don't have the history, full context, and other controls that I do for examples generated in my T-groups. So how are we to know for sure that Wolf's comment wasn't just a simple pun, and if it wasn't, how are we to know what Wolf's view of the Clinton affair really is? Under the circumstances, we would have to follow Wolf's reports to accumulate an ongoing history and context. This would provide additional information by which we could begin to verify the analysis of Wolf's slip of the mind.

TAKE A LOAD OFF, DOLLY

Watching TV talk shows can also reveal subliteral meaning. Most talk shows are, after all, relatively unscripted social conversations. Subliteral meaning can also be seen in commercials. Indeed, it's no secret that advertisers consciously use symbolism—Freudian and otherwise—in their ads. A great deal has been written on symbolism and the use of puns in advertising. Although most of the following TV commercials may seem fraught with "Freudian symbolism," I am more concerned with the way those who create the ads "subliterally" communicate meanings to your unconscious mind.

Years ago on the late night Johnny Carson show, he was welcoming a well-known female Country Western singer. As she walked toward Johnny, it was obvious that she had extremely large breasts. Johnny seriously welcomed her saying, *"Sit down and take a load off your feet."* He had no more than gotten the words out of his mouth, when he apparently realized what he had "really," i.e., unconsciously, said: *Those huge breasts must be heavy to carry around. You had better sit down and relieve yourself of that* load! You could see Johnny's face turn red. He fumbled around trying to cover it up, but to no avail.

This example illustrates the process of an unconscious meaning slipping into the conscious mind. When he recognized what he had really said, Johnny blew the scene by socially revealing to his guest his unconscious meaning. His guest was the Country Western singer, Dolly Parton. This example also illustrates what is perhaps a rather common perception by males of big breasted women, that they need to relieve themselves of their burden. For a similar example using a similar phrase, see the illustration "Unconscious Seduction" later.

HURRICANE BABE

On the *Good Morning America* show one day,[2] an anthropologist was explaining to Sandy Hill, the attractive co-host of the show at that time and to the handsome John Lindsay, ex-mayor of New York City and a roving high-society "socialite," about a primitive tribe where the people seldom engaged in sexual intercourse. Both thought that this was quite hilarious and proceeded to engage in uneasy, giggly, and coy verbal banter. The sexual tension brought about by the topic was clear. Then, John Coleman came on with the weather and uncharacteristically began his report by saying "Can you see John and Sandy in this satellite photo? No, you can't of course," he said, adding, "but you can see Hurricane Babe."

It's likely that Coleman had obviously been fantasizing some hanky-panky between John Lindsay and Sandy Hill. Now, Sandy, without batting an eyelash, had held her own in the sexual innuendo-like banter with John Lindsay. Like the eye of a hurricane, Sandy had publically weathered the potentially embarrassing sexual storm. Coleman's primitive visualization of sex between John and Sandy was verbally projected, as onto a Rorschach ink blot card, onto a photo produced by a technologically advanced society. In fact, Coleman himself was electronically hooked into the studio by satellite. Subliterally, the socialite John Lindsay is associatively linked with Coleman's introduction by mentioning the satellite (equivalent to socialite) connection. The hurricane represents John and Sandy's stormy banter. Indeed in his mind's imaginative eye, John Coleman had seen, via satellite, sex with a hurricane babe!

THE BEST WRAP AROUND

The people who design and carefully construct advertisements know that meanings get wrapped around our psyches in various ways, some obvious and some not so obvious. When the Reynolds Company introduced a new product for wrapping food to keep it fresh (the product is now well known as Reynolds Wrap), they ended their ad by simply saying, "Reynolds Wrap, The Best Wrap Around." When I heard this phrase, I first heard what the Reynolds ad designers wanted me to hear, namely, that "The Reynolds product was the best on the market." But it wasn't that simple. The ad generated at least two other levels of subliteral meaning.

The first is based on sound symbolism, or a kind of pun-meaning. This meaning tells the listener that the talk they are listening to is the best. That is to say, the words they are listening to constitute the best (w)*rap* around, that it's truthful. The connection here, of course, is to the double meaning of the word *rap*, (1) to have a conversation and (2) a popular musical form characterized by spoken, rhyming lyrics. The ad's last meaning I believe was intended to be a sexual association. That is, the phrase "wrap around," is semantically connected to a network of sexual associations. The nonconscious subliteral connection is to sexual embrace, to arms and/or legs being wrapped around as in sexual embrace. Indeed, Reynolds implied that this kind of sexual wraparound is the best wraparound. I am tempted to add my own commercial here, that subliteral talk, too, is the best (w)rap around.

If all of this talk of subliteral sexual content to ads sounds far fetched, the history of advertising clearly shows that since the early 1950s it has been heavily Freudian, and advertising agencies have used their understanding of psychoanalytic symbolism. In addition, the field has extensively used their understanding and adaptation of associative psychology, where ideas and images are connected to each other by association. Their belief is that using unconscious symbolism will function like a subliminal message or like a posthypnotic suggestion for viewers to buy their product. Such sexual ad talk can become even more bizarre. With this said, now let's look at what I consider a blatant example of subliteral sexual communication in a TV ad.

TICKLE ME FRENCH

The following ad ran a number of years ago. As I explain the ad, it may seem terribly obvious, but people only half watch these ads, thus often consciously missing the "subliteral" meanings. I checked with a number of my friends at the time the ad ran, and they seemed genuinely surprised at my analysis.

The ad was for a new roll-on deodorant for women called *Tickle*. This ad employed visual subliteral meaning instead of language. The container—like so many women's cosmetic containers—was an "obvious" phallic symbol with a huge ball-like head. A white female with an ever so slight French accent says that "This is like no other one. It has a bigger ball than most." Then she touches the head with the tip of her finger very hesitantly, withdrawing it rapidly as she giggles. The next scene shows a white woman slowly sliding on a turtlenecked sweater. The final scene shows an African-American female on a baseball field, throwing a ball into her baseball glove. This collage of images is no accident, of course. Every detail of an ad is consciously designed.

The container is not only made to resemble a male penis but is made to look like what is called a "French tickler," i.e., a male prophylactic device, a "safe." Some "French ticklers" have minute protrusions along the shaft to stimulate the woman during intercourse. Hence, the French accent and the product's name *Tickle*. What is more, saying it has a big "ball" is subliterally connected with an associative meaning for sexual intercourse, as in "to ball" someone. In standard Freudian symbolism, a baldheaded male signifies sexual potency (e.g., Yul Brynner), presumably because he's a walking erect phallic symbol.

The forbidden fruit of touching the male penis is symbolized by the woman touching the container's head quickly and "withdrawing" her finger giggling. Still more, the male penis has been popularly symbolized as a worm. There is even a joke about the male penis being a worm with a turtlenecked sweater on. Thus, the scene showing the women slowly and slinkily sliding a turtlenecked sweater over "her" head is subliterally connected by association with the imagery of the foreskin of the penis being pulled back from the head.

In the final scene, the black female in the base"ball" field (equivalent to "ball" and "feel") throws a white baseball into a "colored" glove. Subliterally the baseball is the white male penis going into an African-American vagina, i.e., a white male having a ball, or "balling," a black female.

Subliterally tying the ad altogether in an associative matrix of similarity of sound and associative images, we have tickle-turtle-giggle; ball-bald, field-feel. Other more peripheral subliteral associations related to the baseball imagery are "scoring" equal to laying a female," i.e., winning her; the judgment of being "safe" at the plate; "sliding into" home base; a double "header," i.e., big-ball-game; sexual intercourse being the activity of going "in" and "out," i.e., inning (represents winning) of a game, you're "out"; of "mounting" and being at the "top of the inning;" and of course "strikes," i.e., sex being related to aggression. Thus, the ad is a masterpiece of symbolism and associative connections "subliterally"communicated around sexuality.

SEXUAL STEREOTYPES AND SEDUCTION DYNAMICS

Whenever men and women gather, one enduring concern is social and sexual dominance. The degree of dominance and influence in social situations depends on a number of factors. These include the kind of situation, the topic being discussed, the assigned roles, and the relative number of women and men present. Given the history of humankind, the primary, or at least the overt concern typically revolves around male dominance of and influence over women. Other deeply rooted stereotypes about gender and sexual preference also run deep.

But perhaps the deepest sexual drama is about seduction. Since the beginning of time, sexual seduction is one of the grand eternal archetypal dramas in human *affairs* (the pun *is* intended). Seductions can be obvious, or they can be subtle. They can be conscious or unconscious, and they can be carried out verbally or just with our body language. Finally, they can be real or simply in the mind of the beholder. In groups of mixed gender composition, sexual seduction and rivalry dramas are not uncommon. These dramas of sexual seduction and rivalry especially seem to go with power and authority. Followers often lust after a leader, and/or leaders lust after their followers.

OH, NOT ME

Freud not only recognized the role of sex in human affairs, he recognized the role of double meanings and pun-like processes for creating these meanings. Double meanings can express two different meanings while at the same time not altering the original meaning. In his book, *Jokes and Their Relation to the Unconscious,* Freud gives the example of asking a youthful patient whether he has ever masturbated. The patient answered, "O na, nie," i.e., "Oh, not me." This was a double meaning with the word *onamie,* which one of its German meanings translates to masturbate.[3] This is a kind of subliteral *use of oronymic* meaning (recall from chapter 7 the sentences: *The good can decay in many ways/The good candy came anyways).*

TWO VIRGINS

Sometimes sexual meanings are created by slips of the tongue that combine two different words or meanings as in a portmanteau. An example of this occurred in my office one day. My colleagues and I were engaged in a conversation about hard-core child pornography. One colleague said that she had recently seen a poster of two nude children who were about two years old. The discussion continued about the morality of using children as sexual objects. The question was raised as to why people need such things. There was a very brief pause, and a male colleague said, *"I guess people need diversions."* Now, the spoken word *"diversion"* came out with a slur, which sounded like *di-virgins*. Unconsciously, the two nude pornographic babies were represented by (di) equals *two* (versions) equals virgins—or two diapered virgins. What can I say? I don't make these up. I just analyze and report them.

THESE BOOTS ARE MADE FOR WALKIN'

A group was nearing the time when the required midterm paper was due. In the paper, they had to describe the interpersonal, communication, leadership, and group level dynamics they had learned and observed up to that point.

"Do all of you have your papers done," it was asked? There was much talk in separate discussions around this issue. Silence ensued. Then there was talk of writing the paper in "Your own personal terms instead of using the language in the instructor's textbook." A male who had been counterdependent throughout the sessions proclaimed that he didn't use the book at all. An attractive female sitting beside me defended my book and said that she used it a great deal in writing her paper. Then, the dominant and counterdependent male went around the group asking how much each used the book and he assigned a grade accordingly. If a person didn't use my book, he gave that person an "A." If the person used it a lot, he flunked the person. Then, the group briefly broke into separate conversations and someone was heard to say, "You have a dirty mind." Silence again. The attractive female said that the paper was "Not that hard to do." There was much laughter and subgrouping.

I was asked if anyone ever flunked the course. Another said to me, "I heard you don't give A's," to which there was much anxious laughter. Then, the attractive female reached over and put her hand on my shoulder. There

was a brief but very heavy pause. Then, the counterdependent male jokingly exclaimed, "I heard you're a lecherous old man." Then, a member
said to the male, "Oh, you're not going to get an A." The male responded
that he didn't want anyone to give him anything. "That's why," he said, "I
don't live with my mother and father, and my brother who is an ass." He said
he lived with a girl and another guy. A member said, "Ho, ho! I've heard
about that kind of thing?" Again, much laughter. "That's from the new
school, that's the new in thing," it was said. Silence.

Then, talk ensued of getting drunk over the weekend. The dominant
male said that it took him forty-five minutes Saturday night "to figure out
that the dance floor at Creek Side was flooded." The older female said that
it could be dangerous with the "Musical instruments plugged in," that "you
could get electrocuted in bare feet." The dominant male said that Creek
Side was a "meat market," i.e., for "pickups. No one belongs in a place like
that." The dominant male, who was a bartender, then said, "You can come
to my bar. I don't throw people out. I let them do what they want."

Then, the conversation changed to how to pick up women. The dominant male said he "Used the indirect method." "How does that approach
work," it was asked. He went on to say that girls want a "free ride. At the Jail
House" [bar] he continued, "I went over to some girls and said some guys
wanted to talk to them, and in the course of conversation I said that they
were not acting like the rest." He made a point of saying that he was sitting
in one of the high-backed chairs in the bar. In response to the term "pick-
up," the older woman asked what happened to "dating." It was said that dating is "out" now. It was suggested that she go down to "3rd Street" (the
prostitution area) and observe what goes on there. The dominant male
talked of impressionable girls who come into his bar saying "When young
girls come into the bar, that child's mind is impressionable." He went on to
explain that his motives were "pure." However, he said if he were really
"horny" (i.e., sexually aroused) he would say so.

Again the group broke into separate conversations. Then, the male
suggested that they all meet at his bar over the weekend. He said that the
older female could bring her husband and that a cute girl would be provided for him to pinch. There was a discussion about what if they said inappropriate things or what if they got "drunk" and then had to come back into
the group on the next day. One member said that he might get drunk and
"pee all over the floor," for example. Silence. In an attempt to return to the
here-and-now group situation, the older female said that she titled her paper "To be or not to be." Some discussion of this title ensued. More sub-

grouping ensued and someone was heard saying to another member, "You're the seductive type."

Then a male who had been silent during the whole session said, "On Wednesday we can explore what we did today. Did anyone read how laughter reduces tension." The dominant male member said that "Laughter forms a barrier. It kind of says "don't touch me." Silence. Then in a rambling tone he said, "My goal was 10 pages typed . . . What is your immediate goal?" Then, he noted, "We are all sitting on the edge of our seats ready to go. What's the reason for this?" No answer. Silence. Then, he looked at his boots and said, "These boots have been over the mountains to San Diego. They've thrust the hills with a 45-pound pack on my back." End of session.

This conversation demonstrates sexual rivalry and competition dynamics which are integrally intertwined. Some of these dynamics are relatively obvious, but others require a subliteral analysis to recognize their meaning. The overt sexual dynamics for the entire session were precipitated at the very beginning of the session by the attractive female (1) sitting next to me, (2) defending my book to the counterdependent male, and (3) most of all by placing her hand on my shoulder. That the male was overtly competing with me was clearly reflected (1) by his saying he didn't read my book, (2) by his assigning grades to members based on how much they relied on my book to write their papers, and (3) by jokingly referring to me as a lecherous old man. Other sexual and competition dynamics were more covert or unconscious.

Semantically, it's interesting that the male used the phrase "don't touch me," in describing laughter as a defensive barrier to really communicating. I suspect this phrase is connected to the young attractive female who had reached over and put her hand on my shoulder. Additionally, the male's phrase, "thrust the hills," also has obvious sexual connotations. It's clearly an odd choice of words, at best. Such lexical selections should alert us to ask, out of all the possible choices of words, why was this particular word chosen? Given the context of the conversation, to answer that it was coincidental or that it "just happened" doesn't explain anything.

The counterdependent male noting that "I don't live with my mother, father, and my brother who's an ass," subliterally means mother represents the older female in the group, father represents me, and brother is the younger male. That myself and the older woman are represented as father and mother figures is perhaps obvious because of our age differential. But what supports that the younger male is represented as his brother who is an ass? The answer is that he thought the younger male who told him he would not get an "A" after calling me a lecherous old man was an ass for being so obsequious. The counterdependent male saying that "He lived with a girl and another guy," subliterally means the young female and myself. Thus, the 3 of us constituted the sexual and leadership triangle in the group. This triangle is also subliterally referenced in the numerical statement about the prostitution area on "3rd Street," i.e., the older woman, the young female, and myself.

At this point the older female unconsciously recognized what was going on sexually by the competitive male's remark that "It took him forty-five minutes Saturday night to figure out that the dance floor at Creek Side was flooded." This is indicated by her saying that "It could be dangerous with the musical instruments plugged in, you could get electrocuted in bare feet." Her apparently literal statement subliterally warns the male that his sexual competition could be dangerous.

Now, being somewhat older than the others in the group and because he was a bartender, it was clear that he understood the role of status and power in sexual attraction and thought that this was what was going on with the young attractive female in relation to me. This was indicated by his statement, "When young girls come into the bar, that child's mind is impressionable," represents the young female who he thought was sexually enamored by my status and power and was thus impressionable. This is indicated by the plural shift from "young girls" in the beginning of the sentence to the singular "that child's" mind is impressionable.

To say that the older male was simply counterdependent, however, is somewhat of an oversimplification. Human motivation is seldom one-dimensional. On a literal or conscious level, he was counterdependent, but on a subliteral or unconscious level he simultaneously disidentified and identified with me in my role as leader which he was trying to usurp. This is indicated by his statement to the group that "You can come to my bar. I don't throw people out. I let them do what they want." This was a subliteral reference to the literal discussion of grades and flunking the course and my having outlined on the board the dynamics of the group up to that point and suggesting what the group might do to change their behavior. In other words, he wouldn't flunk anyone, or tell anyone what to do like I supposedly did. Further in the discussion about picking up women in bars, he said he, used the "indirect method." The question is, why did he use this particular phraseology? The answer is that in both of my comments in the group and in my textbook I discussed T-group leadership as nondirective. The phrase nondirective is often translated in members' minds as also being indirect leadership. Thus, the phrase is a link to the here-and-now group.

That my analysis of subliteral meaning is likely correct is indicated by the number that was mentioned in the conversation. The dominant male's comment that it took him "45 minutes Saturday night . . . ." represents the 4 males and the 5 young females in the group. Although there were seven females in the group, the older female and the younger female are not included in the reference to "forty-five." The older female is not counted because (1) she is not a sexual object for the young macho male and (2) she has already been counted in the triangle. The younger female is not included in this number is because (1) she is also slightly older than the rest of the young females and (2) because she, too, is part of the triangle. Thus the 5 younger females constitute a group of their own, just as the males do, hence "forty-five."

Other numbers that were mentioned also have subliteral meanings that support the subliteral topical and linguistic analysis of this conversation. The dominant male's statement regarding the term paper that "My goal was 10 pages typed, what is your immediate goal?" represents the 11 members in the group, minus himself which adds up to 10. He psychologically excludes himself because he has already referenced himself with "My goal . . ." There's still more to this subliteral story.

Just as the session was about to end and members were beginning to leave, apparently out of nowhere and looking at his military type boots, the male said, "These boots have been over the mountains to San Diego. They've thrust the hills with a 45-pound pack on my back." The reference to the "pack on my back," means he thinks that by his voluminous talking and leadership that he has been carrying the group on his back.

The resounding crescendo of his parting words is his statement that, "These boots have been over the mountains to San Diego," is a final subliteral sexual reference to the young female. In general terms his (military type) boots having been over the mountains to San Diego is a reference to his fantasy about the young female's body. In addition, I might note that if this sounds like I'm stretching the analysis beyond all reasonableness and reading too much between the lines, it needs to be asked why he selected San Diego as the city, and why he selected the military imagery of a back pack and called attention to his military boots? The answer is that in an earlier session the young female had informed the group that she was married and that her husband was in the military. Moreover, she said that he was being transferred to Corpus Christi, Texas, but that she would like to go to San Diego.

WOMEN UNDER THE INFLUENCE

In this conversation from one of my T-groups, the group had only two male members other than myself. One of the males had been quite verbally dominant throughout the sessions. Although the female majority of the group was wholly disgruntled with me for not providing structure, it was respectful (i.e., retained a dependency relation to me, the authority). Thus, the group members were not satisfied with their progress, and the dissatisfaction increased upon returning from a vacation.

As a consequence, the group members were not working as a unit and couldn't seem to return to the level of functioning that they had achieved before the vacation break. They felt badly about that and were always obliquely apologizing to me. At this point, the essential here-and-now concerns of the group were (1) the group had died over the vacation, (2) an artificial attempt was being made to bring it back to life, (3) ambivalence about the manipulation to revive it, and (4) the continuing concern about dominance and control.

There was talk about "it's like what we had has come apart," or "the group has died," and "coming back to life after vacation is difficult," and "it's like beginning all over again." Then after a flurry of topics, the group settled upon discussing a movie entitled, "Women Under the Influence." The next topic was about the movie, "Dr. Frankenstein." Discussing the movie, "Dr. Frankenstein," a number of specific subliteral references are revealed about the feelings in the group, especially the women. The basic subliteral structure was: Dr. Frankenstein represents me. The monster is the group.

Talk of "Bringing the monster back to life," means *the group,* That it "is a difficult task even for Dr. Frankenstein" means *it's a difficult task even for me.* In talking about Dr. Frankenstein, it was also said that "scientists must have patience," *a double reference.* First, I (represented by Dr. Frankenstein) must have not only "patience" but (like a Dr.) have *patients.* In addition, for Dr. Frankenstein (representing me) to construct the monster (means the group), he must have used a lot of bodies (means patients , i.e., members). Also, like the monster, there was talk about the group having to be "shocked" to bring it to life. Finally, the dominant male member" is *Igor,* Dr. Frankenstein's (i.e., my) helper. Subliterally, the monster like the group is made up of human parts, meaning *group members.* The monster, of course, being brought back to life means "it's like beginning all over again" in the group. The group and the monster are also like movies, i.e., they were all constructed, i.e., are unnatural, artificial. The themes of unnatural and artificial are a frequent perception about T-group functioning.

After I had advanced the general interpretation that the group was the "monster" and that I was Dr. Frankenstein, a couple of members immediately, but jokingly, referred to the dominant male member as *"Igor."* This demonstrates that subliteral meaning is often not far from consciousness.

The subliteral meaning of the movie, "Woman Under the Influence" represents *the women in the group being dominated by the males.* At first glance, it may appear that the two movies subliterally dealt with separate issues, the *Woman Under the Influence* movie subliterally discussing gender issues and the Dr. Frankenstein movie subliterally addressing other issues in the group. But because these two movies were mentioned together, they were psychologically connected. Just as *Women Under the Influence* dealt with the group issue of the two males who were perceived as dominating the largely female group, so too, the Dr. Frankenstein movie, also dealt with domination and gender. Dr. Frankenstein (means me) and his assistant, Igor (means the other dominant male) dominated nature (means the females), and in effect, the people in the town (means the rest of the group) where Dr. Frankenstein carried out his experiments. Thus, both movies were about the domination of the females in the group.[4]

VICARIOUS SEX

The following illustration is from a single parents group that was conducted and subliterally analyzed by a colleague.[5] A female member of the group was the mother of a 17-year-old daughter, who was her only child. She was a devout Roman Catholic. Her husband had been dead for over a year, and during the last several years of her marriage she did not engage in sexual intercourse with her husband. Nor had she had sex since her husband's death. Her daughter had been recently dating a boy quite steadily and seriously. Throughout the sessions, she expressed constant worry about her daughter having intercourse with her boyfriend and becoming pregnant. She repeatedly said that she couldn't trust her daughter, even though she was very trustworthy in all other respects. She feared that her daughter would violate her deeply held religious values with respect to not engaging in sex until after marriage.

The counselor suggested to her that "Sometimes a parent without a partner becomes jealous of a child (daughter) who she thinks is, or may be, getting what she isn't." The sexual connotation of this comment became obvious and the counselor mentioned the implication. Her response was: "I think . . . guess? . . . you're right." Then, she switched the topic, as time was running out for the session. Just before the group got up to leave, however, she said: "You know . . . (her daughter's boyfriend's name) . . . belongs to a club called the 'Explorers' (suggesting that he wasn't a delinquent) but," she emphasized, "he is cocky." The session ended.

The woman had directly revealed her emotional issues around separation and loss. First the loss of her husband and now the psychological loss of her adult daughter to a man. She had also directly revealed her sexual frustration and tentatively admitted a jealousy that her daughter might be enjoying what had been missing in her life, not only for the sixteen months following her husband's death, but also for the last several years of her marriage—sex.

A subliteral analysis of her last statement about her daughter's boyfriend belonging to a club called the "Explorers" and the further emphasis that "he is cocky," can be seen as subliterally supporting her tentative agreement with the counselor's interpretation that she was perhaps unconsciously feeling jealous of her daughter who may be having a sexual relationship.

Phonetically, the term *Explorers* can be parsed into *"explore her,"* and the reference to *cocky* (given the context) subliterally likely means *cock* in the vernacular, referring to a male's penis. Thus, the mother feared that the penis of her daughter's boyfriend would *explore her* daughter, an event which would simultaneously violate her conscious religious values while unconsciously desiring a sexual relationship herself.

UNCONSCIOUS SEDUCTION

In response to changing my seat at the start of the last session, explaining as I did so that a group leader should always be able to see each member clearly, at the start of the next session an attractive young female member sat in the seat directly across from me. With a nervous laugh she said, "we can really look into each other's eyes now." There followed a heavy silence. In an apparently unrelated vein, a slightly older female member sitting next to the younger female said to the group, "I have a problem that I would like your opinion on." She told of going with a married man who was separated from his wife and "the other night she (his wife) was peeking in through this window" at them. At this point I took off my jacket and placed it on the back of my chair. Almost immediately, the older female member who told of going with the married man, took off her pullover sweater, sharply exposing as she did so the outline of her rather large breasts against her tight jersey shirt. Then, a male member said that he thought she ought to talk about it "and get it off her chest."

Throughout the group sessions, the two female members had exhibited a great deal of grooming and primping behavior (called "preening" by those who study animal behavior). Such behavior in social situations is considered sexual in connotation by many psychologists and anthropologists— a flirting invitation. Throughout the previous sessions, she had made eye contact with me more than other group members. In addition, the two dominant males had been vying almost openly for leadership of the group (which consisted of 8 females and 5 males). What this conversation means may already be obvious. Seduction is at work here.

The young female's statement to me that "we can really look into each other's eyes now," means either a romantic feeling or fantasy on the part of the younger female member involving me or feelings she believed that I may have toward her. The discussion that followed immediately by the older woman about her "going with a married man" represents her feelings toward the other female's previous remark to me of "looking into each other's eyes." It suggests a rivalry for my sexual attention. Removing my jacket can be suggestive of seductively undressing.[6] The older female then taking off her sweater is a reciprocal seductive response in this sexual drama.

Just as in the story she related about the eternal triangle of husband/wife/lover, so too, in the group I, the young female, and the older female are the sexual triangle. The older woman's response put the younger female (representing my wife) and me (representing her husband) on notice that she too (as the third part of the triangle) was in on the competition. The remark, "get it off your chest" by the male subliterally indicated the male noticing the female's breasts when she seductively removed her sweater. The "peeking in the window" represents the older female observing the ostensible relationship between the myself and the younger female, just as the wife was peeking in at the husband (represents me) and herself (means subliterally transformed, the younger female). The remark of "peeking in" was stimulated by the younger females remark to me of "looking into each others eyes." The dynamics which this subliteral interpretation reveal are (1) the rivalry between two female members toward the leader and (2) the male's sexual feeling about the female members.

This conversation also illustrates the shaping of topic and word selection by physical happenings in a conversation (see Appendix, 5. Parallel Psychomotor Operations). For example, the remark, "get it off your chest" was precipitated by the older woman physically taking off her sweater. In terms of imagery reflecting physical action, the remark by the older woman about the wife who was "peeking in through this window" was precipitated by (1) my remark at the previous session about sitting so I could see all members clearly and (2) the younger female's opening remark to me of "looking into each other's eyes now." Finally, in terms of validating procedures, the remark about "peeking in through *this* window" is significant. The adjective *"this"* which is used to refer to a person or thing which is present, was used instead of the appropriate indefinite article *"a,"* i.e., instead of saying peeking in through *a* window, *the* window, or *that* window. This temporal shift psychologically links the literal topic to the here-and-now situation (see Appendix, 6.5. Temporal Shift Operations).

GAY SEXUAL STEREOTYPE

Just as in our perceptions of ethnic and racial relations, we still harbor stereotypes and other feelings about a person's sexual preference. Let me begin with a subliteral conversation that involves a subliteral perception *of the person listening* and the person doing the talking.

PLAYING IT STRAIGHT

Recently, a woman I know was in a store that she frequents and was waiting to pay for her purchase. In front of her was a man wearing a T-shirt that had "Secret Service" embossed on it. He was inquiring about a product. The woman knew the store clerk who is gay. Though the clerk's demeanor is not the typical stereotype of a gay male who acts extremely effeminate, his behavior could be seen as such, and thus it wouldn't be unreasonable for someone to suspect that he might be gay, especially by a macho male. The clerk had just finished a long and rather dramatic explanation of a product to some other customers. Then, it was the man's turn. As the clerk was answering the man's question about the product he was inquiring about, the man said to the clerk, "Be straight with me, now, is this a good product," by which the man literally meant, don't just give me a sales pitch to sell the product, is it really good? The woman observing all this said the clerk did a clear double-take on the man asking him to be "straight" with him. Three common meanings of the word straight, of course, are (1) to be socially conventional or normal, (2) to be honest, and (3) to differentiate someone who is heterosexual from someone who is homosexual. The gay clerk certainly consciously understood this meaning. The question is, was this a subliteral statement reflecting that the man unconsciously recognized that the clerk was gay?

Not having more information, I can't absolutely assess that the statement was in fact subliteral. However, given (1) that the instance occurred in a small and rather provincial town, (2) in a state where there had recently been a referendum on gay rights legislation, and (3) in a town where there had been beatings of gay men, it seems reasonable to assume that the word straight was selected was no accident. Judging from the clerk's double-take, it certainly didn't seem to be an accident to him. The clerk's unconscious tuned in on the possible subliteral meaning, which became conscious.

Then, there is the matter of the man's T-shirt which was embossed with "Secret Service." After the man's statement, the clerk asked the man if he was in the Secret Service. The man said "No," he wasn't. Why would the clerk ask the man if he was a Secret Service agent? Perhaps the clerk's subliteral mind picking up on the word straight was in part based on the man's T-shirt. Although it's no longer illegal in most states to engage in homosexual activity, it is still illegal in some states to engage in anal sex (called sodomy). Perhaps the clerk was reacting to this illegal association on some unconscious level.

Finally, the noun "service" is also used by both gay and heterosexual males to refer to providing sexual activity to another, as in servicing someone. In fact, in most dictionaries this is one of its meanings (but it's usually defined as having sex with a female). If the illegal aspects of my analysis of term *servicing* seem farfetched, consider that in the area where this subliteral example occurred, every so often there is a news item that the police are cracking down on an interstate highway "service" area where gay men meet to have sex, i.e., to *service* each other (I don't recall similar news items about heterosexual gathering places, like lover's lanes).

UNRESPONSIVE

Yet another example. A group was in progress and a female member, who was being trained to work in counseling groups at her workplace, asked me, "Were you absent last time on purpose to see what our response would be?" I replied that, "No," I wasn't absent on purpose. I was just about to explain that typically I plan to be absent a couple of times during a semester, when the dominant male member sarcastically interjected saying, "Oh, come on, don't give us that." There followed a heavy silence because, typically, statements that appear to challenge a leader are both consciously and unconsciously felt by other members to be "dangerous." They fear that it may bring retaliation not only to the member who made the statement, but upon them as well.

Then, the female member began talking about the counseling group where she worked. She said she felt "so sorry for this one member. He is a homosexual and he announced it at the first meeting." She went on to say, "This made me wonder if he really felt comfortable with it," adding that in the counseling group there's a "male member who is always making remarks about this homosexual, but the fellow who is homosexual will not respond to them. He just sits there passively. I feel so sorry for him." Then, she explained that she didn't know whether to say something to the male who was making remarks about the homosexual or not, as she was "just beginning to establish a good relationship with him" (the person in her counseling group). Silence. Some small talk ensues, and the session ends.

In previous sessions, the dominant male member had frequently made derogatory and chiding remarks to me to which I didn't respond. Each time this occurred, the female member looked aghast at me, clearly expecting me to reply to his remarks. She had also mentioned in previous sessions that she felt that she and the dominant male member in the group were just beginning to establish a comfortable relationship.

The woman's reference to the gay male in her counseling group represents me, as, like him, I will not respond but just sit there passively. The "male member who was always making remarks about the homosexual" is the dominant male member who makes remarks about me. "The homosexual does not respond to them" means me who doesn't respond meaning "I just sit there passively." Therefore, her remark of "feeling so sorry" for this member means feeling sorry for me. Members frequently feel perplexed and sorry in such group situations where the trainer is nondirective and passive. (The British group analyst, Alfred Bion, once said, "that groups do not understand a leader who neither fights nor runs away.") That the gay male announced his role at the first meeting of her counseling group stands for my announcement at the first meeting that my role was not that of an active member. Her wondering whether the gay male was comfortable with his role means that she is wondering whether I am comfortable with my role, i.e., being addressed in such a manner by the male in the group.

The female member not knowing whether to say something to the male in her counseling group making the remarks about the gay male because she is "just beginning to establish a relationship with him" refers to the dominant male member in this group with whom she is just beginning to establish a good relationship. Recall that in a previous session she mentioned that she and the dominant male member were just beginning to establish a comfortable relationship. This episode demonstrates the dynamic of the female member's feelings toward (1) me in terms of a person and as a trainer and (2) the male member. It may also reflect some concern she has for another group member who could be construed as being gay. No one bothers him, but he did just sit there passively, too.

Once again, the particular language unconsciously selected linguistically signifies the topic's linkage to the here-and-now group. In the woman's statement about a male in her counseling group, who is always making remarks about a gay male, instead of saying "*the* homosexual," or "*a* homosexual," she used the pronoun "*this*" in referring to the gay male. Thus, she psycholinguistically shifted the reference to reflect subliterally a here-and-now meaning. Likewise, in the statement, "but the fellow who is homosexual will not respond to *them,*" which literally refers to the other male's comments, subliterally means that in my nondirective leadership style I do not respond to members, i.e., them (see Appendix, 6.5. Temporal Shift Operations; 6.6. Pronoun Shift Operations).

There is yet another level of subliteral meaning to this episode. During the group discussion previously mentioned, I didn't feel as though I had identified all aspects of the subliteral meaning connected to the gay male topic. Thus, I asked the woman to make an appointment to see me in my office. In response to my request that she reiterate the story she told about the gay male in her counseling group, she said that he did not return to the counseling group. She went on to day that "He's very intelligent." As a matter of fact, she said, "He's the most intelligent person in the group so I guess he wasn't getting anything out of the group." Interesting, during the session, just before meeting with me in my office, the woman had expressed that she "wasn't getting anything out of the group and that she felt like not coming to the group anymore."

Thus the gay male also represents this female member, i.e., being older than most of the members, she felt she was more "intelligent," in the sense of having more experience, and that like him she, too, felt like not attending the group any longer. Thus like him, she is different because she is older and more "intelligent," i.e., experienced. Further support that the gay male subliterally represents me is the woman's comment that "He's the most intelligent person in the group so I guess he wasn't getting anything out of the group." Contextually, groups often mention that professors are very intelligent. More specifically, groups often talk about their belief that because I have conducted these groups for years, that I probably don't learn anything new and that I am probably bored (neither of which is correct).

The literal topic about gays becomes a multilevel set of subliteral meanings and a window into the deeply-rooted stereotypes in our culture. The stereotypes here are that gays are (1) effeminate, (2) passive, (3) emotionally "female," (4) deviant, and (5) highly intelligent. Just as with racial and ethnic stereotypes (see chapter 9), these deeply rooted emotional beliefs become generalized to other situations that are perceived as similar.

CONCLUSION

All of these subliteral topics were transformations of basic concerns about sexuality, including domination, competition, stereotypes, sexual preference, physical touching, disrobing, and about genitalia. Each different topic was a permutation or variation revolving around a single complex of emotional concerns. We also saw that subliteral transformations were carried out by using various cognitive and linguistic operations. These included the use of (1) movie themes reflecting here-and-now meaning, (2) pun-like sounds, (3) the use of words that have multiple underlying meanings, (4) the physical events precipitating corresponding or subliteral topics and meanings, (5) the use of plural and pronoun shifts, and (6) oronymic use of words. *And once again,* we saw that much can be learned about particular unconscious feelings and thoughts and interpersonal relationships by listening subliterally.

CHAPTER 11

DREAMS AND DREAMING

THE SLEEPING SUBLITERAL MIND

In this chapter, I show how subliteral meaning is present in dreams. First, I reanalyze two dreams containing numbers that Freud presented in his book *The Interpretation of Dreams*. Then, I show how subliteral meaning is present in people's dreams about social and group situations. I approach this chapter with nearly the same angst as I approached chapter 5 on the subliteral meaning of numbers—and for some of the same reasons.

INTRODUCTION

There is no shortage of pop psychology books on the interpretation of dreams. In the Introduction, I expressed concern that my subliteral findings would be associated with pop psychology, where all manner of speculations and theories are put forth as psychological fact. This brings me to the second reason for my angst, the hoary problem of meaning, in this case, the meaning of dreams. Freud's book, *The Interpretation of Dreams,* notwithstanding—there is a continuing spate of pop psychology books on the meaning of dreams. As I have warned elsewhere,

> the study of dreams is an area of research that seems either to stimulate almost boundless, yet imaginative, theories regarding the meaning and function of dreaming; or conversely, it stimulates an equally boundless and irrational skepticism, denying any meaning or function to dreaming whatsoever. On one hand, there are those who believe certain dreams are evidence that they fly off to Jupiter and Mars in the middle of the night without physically leaving their beds, becoming kind of disembodied astronauts, as it were; and on the other hand, there are those who believe dreaming to be simply the result of the spontaneous and random firing of subcortical neurons, a kind of Fourth-of-July nocturnal fireworks of the mind.[1]

This quote shows the extreme split that exists in the study of dreams. On the one hand, there are those who attribute all manner of meaning to dreams, from dreams that tell us how we were feeling while we were in the womb, to those that apparently describe how we felt in a past—reincarnated—life. On the other hand, there are those who believe dreams have no meaning whatsoever. Then there are those, like myself, who think that the evidence suggests a middle of the road approach.

Again, I want to clearly separate the subliteral analysis of dreams about the group from the pop psychology of dreams. In chapter 7 on *The Sounds of Reason,* I addressed the issue of subliteral meaning based on pun-like sounds. The same arguments I made there can be applied to meaning in dreams. I will deal with this issue in more detail at the close of this chapter. In the meantime, let me say a few introductory words about the study of dreams.

In recent years the study of dreams has become a legitimate area of research, no longer confined to the psychoanalytic couch, with all manner of fast-and-loose interpretative meanings attributed to them. Dreams and the physiological process of dreaming are being studied in sleep laboratories where people are wired up to electronic equipment like electroencephalographs (EEG) which measure their brain waves while sleeping, and are awakened when they enter the dream state and asked to report what they are dreaming. Moreover, extensive research on physical and mental health issues are being related to dream content.[2] Notice that I used the phrase "dream *content,*" not dream interpretation or the meaning of dreams. This is an important distinction. Dream content analysis, in contrast to dream interpretation, has long been a recognized and legitimate area of research.[3]

The content analysis of dreams is simple. In reports of dreams, all items in the dream, for example, trees, cars, people, places, and other images, are identified and logged. There have been some interesting findings of the content differences in people's dreams based on their ethnicity, age, and gender, and along a number of other dimensions. For example, one of the long-term findings has been that the settings of female dreams tend to take place indoors, whereas the setting of the dreams of males tend to take place outdoors. Another long-term finding of the difference between male and female dreams has to do with the content of sex in dreams. When males dream of having sex, it's often with a female they don't know. Females, on the other hand, dream of having sex with a person they know. This is content analysis, not dream interpretation.

As with the subliteral analysis of group narratives, the analysis of dreams about the group is based on the five areas that I outlined in chapter 8 that involve (1) knowledge of group or social dynamics in general, e.g., (a) group level dynamics, and (b) leadership and authority dynamics;

(2) data about the specific group or conversational situation, e.g., (a) sub-grouping and coalition forming, (b) the composition of the group, (c) the stage of development achieved by the group, and (d) knowledge of the dynamics in past conversations; (3) knowledge from social psychological research, e.g., (a) expectations and beliefs that people have about social situations, (b) how they should function, (c) norms of acceptable social behavior, and (d) general knowledge about various tensions and conflicts in human relationships; (4) knowledge about demographics, the history, and stereotypes of specific groups of people including (a) race and ethnicity, (b) gender, (c) sexual preference, and (d) age; and (5) knowledge about individual members in the social situation, e.g., (a) what each has consciously said and done in past sessions, and (b) knowledge about thoughts and feeling that are not being expressed or that are unconscious.

As with subliteral narratives, this knowledge, along with knowledge of the subliteral cognitive operations, makes analyzing dreams about the group possible. As I show in a moment, the subliteral analysis of dreams is closer to content analysis than it is to dream interpretation. In analyzing dreams about group and social situations, I approached the reported dream just as I do a description of a group narrative. This description of the group, then, is mapped onto what's known about the dreamer and the actual here-and-now situation that the dream is about. In this sense, the analysis of dreams about the group is basically the same as analyzing observations and descriptions of the group presented so far. And the reason for paying attention to dreams about social situations is also the same: dreams can tell us what we and others are feeling and thinking unconsciously. Now, I begin by reanalyzing two dreams that Freud presented when he discussed numbers.

TWO FREUDIAN DREAMS REVISITED

Although selective portions of *The Interpretation of Dreams* continue in use with varying degrees of modification by clinicians and researchers, what Freud suggested regarding the psychodynamic and cognitive function of numbers in dreams has since been virtually ignored even in the dream interpretation literature. As I explained in chapter 5, even in the psychoanalytic literature, what little mention there is of numbers in dreams treats them as if they have either a fixed "symbolic" meaning similar to the cosmological and mythological view of numbers, as a simple dream mechanism of associating birth dates and the like, as sexual symbolism where, for example, the number "3" equates to male genitalia, or as simple puns, where the number "50" semantically equates with the word "filthy," i.e., fifty equals filthy.[4]

Despite his serious methodological shortcomings, Freud discovered that numbers in dreams function cognitively. His aim being principally therapeutic, however, he was not overly concerned with numbers as cognitive data but rather as symbolic meaning structures. Freud did not consider that numbers in dreams functioned at all like they do in the waking state, simply reflecting an accounting of objects. He says,

> When we take together these and some other examples which I shall give later [p. 448 ff.], we may safely say that the dream-work does not in fact carry out any calculations at all, whether correctly or incorrectly; it merely throws into the form of a calculation numbers which are present in the dream thoughts and can serve as allusions to matter that cannot be represented in any other way. In this respect the dream-work is treating numbers as a medium for the expression of its purpose in precisely the same way as it treats any other idea, including proper names and speeches that occur recognizably as verbal presentations.[5]

In fact he didn't think the mind functioned during dreaming like it does in the waking state. He was not correct, as we shall see. Despite his theoretical beliefs about how the mind worked during dreaming, we will see that his actual analysis shows that the use of numbers in dreams is similar to the way numbers are used in the waking state and in subliteral conversations.

Unfortunately, Freud discovered only a small number of examples, which perhaps is all the more to his credit for formulating any theory regarding the function of numbers in dreams. This paucity of cases limited his findings with regard to a method of analyzing and validating them and their scope in terms of meaning. My purpose in the analyses of the two following dreams presented by Freud is not to "reinterpret" the meaning of the dreams but to reanalyze them and to extend the meaning Freud gives to the numbers in the dreams to show how numbers function in the same subliteral way that I've demonstrated they function in waking subliteral conversations.

FREUD'S 3 FLORINS 65 KREUZERS DREAM

In the dream involving the monetary amount of 3 florins and 65 kreuzers, one of Freud's patients dreamed that she was about to pay a bill.[6] The patient's daughter in the dream took 3 florins and 65 kreuzers from her (mother's) purse and the dreamer asked her daughter what she was doing becauuse it cost only 21 kreuzers.[7] Without going into a lengthy explanation of the background material, according to Freud the "3 florins and 65 kreuzers" combine to make 365 days—or one year—the amount of time that the patient had been asked by the headmistress of her daughter's school if she would like her daughter to stay. The "3 florins" also means the end of her daughter's school year in three weeks. In addition, the "3 florins" also represents the dreamer's own treatment that was ending in three weeks. The "21 kreuzers" is interpreted as another reference to the three weeks, i.e., 21 days. According to Freud, the numbers were expressed in terms of money because both her daughter's school fees and their treatment fees were of primary concern to her.

Freud's analysis of numbers in this dream was in principle, brilliant. I say "in principle" because, though he recognized the cognitive function of these numbers, his analysis of their meaning was not based on a systematic method. Thus, he "interpreted" their meaning. Nevertheless, his interpretation was likely correct. Why do I think it likely that he was correct? I think he was correct because, as I explained in chapter 5, numbers are much more concrete than words and can be mapped more reliably onto situations to which they correspond. At the very least, his interpretation of the numbers is very persuasive.

My research on the cognitive function of numbers suggests an analysis of Freud's interpretation based on the function of numbers that I've observed in subliteral narratives.[8] I suggest that the numbers are subliteral representations of the people involved in the dream imagery, just as numbers subliterally represent the composition of the people in a social conversation. Thus to show that the numbers in the dream have subliteral meaning does not require dream interpretation to analyze them, though certainly Freud's interpretation can be another level of the meaning of numbers. Now, let me reexamine the two dreams presented by Freud.

As in waking conversations, let's see what the composition or membership of the "conversation" in the dream was. The first "subgroup" of people in the dream content is (1) the patient, (2) the daughter, and (3) the headmistress. Second, there was the subgroup of (1) the patient, (2) the daughter, and (3) Freud. The "3 florins" subliterally represents (1) the patient, (2) the daughter, and (3) the headmistress. The "21 kreuzers" structurally differentiates the representation of (1) the patient, (2) the daughter, and (3) Freud (because he is indirectly involved in the concern of the dream about money), that is, the "21" kreuzers structurally differentiates the female/male subsets of this second subgroup. The "2" (of the 21) represents the two females, and the "1" (of the 21) represents the male, Freud. The "3 florins" (representing 3 females) is contextually associated in the manifest content with "female" because they were taken from a purse, whereas the 21 kreuzers were not. They were simply mentioned as the correct amount of the cost of the daughter's schooling. Then, the "21 kreuzers" was neither simply a repeat of the number 3, nor a simple association but was a further constructive cognitive process.

Recall we saw this exact structural use of the number "21" in chapter 5 in the topic of being "under 21" years of age, in which the "2" in the "21" represented two males and the "1" equaled the one older female. We also saw the same kind of structural differentiation in the topic about "3 of the 10 People" who came into a bar, where the "3" represented the three leaders in the group and the "10" represented the ten other members. As for the reference to "65" kreuzers, the "6" represents the two subgroups of three each, equal to a total of 6 people. The "5" is probably a recognition of a further differentiation of the total of the two subgroups, by subtracting either Freud or the headmistress (or it may translate into a total of 11, which, in any event, adds to the same thing). Admittedly this last "interpretation" of the number "5" is problematic. At this stage of knowledge about exactly how the subliteral mind works, there is much more to be discovered.

FREUD'S 1 FLORIN, 50 KREUZERS DREAM

The dream involving the monetary amount of 1 florin 50 kreuzers[9] can be analyzed subliterally similar to the previous dream: A woman, Elsie L., who was almost the same age as the dreamer, had just become engaged. The dreamer said that

> "she was at the theatre with her husband. One side of the theater stalls was completely empty. Her husband told her that Elsie L. and her fiancé had wanted to go too, but had only been able to get bad seats—three for 1 florin 50 kreuzers— and of course they could not take those . . . ."

As an immediate and obvious stimulus for these numbers, Freud points out that on the previous day the dreamer's sister-in-law had been given a present by her husband of 150 florins. By way of a series of tenuous associations and an equally tenuous reconstruction of the dream thoughts, Freud suggests that 150 florins is a hundred times as much as 1 florin 50 kreuzers, which Freud then says is evidence that she must have said to herself (i.e., reconstructed dream thoughts) that she could have had a husband who was a hundred times better if she (the dreamer) had waited. By way of fiat, Freud tells us that the "three" florins equals the three-month difference between the age of the dreamer and her friend, Elsie L.

Now the tenuousness of the associated dream material and the lack of more detailed information notwithstanding, a subliteral approach to these numbers is as follows. First the "1" of the "1 side of the stalls" and the "1" of the "1 florin" probably structurally represent the identification aspects of the dreamer with her friend of whom she is jealous. The "3 seats" subliterally refers to the 3 couples associated with the dream (1) the dreamer and her husband, (2) the friend and her escort, and (3) the sister-in-law and her husband. The "1 florin 50 kreuzers" subliterally add to 6, the exact number of people concerned, that is, 1 + 5 (zeros are often canceled, or they are used to represent another category) equals 6. Thus, the numbers structurally represent the composition of the dream's social situation. Moreover, the "1 florin 50 kreuzers," is a structural differentiation. The "1" represents the dreamer, and the "5(0)" represents the 5 other people.

Once again, my reanalysis of Freud's two dreams shows that subliteral operations function in the dreaming state as they do in constructing subliteral meaning in conversations. Methodologically, Freud began to recognize that the meaning of numbers could be analyzed by their associative contexts, but more importantly from a cognitive point of view, he began to recognize their structural characteristics, as implicitly indicated by the fact that he recognized that the "3" florins which was separated from the "65" kreuzers was, he believed, used as single number, 365. In a later dream analysis, he began to formulate an explicit rule. He says of a number that was presented separately that "the mere fact that in reporting the dream the dreamer broke up the number . . . . showed that its components had separate meaning."[10] If Freud had continued to recognize that arithmetical representations and their visual-linguistic counterparts have a set of logical operations quite different from what we understand as standard logic, *The Interpretation of Dreams* would be a somewhat different book, at least methodologically. Freud, however, was limited by the scientific zeitgeist in which he was working. The sway of simple associationism was in full swing. Thus he was too focused on associations and not on thoughtful cognition. In addition, he was very much the clinician and therefore concerned with therapeutics and content.

Finally, underlying the selection of numbers in dreams are affective schemas that select and organize them, just as emotional schemas in subliteral narratives. In the first dream described by Freud, one of the affective schemes was a concern about money, hence the representation of numbers through the medium or vehicle of currency that reflected his patient's concern over money relative to her daughter's school fees and her fee to Freud.

One final point. By Freud's analysis of these two dreams we see that he implies that there is unconscious perception and cognition. His many analyses of slips of the tongue also imply unconscious perception and cognition. But as we see in chapter 12, his theory of the unconscious precludes unconscious perception and cognition of reality. Freud's theory (or theories) of the unconscious is often contradictory. His theory says one thing, and his actual practice says quite another. It's difficult for science and therapeutics to work together.

DREAMS ABOUT GROUP CONVERSATIONS

We have seen that, just as with regular subliteral stories, dreams also have subliteral meaning. A content analysis of dreams about a group shows that, like many subliteral stories, dreams about a group are frequently represented as an automobile, a bus, a house, a house trailer, a bathtub or a swimming pool with a number of people in it, or a mental hospital or ward. One person represented a group as an octopus, and the group members were its tentacles. Thus, objects or places in dreams that contain groups of people is one sign that it may be a subliteral representation of the social situation. Other social situations that reflect a "collectivity," like business meetings, clubs, and athletic teams, are often used to represent a group. Some dreams are very brief, and some are quite extensive. Some are not about the group as a collective unit, but about interpersonal relationships in the group, some are an amalgam of both levels, and some are just about the leader. Now, let's look at some of these dreams.

I present the dreams exactly as written up by the dreamers. Recall that the subliteral analysis of dreams about a group is accomplished by exactly the same method as analyzing regular subliteral narratives, which is to map the dream on the known facts about the dreamer and the dynamics of the group.[11] One final point. Like subliteral narratives, dreams are complex and may be about multiple issues and concerns, so they often can't be categorized in terms of one issue or concern.

DREAMS ABOUT THE CLIMATE OF THE GROUP

Dream # 1

I find myself walking around in an asylum. I am one of the patients. I'm walking around looking at the other patients. I do not know anyone, but I am getting along well with them. I feel right at home. I wake up.

The content of this dream, which occurred in the initial stages of a group, is clear. It takes place in a mental hospital (representing the group), and the dreamer is a patient. He is obviously fairly new to the asylum (means the initial stage of the group) because he doesn't know anyone, but, nevertheless, he is getting along with the other patients (representing group members). In fact he feels relatively comfortable. This dream is saying exactly what it appears to be saying about the dreamer's feelings about the here-and-now group being dreamed about.

Now the question becomes, why the imagery of a mental hospital? As we have seen in previous chapters, subliterally representing the group as "crazy" mental patients isn't uncommon. The reason for this imagery can be explained by the way people experience T-groups and other loosely structured situations. It tends to be disorienting. This disorientation is often unconsciously experienced as "crazy," as "weird," with peoples behaviors like being "drunk." Despite this disorientation, however, the dream tells us that the dreamer is feeling relatively good about the group experience.

Dream # 2

I was in the entrance of a church and several people entered with babies. As they entered the church, each child was put into a high-chair and I was there to baby-sit. Then they entered the church—yet it wasn't a church. When I looked into the church, it was an ice rink. Later I turned and looked in a window and saw inside another house across the street. In the house, was a family. I watched them for a while, then they realized I was watching, so they shut the curtain. From here I returned to observing the skating rink.

In this dream, the group is represented as a church, and the babies are the group members, which the dreamer feels like he is baby-sitting. The imagery of the group also being an ice rink, probably reflects the dreamer feelings about the "cold" interpersonal climate of the interaction at this point in the group's development. The imagery noting that the dreamer was looking through a window into a house across the street probably is a reference to my emphasis that members be both participants and observers. In other words, this imagery is one of being psychologically removed (i.e., observing). The imagery about when the people realize he is observing them they shut the curtain, refers to his awareness of the fact that group members (like most people) do not reveal their "true" selves if they know that they are being observed. The final image of "returning to observing the skating rink," refers to his accepting that he will observe what he can under the circumstances. It is also likely that the imagery of skating refers to his being unsure of himself, i.e., unstable footing on the slippery ice.

Dream # 3

It is a beautiful crisp day at the ocean. On the beach sits a big yellow tent made of nylon (Goretex). It is the exact shape of an olive and it has a wooden platform that's also yellow (one of my favorite colors, by the way). The inside naturally is hollow and filled with black chairs that are arranged in a circle. The chairs are an awkward shape. Each chair is occupied except for the one intended for me. I am not sure who the group is. I only know (sense) that it's familiar. I recognize only one person in the group (Mary in my Human Relations class).

I am floating above the tent which enables me to have a top view of what's going on. The outside sea breeze is blowing fiercely at the tent causing it to crumble inward. I feel an overwhelming responsibility not to let the tent crumble together and suffocate the group. (The only way out of the tent is through the top). I unsuccessfully grab desperately at the tent trying to gather all of the top part of it so I can blow air into it like a balloon. At this point I was aware of feeling really frustrated and overwhelmed and hindered. And really it's unrealistic, but I attempt it anyway. However, the outside wind is in control. I blow and blow using up a great deal of energy, only to fail.

Before I know what happened, I am no longer floating over the tent. I was aware that I was gone but in my dream I was still able to see what was going on. When I returned, I noticed that even in my absence the tent was still standing. In fact it was just fine. It wasn't perfectly round and the outside wind was still blowing on it but not enough to cause any drastic harm to anyone in the group. It was at this point when I realized that there was a certain stability that I didn't know existed in the group and tent. There was a great sense of relief and some joy when I saw that the tent was still standing.

I floated in through the top and settled gently into the chair. I was comfortable at last. The group wasn't aware of all that went on with me and that didn't even make a difference because I felt really settled inside. In my dream it seems I had to sit in that chair several times before it caused me to have bad neck and backaches. This was the first time I was relaxed and comfortable. Mary was the person who said that it was OK for me to stop blowing, that it wasn't all my responsibility. She said things would be better if we all worked together. . . . As I write this part, I can't remember where in my dream this took place, I just remember she was the person who reassured me.

Like many dreams about the group, this dream has many obvious elements, and some not so obvious. The dream gives us linkages demonstrating that it's about the here-and-now group. In the dream, (1) the chairs are arranged in a circle, (2) the dreamer senses that the group is familiar, (3) the dreamer recognizes one person in the dream who is actually someone from the group (i.e., from her Human Relations class), and (4) the theme is that people should all work together.

The group is subliterally represented as a tent. That the tent is made of nylon indicates that the group is strong, yet flexible. This is indicated by the fact that after the dreamer's feelings of anxiety about the fragility of the tent, she noted that the wind was not strong enough to cause any harm and comes to the realization that there was an inherent stability about the group that she didn't understand previously. But before this realization, the imagery was of strong winds that caused the tent to collapse. This is a reference to her anxiety about the conflict in the group and about this kind of T-group experience in general. That (1) the chairs were black, (2) an awkward shape, and (3) that the tent was not perfectly round also indicates negative feelings about the group situation. Even during these feelings, the dreamer feels positive about the group, as indicated by the fact that the tent is her favorite color.

The dream also shows that the dreamer felt a great responsibility to make the group function effectively. This is indicated by (1) her feeling responsible for not letting the tent collapse and (2) feeling frustrated at the task. She also felt hindered and overwhelmed by the responsibility and tries frantically to blow life (air) into the group like a balloon, only to fail. The imagery of floating above the tent is a subliteral reference to her knowing that if she is going to help the group that she must be objective and become like an observer, as I had indicated a number of times to the group. Though she realizes that trying to save the group all by herself is "unrealistic," she tries, anyway, only to realize later that the group has an inherent strength of its own. The dreamer also makes clear that, as in the dream where the group "wasn't aware of all that went on with me," the here-and-now group was not aware of her feelings. Finally, she stops floating above the tent and trying to breath life into it, settles down inside, feeling good about the group because she now realizes it's not her responsibility alone.

This dream is really two dreams in one. The major change of scene in the dream from negative concerns and feelings to the final scene with positive imagery probably reflects the dreamer's emotional progress in the group. The first scene expresses early feelings and concerns, and the last scene expresses current feelings about the group.

DREAMS ABOUT INDIVIDUAL CONCERNS

Dream # 4

I was jogging alone on a road one morning, when I saw Pam. She was sitting with her arms around her knees on a lawn about two feet above the roadway. I stopped and lay down on my stomach about two feet away from her right side. She was facing the road. I asked her if she thought that our human relations class was weird and different. She agreed. We continued talking as the dream faded out. I knew she would talk if we were alone.

The dream refers to the dreamer's relationship with a group member, and like the previous dream it's about getting to know the "true" selves of the group members. This is indicated by the informal setting of the dream and by the female group member sitting above the roadway which she was looking out over, showing that she was not yet emotionally part of the group (this was only the third session of the group). Typically, members believe that the group situation is artificial, and if they could only talk to members on a one-to-one basis, they would be able to relate to each other better. This is indicated by the dreamer's last comment saying that a member "would talk if we were alone." Finally, the dream communicates the feelings that most members have about the T-group experience: that it's weird.

Dream # 5

> I found myself in a state of being half awake and breaking out in a cold sweat. I feel I'm being backed into a corner by a bunch of angry people, expecting me to come up with a topic for others to talk about.

The meaning of this dream was analyzed by the dreamer. The dreamer asked: "Are they looking at me to be leader, or is it that I want to be the leader, but I can't find a way to express it? Or is it something else? The dream was kind of frightening. I didn't get much sleep. Everyone was yelling at me. Why? Does it have to do with the last meeting? Was I disturbed because I felt I was being rebelled against? For the first time, I felt bad about the group. Maybe when they so-called 'ganged up' against me, I felt weak? Maybe I couldn't retaliate." This dream clearly tells us that the person is experiencing conflict about his leadership role in the group.

Dream # 6

> I was in a class taking an exam when Helen, Mary, and Martha came to the door. They were just looking into the room and the teacher went over to ask what they wanted. Mary proceeded to ask if they could talk to me. For some reason I felt afraid to go. I just wanted to take the exam, but the teacher told me I had to go, so I went. When I got into the hall, they just looked at me, and the next thing I remember, I was running away from them because I was being chased. The chase continued all over the school and finally ended when I tripped up the stairs to the third floor, and I wake up. I do remember feeling as if no one was willing to help, as I was running away from them and feeling scared when I woke up.

First, this dream tells us that the dreamer is concerned about being evaluated by (1) me, as indicated by the reference to taking an exam and (2) other members, as indicated by her dream image "they just looked at me."

Second, the dream indicates that the dreamer recognizes that members are not doing what they should to help the group develop. This is indicated by the image of "no one was willing to help us." Third, the dream probably refers to the issue of confidentiality of the group discussions, as indicated by talking to people who are not part of the group. Third, it is clear that the dreamer does not yet see herself as part of the group, as indicated by her running away from the people. It also tells us that she would like more help.

DREAMS ABOUT THE LEADER

Dream # 7

On an island and Dr. H is there. We sit in a group, and he asks us if it's important to say "Hi" to people or not. Sue says it isn't because it's stupid. I yell at her and say it is important because what are you going to say to someone if you just meet them? You can't just jump right in and start talking about something important. I apologize for yelling at her, and then Dr. H says there is a hurricane coming and he has to leave. We end the group and leave. I ask if he needs anything taken to his truck (he is moving his stuff so it won't get ruined). His plants and books. He says the plants stay where they are, but I can take the books. I take some and put them in a room that can move (like a car?). Lucy and her boyfriend take some too and throw them in a corner. Dr. H gets mad because they're so messy. He reorganizes his books, and when he finishes he goes and gets the rest of his stuff. I help him bring it in the room, and I ask him where his wife is. He said, "normally by this time she would be home." I assume she's dead and say I'm sorry (or at least think it).

Dr. H, of course, is a literal reference to me, and it's literally clear that it's about the here-and-now group situation. The remark about whether it's important to say "Hi," to people before just jumping in and starting to talk about important things is a subliteral reference to the purpose of the group which is interpersonal communication skills. The dreamer makes it clear that she thinks such skills are important by her retort to a member who says that there is no reason to say "Hi." This may indicate that, unlike the dreamer, a group member doesn't think that what's being taught is important. The reference to a hurricane is a subliteral reference to the dreamer's experience of interpersonal conflict in the group. The reference to my leaving the group because of the hurricane is a subliteral expression of the dreamer's perception and feeling about me abandoning them by not stepping in and resolving the conflict. The reference to the rest of the members leaving reflects an underlying fear that the conflict will lead to the group disbanding—either in reality or by simply not functioning effectively.

The dreamer, asking if I need anything taken to my truck, tells us that, once again, she is identifying with me and with the purpose of the group. The reference to my having a truck (which in reality, I didn't have) is probably a subliteral reference to her perception that though I am being nondirective in the group, I am nevertheless "working," or helping the group to grow or develop. A truck is considered a work vehicle as opposed to a car. The plants refer to the group members (i.e., growing, developing, or learning). My books in the dream refer to the texts that I developed for the course. My saying that she can take my books tells us that she is learning something in the group, though she still is unsure of her new knowledge. This is indicated by the room where she takes the books which is one that moves (i.e., unstable, unsure). It's also probably a reference to the group progressing and moving forward. Her reference to moving my "stuff so it won't get ruined," is probably a reference to my textbooks not being read and applied by most of the members. This is indicated by the image of a female and her boyfriend throwing my books in a corner.

That I become angry at them for throwing my books in the corner is a reference to her unconscious fear that I am angry at the group members for not paying attention to my books and learning the skill that she should be learning (this is a typical unconscious perception, like a parent being angry with a child). The reference to the books lying there in a mess and my reorganizing them is a reference to the disorganized state of the group process. The dreamer helping me is a further reference to the fact that the dreamer is learning skills.

Finally, the dreamer asking me where my wife is, then saying that she's dead, and that she is sorry is probably a reference to her self-perception of not being a very good ally to me in the group (because she is unsure of her knowledge).

Dream # 8

I was standing in a doorway of a huge auditorium just below the stage. A speech was being given by a student. The whole setup reminded me of a protest rally. The audience stood and yelled angrily in agreement with the speaker, holding clenched fists above their heads. I couldn't hear the speaker so I don't know the subject of the speech. Dr. Haskell entered from back stage with a machine gun on a strap over his shoulder. He stood under the lights and never said a word, but everyone knew that he was taking over the meeting and would shoot. I walked on stage and approached him from behind. When I was in back of him I stepped to the side and threw a punch with my left hand and caught him on the right side of his face and nose.

Once again, the group is being represented by a "container," a room/auditorium. The dreamer noted that he was standing in the doorway indicating that he does not yet consider himself a part of the group. That a speech was being given by a student in the atmosphere of a protest rally where the audience was yelling angrily and shaking clenched fists indicates that the dreamer is quite dissatisfied with the group experience and feels like protesting my nondirectiveness. That he couldn't hear the speech and thus didn't know the subject of the speech indicates uncertain and unclear knowledge.

The image of me entering from back stage with a machine gun is a clear reference to me as the authority. In addition to this, my standing under the lights indicates my prominence in the group. The reference to me taking over the protest rally and shooting if anyone objected, is a reference to the perception that I am indirectly (coming from backstage) really running the group—as "everyone knew." That I am somehow indirectly manipulating the group is a common unconscious perception (not only of me but of leaders in general). The final image of the dreamer punching me in the nose clearly expresses his feelings about me.[12]

CONCLUSION

We have seen that numbers in dreams function the same as in waking subliteral narratives and that the "cause" of numbers being selected for the dream is the same as subliteral numbers in waking narratives, to express unconscious feelings and concerns. We saw, too, that dreams about social or group situations can be subliterally analyzed in the same way as the group and social conversations presented throughout this book. Accordingly, these dreams can tell us about the dreamer's thoughts and feeling that are otherwise not available to us and might not even be available to the dreamer. Thus, like recognizing our own subliteral meanings in our conversations, we can find out about ourselves and about others.

In addition, the way a group or social situation is represented in dreams is the same as the way they are represented in waking narratives. As in waking narratives, the group in these dreams is represented as a "container" that holds people. We saw this where the group was represented as an auditorium, a church, a mental hospital, ice rink, and a tent and the group's members were represented as protesters, babies, patients, and just plain members of a group as in the dream about the tent. We saw conflict being subliterally represented as strong winds, as a hurricane, and as protesting. We also saw members feelings about their roles in the group represented as baby-sitting, not being a good ally of the instructor, being unsure of themselves, and either feeling a part of the group or feeling alienated.

In this particular collection of dreams, I was literally represented as myself, and the dreamer's feelings about my role were represented by me having a machine gun, reflecting feelings that they thought I was angry at them. Other content in the dreams, like chairs being black or an awkward shape, also subliterally express the dreamer's feelings. Although the color black expressed negative feelings, the yellow color of the tent expressed the dreamer's positive feelings, as indeed, the dreamer commented that it was one of her favorite colors. Finally, dreams about a group or social situation can reveal a person's progress in feeling that they psychologically belong or have adjusted to the group situation.

POSTSCRIPT: UNCONSCIOUS MEANING REVISITED

Like the controversy over the idea of a smart unconscious mind, there has long been a similar controversy over whether dreams have meaning. The previous analysis shows that dreams about the group can be analyzed with the same approach as analyzing subliteral narratives in social conversations. Both are created from the same set of unconscious processes that I described in chapter 8 on the subliteral unconscious mind. Thus, it's important to revisit the problem of unconscious meaning, only this time as it relates to analyzing subliteral meanings in dreams. Before I outline the problem of analyzing meaning in dreams, I would like to make it clear that, unlike many of my more hard-nosed colleagues, I think that some dreams have meaning. Unlike many of my more mystical colleagues, however, I don't think all dreams do, nor do I think we really fly off to Jupiter and Mars in our dreams.

THE RANDOM CAUSE OF DREAMS

The main reason for the hard-nosed approach which maintains that dreams have no meaning is partly because it has been clearly demonstrated that dreams are generated by neurological circuits in our brain stem that periodically (about every 90 minutes) fire a barrage of random signals that spread throughout many areas of our brain.[13] This barrage of signals, caused by their firing, stimulates many areas of our brain, including feelings and memories. Now, it's important to note that this array of neuronal firings is random. Based on this random array of neurological signals, it's concluded that therefore the dreams resulting from these random signals must also be random. Hence, in this view, dreams have no meaning. The description of the cause of dreams is correct. The conclusion is wrong.

One extreme view says that not only do dreams have no meaning, but that the function of dreaming is to erase information in our brain that's not needed. This view was initially put fourth by Sir Francis Crick and Graeme Mitchison,[14] which they later expanded in a book I edited on *Cognition and Dream Research*.[15] If you remember your biology course, you may recall that in 1953 James Watson and Francis Crick[16] discovered the helical structure of the DNA molecule which contains all of the information responsible for our genetic development and subsequent characteristics. This discovery is considered by many scientists the most important discovery of the twentieth century in biology. It won them the Nobel prize in 1962. Now, if you are wondering what Crick is doing theorizing about dreaming, the connection is that he has been conducting research on simulating the function of neural networks in the brain. In so doing, he (and others) believe they have simulated the neuronal activity of dreaming in these artificial networks. In any event, this kind of research leads many to assume that dreams have no meaning. This, again, is incorrect.

The same arguments that I made in chapter 7 that some slips of the tongue are meaningful can be applied to the meaning of some dreams. Recall the argument was that because linguists and cognitive scientists can show a lawful set of linguistic processes underlying slips of the tongue, this shows that slips have no psychological meaning. But, it doesn't logically follow that because there are lawful linguistic mechanisms underlying slips and errors, unconscious meaning is ruled out. The same kind of argument applies to Crick's neurological explanations of the function of dreams. Because Crick's theory is largely based on simulated neural networks, the erasing of information in fact refers to an extremely microlevel of neurological "garbage" that's accumulated in the network.

Thus, even if the idea of the erasure function of dreaming is valid, it would be likely to have no appreciable effects on a macrolevel of dream memories. This is why. In quantum and subatomic physics, it's thought that physical matter is made up of particles which are constantly coming and going out of existence. Further, it is thought that the underlying processes are random, and our knowledge of them is based on mathematical probabilities, not *cause*.

On a macrolevel of physics we can explain the movement of planets and other solid and relatively permanent objects by Isaac Newton's theory. Now, if I may be permitted some slight—but only slight—hyperbole to make a point. Just as the apparently random and continuing subatomic destruction of atoms, electrons, mesons, and other subatomic quantum particles coming into and going out of existence doesn't change planetary orbits,[17] neither does it significantly change the shape of the chair on which I'm now sitting. Likewise, the microerasing of neurological "garbage" is not likely to affect macro memories of which dreams are made. Once again I belabor this point because it's crucial to the entire idea of subliteral meaning.

And one more time, I am not saying that all dreams have meaning, only that some do. Just as some slips definitely have meaning, some don't. So too, some dreams have meaning, some don't. The problem is how we know when they do and when they don't. Now, let me explain why I think some dreams have meaning.

HOW SOME DREAMS HAVE MEANING

Though many people already agree that dreams have meaning, this is not simply preaching to the choir, so to speak, to the already convinced. Understanding the reasons for believing that some dreams have meaning is important for understanding's sake alone, and also for defending oneself when high tech and other sceptics laugh when you claim that a dream you had may have meaning.

In greatly abbreviated form, my argument goes like this.[18] In our waking state, our brain is being barraged by stimuli every moment. Auditory, visual, sensual, and a host of other stimuli impinge on our sensory apparatus. Because we can't attend to all of this information at once, we must preconsciously select and order it. In doing so, only certain stimuli reach our consciousness. Therefore, we must selectively take this random array of information, and by selectively ordering it on the basis of a particular focus or concern, we make sense of it. In other words, during our waking state, this myriad and multiplicity of incoming information from the world around us is selected and organized on the basis of the needs and concerns that we have at any given time. Thus, if we are listening to a person talking, we filter out or prevent other sounds and activities happening around us from reaching our consciousness. Thus, we take an inherently random barrage of information and render it consciously meaningful. I am suggesting that our brain simply does the same thing while we are in the dream state. Enter what we call the dream.

If, as most of the rigorous cognitive research on dreaming suggests, the brain's basic cognitive operations which function while we are awake are the same as those in force when we are dreaming (as measured by brain waves, the dreaming state is essentially undistinguishable from the waking state), then it's reasonable to infer that the random stimuli being sent from the lower brain centers during the dreaming state are similarly organized to create meaning. Granted, just because this random array of stimuli is organized, it still doesn't mean that it's meaningful in the sense that a dream has unconscious meaning. Without further consideration, this organization is simply a recognizable pattern or set of patterns from memories that are stimulated. Lesser hard-nosed researchers accept this argument, because they can still say that the dream has no meaning beyond a recognizable set of stimulated memory patterns.

The significant point being missed in the previous argument, however, is this. If the brain works essentially the same during dreaming as it does while awake (as most rigorous research suggests it does), then it is reasonable to assume that the organization of the random stimulation of memories does not just reflect a remembered or constructed pattern. It is reasonable to assume that this is not the case because, just as in our conscious state, there are likely emotional or feeling schemas or emotional concerns in the dreaming state that organize the random stimuli into dreams which reflect these concerns. The meaning of such dreams would be analogous to thoughts we have when we silently think to ourselves.

Organizing these random stimuli on the basis of unconscious feelings and concerns may be explained further by an unconscious monitoring "executive,"[19] just as some such executive system is required in the waking state. In chapter 8, I adopted Ernest Hilgard's metaphorical concept of a "hidden observer," where there is a part of our unconscious that does the planning for the conversations in which we engage and the stories we tell or write. This executive monitoring should also apply to the dreaming process. The basic difference is that thoughts and stimuli ordered during the waking state are, by social consensus, considered real, whereas those ordered during the sleep state are considered imaginal and idiosyncratic to the individual. It is doubtful, however, if neurocognitive processes or brain tissue make this rather fine philosophical distinction. On this level, thoughts are thoughts, and images are images, all equally "real" to the brain.

Finally, I mentioned at the beginning of this chapter that from my perspective the problem is not whether some dreams have meaning or not, the problem is knowing which ones have meaning and which ones don't and how we know the difference between the two. There are probably as many systems of dream "interpretation" as there are interpreters. At least in analyzing dreams about the group, we have a relatively concrete set of here-and-now circumstances on which to map the contents of the dream, leading to the dream's meaning.

CHAPTER 12

SUBLITERAL THERAPEUTICS

THE NEW PSYCHOTHERAPY OF ROBERT LANGS

I am including this chapter on the work of the psychiatrist Robert Langs because as I was discovering subliteral narratives, about the same time he was independently discovering similar unconscious communications from his patients. He claims that what I call subliteral communications from patients can be used therapeutically. Langs calls these unconscious communications from patients *derivatives,* presumably because they derive from the unconscious. If Langs is correct in his observation, then subliteral communications could be useful to mental health counselors as a method of obtaining information from clients not otherwise obtainable, or as a new way of doing therapy. This could be a major new development and application of subliteral phenomena. Based on his discovery of unconscious communications being therapeutic, Langs founded a new school of psychodynamic therapy called Communicative Psychotherapy.[1] Understanding this form of subliteral communication will also help to further clarify how subliteral meaning works.

In this chapter, I briefly introduce Langs's approach to subliteral communications. Then, I describe (1) his theory of derivatives and his method of validating them, (2) his theory of the unconscious, and (3) what he calls trigger analysis and frame setting. I limit my focus, however, to these three aspects of his theory for two reasons. First, these are the three aspects of Communicative Psychotherapy that relate directly to my theory of the subliteral mind, and secondly, because in my view, these three aspects constitute the bedrock of Communicative Psychotherapy as a theory and as a therapeutic technique. Finally, I briefly address the significance of my subliteral findings to Langs's theory of psychotherapy. But before I do this, I feel compelled to make a few prefatory comments.

INTRODUCTION

When I learned about Langs's discovery of unconscious communications and its therapeutic possibilities, it put me in a terrible dilemma. On the one hand, it was gratifying that subliteral phenomena were being researched and applied in another potentially significant way. Langs's insight that subliteral narratives could be used therapeutically was exciting. Beyond some general, but increasing, references in the literature about the use of "metaphors" in psychotherapy, as I mentioned in chapter 2, I hadn't given much thought to subliteral narratives in therapeutic applications.[2] On the other hand, Langs also referred to his new psychotherapy as Communicative Psychoanalysis. This was disconcerting. Throughout this book, I have made no secret of the fact that I am not overly enamored by psychoanalytic theory. But more than this, I was (and still am) concerned that subliteral phenomena would become associated with pop psychotherapy and psychoanalysis (see later). With this said, now, let me begin to explain Langs's framework for unconscious communications in more detail.

Langs's formulation of derivative communications has engendered considerable heated controversy even amongst psychoanalysts. Unlike most other schools of psychoanalysis, however Langs has been concerned with the *science* of psychoanalytic *practice*, even to the extent of conducting mathematical research on transcribed protocols of patient sessions.[3] He has also developed a method of testing derivative communications within the therapeutic sessions. Interestingly, in addition, Langs developed a Darwinian evolutionary framework for explaining the biological origins of derivative phenomena.[4] Langs is no pop psychoanalytic guru.

For purposes of this chapter, I will have to set aside many important and technical aspects of his theory and summarize others. For readers further interested in Langs's Communicative Psychoanalysis, his own books[5] are available. As beginning reading, I recommend his *Unconscious Communication in Everyday Life.*[6] For an excellent introduction to Langs, I recommend David Livingston Smith's book, *Hidden Conversations: An Introduction to Communicative Psychoanalysis.*[7] Communicative Psychoanalysis is based on verbal unconscious communications from patients. According to Langs, these unconscious communications are about three things. First, they are about patients revealing problems to which they don't have conscious access. Secondly, they are communications from the patient about the therapist's behavior in the therapeutic sessions, and third, they are communications telling the therapist whether his or her therapeutic interventions, suggestions, and interpretations are correct. This last category is one of the more bizarre and questionable aspects of his theory.

At this point, those who have a popular understanding of psychoanalysis may respond to Langs's claim of unconscious communications from patients with, "So, what's new? Freud said this years ago, didn't he?" The answer is: "No, he didn't." The fact is, neither what I have presented regarding subliteral language nor Langs's discovery of derivative communication fits any Freudian theory of the unconscious mind, nor any modern formulations of it. Nor does it fit any other school of psychoanalysis. In large measure, Langs's view of the unconscious is what all the controversy is about in the psychoanalytic community—along with his claim that derivative or unconscious communications can be used therapeutically—not to mention his view that a patient's unconscious mind knows what is therapeutically correct.

Now, because unconscious messages from patients are the very core of Langs's theory, analyzing the content of these messages from the unconscious is crucial. This is where my subliteral method comes into the Communicative therapy picture. As I outline below, the recognition of derivatives by Communicative therapists is rather general and global, like the early observations of subliteral communications found in the group dynamics and group analytic psychotherapy literature briefly noted in chapter 2. If the content of unconscious messages is therapeutically important, then the more detailed recognition of the cognitive operations that create that content, the better.

LANGS'S THEORY

To understand Langs's theory of the unconscious and its implications, it's useful first to understand his concept of derivatives. Like subliteral communication, derivatives are communications of "encoded" unconscious material from a patient to a therapist that may be in the form of imaginary or real stories about people, past events, life situations, or of the therapeutic session. These unconscious communications are selected for a therapy session as comments on the patient's past or as comments on the various aspects of the here-and-now therapy session. Let me illustrate Langsian derivatives by using examples from David Smith's book.[8]

DERIVATIVE COMMUNICATION

After listening to a lengthy and inappropriate interpretation by a female analyst, a male patient consciously responded to it by saying that it seemed to make sense. Then, after a pause, the patient switched to an apparently different subject and in telling a story about his wife, said, "My wife is a bad public speaker."[9] According to the principles of Communicative Psychotherapy, this is a derivative about the therapist's verbal intervention or interpretation, demonstrating that the patient felt the (female) therapist, who is unconsciously represented as being like his wife, did not express herself clearly or correctly in her therapeutic intervention. The here-and-now context of the situation (i.e., the therapist poorly communicating the intervention) is what Communicative therapy calls a "trigger." Triggers help to recognize derivative communications from the patient. Triggers are what I generally refer to as events in the here-and-now conversational situation that are the stimuli which precipitate subliteral meaning (see later).

Another example of a patient's derivative communication is from a therapist who made (from a Communicative Psychotherapy perspective) an inappropriate interpretation. After the interpretation, the patient launched into the following story:

> You know, I was saying to Nick that in the flat, or anywhere for that matter, there always seems to be a radio playing and it's either too loud or too soft. . . . It's like that with all media things with me. I use my glasses to watch TV. Yet sometimes even with my glasses on there's a blurred image.[10]

As David Smith observes, the patient pauses, then begins with a manifest comment that the interpretation is "interesting," and then begins to tell a story about radios that have no apparent connection with the content of the therapist's interpretation.

The general themes in this derivative are of (1) things not *sounding* right, (2) a radio which is either too loud or too soft, and (3) a blurred image. From both Langs's and my perspective, it's clear that the patient's derivative about things "not sounding right" is a communication to the therapist that her interpretation didn't sound correct to him. The reference to a "blurred image" means that the therapist's image of him (the patient) was blurred or, again incorrect. Langs would interpret this more stringently, maintaining that the patient's message demonstrates that the therapist's interpretation was definitely not correct. Thus, according to Communicative Psychotherapy, derivatives are not just the patient's unconscious opinion, they represent valid information about the therapy situation. The question is, how does Langs know this?

VERIFICATION OF DERIVATIVE COMMUNICATION

In keeping with Langs's continuing efforts to bring scientific methods to bear on psychoanalysis, he supports his interpretation of unconscious messages by a simple but ingenious verification method that occurs within the therapeutic session. As David Smith notes, "To my knowledge Langs is the only psychoanalytic writer to have consistently employed and refined this approach to the verification of psychoanalytic hypotheses."[11] For example, following a patient's initial unconscious communication and the therapist's response to it, a patient's subsequent unconscious message will either be one of positive or negative imagery. If positive, the unconscious communication is thereby considered to have validated the therapist's intervention or interpretation. Conversely, if the subsequent unconscious message is negative, then the therapist's response is considered to have been incorrect. By way of an example, I will continue Smith's account of the above patient's derivative. After his initial derivative, the patient then says, "It's like going to church. You go with a lot of faith and often you're disappointed."[12]

Because the imagery of this brief story is one of loss of faith and disappointment, the message is interpreted as not validating the therapist's intervention. Then, recognizing the mistake, the therapist addresses the patient's derivative by responding to the patient's unconscious communication by saying,

> Steve, this seems to be very much to do with what's going on here between us. You're telling me a lot, but I don't seem to be getting the message quite right, hence your reference to the blurred images on the TV and the distorted sounds from the radio. Maybe you're disappointed in my interpretation, in my lack of understanding.[13]

Then, the patient responds with another unconscious communication:

> You remember I told you about how I try to go for a swim at least once a week. Well, I didn't tell you that for a long time I couldn't swim. Then one holiday I decided to learn. I went for lessons. I thought it would be pure pleasure, but I was wrong. There was a helluva lot of pain, but actually I recovered quickly afterwards. The instructor did his best and I learned a lot from him. *In the end I thought it was worth it. It was worth it in the end.* [Italics added][14]

Now, the theme of the patient's story has changed. The content of this message is about learning something new and concludes that it's worth it. As Smith observes, unlike the first narrative, this derivative is full of positive imagery and thus validates the therapist's previous communication to the patient. Apparently, this invalidating and validating process is found consistently in therapeutic sessions. It's working with these derivatives that, somehow—it's not known how—presumably results in effective treatment.

Assuming for the moment that Langs's therapeutic method works, increased insight into the patient's subliteral messages would facilitate treatment. Thus, from a subliteral perspective, merely understanding the general meaning of derivative themes is not sufficient. If I were a therapist, I'd like to know more. For example, in the previous derivative, I'd like to know more about what the patient meant by the words (1) "saying to Nick that in the flat," (2) or "anywhere for that matter," (3) I didn't tell you that for a long time "I couldn't swim," and (4) "one holiday I decided to learn." It would seem that these uninterpreted parts of the patient's derivatives might hold important keys into the patient's problem and his successful treatment. This is where a thorough understanding and application of my subliteral method could enhance Communicative Psychotherapy.

THE LANGSIAN UNCONSCIOUS

As I alluded to before, receiving these kinds of messages from the unconscious mind is not standard fare, even for psychoanalysts. Neither is an unconscious that perceives and thinks like our conscious mind standard fare for psychoanalysis. Although it's certainly not necessary to convince psychoanalysts that an unconscious mind is real, to convince most of them of Langs's theory of an unconscious that perceives the outside world and thinks and reasons like the conscious mind, however, is apparently quite another matter. The reason for this is that Langs's theory of the unconscious differs fundamentally from the classic psychoanalytic unconscious with its seething caldron of primitive and innate *id* impulses or just about any other variant on a psychoanalytic unconscious. Most certainly it differs from any of the nonconscious processing models of the mind of mainstream cognitive psychology.

There are basic ways, then, Langs's view of the unconscious mind fundamentally differs from most others. First, Langs's theory of the unconscious asserts that it functions perceptually and cognitively. This means that it perceives the external world independently of—and prior to—our conscious perceptions. Secondly, it cognitively responds to those perceptions by appraising stimuli, which means that it *thinks and reasons* just like the conscious mind. According to Langs, it not only perceives the world but makes judgments regarding emotional stimuli *more validly than the conscious mind,* at least within the therapeutic context. Further, Langs imbues the unconscious with a psychoemotional "wisdom" beyond that of our conscious rational mind, a wisdom that he intriguingly theorizes is based in evolutionary biology.[15]

Again, despite common misconceptions about the Freudian unconscious—except for Freudian slips of the tongue and possibly the chapter on Dream Work in his *Interpretation of Dreams*—a perceptual and cognitive unconscious is alien to a psychoanalytic theory of the unconscious. It helps in understanding this to look briefly at Smith's review of the psychoanalytic history dealing with the development of the theory of the unconscious mind. Necessarily, the following account abbreviates Smith's more detailed review.[16] As Smith notes,

> That psychoanalysts do not entertain a theory of unconscious perception is not a mere oversight on their part. It is deeply rooted in the philosophy of mind to which Freud subscribed.[17]

There are, however, what can be seen as precursors or forerunners of unconscious perception and derivatives in Freud's writings. Smith observes that in *The Interpretation of Dreams* Freud revises an earlier view of the unconscious which allows for "revision" of perceived information before it enters into the conscious mind. As Smith notes, this implies that Freud "was toying with the idea of nonconscious perception during this period. In the end, however, Freud concludes that perceptual information must pass through the conscious mental system before being passed into the unconscious mental system."[18] According to Smith, in 1913, Freud apparently once considered unconscious perception a skill. Smith says,

> Here Freud sees unconscious perception as a technical skill which can be consciously brought to bear on the listening process: the analyst is advised to actively 'turn' his unconscious toward that of the patient. Is Freud only speaking metaphorically? It is difficult to understand how so malleable and accessible an unconscious could be reconciled to his notion of the unconscious part of the mind as neither easily influenced nor directly accessible to the conscious part of the mind.[19]

In any case, says Smith, in 1913 Freud took a more consistent stance. We find Freud saying,

> I have had good reason for asserting that everyone possesses in his own unconscious an instrument with which he can interpret the utterances of the unconscious in other people.[20]

Let's get this straight. Now, Freud is saying that the unconscious mind of one person can correctly interpret the unconscious meaning of another. So, at this point if you are confused about what Freud "really" meant when he used the term unconscious, so am I—and, understandably, so was he, and so are many other people.

In any event, in Smith's brief historical look at the psychoanalytic theory of the unconscious, we can see what I was getting at in the chapter on the Subliteral Mind, namely, there has been a confusion of tongues, so to speak, about what the term "unconscious" means in psychoanalysis. In fact, one could probably go through the corpus of Freud's writings and find justification for just about any definition of the unconscious that we might want. Finally, Langs maintains that the perceptual unconscious lies embedded in what he calls the emotion processing mind.

The bedrock for derivatives is the unconscious perception and processing of emotional material. It's clear that this is not the irrational emotional caldron of the Freudian *id*. It is more like the emotion that we consciously experience. Somehow unconscious emotional material becomes transformed into linguistic derivatives. I've already noted that Langs's notion of derivatives has provoked considerable controversy. Although Langs independently discovered derivative communication, in reviewing the history of psychoanalysis, Smith has found what he considers precursors to derivative communications which Freud and other therapists either ignored or dismissed because they were not compatible with what they thought was the correct psychoanalytic theory of the unconscious.

There was one exception: The psychoanalyst, Sándor Ferenczi's early observations of what Langs calls derivatives. This early history was first documented and extended by Piers Myers.[21] Formerly one of Freud's closest colleagues, Ferenczi was "excommunicated" after writing a paper on unconscious communication. Perhaps somewhat understandably, Ferenczi's claims of unconscious communications from patients were dismissed as his "ideas of persecution" similar (as Smith describes it) to a paranoid's perception of a television program that sends him encoded messages. Langs's announcement of unconscious communication from patients has frequently been met with a similar response. As a consequence, apparently most of the psychoanalytic community has largely ignored Langs's work, despite the fact, as Smith's historical review suggests, that Freud came close to discovering derivative communications from his patients on multiple occasions.

In one of his many examples, says Smith,

> "The last of Freud's forms of indirect confirmation is by far the most interesting, and has been almost entirely neglected within the psychoanalytic literature. Freud presents it through an account of a 'small extra-analytical experience'. Freud says,
>
> It concerned one of my colleagues who—it was long ago—had chosen me as a consultant in his medical practice. One day, however, he brought his young wife to see me, as she was causing him trouble. She refused on all sorts of pre-

> texts to have sexual relations with him, and what he expected of me was evidently that I should lay before her the consequences of her ill-advised behaviour. I went into the matter and explained to her that her refusal would probably have unfortunate results for her husband's health or would lay him open to temptations which might lead to a break-up of their marriage. At this point he suddenly interrupted me with the remark: 'The Englishman you diagnosed as suffering from a cerebral tumour has died too.'[22]

According to Smith, at the time, Freud didn't understand the meaning of the man's remark. The man had recollected an event about Freud, a recollection which seemingly had no apparent relevance to the situation. Freud later understood the unconscious significance of the man's statement. As Freud said, "The man was evidently intending to confirm what I had been saying; he was meaning to say: 'Yes, you're certainly quite right. Your diagnosis was confirmed in the case of the other patient too.'"[23] In other words, says Smith, Freud believed that the man's unconscious found a way to communicate an agreement with Freud's diagnosis. It was expressed indirectly and unconsciously by evoking a memory that served as an encoded expression of confirmation of Freud's diagnosis.

In interpreting the man's remark, Freud took the *theme* of the apparently irrelevant association and applied it to his here-and-now situation, that *is*, he understood that *his patient unconsciously regarded him as having correctly 'diagnosed' his marital situation.*[24] Freud's next comments are extremely suggestive. Freud recognized that it was, "an exact parallel to the indirect confirmations that we obtain in analysis from associations." In fact, according to Smith, late in his career Freud was in the habit of monitoring the free associations of patients which followed an intervention for just such disguised, unconscious communications for confirmation or disconfirmation of his interventions.[25]

Thus, again, we can see that there were precursors and indications that Freud and other psychoanalysts recognized brief instances of unconscious communications but considered them anomalous because of preconceived theoretical beliefs. But the appearance of one robin doesn't make it springtime.

TRIGGER ANALYSIS AND FRAME SETTING

Now, the question is, how are derivatives recognized? Derivatives are recognized by using what Langs calls *triggers*. Triggers are behaviors or events that occur within or impinge on the therapeutic situation. Quite early, Langs developed a here-and-now interpersonally interactive view of the therapeutic setting. For example, in both of the previous illustrations of derivative (stories), the first by a patient who said, *"My wife is a bad public speaker,"* and the second story about *"a radio playing and it's either too loud or too soft,"* the triggers were the therapists' analysis of the patients' previous conscious communication. In short, Langs's theory suggests that patient communications within the therapeutic setting are responses to the here-and-now interaction and not simply transference reactions emanating out of the patient's history. Then, trigger analysis is similar to my approach to analyzing subliteral communications by mapping the communications onto the concrete conditions in a here-and-now group situation.

The notion of *frame* is another important aspect of Communicative Psychotherapy. The *frame* is an elaborate set of rules and physical boundaries around the therapeutic session that Langs suggest must be adhered to. The psychoanalytic frame is a system of ground rules which define, demark, and constitute the analytic situation. The 'secured' or 'ideal frame' is the set of ground rules that are presumably unconsciously held and desired by the patient. When these rules are not adhered to, patients often respond with derivative communications about the frame infringements. Langs has been severely criticized as being too rigid about these rules.

Although the entire set of rules and boundary conditions are considered necessary for Communicative Psychotherapy, for my purposes here, I am concerned only with two aspects of the Communicative Psychotherapeutic *frame* as it relates to my findings on subliteral cognition and communication. The two most significant frame conditions are (1) that the patient lies on a couch and the therapist is out of the patient's range of vision, and (2) the therapist is completely silent until the patient offers a derivative communication. Just as in the nondirective style of conducting T-groups (and, I might add, in the near classic style of psychoanalysis), some aspects of the Communicative Psychotherapeutic frame create similar conditions of uncertainty, ambiguity, and anxiety out of which subliteral communications are optimally generated.

THE FUTURE OF SUBLITERAL THERAPEUTICS

In the opening paragraphs of this chapter, I said that Langs's discovery of unconscious communications from patients may have a therapeutic application that is very exciting. I also said, however, that I had never been enamored with much of psychoanalytic theory in general and therefore, was reticent to have my work linked to psychoanalysis. I say this as a cautiously friendly critic of psychoanalysis who believes that some of its basic ideas have scientific and neurological research to support them,[26] and that other specific psychoanalytic ideas may be verified in the future,[27] albeit with such extensive modifications that it will no longer make sense to call the entire corpus of findings psychoanalysis—at least as we have come to understand the term (recall my noting in another chapter that to label all unconscious things Freudian is like calling modern mathematics Pythagorean). So where does all this leave the future of the subliteral mind in relation to therapy? Before I answer this question, this is an appropriate time to put into perspective the issue of pop psychology that I've addressed from the beginning of this book.

CAUTION: THERAPEUTIC WONDERLAND AHEAD

I've noted that Langs's linking his method to psychoanalysis was not only unfortunate but necessary (which, again, I explain later). Over the years, pop and not-so-pop psychotherapists and psychoanalysts have made all manner of wild claims, especially about the unconscious mind. For example, it's said that the unconscious mind has powers of extrasensory perception (ESP), like seeing into the future, reading minds, and a host of other New Age phenomena like possessing memories of past (reincarnated) lifetimes—indeed, even future lifetimes. Psychoanalysis has become a pop-culture pastime and near parlor game activity, and also the brunt of jokes.

It's this "hermeneutic wonderland" of many psychoanalytic practitioners and the further dilution of Freud's ideas by an instant certification of credentials on which much of what the public understands about the unconscious. As for who is a psychoanalyst and what ties them all together, I can't say (and neither can they, for that matter). It seems that a psychoanalyst is a therapist who believes in an unconscious mind, infantile sexuality, and transference between patient and therapist—maybe with an oedipal complex thrown in for good measure.

In recent years, an even broader spectrum of those who consider themselves psychoanalytic practitioners have arisen and have added all manner of other wild claims about the unconscious mind. Although technically speaking, in the beginning—with rare exception—psychoanalysts were, like Freud, those with a medical degree, an M.D. Now some schools offer a B.A. in psychoanalysis, and some Psychoanalytic Institutes offer even lower level certificates. Although it's true that Freud considered the training of what he called "lay analysts," I don't think the kind of B.A.'s and certificates being offered in psychoanalysis, however, are what he had in mind (Freud is probably rolling over in his grave). I invite the reader to go on the Internet and do a search of the World Wide Web (www) references not just on psychoanalysis, but on psychotherapy in general. What you will instantly hear is a great sucking sound, usurping all possible meaning of the terms psychoanalysis and unconscious into a swirling vortex of verbiage. It's scandalous, really.

Now, I want to make it very clear that I don't mean to imply that all psychoanalytic theory and therapy belongs to this pop heritage. It doesn't. It's just that most of it does. Neither am I implying that all psychotherapy is invalid, only that most seems to be. Further, it's not that psychotherapy can't be made valid, it's just that most of it isn't.[28] There has been a rich history of experimental work on a psychodynamic unconscious that has existed almost from the time when psychoanalysis was introduced into the United States, and which has continued up to the present. This research had been conducted by psychoanalysts and also by psychologists.[29]

There is yet another reason that Langs' linking his insight to psychoanalysis is unfortunate. Many mental health counselors may find Langs's use of unconscious communications fascinating and want to apply it to their own work with clients, but because they may not be trained in psychoanalysis—whatever that means these days—they may not feel comfortable with their professional skills. In my view, this concern is not warranted (there are ethical concerns, however, that are warranted. I discuss these in the Concluding Ethical Postscript at the end of this book). These concerns are not warranted because unconscious communication as a therapeutic method is not inherently tied to psychoanalysis. Psychoanalysis is simply an overlay on the therapeutic use of unconscious communications.

UNCONSCIOUS COMMUNICATION AND ITS THERAPEUTIC OVERLAYS

Langs's discovery of derivatives and my subliteral material share a fundamental commonality, unconscious communication. There the similarity ends. Both were conceived from different parentage, thus were raised in a different environment, and therefore are destined to develop quite differently. Langs's theory was born in therapy, and mine in the small groups dynamics laboratory. Langs's goal was therapeutic, mine was to understand cognitive and social processes. Although these differences can be rich in further possible discoveries, nevertheless, they can lead to serious problems,

problems that need not occur. They need not occur because linking Langs's derivative communications to psychoanalysis is not necessary because even if subliteral or derivative communication can be used therapeutically—and this is a big "if" at this point—there are no inherent reasons to superimpose psychoanalytic concepts on the subliteral meaning. Understandably, Langs links derivatives to psychoanalysis because this is his training, after all, and because he discovered derivatives in the context of psychoanalytic therapy. In short, the link is an accident of history.

The cognitive operations underlying Langs's derivatives and my subliteral phenomena are the same. If they can be used therapeutically, the therapeutic mechanisms would not specifically depend on psychoanalytic theory and interpretation. Indeed, there is no need to overlay them with any therapeutic theory at all. As we saw in the previous therapeutic examples, no psychoanalytic-specific interpretation was necessary. Although subliteral communications can be overlain with any given theory, the point is, it doesn't need to be. I say this understanding quite well that all interpretation is implicitly based on some "theory" even if we are not aware of it. In any event, the phenomenon stands by itself. Accordingly, if unconscious communications can be used therapeutically, then cognitive research—independent of any therapeutic theory overlay—needs to be conducted to further understand and develop a valid and effective cognitive therapy based on these unconscious communications.

Finally, at the risk of seemingly belaboring the separation of subliteral and Langsian derivative phenomena from psychoanalysis, let me indicate a couple of final practical reasons why the separation is necessary. First, given the negative scientific track record of psychoanalytic theory and its treatment effectiveness history, it doesn't make an appropriate base for such a potentially important therapeutic method. Unconscious communication as a therapeutic method is too potentially important to be left to the vicissitudes of any specific therapeutic theory. Secondly, because of this long history, most rigorous researchers have historically distanced themselves from conducting research on anything even remotely sounding psychoanalytic. The historic linking of the unconscious mind and of the analysis of dreams to psychoanalysis retarded cognitive research into these areas for decades. Thus to link either subliteral phenomena or unconscious communication and its therapeutic possibilities to psychoanalysis is to sever important links to legitimate research efforts. This in turn would relegate subliteral findings to the accumulating scrap heap of pop psychology and again retard research for decades.

POSTSCRIPT

I mentioned in chapter 2 that scientific discoveries are sometimes made nearly simultaneously by two people. The classic example is the theory of evolution by Charles Darwin and Alfred Russell Wallace, the biologist who had independently discovered natural selection, who had been influenced by some of the same authors as Darwin, and who had expressed the theory of evolution using almost the same words. Although Darwin and Wallace admired each other, what separated them was their different views of the human mind. Similarly, my subliteral phenomena and Langs's derivatives, though born separately and raised quite differently, are siblings. It is appropriate, then, to close this chapter with the following quote. Charles Darwin is reputed to have written to Alfred Russell Wallace, "I hope you have not murdered too completely your own and my child."[30]

CONCLUDING ETHICAL POSTSCRIPT

As the illustrations presented in this book clearly demonstrate, listening subliterally can be interesting, sometimes humorous, and provides a window into the unconscious workings of our minds. It can also be a powerful tool for discovering very personal hidden feelings and experiences in people's lives, so potentially powerful in fact, that I feel ethically obligated to sound a note of caution.

Scientists have an ethical responsibility for their work. I remember as a first-year graduate student taking a seminar on ethics in science. The Manhattan Project, which developed the atomic bomb that was later dropped on Hiroshima and Nagasaki in WWII, is perhaps the modern poster child for ethics in science. Albert Einstein and J. Robert Oppenheimer, the director of the project, wrote to the President expressing their ethical and moral concerns. More recently, the continued ethical controversies about the environment, using animals for experiments, and human cloning, clearly point out the ethics involved in scientific research.

I recall that in the seminar I posed the question, what if I happened to discover a complex chemical formula for a pill that would enable anyone to read other people's minds? Think of the implications of this discovery. Do I publish my formula for this pill, or do I flush it down the toilet? There was then, and there is now continuing controversy about where the ethical boundaries of science lie. In that seminar, there were many students who felt strongly that I should destroy the formula. My position then and now is that the formula should not be destroyed because, as we know from the history of science, someone else would probably discover it eventually and might keep it secret for their personal or national gain.

Ironically, now I find myself, not with a chemical formula for reading minds, but with a psychological method that is similar in many ways.

Writers have this ethical dilemma, too. I remember the Woody Allen movie, *Deconstructing Harry,* about a writer who published in his novels all of the personal information that his friends had shared with him that he should have kept confidential. Although it may be appropriate to climb a mountain simply because the mountain is there, unlike scientific discoveries, it's not always appropriate to reveal a subliteral meaning simply because it was recognized. I have many subliteral stories that I did not present in this book, stories from friends and colleagues. I didn't present them because I couldn't disguise them sufficiently so that the person telling the narrative or the people to whom they referred wouldn't recognize the situation. There are a number of reasons why revealing such information might be harmful.

First, the hidden meaning found in subliteral conversations is frequently hidden for a reason. A person's conscious mind either didn't want you or others to know the thought or feeling, or their unconscious mind didn't want their own conscious mind to know. Listening subliterally, then, is like having someone tell you something in confidence. Secondly, revealing subliteral meanings can be embarrassing for the person. It can also be personally or socially harmful.

That it's sometimes inappropriate to reveal subliteral meaning is illustrated in chapter 4, where a group member told about her dying friend. It would have been inappropriate for me—even in this educational setting—to have asked the group or the member whose friend was dying, if they recognized the subliteral connection between the topic of the dying friend and having to pressure him to talk with their discussions about silent members in the group and about boyfriends who were uncommunicative.

Though the member introduced the topic of her dying friend and though it would have provided an added example for the group members to understand subliteral conversation and the group dynamics further, I didn't consider it educationally justifiable. If, however, the group had been a counseling group dealing with issues of separation and loss or grieving, then it would have been appropriate to link the subliteral meaning of the topics to the member's story of her dying friend. Indeed, it could have provided a powerful therapeutic experience.

Third, at this point we don't always know on what level subliteral meanings have significance. For example, in chapter 9 I cautioned that often subliteral references to ethnic racial stereotypes may not necessarily mean that the person speaking is prejudiced in a negative sense. Instead, such references may reflect deep cultural stereotypes that most of us have had culturally ingrained in us and which may be automatically evoked in certain circumstances. Or they may simply reflect an unconscious recognition of human differences.

Finally, though I have developed a systematic method for analyzing and validating subliteral meaning, it's not an exact science, and the subliteral analysis of a piece of literal conversation may not be correct. It's often the case that verification of a subliteral meaning may be an ongoing process.

Appendix

Overview of Analysis, and Validation Operations

This Appendix is a modified and updated version of my main article on subliteral methodology which appeared in the journal *Small Group Research*.[1] The article laid out the cognitive and linguistic operations that I developed at that point for analyzing and validating subliteral meaning. I have included them here as an appendix for four reasons. First, it serves as a source when I refer to a particular operation in some of the many examples that I use throughout this book. To have applied all of the aspects of this methodology in each subliteral illustration would have been much too cumbersome, tedious, and would have broken the flow of the narratives. Secondly, I include it because it was important to me that readers could verify for themselves the interconnectedness of the many strange and sometimes bizarre cognitive operations in this book. Third, this appendix shows that the subliteral narratives are based on a systematic, scientifically controlled method and are not just fanciful interpretations. Fourth, I included them so that interested readers could check on my analysis of an illustration or use it as a reference source when they subliterally listen to conversations in their own personal or professional lives. Finally, this appendix will serve as a highly concentrated summary and overview of the subliteral approach to language, meaning, and mind.

I have modified the list of the various operations from their original form for a number of reasons. First, I have modified them to make them more readable. Second, I have added new findings since the original publication. The main reason I modified the list, however, is that although all of the cognitive and linguistic operations are not illustrated in this book, nevertheless, I wanted to include the entire set of operations, so that readers could get a general idea of the complete scope of the method. I would like to point out that I have consistently found these operations across many different sets of data.

In addition, I have categorized and numbered the operations for easy reference. In doing so, I have maintained the original category and numbering system used in the original article. I have done this to keep a continuity between this updated version and the original, so that the interested reader can easily refer to the original material. Some of the changes are simply rewording of the material. Other categories have been added since the original version. I mark with an asterisk [*] only these added categories Finally, in briefly illustrating the operations, I have used mostly examples from the chapters in this book. Others, however, are not in the book. I included these, however, because, again, I wanted to include the complete array of operations.

I. General Optimal Conditions and Considerations for Generating and Recognizing Subliteral Phenomena

0.1.* General Conditions and Cues

0.1.1. Optimal Conditions Although subliteral material can occur under most conditions, the optimal conditions leading to subliteral expressions are conditions of (1) low social structure, (2) ambiguity, and (3) uncertainty. The more a conversational situation is free-floating, the more likely it is that unconscious processes will be activated and subliteral meaning generated.

0.1.2. Affective Arousal and Loading Under the previous conditions, affective or emotional arousal levels (1) increase, (2) create a cognitive state in which nonconscious affective and linguistic schemas are activated.

0.1.3. Intra- and Interpersonal Conflict The more conscious or unconscious conflict that exists within an individual and between or among members of a conversation, the more likely it is that subliteral material will occur.

0.1.4. Censoring The more social taboos, rules of etiquette, and other social rules that preclude the open expression of feelings and ideas, the more likely subliteral narratives will occur.

0.1.5. Pauses and Silences The more awkward silences and pauses in a conversation, the more likely it is that subliteral material will be generated.

0.1.6. Contiguity Association   A topic is often subliteral if it is associated in time, i.e., merely comes after another topic (especially after a silence or pause in a conversation).

0.2.* Other Initial Theoretical Considerations

0.2.1. Topic and Language Selection   The previous conditions leading to the activation of affective and linguistic schemas result in a merging with and a shaping of the unconscious selection of (1) topics, (2) specific words, phrases, and (3) other linguistic operations.

0.2.2. Oral Speech   In recognizing subliteral meaning, analyzing the literal language from which it derives must be approached as oral speech, not as formalized written language. The distinction between "speech," on the one hand, and formalized, written, grammatically correct linguistic productions, on the other, is an important distinction In analyzing oral speech, speech errors, sounds, inflections, and memory distortions are important factors (See 7.4. Memorial and Perceptual Operations).

0.2.3. The Unconscious   As used in relation to generating subliteral material, the term unconscious includes (1) what is commonly meant by the term, which involves deep, unaccessible, mental and emotional material; (2) consciously unattended to material; and (3) thoughts and feeling that are intentionally withheld from public view because of fear, social etiquette, or social taboos. Although conscious thoughts and feelings that are withheld may be relatively conscious, they still are associated with conflict and thus initiate the processes that generate subliteral material.

0.2.3.a. Unconscious Cognition   The subliteral unconscious is a cognitive unconscious. This means that perception, thinking, and reasoning occur before the conscious awareness of input. Thus, the subliteral unconscious functions cognitively in the same way as conscious cognition.

0.2.3.b. Unconscious Conversations   Unconscious or subliteral conversations occur between members, that is, a listener's unconscious mind understands the subliteral level of meaning in the literal narratives spoken by another person and responds subliterally, just as in conscious conversation.

0.2.3.c. Oscillation   The subliteral unconscious is not a static set of processes. It slips and slides from a deep unconscious state, which is inaccessible, to a nearly conscious state, to being partially conscious.

II. COGNITIVE OPERATIONS

1. ANALOGICAL AND ISOMORPHIC OPERATIONS

1.1. Analogical Matching Operations Literal words, phrases, and stories in conversations are compared to (1) the membership composition of a conversation, (2) the inferred psychodynamics, and (3) other contextual information. This matching is done using both concrete and abstract similarity relationships between the words, phrases, stories, and the actual here-and-now conversational situation.

Instantiation A topic of journalism is selected for a narrative. The narrative topic is matched to the fact that group members are *writing notes* (concrete correspondence) on the verbal interaction (abstract relationship). Thus, the topic of journalism is initially hypothesized as a subliteral match to the act of note taking occurring in the discussion. The hypothesis may be further supported when *contextual* (See 2. Contextual Frame Analysis) evidence suggests a match between the topic and an affective concern of members that they are secretly being written about.

1.2. Isomorphic Mapping Operations The hypothetical match is, then, further mapped onto the composition structure of the interaction (concrete relationship). Mapping is a higher order extension of the matching process.

Instantiation If the literal verbal material specifies "3 journalists" when only 3 group members are taking notes and no other triadic composition structure is evident, then the initial validity of the mapping of the topic of journalism subliterally equates to the here-and-now situation and is tentatively hypothesized.

1.3.* Double References In matching and mapping, double references may be involved. A double reference means that a literal narrative subliterally applies to two separate referents simultaneously.

Instantiation   A literal topic about being "under 21" may refer (1) to younger members in a discussion, who in fact are under 21 years of age, and (2) to 3 dominant members in the discussion, i.e., $2 + 1 = 3$ (See 8.4. Single Number Operations; 8.5. Addition Operations, 9.4. Relative Categorical Operations).

2. CONTEXTUAL FRAME ANALYSIS

The context of a situation is important to the analysis of subliteral meaning. Context includes understanding the history of the situation, its developmental aspects, people's expectations, and knowledge of social and group dynamics.

2.1. Historical   Matching and mapping information surrounding, or external to, the immediate narrative situation is important evidence for understanding, analyzing, and validating subliteral meaning.

Instantiation   If in previous discussion sessions, open and unresolved discussions over the concern of writing notes during conversations has been evident, then the context evidentially supports the literal topic of "journalists" as a subliteral narrative.

2.2. Developmental Stage   The content of hypothesized subliteral meaning is matched with concerns and issues that are correlated with the stages of group development. Concerns and issues that are expressed are typically consistent and congruent with the stage of development that the interaction has reached.

Instantiation   In the initial stages of a discussion or long-term social gathering, literal narratives are typically about power and authority, about *"a new job,"* or *"being newly weds,"* or other topics having to do with "beginnings." Later stages involve stories about conflict, as in talk about movies like *Star Wars,* about *disaster movies,* or about *groups breaking up.* Then, as the conflict situation resolves, narratives often shift to talk of *traffic problems, growing plants,* or about *building houses.* Finally, as a group nears its end, narratives may be about *separation and loss* or about *death.*

2.3.* Expectations   In analyzing literal narratives for subliteral meaning, it is important to understand the expectations that people have about the narrative or social situation.

Instantiation   It is known that behavior in social situations is often influenced by people's expectations and beliefs about (1) groups and how they should function, (2) leadership and authority, and (3) acceptable social behavior. They also have stereotypes about (1) gender, (2) sexual preference, (3) race and ethnicity, (4) age, a host of other expectations and beliefs about (5) sexual tensions in relationships, and (6) human conflicts in general.

2.4.* Knowledge Base   Although much of subliteral analysis is based on fairly direct observation of the actual dynamics in a here-and-now group situation, analyzing subliteral meaning is based on four different kinds of data about the narrative situation.

Instantiation   It is known that knowledge about (1) collective or group level dynamics, (2) leadership and authority dynamics, (3) data about the specific group, e.g., (i) subgrouping and coalition forming, (ii) the composition of the group, (iii) the stage of development achieved by the group, and (iv) knowledge of the dynamics in past sessions; (4) knowledge from social psychological research, e.g., (i) expectations and beliefs that people have about groups and how they should function, (5) norms of acceptable social behavior, (6) social stereotypes about (i) gender, (ii) sexual preference, (iii) race and ethnicity, and (iv) age; (7) general knowledge about (i) various tensions in human relationships and (ii) human conflicts in general; (8) knowledge about individual group members, e.g., (i) what each has consciously said and done in past sessions and (ii) about thoughts and feeling that are not expressed or that are unconscious.

2.5.* Selection Response Field   In all literal narratives the number of topics, words, and phrases that could be selected for the conversation is practically infinite. Thus, for all topics and the specific language used to express them, we must ask why the particular and specific topic, word, or phrase was selected as opposed to others. Both context and purpose (conscious or unconscious) create constraints on selection. Using the history and context of the narrative situation, along with knowledge of the previous categories, provides a basis for understanding the constraints on the selecting of topics.

Instantiation A topic about a childrens TV program, called *Mr. Roberts,* is selected for a discussion because (1) it combines a members' basic and immediate feelings about the narrative situation, which in this case is primarily a concern with the leader, hence selecting a TV program that has a clear leader in its title; (2) the member who selected the topic is surprised by the presence of a television and a microphone, hence, increasing the possibility of narrowing the response field to a remark about television; (3) the member is also surprised at seeing a child in the group, further narrowing his response field to children's television programs; (4) the member had been counterdependent and considered the process childish; (5) the trainer's name, "Robert," narrows the response field to a children's television program that has a leader whose name begins with at least an "R."

3. PSYCHOSOCIOMETRIC OPERATIONS

3.1. Resonance Operations Resonance refers to a person in a conversation who is psychoemotionally involved in the concern to which the subliteral meaning of the conversation or topic refers. Subliteral stories are not expressed by people who, by historical and contextual analysis, do not have an affective or emotional involvement in the concern that the subliteral material expresses.

Instantiation A member, not concerned about note taking in a discussion will not generate subliteral material referring to a literal topic of "journalists." Such topics are generated only by those who are known to have a concern about note taking.

3.2. Sociometric Operations A variant on the previous operation is that the *content* of a subliteral topic will isomorphically match or correspond to the literal or actual relationship of the person who produces the material to the person's status in the discussion.

Instantiation   Negative subliteral narratives about "3 journalists" are invariably generated only by nonmembers of a triadic subgroup. Conversely, positive subliteral narratives about the triadic structure are made by members of that subgroup or other group members who have demonstrated positive resonance to the triad.

3.3. Gender Operations   Literal narratives that identify gender match the actual gender composition in the discussion to which it subliterally refers.

Instantiation   When it is hypothesized that the literal topic of "3 journalists," two of whom are female and one male, is a subliteral reference to the 3 people in a discussion, the subliteral reference will match the actual here-and-now gender composition of two females and one male taking notes.

4. ASSOCIATIONAL OPERATIONS

4.1. Semantic Association Operations   Affective semantic evaluations contained in, or which are about, a literal or actual conversational situation will consistently match the subliteral affective evaluations by the members who generate the literal material.

Instantiation   A literal report about "3 journalists" that contains a negative reference will subliterally correspond to 3 members of a conversation who are taking notes and toward whom the remaining members have negative feelings (see 4.2. and 4.3.).

4.2. Dimensional Evaluative Vector Operations   Literal references in narratives that are associated with spatial dimensions like "up" or "down," with the dimension "up," equaling positive, and the dimension "down," equaling negative, reflect affective evaluations that isomorphically correspond to positive or negative evaluations of the three members in a literal conversational situation that it subliterally references.

Instantiation   3 members who take notes are affectively experienced by other members as negative. Accordingly, the literal topic of "3 journalists," which is subliterally about 3 members in a here-and-now situation, is consistently and contextually associated with being "down in back" as opposed to "up front."

4.3. Dimensional Vector Equivalence Operations   Subliteral topics are systematically and consistently associated with other equivalent spatial dimensions, like "left," as opposed to "right."

Instantiation   In addition to "3 journalists" being "*down* in back of," subliteral references can be tracked to the associated cognitively equivalent vectors of being on the "left" as opposed to "right" which, respectively, are associated with being in "back" of as opposed to being in "front." Vectorial tracking is consistent across multiple permutations of the literal topic of "3 journalists" (see 9.8.) and its subliteral referents.

5. PARALLEL PSYCHOMOTOR OPERATIONS

Parallel psychomotor operations are significant adjuncts to establishing the validity of subliteral meaning. Being outside the linguistic production system, these unconscious isomorphic psychomotor operations add another level of matching and mapping operations.

5.1. Ocular Operations   Literal topics are often indicated and simultaneously accompanied by nonconscious micromovements of a speaker's eyes.

Instantiation   Indicating subliteral meaning to the literal topic of "3 journalists," speakers may briefly shift their gaze when talking about the literal topic of "3 journalists" in the direction of the 3 members to whom the topic's subliteral meaning refers (consistent with 3.2.).

5.2. Gestural Operations   Literal topics are often indicated and simultaneously accompanied by nonconscious hand movements.

Instantiation   Indicating subliteral meaning to the literal topic of "3 journalists," speakers may unconsciously point in the direction of the 3 members to whom the subliteral meaning refers (consistent with 3.2.).

5.3. Body-Positioning Operations   Literal topics are often indicated and simultaneously accompanied by nonconscious body positions and movements.

Instantiation   Generating a literal report of "climbing mountains," being "king of the mountain," and "being on top," a speaker may sit on the top of the backrest of a chair (with his or her feet in the seat) structurally and physically reflecting the member's perception of their literal high-status position in the group.

6. LINGUISTIC AND NOMINAL OPERATIONS

6.0.* Deep Structure Representation   There are many normal sentences whose surface structures have multiple deep structures or internal representations that generate multiple semantic surface structures of "literal" meanings. The following classic sentences in the field of linguistics demonstrate such multiple internal representations that underlie a single surface structure:

1. *Surface structure:* **The shooting of the hunters bothered him.**
   Representation 1: The killing of the hunters bothered him.
   Representation 2: The sound of the hunters shooting their guns bothered him.
2. *Surface structure:* **Flying airplanes can be dangerous.**
   Representation 1: Flying in airplanes can be dangerous.
   Representation 2: Airplanes flying in the air above you can be dangerous.

The deep structures or internal representations of the surface structures of these classic sentences are formal equivalents to the subliteral internal representations of literal (surface structure) meanings;

Instantiation   A phrase whose surface structure is the name of a journalist, Harry Reasoner, can have a second or internal representation:

Surface Structure: **The journalist Harry Reasoner.**
Representation 1: His name is Harry Reasoner.
Representation 2: He is a *hairy reasoner.*

The researcher is being internally represented as a bearded person (i.e., *hairy*) who is a reasoner about the group process (see 6.1., 6.2., 6.3., 7.1., and 11.2.).

6.1. Nominal Semantic Operations

6.1. Nominal Semantic Operations   Names in literal narratives can be subliteral references to members in a conversation and can be recognized by being the same name or by a modified representation of the member's name.

Instantiation   A literal topic about the movie director Stanley Kubrick is used to represent subliterally a member whose name is Kulick.

6.1.1.* Initials   Initials in literal narratives can be subliteral references to members in a conversation and can be recognized by being letters that are part of a literal topic or by the first and last letter of a first and last name. Initials may be in the correct order or be reversed.

Instantiation   The literal name of a writer and author, "*H*arold *R*obbins" is generated as a subliteral reference to a trainer writing notes. The first letters in the first and last name represent the trainer's initials, *R. H.* (see 6.1., 7.1. on reversals; consistent with 2.2., 3.1., and 3.3.).

6.1.2.* Embedded Names and Initials   Names or initials in literal narratives that are subliteral references to members in a conversation may be embedded within another name or phrase.

Instantiation   The use of the phrase *foolhardy* is used subliterally to represent a person whose last name is *Hardy*.

6.1.3.* Fusions of Names and Initials   Names or initials in literal narratives that are subliteral references to members in a conversation may be fused within another name or phrase.

Instantiation   The word *sunlight* is constructed from two members' names. One is that of an older woman whose name is *Firestone* (represented by sun; i.e., a big stone of fire), and the other name is that of a male, young enough to be her son (represented by sun), whose name is *Wright* (i.e., phonetically or by rhyme equal to light;); hence, */Firestone/* + */Wright/* equals *sunlight* (see 6.2.1. *Portmanteaus*).

6.2. Phonetic Operations   Literal narratives are often rendered subliteral by phonetic transformations similar to puns and plays on words.

Instantiation   A literal name, "Harry Harris," is a subliteral reference that describes 2 trainers in the discussion. The first name /Harry/ is phonetic for */hairy/*, which describes the first trainer who had a beard. The last name /Harris/ is phonetic for */hairless/*, which describes the second trainer who did not have a beard.

6.2.1.* Portmanteaus   Similar to 6.1.3., portmanteaus or portmanteau-like words and meanings are often constructed by merging the sounds and meanings of two different words.

Instantiation   In a conversation about hard-core child pornography and a poster with two nude infants who are about two years old, it is said, *"I guess people need diversions."* The spoken word *"diversions"* is pronounced with a slur, making it sound like *di-virgins.* Subliterally, the two nude babies on the poster were represented by: (di) equals */two/* (versions) equivalent to */virgins/*—or two virgins.

6.2.2.* Homophones   Like the */hairy* Harris/ *hairless* illustration, there are hundreds of homophones—words that are pronounced alike but which have different meanings or spellings—that are used to construct subliteral meaning (there are also homographs, words that are spelled alike but have different meanings or pronunciations like *bow,* as in the *bow* of a ship and *bow* as in a *bow* and *arrow*).

Instantiation   In a discussion about psychotherapists, a woman at her podiatrist's office talked about his clients */baring/* their */souls/* to him, while having the */bare/ /soles/* of her feet massaged.

6.2.3.* Oronyms   Subliteral meanings sometimes use a string of sounds that can be heard in two different ways and has two different meanings, e.g., *The stuffy nose / The stuff he knows.*

Instantiation A literal reference to a club called the *Explorers* is subliterally heard as /explore/ /her/.

6.3. Syntactic Ordering Operations The order in which first and last names are presented is often a subliteral reference to the dominance or seniority order of two (or more) persons.

Instantiation The literal name /*Harry Harris*/ is generated to correspond subliterally in the correct order to the senior researcher. Harry stands for /*hairy*/, the bearded *senior* researcher, then the second name Harris stands for /*hairless*/, the beardless *junior* researcher (see 7.4., 10.2., and 12.1.; consistent with 2.2., 3.3., 6.1.1., 6.1.2., and 6.1.3.).

6.3.1.* Paronyms Paronymic words that derive from the same root or stem, like *mean*ie, and *mean*ing—or words that are graphically perceived to be paronymic-like—are used to create subliteral meaning.

Instantiation In a literal discussion about a black Labrador retriever which is a subliteral reference to an African-American female (whose last name is *Baltimore* and about a black person who was said to be from *Baltimore*) who is originally from /*Georgia*/, a subliteral linkage is a reference to a simple gift that is given to her which, it is emphasized, is /*gorgeous*/.

6.4. Verbal Tagging Operations Topics in literal narratives are often tagged to signal an approximation to a reference that would not fit the intended subliteral meaning if it were exactly referenced.

Instantiation The literal narrative, "it was *about* 10 or 11, or *something like that,*" simultaneously subliterally references two subgroups: the 10 group members, which would equal 11 total if the trainer were counted (consistent with 7.4. Memorial and Perceptual Operations).

6.5. Temporal Shift Operations Subliteral references involve temporal shifts that psychologically transform a literal reference to a past event into a psychologically present subliteral event.

Instantiation A literal narrative about "3 guys who /*were*/" talking funny, a reference to three male members in a discussion who are verbally joking with each other in a subgroup of their own, is shifted to the present tense, "3 guys who /*are*/" talking funny.

6.6. Pronoun Operations Like temporal shifts, subliteral references often involve corresponding pronoun shifts, which linguistically link a literal topic to its subliteral meaning.

Instantiation A literal report about "*those* 3 guys who were" acting funny is changed as the narrative progresses to "/*these*/ 3 guys who /*are*/" acting funny or to "/*that*/ guy was" acting funny to "/*this*/ here guy *is*" acting funny, thus indicating that the report is a subliteral reference to the males who are acting strangely in the here-and-now situation (see 6.5. Temporal Shift Operations)

6.7. Noun Shift Operations Literal narratives often involve noun shifts appropriate to the subliteral meaning, which linguistically link the literal topic to a here-and-now interaction.

Instantiation In a literal numerical narrative about "3 of 10" people in a bar, the 3 subliterally references 3 dominant members, and the 10 subliterally references the remaining group membership. The 3 is linguistically referred to as *people,* whereas the 10 is linguistically referred to as *kids.* Because the 3 dominant members are older (and age is an affective concern) the use of the noun *kids* with the reference to "3" would not be subliterally congruent in distinguishing the 3 dominant older members from the rest of the group (see 8.1., 8.2., and 9.5.). The collective noun *people* is age-neutral, whereas the collective noun *kids* is not.

6.8.* Plural Shift Operations Literal narratives often involve plural shifts appropriate to the subliteral meaning, which linguistically link the literal topic to a here-and-now discussion (consistent with 6.7.).

Instantiation In a literal narrative about a black *hole* in space, which is a subliteral reference to a single African-American male in the discussion, the typical use of the plural to describe the phenomena, i.e., black holes, is shifted to its singular form *hole.*

6.9.* Adjectival Shifts   Nouns used in literal narratives are often shifted to adjectives and adverbial form to express subliteral meaning.

Instantiation   In 6.2. Phonetic Operations, the proper noun /Harry/, on a subliteral level, is shifted to the adjective, /*hairy*/.

6.10.* Transitional Topics   Transitional topics are literal narratives that have subliteral meanings which belong to the same category as the here-and-now concern for which the topic is subliteral. These provide direct links to a here-and-now situation.

Instantiation   In a discussion where the unconscious concern is about a here-and-now instructor or a course, the literal topic will be about other instructors or courses, as opposed to literal topics about other authority figures in general.

6.11.* Transitional Linkages   Certain phrases often function as transitional linkages to a here-and-now situation.

Instantiation   Literal topics are sometimes consciously or semiconsciously linked to a here-and-now situation by the phrases "Like in here. . . . . ." or, as in a literal discussion, about mental patients and convicts where it is said that some of these patients and convicts are going to school *"here now."* Such linkages are carried out by 6.8. Plural Shift Operations, 6.7. Noun Shift Operations, 6.6. Pronoun Operations, and 6.5. Temporal Shift Operations.

7. REVERSAL, INVERSION, OPPOSITION, AND MEMORIAL OPERATIONS

7.1. Reversal Operations   Reversals of names and initials in literal reports are cognitive operations that expressing subliteral negation of the person being referenced.

Instantiation   The literal name of a journalist, *Harry Reasoner,* is selected for the narrative to correspond subliterally to a person taking notes in the discussion whose initials are *R. H.* Reversals of the initials is a mode in which to express negative affect toward the referent.

7.1.1.* Textual Expression Operations Reversals are used to express negation only when the text or context in which the initials are used does not involve a negative.

Instantiation In a previous protocol subliterally referencing the trainer's (unreversed) initials *R. H.,* the topic "Rh-negative" blood is selected. Because the negative attribution was linguistically explicit, the initials were not reversed.

7.2. Inversion Operations
Inversions in literal reports, in which something is converted to an opposite, are operations performed to express opposition or disagreement.

Instantiation In a literal narrative about the 9:1 ratio of hyperactive males to females, a discussant notes that the ratio of 9 males to 1 female is the same ratio as the group gender composition. Although the 9:1 ratio was correct, the actual group gender composition was the reverse (9 females to 1 male). In response, a discussant described a work situation in which "the signs on the restroom doors were switched," subliterally indicating disagreement with the previous discussant's observation that the ratio of 9:1 was the same in the *group*. Switching the signs of the restroom door is equivalent to changing the signs on an algebraic equation from + to –.

7.3. Opposition Operations
Literal narratives presented as paired opposites are cognitive operations that subliterally express differences among members of a conversation.

Instantiation An affective subliteral concern among discussants regarding dominant versus nondominant members is expressed by the literal opposing topics of "giants versus dwarfs" or "parents versus children."

7.4.* Memorial and Perceptual Operations
Memorial and perceptual reconstructions occur that render the content and structure of literal reports correspondent with the subliteral referents to which they refer.

Instantiation A reference to a journalist, Harry Harris, is "misremembered." The discussant later reported that the intended name was Sidney Harris (see, 6.2. Phonetic Operations; 6.3. Syntactic Ordering Operations).

8. MATHEMATICAL COMPUTATIONAL OPERATIONS

8.1. Numerical Recomputation   Numbers selected for a conversation correspond subliterally to subgroups within the narrative composition and will consistently vary with fluctuating membership.

Instantiation   The number 6, selected for a discussion subliterally representing a dominant subgroup of 6, is changed to the number 5 when one member is absent (see 12.4.).

8.2. Cipher Operations   On a subliteral level, zeros (beyond those used in the number 10) do not function computationally beyond the number representing the actual size of discussion membership.

Instantiation   A literal number 10,000 is selected for a narrative about a group whose membership is 10. Subliterally, the *10*,(000), represents the 10 members and the 3 zeros in (1 0,) *000* represent a subgroup of 3 (zeros may also function as dual, double, or complex numbers; see 9.2., 9.4., and 9.5.).

8.3. Cancellation Operations   Literal *double numbers,* e.g., 88, 11, 66, etc. may cancel to a single number, e.g., 8, 1, and 6.

Instantiation   The literal number 44 is selected for a narrative to represent a subgroup of 4 that was dominant.

8.4. Single Number Operations   Literal double numbers, e. g., 44, or *dual numbers,* e. g., 51, may function as two single numbers.

Instantiations   The literal dual number expressed as "21 years old" is selected for a discussion to represent a triadic subgroup where the 2 stands for two male members, and the 1 stands for one female member (see 9.4.).

8.5. Addition Operations   Literal double or dual numbers selected for a discussion may add together to equal a sum.

Instantiation   The literal dual number expressed as "21 years old" is selected for a discussion to represent the leadership subgroup of 3, composed of 2 males and 1 female. The dual number first functions as two single numbers and sums to 3: 2 + 1 = 3 (see 8.4.; consistent with 8.2.).

8.6. Subtraction Operations   Subtraction does not occur as a standard subliteral arithmetical operation, it occurs by using cancellation operations or by using ciphers.

Instantiation   The literal number 10,000 is selected for a narrative to represent the 10 members who are present out of a total of 13 members. The 3 zeros represent the 3 missing members (see 8.2.).

8.6.1.* Multiplication operations   Arithmetical division operations also do not occur. Multiplication operations only occur as a variant of addition operations, that is, by the simple repetition of numbers.

9. LOGICOMATHEMATICAL OPERATIONS

9.1. Binary Coding Operations   Logical and categorical distinctions may be performed by numerical coding similar to computer binary codes, in which various combinations of 1 and 0 are used to delineate categories.

Instantiation   The literal number "110 degrees" is selected for a discussion to logically distinguish the compositional structure of a subgroup in a discussion. The two 1's in the *110* equate to the 2 males of a triad, and the 0 equates to the female member (see 9.6.).

9.2. Categorical Structuring Operations   Physical separation between literal numbers distinguishes subliteral referent categories.

Instantiation   In a previous instantiation (see, 8.2. Cipher Operation), in which the number 10,000 is selected for a discussion to represent two subgroups subliterally, the comma structurally marks the separation between a group of 2, and a group of 3.

9.3. Gender Category Operations   Literal numbers are used to distinguish gender classes categorically.

Instantiation   In the literal number "110 degrees" (9.1. Binary Coding Operations), the 1s are used to represent 2 males in a subgroup of 3, and the zero represents the third member who is a female.

9.4. Relative Categorical Operations   Literal numbers used to represent gender categories are relative, not fixed values.

Instantiation   In the previous instantiation, males are represented in the "110 degrees" by 1's and the female by 0s, whereas in the instantiation using "21 years old," the males are represented by the 2 and female by the 1. Subliteral categories are constructed relationally, not simply in terms of their absolute attributes.

9.5. Inclusivity and Exclusivity of Categorical Set Operations
Categorical boundaries that are inclusive on a literal level may be both exclusive and inclusive on different subliteral levels.

Instantiation   On a literal level, a statement about "3 of 10 people in a bar" is an inclusive set, the 3 being a subset of the larger set 10. On one subliteral level the "3 of 10" is also inclusive, in that it references 3 members in a group of 10. On yet another level the "3 of 10" constitutes two exclusive sets, in that it references the total group membership of 13, i.e., 10 + 3 = 13.

9.6. Logically Complex Number Operations   A numerically simple literal number can be a complex subliteral cognitive operation that represents multiple categories.

Instantiation   The complex number "110 degrees," which is a literal reference to the temperature at the top of "3 warehouses," subliterally references the multiple subsets of 3 dominant members in a discussion. First the 110 (1 + 1 + 0) adds up to 3, the complete triadic structure. Second, through categorical structuring, gender category operations, and relative categorical operations, complex numbers distinguish subgroups within the triad: the two 1's stand for the 2 males, the 0 for the older female, the 1 + 10 for the older male + a younger male + older female (who are perceived as a couple or pair). Third, the number distinguishes multiple subgroups within the total group: 1 + 10, the 1 stands for the male; the 10 for the 10 young females; 11 + 0 is the total number of females (including the older female) + the male (now represented by a 0) totaling 12, the entire group (see *9.4.*). The researcher is not included in this aspect of the total count because the topic of 110 degrees was a subliterally reference to obtaining a college degree and thus would not include the researcher (see 10.5.).

9.7. Dimensional Tracking of Deductive Subset Invariance
Logically, if a literal narrative is consistently associated with a given dimensional vector (see 4.3.) such as "down" or "left," then it follows that subliteral subsets of the topic should also be consistently associated with that vector.

Instantiation   In subliterally referencing a dominant triad, the report of "110 degrees" is selected for the discussion. The subsets of the triad are 2 males and 1 older female. Thus, in addition to dimensional association to the 110, references to subsets are also equivalently associated in terms of their dimensional tracking, i.e., reference to 2's and 1's are *down* and *left*.

9.8. Dimensional Tracking of Permutation Invariance   Logically, if a literal narrative is consistently associated with a dimensional vector such as "down," "left," and so on, then it follows that any permutations of the topic should be consistently associated with a given vector.

Instantiation   In subliterally referencing a dominant triad, the two permutations of "110 degrees" and of being "21 years of age" and "3 warehouses" (cited previously) are consistently associated with the dimensions of down and left (by nonmembers of the triad, which is consistent with 2.2., 3.1., and 3.2.).

10. TRANSFORMATIONAL GROUP OPERATIONS

10.1. Transformational Operations   Each literal and basic concern is repetitively transformed into a series of subliteral narratives of which the content representation mode changes, but which retains the same value.

Instantiation   A concern with a dominant triadic subgroup is transformed into (1) 3 warehouses, (2) 3 Greyhound buses, (3) 3 Lucky Spots (a local singing group), and (4) 3 drunken seniors. Each transformation is isomorphic to the literal group triad. The set of transformations constitutes a cognitive transformation group.

10.2. Thematic Transformational Operations   The literal and basic concerns that are transformed in a series of subliteral reports are variations on a basic affective concern, of which each narrative represents a different aspect.

Instantiation   Based on previously expressed concerns about the role of a dominant triad, (1) a narrative about "3 warehouses" represents a concern that the triad is a depository of knowledge about the group dynamics; (2) a "3 Greyhound buses" narrative represents a disconcerting recognition that the triad is "driving" and carrying the entire group discussion; (3) a narrative about "3 Lucky Spots" represents a recognition that the triad is probably favored by the researcher or trainer; and (4) a "3 drunken seniors" narrative represents the judgment that the triad is out of control. Taken together, these narratives constitute a thematic transformational group.

10.3. Permutational Operations   Each literal and basic concern is reflectively permuted into a series of subliteral narratives of which the structural mode of representation changes but which retains the same value.

Instantiation   A concern with a dominant triadic subgroup composed of 2 males and 1 female is permuted into (1) 110 degrees, (2) 21 years of age, and (3) a $20,000 bribe. Each permutation is isomorphic to the literal triad, and its subsets and constitutes a cognitive transformational group. Transformations (10.1. and 10.2.) are primarily semantic in their representational mode and more global in their representation, whereas permutations are primarily numerical representations that permute the rearrangements of subgroup differentiation.

10.4. Permutational Numerical Changes   Literal numbers selected into narratives that correspond isomorphically to subgroups within the total group composition and consistently vary with subgroup member ab-

sences will also change consistently throughout the permutations of the base or literal narrative.

Instantiation   Narrative permutations that correspond to a literal subgroup of 6 such as "6 people were standing" or "6 cars were parked" are changed in subsequent permuted narratives to "5 drinks" and "5 doors down," when one member of the subgroup is absent (see 8.1.).

10.5. Single-Aspect Permutational Numerical Changes   A given subliteral number may, at one time, include a member and at another time exclude the same member, depending on the affective concern at a given time.

Instantiation   When the concern is leadership, the complex number "110 degrees" includes the male trainer when its representation is 11 standing for the two males and 0 standing for the female, when the representation totals the entire group (i.e., $11 + 0 = 12$), it excludes the male trainer, because only the peer membership is working toward a "degree", i.e., a diploma (see 9.5. and 9.6.).

11. MATRIX AND LATTICE STRUCTURE OPERATIONS

11.1. Matrix Structure Operations   To analyze and understand the internal cognitive structure manifested in these narratives, the different aspects of literal narratives from which the subliteral levels are partially derived, can be assigned to cells within a cognitive base matrix notated as M_1, M_2, M_3, and M_4.

Instantiation   See figures in the text.

11.2. Lattice Structure Operations   A lattice structure is composed of the base matrix (M_0,) and a series of matrices (M_1, M_2, M_3, M_4), the cells of which contain the different levels of subliteral material that isomorphically correspond to the cells in the generative base matrix. Each tier is a harmonic.

Instantiation   See figures in the text.

12. MULTICORRELATIVE TRANSFORMATIONAL VALIDATION

12.1. Internal Order Structure   In part, validity and falsification of subliteral narratives are established by operations similar to establishing mathematical proof, that is, internal isomorphic correspondences are deductive or derived transformations, correlations, and relationships, which constitute the structure of an ordered series based on cognitive operations and on rules of inference.

Instantiation   See 9. Logicomathematical Operations and 10. Transformation Group Operations.

12.2. External Order Operations   Unlike mathematical proofs, establishing the validity and falsification of subliteral narratives requires external structures corresponding to the literal narrative situation. (See 2. Contextual Frame Analysis).

Instantiation   Context: (1) the atypical situation of two trainers/authorities in a discussion; (2) members will be concerned with this situation. *Rule:* Literal references to "2" or "pairs" may reference two researchers in the group. (2) Context: Members are largely concerned with authority relationships in the initial stages of group development. *Rule:* Reference to "2s" or "pairs" decreases as the group develops. (3) Context: (1) open discussion about note taking in the group; (2) the two researchers are taking notes. *Rule:* Literal topics will be discussed that thematically relate to writing or storing information.
   Internally consistent order structures are important for establishing reliability, whereas external order structures are important for establishing validity. Without external correspondence, the mathematical proof-like internal order may be interesting, but it does not refer to any empirically valid reality.

12.3. Intra- and Internarrative Structure   Narratives within a given affective concern structure in a discussion as well as among different affective concern structures and different discussion sessions will consistently use the various cognitive operations.

General Instantiation   Narratives that exhibit transformations, permutations, and deductive subsets, both intra- and interdiscussion topics, will appropriately exhibit consistent semantic, dimensional, associational, evaluative tracking, resonance, sociometric, gender, noun, pronoun, temporal shifts, reversals, oppositions, inversions, and psychomotor and computational operations.

13.* VERIFICATION AND FALSIFICATION

13.1. Nomological Network   Validation and falsification procedures derive from being sufficiently tied to a network of procedures that exhibit a high degree of formal adequacy of the correspondences and the plausibility of the entire analysis. Thus, validation is a network concept composed of an interconnecting network of relationships, what the philosopher of science Herbert Feigl classically referred to as a nomological network. Making a similar point on validation procedures in his classic work, *The Structure of Science,* Ernest Nagel suggested that "a sufficient condition for a theory to be testable and to perform its function in inquiry is that enough of its theoretical notions be associated with coordinating definitions." Substituting the term *theory* for methodology, the point is that it is not a requirement of validation that every piece of a research puzzle be subject to a complete set of validating procedures. Moreover, as Roy Lachman and his colleagues note, if cognitive psychology is going to make progress, it will have to give up the hope of validating each and every construct, just as in modern physics, not only will empirical outcomes weigh in the judgments but so will *formal adequacy,* sufficiency, plausibility, and other values.[2]

The following validating methodology is based on these methodological premises. Each report must be evaluated, not in isolation, but in relation to direct and indirect relationships and procedures in a network of relationships. The methodology is based on (1) internal relationships of invariance constituting formally consistent sets and transformations of cognitive structures similar in form to establishing arithmetic proofs and (2) external relationships of isomorphic correspondences to empirical group interaction data. Thus, the method is neither causal nor linear but based on internal and external consistency and the invariance of formal structure. Methodologically, normal sampling procedures are not relevant for structural analyses, such as the present method, because the purpose is not to suggest that all or most topics are subliteral, but rather that the form they take is valid.

13.2. Levels of Verification   Verification consists of two basic levels. Level 1 involves relatively simple correspondence operations between the literal narrative and the actual group situation, context, and stage of group development and is composed of analogical matching and mapping operations (1.1. and 1.2.) and contextual operations (2.1. and 2.2.). Level 2 involves complex interrelationships among lower order structures and is composed of psychosociometric operations (3.1., 3.2., and 3.3.); associated operations (4.1., 4.2., and 4.3.); parallel psychomotor operations (5.1., 5.2., and 5.3.); linguistic operations (6.3., 6.5., 6.6., and 6.7.); reversal and inversion operations (7.1. and 7.2.); mathematical computational operations (7.4. and 8.1.); logicomathematical operations (9.7. and 9.8.); transformation-group operations (11.1. and 11.2.); and multicorrelative transforms (12.1., 12.2., and 12.3.).

Operations 6.1., 6.2., 6.4., 7.3., 8.2., 8.3., 8.4., 8.5., 8.6., 9.1., 9.2., 9.3., 9.4., 9.5., and 9.6. are not directly involved in validation and falsification. They are relatively simple descriptions of cognitive operations.

Exemplar instantiations   Level 1 operation 1.1 is a relatively simple matching of (1) the literal narrative of journalism with the (a') group concern about the member taking notes, whereas Level 2 operation 9.8. in which, if the given subliteral narrative is associated with the dimensional vector down, other permutations of that narrative should also be associated with down, thus taking the form of "if -then" statements (i.e., if all X is associated with Y, then X' should be associated with Y).

13.3. Falsification   Falsification of hypotheses regarding subliteral material, like verification, derive from specific methodological operations and procedures of analysis. Failure to meet verification requirements generally implies falsification. Minimally, falsification requires meeting the standards of 1.1., 1.2., 3.1., 3.2., 4.2., 4.3., 10.1., 10.2., and 10.3.

Instantiation   A hypothesized topic of "8 males dominating a group" (negative attribution) is falsified if (1) there is no group of 8 males which is dominating a discussion (1.1. and 1.2.); (2) the discussants who generate the topic demonstrate no concern about domination in the group (3.1.), (3) the topic is generated by one or more of the eight males (3.2.); (4) no dimensional evaluative vector operations are evident (4.2. and 4.3.); and (5) there are no other transformations of the topic (10.1., 10.2.).

III. THE SUBLITERAL MIND

The subliteral mind is a set of unconscious processes. It is composed of (1) the Genesis Matrix, which includes (i) mental maps, called schemas, (ii) invariance transformations, and (iii) psychodynamic functions and (2) a Subliteral Executive Function.

14. THE GENESIS MATRIX

Within the genesis matrix is a set of unconscious functions that direct the subliteral cognitive and linguistic operations described previously.

14.1. Schemas   At their base, schemas are neurological templates or circuits formed as information enters the brain. Input needs to be ordered in some way to make it manageable. This created order or pattern is called a schema. On various neurological levels, there are many schemas, including linguistic schemas, emotional schemas, postural schemas, motor schemas, face recognition schemas, and memory schemas. Schemas function as mediators or go-betweens that link our inner experience and input from the external world. They may also function as mediators or go-betweens in our internal worlds.

14.1.1. Abstract Schemas   Schemas tend to abstract representations of the world. By way of an analogy, they are like an arithmetic operation where 1 + 1 = 2 is an empty abstract form into which can be plugged an infinite number of things: peaches, plums, humans, or Buicks. The operation renders all the differences among these things irrelevant.

14.1.2. Sensuous Schemas   Sensuous schemas consist of sensuous elements involving physical or *felt* bodily experiences.

14.1.3. Feeling Schemas   Though sensuous schemas consists of emotion or feeling on some level, which often involves muscular or physical sensation, feeling schemas are relatively separate. Feeling schemas are second-order experiences involving cognition. Feeling schemas are central to creating subliteral narratives.

14.1.4. Linguistic Schemas   These involve the three main parts of language, semantics, which regulates word meanings, phonology, which regulates the use of sound, and syntax or grammar, which regulates order among words.

Depending on the particular set of conditions and context, these schemas, individually or collectively, influence semantics, phonology, and syntax to produce a particular subliteral word, phrase, sentence, or story. These schemas come together on various levels to form the Genesis Matrix.

14.2. Invariance Transformations   Implied in the notion of schema is a mechanism for creating invariance, where different "things" are made "identical," the "same as," or "like" some "thing" else. The term transformation is used in its mathematical sense where invariance or constancy is maintained. Invariance transformations enable the mind/brain to recognize a musical composition though it's played in a different key.

14.3. Psychodynamics   Psychodynamics refers to understanding psychological material related to a literal narrative. Psychodynamics enables the analysis of subliteral meaning.

14.3.1. Individual Psychodynamics   Psychodynamics refers to conflicting thoughts and feelings that may be occurring on an unconscious level and involve unconscious motives.

14.3.2. Contextual Narrative Psychodynamics   This level of psychodynamics involves knowledge of past and present group or social dynamics which may be occurring that enable the analysis of subliteral meaning.

15. SUBLITERAL EXECUTIVE FUNCTION

The executive function is an unconscious control program that plans and tracks, the many subliteral narratives, their variations, and their correspondences.

NOTES

INTRODUCTION

1. Plato, *Meno. In Great Dialogues of Plato.* (trans. by W. H. D. Rouse) (New York: New American Library, 1956).
2. I define pop psychology as (1) psychological information, (2) widely disseminated to the general public, (3) that is simplified and distorted, (4) has little or no rigorous evidence to support it, (5) but which is disseminated as true. I define a "psychologist" here as any mental health professional who conducts any form of counseling or psychotherapy.
3. Mcdonald, K. A. "Americans Have Interest in But Ignorance of Science, Study Finds," *The Chronicle of Higher Education* 17 July 1998, p. A22.
4. Sagan, C. *The Demon-Haunted World: Science as a Candle in the Dark* (New York: Random House, 1995).
5. If this were another kind of book or scientific article I might spend considerable time outlining precisely what kinds of findings might constitute disconfirming evidence. To do this here, however, would turn this book into something it wasn't designed to be.

CHAPTER 1
SLIPS OF THE MIND: INTRODUCTION TO UNCONSCIOUS MEANING IN EVERYDAY CONVERSATIONS

1. Piaget, J. *Play, Dreams and Imitation of Childhood.* (New York: W.W. Norton, 1962).
2. Haskell, R. E. "The Matrix of Group Talk: An Empirical Method of Analysis and Validation." *Small Group Behavior 2* (1982) 419–443.
3. See, for example, Culler, J. *On Puns: The Foundation of Letters* (London: Basil Blackwell, 1988).
4. Haskell, R. E. "Structural Metaphor, and Cognition" in *Cognition and Symbolic Structures: The Psychology of Metaphoric Transformation,* R. E. Haskell (ed.) (Norwood, New Jersey: Ablex, 1987), pp. 241–255.
5. Haskell, R. E. "The Matrix of Group Talk: An Empirical Method of Analysis and Validation." *Small Group Behavior 2* (1982).
6. Lakoff, G. and Johnson, M. *Metaphors We Live By* (Chicago: University of Chicago, Press (1980); Langacker, R. W. *Foundations of Cognitive Grammar (Volume II). Descriptive Application.* (Stanford: Stanford University Press, 1991).
7. See, Ricoeur, P. "The Metaphorical Process as Cognition, Imagination and Feeling" in *On Metaphor* S. Sacks (ed.) (Chicago: University of Chicago Press, 1979), pp. 141–157; Ricoeur, P. *Freud and Philosophy: An Essay on Interpretation* (New Haven: Yale University Press, 1970).

8. CNN, *Burden of Proof,* 7 August 1998. 12:30 pm. EST.

9. CNN, 13 September 1998, 1:16 pm, EST.

10. It often happens in popular culture that certain words and ideas come to be exclusively associated with certain authors. This is the case with slips of the tongue. However, such so-called Freudian slips, which indicate unconscious meaning behind the slips, were recognized long before Freud. For example, it is well known that Shakespeare recognized unconscious meaning behind slips of the tongue. Freud owes—and indeed acknowledges—his debt to the great literature he read.

11. Chomsky, N. *Syntactic Structures* (The Hague: Mouton, 1957).

12. Chomsky, N. *Language and Mind* (New York: Harcourt Brace Jovanovich, 1972).

13. It should be noted that structural linguistics did not deal with grammatically incorrect sentences, only correct ones. Accordingly, it could not deal with metaphorical or subliteral meanings because they may not conform to correct grammar.

14. Carroll, L. *Through the Looking Glass* (New York: Random House, 1946), p.94.

15. See, Pollio, H. R., Barlow, J. M., Fine, H. J., and Pollio, M. R. *Psychology and the Poetics of Growth: Figurative Language in Psychology, Psychotherapy and Education* (Hillsdale, N.J.: Lawrence Erlbaum, 1977).

16. Crosby, F., Bromley, S. and Saxe, L. "Recent Unobtrusive Studies of Black and White Discrimination and Prejudice: A Literature Review" *Psychological Bulletin 87* (1980) 456–563.

17. Norman, D. A. "Twelve Issues for Cognitive Science" *Cognitive Science 4* (1980) 1–32.

18. Bruner, J. *Acts of meaning* (Cambridge, Massachusetts: Harvard University Press, 1990), p. 3.

19. Ibid., p.77.

20. Blumenthal, A. "Psycholinguistics: Some Historical Issues," in *Structures and Transformation* eds. K. Siegel and G. Rosenwald (New York: Wiley, 1975), pp. 1–15.

21. Martindale, C. *Cognition and Consciousness* (Homewood, Illionis: Dorsey Press, 1981) p. viii.

22. Baars, B. J. *The Cognitive Revolution in Psychology.* (New York: Guilford Press, 1986), p. 411.

23. Gardner, H. *The Mind's New Science: A History of the Cognitive Revolution* (New York: Basic Books, 1985) p. 380.

24. Werner, H. and Kaplan, B. *Symbol Formation: An Organismic Developmental Approach to Language and the Expression of Thought* (New York: Wiley, 1963).

25. Broen, W. E. and Storms, L. H. "Lawful Disorganization: The Process Underlying a Schizophrenic Syndrome," *Psychological Review 73* (1966) 265–279.

26. Baars, B. J., Cohen, J. Bower, G. H. and. Berry, J. W. "Some Caveats on Testing the Freudian Slip Hypothesis: Problems in Systematic Replication" in *Experimental Slips and Human Error.* Bernard J. Baars (ed.) (New York: Plenum Press, 1992) p. 308.

27. What Baars' insightful comment about laboratory methods perhaps being too "blunt" means is that current methods for trying to reproduce unconsciously motivated (Freudian) slips experimentally are missing some unknown factors and thus fail to show unconscious motivation underlying slips of the tongue. I think Baars is correct. In my view there are two very important variables missing in most laboratory experiments. The first is that, unlike slips that occur in everyday settings, laboratory experiments often (a) don't use material that's sufficiently meaningful to subjects on a personal level, (b) the material isn't sufficiently connected to a meaningful social and affect-ladened context, and thus (c) the material isn't sufficiently a part of the subject's ongoing deep cognitive processing. Finally—and I really hate to hear myself saying this—it's unfortunate that for many cognitive scientists, if an effect can't be reproduced in the laboratory setting, then it does not exist.

28. See, for example, Lazarus, R. "Thoughts on the Relations Between Emotion and Cognition" *American Psychologist 37* (1982) 1019–1024; Zajonc, R. B. "Feeling and Thinking: Preferences Need No Inferences" *American Psychologist 35* (1980) 151–175.

29. Piaget, J. *The Affective Unconscious and the Cognitive Unconscious* (1973) p. 39.
30. Although the data here were not experimentally elicited, it is possible to generate subliteral phenomena experimentally by introducing variable conditions. A confederate, for example, could be planted in a group and instructed to act in certain ways, or affect-arousing objects could be introduced (e.g., a video camera). Then, hypotheses could be formulated about the type of topics generated in response to experimental manipulations. In any event, a prior methodology is required to analyze and verify subliteral reports even when they are generated experimentally.
31. Cassirer, E. *Mythological Thought* (London: Yale University Press, 1955).
32. Levi–Strauss, C. *The Savage Mind* (Chicago: University of Chicago Press, 1966).
33. Weimer, W. and Palermo, D. S. (eds.), *Cognition and the Symbolic Processes* (Hillsdale, New Jersey: Lawrence Erlbaum, 1974) p. 440.
34. Neisser, U. *Cognition and Reality: Principles and Implications of Cognitive Psychology* (San Francisco: W. H. Freeman, 1976).
35. Haskell, R. E. "An Analogical Methodology for the Analysis and Validation of Anomalous Cognitive and Linguistic Operations in Small Group (Fantasy Theme) Reports" *Small Group Research 22* (1991) 443–474.

CHAPTER 2
THE DISCOVERY OF SUBLITERAL MEANING:
A PERSONAL AND SCIENTIFIC ODYSSEY

1. See, for example, the classic work of T. Kuhn. *The Structure of Scientific Revolutions* (Chicago, University of Chicago Press, 1970).
2. Mcdonald, K. A. "Americans Have Interest in But Ignorance of Science, Study Finds," *The Chronicle of Higher Education* 17 July 1998, p. A22.
3. See, for example, Sperry, R. W. "Brain Dissection and Consciousness," in *Brain and Conscious Experience*, J. C. Eccles (ed.) (New York: Springer-Verlag, 1966).
4. Haskell, R. E. "An Analogic Model of Small Group Behavior," *International Journal of Group Psychotherapy 28* (1978) 27–54.
5. See, for example, the following early works: Fine, H., Pollio, H., and Simpkinson, C. "Figurative Language, Metaphor and Psychotherapy," *Psychotherapy: Theory, Research and Practice 10* (1973) 87–91; H. R. Pollio, J. M. Barlow, H. J. Fine, and M. R. Pollio, (1977). *Psychology and the Poetics of Growth: Figurative Language in Psychology, Psychotherapy and Education* (Hillsdale, New Jersey: Lawrence Erlbaum 1977); Gordon, D. *Therapeutic Metaphors* (Cupertino, CA: Meta Publications 1978); Rossi, E. (ed.), *The Collected Works of Milton H. Erickson* (New York: Irvington, 1980).
6. Haskell, R. E. "Empirical Structures of Mind: Cognition, Linguistics and Transformation" *The Journal of Mind and Behavior 5* (1984) 29–48.
7. Haskell, R. E. "The Matrix of Group Talk: An Empirical Method of Analysis and Validation" *Small Group Behavior 2* (1982) 419–443.
8. Haskell, R. E. "Thought-Things: Levi-Strauss and the Modern Mind," *Semiotica: Journal of the International of the Semiotic Association 55*, 1/2 (1985) 1–17.
9. Haskell, R. E. "Cognitive Structure and Transformation: An Empirical Model of the Psycholinguistic Function of Numbers in Discourse," *Small Group Behavior 13* (1983) 165–191.
10. See, Kahn, D. *The Codebreakers: The Story of Secret Writing.* (Scribner, New York, 1967).

11. Bales, R. F. *Personality and Interpersonal Behavior* (New York: Holt, Rinehart & Winston 1970).

12. Mann, R. *Interpersonal Styles and Group Development* (New York: Wiley 1967); Slater, P. *Microcosm: Structure, Psychological and Religious Evolution in Groups* (New York: Wiley 1966); Mills, T. *Group Transformation* (Englewood Cliffs, New Jersey Prentice-Hall, 1964).

13. For those interested in reading the fascinating early material in various fields, see, Bormann, E. G. "Fantasy and Rhetorical Vision: The Rhetorical Criticism of Social Reality," *Quarterly Journal of Speech 58* (1972) 396–407; DeMause, L. "Historical Group Fantasies," *Journal of Psychohistory 7* (1979) 1–70; Dunphy, D. "Phases, roles, and myths in self-analytic groups," *Journal of Applied Behavioral Sciences 4* (1968) 195–225; Farrell, M. P. "Collective Projection and Group Structure: The Relationship Between Deviance and Projection in Groups" *Small Group Behavior 10* (1979) 81–100; Gibbard, G., and Hartman, J. "The Significance of Utopian Fantasies in Small Groups," *International Journal of Group Psychotherapy 23* (1973) 125–147; Hartman, J. and Gibbard, G. "A Note on Fantasy Themes in the Evolution of Group Culture," in *Analysis of Groups,* eds. G. Gibbard, J. Hartman and R. Mann (San Francisco: Jossey-Bass 1974); Mohrmann, G. P. "An Essay on Fantasy Theme Criticism," *The Quarterly Journal of Speech 68* (1982) 109–132; Morocco "The Development and Function of Group Metaphor," *Journal for the Theory of Social Behavior 9* (1) (1979) 15–27; Schutz, W. *Here Comes Everybody: Body, mind and Encounter Culture* (New York: Harrow, 1971).

14. See Durkin, H. E. *The Group in Depth* (New York: International University Press 1964); Foulkes, S. H. and Anthony, E. J. *Group Psychotherapy* (Baltimore, Maryland: Penguin 1957); Mullahy, P. *Psychoanalysis and Interpersonal Psychiatry: The Contributions of Harry Stack Sullivan* (New York: Science House, 1970); Whitaker, D. S. and Lieberman, M. *Psychotherapy Through the Group Process* (New York: Atherton, 1964); Yalom, I. *The Theory and Practice of Group Psychotherapy* (New York: Basic Books, 1970).

15. Myers, P. "Sándor Ferenczi and Patients' Perceptions of Analysis," *British Journal of Psychotherapy* 13(1) (1966) 26–36. I would like to acknowledge professor Piers Myers of Regent's College, School of Psychotherapy and Counselling for recently calling my attention to Ferenczi's work.

16. Socrates said, "I am myself a great lover of these processes of division and generalization; they help me to speak and to think. And if I find any man who is able to see a 'One and Many' in nature, him I follow, and 'walk in his footsteps as if he were a god' " (Plato, *Phaedrus* [W. E. Helmbold & W. G. Rabinowitz, trans.) [New York: Bobbs-Merrill, (1956)] Later Aristotle echoed the same view: "The greatest thing by far is to be a master of metaphor. It is the one thing that cannot be learned from others. It is the mark of genius" (Cooper, L. The Rhetoric of Aristotle [New York: Appleton-Century-Crofts, 1960] p. 101.).

17. Oppenheimer, J. R. "Analogy in Science" *The American Psychologist* 2 (1956), p. 3.

18. Hesse, M. *Models and Analogies in Science* (New York: Sheed and Ward, 1963).

19. Haskell, R.E. "Anatomy of Analogy: A New Look," *Journal of Humanistic Psychology, 8* (1968) 161–169; see also R. E. Haskell (ed.) *Cognition and Symbolic Structures: The Psychology of Metaphoric Transformation* (Norwood, New Jersey: Ablex 1987).

20. See, for example, Gentner, D. "Structure Mapping: A Theoretical Framework for Analogy," *Cognitive Science 7* (1983) 155–170; Gick, M. L. and Holyoak, K. J. "Analogical Problem Solving," *Cognitive Psychology 12* (198) 306–355.

21. Haskell, R. E. "Analogical Transforms: A Cognitive Theory of the Origin and Development of Equivalence Transformation, Part I," *Metaphor and Symbolic Activity 4* (1989) 247–259.

22. Freud, S. [1900] *The Interpretation of Dreams* (1st English ed.) (London: George Allen & Unwin, 1954).

23. Freud, S. *The Psychopathology of Everyday Life* (trans. by J. Strachey) (New York, W.W. Norton, 1960); Freud, S. *Jokes and their Relation to the Unconscious* (trans. by J. Strachey) (New York: W.W. Norton, 1963).

24. Haskell, R. E. "The Analogic and Psychoanalytic Theory," *The Psychoanalytic Review 55* (1969) 662–680.

25. Vico, G. *The New Science* (T. G. Bergin and M. H. Fisch, trans. and abridgers). (London: Cornell University Press, 1948) (Original work published 1744).

26. Levi-Strauss, C. *Structural Anthropology* (New York: Basic Books, 1963).

27. Snell, B. *The Discovery of Mind* (New York: Harper & Row, 1960).

28. Jaynes, J. *The Origin of Consciousness and the Breakdown of the Bicameral Mind* (New York: Houghton Mifflin, 1976).

29. Ibid.

30. Ibid. p. 47.

31. Ibid. p. 361.

32. Ibid. p. 364.

33. Vico, *The New Science*, p. 375.

34. Ibid. p.218.

35. Jaynes, *Origins of Consciousness*, p. 371.

36. Vico, *The New Science*, p.409.

37. Jaynes, *The Origins of Consciousness*, p.51.

38. In addition to my having come across both Vico and Jaynes and their having so many similarities, there are other interesting personal parallels between these two men's lives. See, Haskell, R. E. "Vico and Jaynes: Neurocultural and Cognitive Operations in the Origin of Consciousness," *New Vico Studies 11* (1993) 24–51.

39. Ibid.

40. See, for example, Danesi, M. *Giambattista Vico and the Cognitive Science Enterprise.* (Emory Vico Studies, Vol. 4) (New York: Peter Lang, 1995).

41. Haskell, R. E. "An Analogical Methodology for the Analysis and Validation of Anomalous Cognitive and Linguistic Operations in Small Group (Fantasy Theme) Reports," *Small Group Research 22* (1991) 443–474.

CHAPTER 3
OF CRYSTAL BALLS AND THE MIND OF GOD:
AUTHORITY AND LEADERSHIP CONCERNS

1. Campbell, J. *The Hero with a Thousand Faces,* 2nd ed. (Princeton, New Jersey: Princeton University Press, 1968).

2. Levi-Strauss, C. *The Raw and the Cooked: Introduction to a Science of Mythology,* I (New York: Harper Row, 1969).

3. Slater, P. *Microcosm: Structural, Psychological and Religious Evolution in Groups* (New York: Wiley, 1966).

4. Mann, R. *Interpersonal Styles and Group Development* (New York: Wiley, 1967) p. 3; Frazier, J. G. *The Golden Bough* (London: Macmillan, 1900).

5. Schutz, W. *Here Comes Everybody: Body Mind and Encounter Culture* (New York: Harrow, 1971).

6. I would like to thank my colleague, John Heapes, for this illustration.

CHAPTER 4
MARKS OF CAIN AND ABEL:
PEER AND INTERPERSONAL CONCERNS

1. *The Merv Griffin Show*, 14 September 1977.
2. Haskell, R. E. "A Phenomenology of Metaphor: A Praxis Study into Metaphor and Its Cognitive Movement Through Semantic Space" in *Cognition and Symbolic Structures: The Psychology of Metaphoric Transformation* R. E. Haskell (ed.) (Norwood, New Jersey: Ablex, 1987), pp. 257–292).
3. The practice of using the titles Mr. And Miss with a first name has a still further interesting aspect. Have you ever wondered why many pop psychologists or media psychologists are known by Dr. + first name? Hence, Dr. Ruth (whose doctorate is an Ed.D.), Dr. Laura (whose doctorate is a Ph.D. apparently in physiological psychology), or Dr. John? We seldom find this mode of address with medical doctors (whose doctorate is an M.D) In my view, this is why: in a democratic society,"experts" are seen as elitist and therefore, suspect. As a consequence, there is pressure to reduce the status differential, to be seen as your everyday "Joe" or "Mary," while at the same being seen as "someone who knows," as having expertise. This is a difficult line to walk. If you are seen as merely the everyday Joe or Mary, just one of the populace, then there is no reason to listen to you. On the other hand, if you are seen as "the authority," you may invoke an authority reaction, or worse yet, you may be seen as an "ivory tower" scholastic. The solution to this dilemma is to become known by "Dr. + first name." Hence, Dr. Ruth. With this form of address, the "Dr." establishes one's authority and at the same time the first name establishes familiarity and equality. Over the years, students have figured this dilemma out, too, with variations. Students have variously addressed me as "Dr. Rob," or "Dr. H," or for some, simply "Doc" seems to establish a comfortable level. Welcome to Mr. Rogers's neighborhood.
4. Tuckman, B. W. "Developmental Sequence in Small Groups," *Psychological Bulletin 63* (1965) 384–399.

CHAPTER 5
FIGURES OF SPEECH: NUMBERS IN THE MIND

1. Haskell, R.E. "Cognitive Structure and Transformation: An Empirical Model of the Psycholinguistic Function of Numbers in Discourse," *Small Group Behavior 13* (1983) 165–191.
2. See Dantzig, T. *Number: The Language of Science.* (Garden City, New York: Doubleday Anchor Books, 1930).
3. See, for example, Cassirer, E. *Mythological Thought* (London: Yale University Press, 1955).
4. For examples of the pathological use of numbers in schizophrenia, see Kasanin's classic work, Kasanin, J. S. (ed.), *The Language and Thought of Schizophrenia* (New York: W. W. Norton, 1964).
5. Fodor, N. "The Psychology of Numbers," *Journal of Clinical Psychopathology 8* (1947) 525–556; Jung, C.G. *Dreams* (trans. by R. F. C. Hull) (Princeton, New Jersey: Princeton University Press, 1974); Stekel, W. *The Interpretation of Dreams* (New York: Liveright, 1943).
6. Gutheil, E. *The Handbook for Dream Analysis* (New York: Liveright, 1951).
7. Freud, S. [1900] *The Interpretation of Dreams* (1st English ed.) (London: George Allen & Unwin, 1954).

8. See, for example, Shepard, R. N., Kilpatric, D. W., and Cunningham, J. P. "The Internal Representation of Numbers," *Cognitive Psychology*, 7 (1975) 82–138.
9. See also chapter 11 for a similar operation found in dreams.
10. Prepositional phrases are composed of a preposition and its object, which often have adjectival or adverbial properties.
11. Quoted in Palmer, R., *Hermeneutics* (Evanston, Illinois: Northwestern University Press, 1969), p. 140.

CHAPTER 6
FEELING AND EMOTION: MISSING LINKS IN A GREAT PSYCHOLOGICAL DIVIDE

1. I am not implying that Descartes should not have made this great divide, just that we shouldn't have burned our bridges behind us. Without this great divide I probably wouldn't be writing this book on a computer.
2. See, Ricoeur, P. "The Metaphorical Process as Cognition, Imagination and Feeling," in *On Metaphor* S. Sacks (ed.) (Chicago: University of Chicago Press, 1979), (pp. 141–157); Ricoeur, P. *Freud and Philosophy: An Essay on Interpretation* (New Haven: Yale University Press, 1970).
3. Ricoeur, "The Metaphorical Process as Cognition, Imagination, and Feeling," p. 154.
4. Haskell, R. E. "Analogical Transforms: A Cognitive Theory of the Origin and Development of Equivalence Transformation Part I, II." *Metaphor and Symbolic Activity* 4 (1989) 241–211.
5. Piaget, J. "The Affective Unconscious and the Cognitive Unconscious," *Journal of the American Psychoanalytic Association 21* (1973) p. 39.
6. Langer, S. *Philosophy in a New Key* (New York: Mentor Books, 1942).
7. Boon, J. *From Symbolism to Structuralism* (New York: Harper Torchbooks, 1972).
8. Gadamer, H. *Truth and Method* (New York: The Seabury Press, 1975).
9. Cited in Cassirer, E. *The Philosophy of Symbolic Forms, Vol. I. Language* (New Haven: Yale University Press, 1955).
10. Watson, J. *The Double Helix: A Personal Account of the Discovery of the Structure of DNA* (New York: Atheneum, 1968).
11. Gardner, H. *The Mind's New Science: A History of the Cognitive Revolution* (New York: Basic Books, 1985).
12. With not a whole lot to do in our society, philosophers are turning their trained minds to nontraditional endeavors. They are increasingly no longer talking about Plato and the nature of what it means to "lead a good life" but are increasingly applying their trade to clarifying and analyzing environmental ethics, to what is called "critical thinking" in education, and more recently, they—like so many today—are becoming "psychological counselors," therapists for helping people cope with modern life.
13. Cassirer, *The Philosophy of Symbolic Forms*, Vol. I, *Language*, p. 81.
14. Vico, G. *The New Science* (T. G. Bergin and M. H. Fisch, trans. and abridgers) (London: Cornell University Press, 1948). (Original work published 1744).
15. Haskell, R. E. "Giambattista Vico and the Discovery of Metaphor," in: *Cognition and Symbolic Structures: The Psychology of Metaphoric Transformation*, R. E. Haskell (ed.) (Norwood, New Jersey: Ablex 1987), pp. 67–82.
16. Vico, *The New Science*, p. 314.

17. Whitehead, A. N. *Science and the Modern World* (New York: Macmillian, 1963).
18. Levi-Strauss, C. *Structural Anthropology* (New York: Basic Books, 1963).
19. See Campbell, J. *The Hero with a Thousand Faces,* 2nd ed. (Princeton, New Jersey: Princeton University Press, 1968).
20. Jaynes, J. *The Origin of Consciousness in the Breakdown of the Bicameral Mind* (New York: Houghton Mifflin, 1976).
21. Vico, *The New Science*, p. 378.
22. Ibid. p. 819.
23. Ibid. p. 699.
24. Ibid. p. 6.
25. Ibid. p. 74.
26. Ibid. p. 86.
27. Jaynes, *The Origin of Consciousness in the Breakdown of the Bicameral Mind.*
28. Ibid. p. 146.
29. Ibid. p. 83.
30. Ibid. p. 69.
31. Ibid. p. 48.
32. Ibid. p. 69.
33. Ibid. p. 51.
34. Ibid. p. 291.
35. Werner, H. and Kaplan, B. *Symbol Formation: An Organismic Developmental Approach to Language and the Expression of Thought* (New York: Wiley, 1963)
36. Beck, B. E. "The Metaphor as Mediator between Semantic and Analogic Modes of Thought," *Current Anthropology 19* (1978) 83–96; see also Beck. B. E. "Metaphors, Cognition, and Artificial Intelligence" in *Cognition and Symbolic Structures,* Haskell, R. E. (ed.) (Norwood, New Jersey: Ablex, 1987), pp. 9–30.
37. Beck, *Metaphor, Cognition and Artificial Intelligence*, p. 84.
38. Ibid. p. 95.
39. Ibid. p. 85.
40. Ibid. p. 84.
41. Marks, L. E. *The Unity of Senses: Interrelations Among the Modalities* (New York, Academic Press, 1978). See also Marks, L. E. and Bornstein, M. H. "Sensory Similarities: Classes, Characteristics and Cognitive Consequences," In *Cognition and Symbolic Structures,* Haskell, R. E. (ed.) (Norwood, New Jersey: Ablex, 1987, pp. 49–65.
42. See for example, Lazarus, R. S. "Thoughts on the Relations Between Emotion and Cognition," *American Psychologist 37* (1982) 1019–1024; Zajonc, R. B. "Feeling and Thinking: Preferences Need No Inferences," *American Psychologist 35* (1980) 151–175. More recently, see Lazarus, R. S. *Emotion and Adaptation.* (New York: Oxford University Press, 1990).
43. Abelson, R. P. (1963). "Computer Simulation of Hot Cognitions." In S. Tomkins and S. Mesick (eds.) *Computer Simulation of Personality: Frontiers in Psychological Theory.* (New York: Wiley, 1963), pp. 277–298.
44. Goleman, D. *Emotional Intelligence* (New York: Bantam Books, 1995).
45. Simonov, P. V. *The Emotional Brain: Physiology, Neuroanatomy, Psychology, and Emotion* (New York: Plenum Press, 1986).
46. LeDoux, J. *The Emotional Brain* (New York: Simon and Schuster, 1996), p.38.
47. Ibid. p. 38.
48. You may recall from your history that the term Trojan horse comes down to us from ancient Greek legend. A huge hollow wooden horse was built with soldiers hidden inside. It

was let into the city of Troy as a gift. Then, the soldiers came out of the hollow horse and opened the gates to the city for the rest of the army to enter. More recently, the term has become high tech, referring to a set of instructions hidden inside a computer program that causes it to fail.

49. In recent years some notable exceptions are Danesi, M. *Vico, Metaphor and the Origin of Language* (Bloomington: Indiana University Press, 1993; Johnson, M. *The Body in the Mind: The Bodily Basis of Meaning, Imagination and Reason* (Chicago: University of Chicago Press, 1987; Lakoff, G. *Women, Fire, and Dangerous Things: What Categories Reveal About the Mind* (Chicago: University of Chicago Press, 1987; Lakoff, G. and Johnson, M. *Metaphors We Live By* (Chicago: University of Chicago Press, 1980; Langacker, R. W. *Foundations of Cognitive Grammar. Volume II: Descriptive Application* (Stanford: Stanford University Press, 1991).

50. First, it should be understood that what constitutes a noun is not simply attributional, e.g., person, place, or thing, but, rather, is determined by its relationship to other linguistic constituents. In their classic studies, Werner and Kaplan concluded that "most abstract words emerge from a concrete sensory-motor affective origin[, and] . . . it is our belief that what is true of words is most probably true of syntactically expressed relations." (p. 60) What this means is that syntax is not inherently given, it's created. Werner and Kaplan's view is not too different from the perspective I have suggested here.

CHAPTER 7
THE SOUNDS OF REASON: THE PUNS
AND POETICS OF EVERYDAY CONVERSATION

1. CNN program, *Burden of Proof*, 7 August 1998.
2. Gadamer, H.-G. *Truth and Method. A Continuum Book* (New York: The Seabury Press, 1975).
3. Plato, *The Republic* (trans. by Benjamin Jowett) (New York: P. F. Collier & Son, 1901).
4. Freud, S. [1900] *The Interpretation of Dreams* (1st English ed.) (London: George Allen & Unwin, 1954), p. 99.
5. Ibid. p. 407.
6. See, for example, Arieti, S. *Interpretation of Schizophrenia* (New York: Basic Books, 1974).
7. Levi-Strauss, C. *The Raw and the Cooked: Introduction to a Science of Mythology, I* (New York: Harper Row, 1969).
8. Lacan, J. "The Insistence of the Letter in the Unconscious," in *Structuralism*, J. Ehrmann (ed.) (Garden City, New York: Doubleday Anchor Books, 1966).
9. Leach, E. *Claude Levi-Strauss* (New York: Viking Press, 1974).
10. The distinction between "speech" and "writing" as different modes of expression has long been an important distinction in the fields of rhetoric and the philosophy of language. See, for example, Baldwin, C. S. *Ancient Rhetoric and Poetic.* Gloucester, Massachusetts: Peter Smith, 1959).
11. See, for example, Trabant, J. "Parlare Cantando: Language Singing in Vico and Herder," *New Vico Studies 9* (1991) 1–16.
12. Vico, G. *The New Science* (T. G. Bergin & M. H. Fisch, trans. and abridgers) (London: Cornell University Press, 1948), p. 230. (Original work published 1744).
13. Jaynes, J. *The Origin of Consciousness and the Breakdown of the Bicameral Mind* (New York: Houghton Mifflin, 1976), p. 364.

14. Haskell, R. E. "Structural Metaphor and Cognition," in *Cognition and Symbolic Structures*, R. E. Haskell (ed.) (Norwood, New Jersey: Ablex, 1987), pp. 242–255.

15. Vico, *The New Science*, p. 378.

16. McLuhan, M. *Understanding Media: The Extensions of Man* (New York: McGraw-Hill, 1964).

17. Anyone who teaches these youths will know what I mean. As the many educational reports testify, an increasing number of students find it difficult to attend to the printed word. Accordingly, many college level textbooks are by design written for an eighth and ninth grade level reader.

18. Litz, A. W. *James Joyce* (Princeton, New Jersey: Princeton University Press, 1972).

19. Haskell, R. E. "Cognitive Psychology and Dream Research: Historical, Conceptual and Epistemological Considerations," in *Cognition and Dream Research*, ed. R. E. Haskell (special book issue of *Journal of Mind and Behavior*) (New York: Institution of Mind and Behavior, 1986), pp. 1–29.

20. Pinker, S. *The Language Instinct: How the Mind Creates Language* (New York: William Morrow, 1994).

21. The term psychoacoustic was used by Marks. I have adapted his concept. Marks, L. E. *The Unity of Senses: Interrelations Among the Modalities* (New York, Academic Press, 1978).

22. See, for example, Brown, R. *Words and Things: An Introduction to Language* (New York: Free Press, 1958); French, L. P. "Toward an Explanation of Phonetic Symbolism," *Word: Journal of International Association* (1977) 305–322.

23. Boon, J. *From Symbolism to Structuralism*. (New York: Harper Torchbooks, 1972); MacLeish, A. *Poetry and Experience*. (Baltimore: Penguin Books, 1964).

24. Marks, *Unity of the Senses*, p. 203.

25. Just to note a few: ad/add, ail/ale, air/heir, aisle/I'll/isle, ate/eight, ante/anti, bail/bale, bait/bate, ball/bawl, bare/bear, be/bee, beach/beech, beat/beet, beau/bow, been/bin, beer/bier, role/ roll, rote/wrote, moan/mown, moat/ mote, weir/we're, wood/would, yoke/yolk, yore/your, tide/tied, right/wright/write, ring/wring.

26. See the example in chapter 9 of a subliteral linkage with the the words *gorgeous* and *Georgia*.

27. See the example in chapter 4, where two people's names, Firestone and Wright were combined into the word *sunlight*.

28. These oronyms are from Pinker, S. *The Language Instinct: How the Mind Creates Language* (New York: William Morrow, 1994). Someday perhaps a linguist will take a systematic look at the structure of the subliteral language in this book.

29. Freud, S. *Jokes and Their Relation to the Unconscious* (trans. by J. Strachey) (New York: W.W. Norton, 1963), p. 42.

30. Bergson, H. *Creative Evolution*. New York: Henry Holt, 1923).

31. See, Baars, B. J. (ed.), *Experimental Slips and Human Error* (New York: Plenum Press 1992); Fromkin, V. A. *Speech Errors as Linguistic Evidence* (The Hague: Mouton 1973); Norman, D.A. "Categorization of Action Slips," *Psychological Review 88* (1981) 1–15. As I noted in chapter 1, Baars is one of the few cognitive scientists who leaves the door open to the possibility of unconscious meaning in slips of the tongue.

32. The Competing Plans Hypothesis is one explanation for slips and errors. This view says that we have two intended but conflicting goals, one of which may not be socially acceptable so it must be inhibited. According to this explanation, the inhibition doesn't work and the socially unacceptable goal (or meaning) "slips" out, so to speak, as in Freudian slips. Now, as others have recognized, the Competing Plans Hypothesis is essentially a psychodynamic explanation, only without the usual Freudian or unconsciously intended dynamics imputed to it.

CHAPTER 8
THE SUBLITERAL MIND: THE UNCONSCIOUS AND THE GENESIS MATRIX

1. For a more complete history and set of illustrations of unconscious processes, see Ellenberger, H. *The Discovery of the Unconscious: The History and Evolution of Dynamic Psychiatry* (New York: Basic Books, 1970) and L. L. Whyte's, *The Unconscious before Freud.* (New York: Mentor Books, 1960).

2. Kihlstrom, J. F. "Commentary: Psychodynamics and Social Cognition—Notes on the Fusion of Psychoanalysis and Psychololgy," *Journal of Personality 62* (4) (1994) p. 684.

3. Haskell, R. E. "Cognitive Psychology and Dream Research: Historical, Conceptual and Epistemological Considerations" in *Cognition and Dream Research*, R. E. Haskell (ed.) (special book issue of *Journal of Mind and Behavior*) (New York: Institute of Mind and Behavior, 1986), p. 19.

4. See, for example, Greenwald, A. G. "New Look 3: Unconscious Cognition Reclaimed" *American Psychologist, 47* (1992) 766–779; Kihlstrom, J. F., Barnhardt, T. M., and Tataryn, D. J. "The Psychological Unconscious: Found, Lost, and Regained," *American Psychologist 47* (1992) 788–791.

5. See Kissin, B. *Conscious and Unconscious Programs in the Brain (Psychobiology of Human Behavior, Vol. I)* (New York: Plenum Press, 1986).

6. See Edelman, G. M. *The Remembered Present: A Biological Theory of Consciousness* (New York: Basic Books 1989); Weiskrantz, L. *Blind Sight. A Case History and Implications* New York: Oxford University Press, 1986).

7. Gazzaniga, M. S. *Social Brain* (New York: Basic Books, 1985); Ornstein, R. E. *The Right Mind* (New York: Harcourt Brace, 1997).

8. Galin, D. "Implication for Psychiatry of Left and Right Cerebral Specialization" *Archives of General Psychiatry 31* (1974). 572–583.

9. Reber, A. S. *Implicit Learning and Tacit Knowledge: An Essay on the Cognitive Unconscious* (New York: Oxford University Press, 1993).

10. Polanyi, M. *The Tacit Dimension* (Garden City, New York: Doubleday, 1966).

11. Brean, H. "Hidden Sell Technique is Almost Here: New Subliminal Gimmicks Now Offer Blood, Skulls, and Popcorn to Movie Fans," 44, No. 13 (March 31), 1958, p. 102.

12. I recall one day when I was engrossed in a book I was reading and my wife asked me to take out the garbage. Consciously, I didn't hear her. About five minutes later, I put my book down and said to my wife, "I guess I'll take out the garbage." I had no conscious recollection of her asking me to do so. Her asking me to take out the garbage acted like a posthypnotic suggestion and is an example of subliminal (unconscious) activation.

13. Plotkin, H. *Evolution in Mind: An Introduction to Evolutionary Psychology* (Cambridge, Massachusetts: Harvard University Press, 1998).

14. Honeck, R. P., Riechmann, P., and Hoffmann, R. R. "Semantic Memory for Metaphor: The Conceptual Base Hypothesis." *Memory and Cognition 3* (1975). 409–415.

15. See Scott Buchanan's wonderful little, but insightful, book, *Poetry and Mathematics* (New York: John Day, 1929).

16. Haskell, R. E. "Analogical Transforms: A Cognitive Theory of Origin and Development of Equivalence Transformation," Part II, *Metaphor and Symbolic Activity 4* (1989) 257–277.

17. There are what is known as connectionist models that don't have executive functions and some mathematical models.

18. See the classic, Miller, G., Galanter, E. and Pribram, K. *Plans and the Structure of Behavior* (New York: Holt, 1960).

19. Hilgard, E. E. *Divided Consciousness: Multple Controls in Human Thought and Action* (New York: Wiley Interscience, 1977).

20. Ibid. p. 185.

21. Ibid. p. 195.

22. Ibid. p. 198.

23. Reber, *Implicit Learning and Tacit Knowledge.*

24. Sartre, J. P. *Being and Nothingness* (trans. H. Barnes) (New York: 1956).

25. Szasz adopts a position similar to that of Jean Paul Sartre (Szasz, 1991, personal communication).

CHAPTER 9
RACE AND ETHNICITY: SUBLITERAL PREJUDICE IN BLACK AND WHITE

1. See, Waller, J. *Face to Face: The Changing State of Racism Across America* (New York: Plenum/Insight Books, 1998).

2. Many of the illustrations in this chapter are from Haskell, R. E. "Social Cognition and the Non-Conscious Expression of Racial Ideology," *Imagination, Cognition and Personality 6* (1) (1987) 75–97.

3. One of the problems in social psychology (and other areas) that's been known for years involves the use of questionnaires to assess people's attitudes and preferences. Responses to questions are notoriously unreliable measures of what people really think. People often give answers they think are expected. In addition, what they believe they think their attitudes or beliefs are often do not reflect what they actually do. For example, who is going to admit—perhaps even to themselves these days—that they have racial and gender prejudices? As a consequence of this state of affairs, social psychologists have begun to develop what are called "unobtrusive methods" of measuring attitudes, i.e., methods that assess attitudes without the person being aware that they are being assessed. My subliteral method is in fact an unobtrusive method for assessing what people really think without them knowing that they are revealing anything, and thus their answers are less subject to distortion. See, Crosby, F., Bromley, S., and Saxe, L. "Recent Unobtrusive Studies of Black and White Discrimination and Prejudice: A Literature Review" *Psychological Bulletin 87* (1980) 456–563; and Webb, E. J., Campbell, D., Schwartz, R. D. and Sechrest, L. *Unobstrusive Measures: Nonreactive Research in the Social Sciences* (Chicago: Rand McNally, 1966).

4. See, Gresson, A. *The Recovery of Race in America* (Minneapolis: University of Minnesota Press, 1995); Gresson, A. *The Dialectics of Betrayal: Sacrifice, Violation and the Oppressed* (Norwood, New Jersey: Ablex, 1982). See also Gresson, A. "Postmodern American and the Multicultural Crisis: Reading *Forrest Gump* as the "Call Back to Whiteness," *Taboo: The Journal of Culture and Education 1* (1996) 11–33.

5. Montague, A. *Man's Most Dangerous Myth: The Fallacy of Race*, 4th ed. (Cleveland: World, 1964).

6. I am all too aware that many people may see my distinction between racial and racist as one without a difference, especially in this particular case. But not knowing more about the person making the statement, there is no way of really knowing whether it was simply a racial association or a racist statement.

7. Herrnstein, R. and Murray, C. *The Bell Curve. Intelligence and Class Structure in American Life* (New York: The Free Press, 1994). See also Gresson, A. "Coda: "Cognitive Elitism" Versus

Moral Courage," in *Measured Lies: The Bell Curve Examined* Kincheloe, J., Steinberg, R., and Gresson, A. (eds.) (New York: St. Martin's Press, 1996), pp. 433–440.

8. See Haskell, R. E. "Social Cognition and the Non-Conscious Expression of Racial Ideology, *Imagination, Cognition and Personality 6* (1) (1987) 75–97.

9. See Haskell, R. E. "Thought-Things: Levi-Strauss and the Modern Mind." *Semiotica: Journal of the International Association of Semiotics 55* (1/2), (1985) 1–17.

10. *The Merv Griffin Show,* 14 September 1977.

11. I wish to express my deep indebtedness to Aaron for his critique of my subliteral findings in the early years of their discovery. I also owe him an even deeper gratitude for tutoring me in racial issues over the years, which both of us often found most frustrating, but from which I have benefited more than he.

12. Over the years, our friendship has been looked upon with suspicion. Some of Aaron's female friends have come right out and asked him if we were bisexual. They simply couldn't understand a black and white male being such close friends. Why else would they be friends? There are, however, numerous close (nonsexual) friendships between black and white males, but this isn't generally known (at least by whites). The exceptions are such relationships among professional athletes and among entertainers, but there it's seen as understandable and legitimate.

CHAPTER 10
SEX, GENDER, AND THE SUBLITERAL MIND:
DOMINANCE, STEREOTYPE, AND SEDUCTION

1. CNN, 20 August 1998 (Evening news, EST).

2. ABC, 7 September 1977.

3. Freud, S. *Jokes and their Relation to the Unconscious* (trans. by J. Strachey) (New York: W.W. Norton, 1963), p.31.

4. For similar themes, see Haskell, R. E. "An Analogic Model of Small Group Behavior" *International Journal of Group Psychotherapy 28* (1978) 27–54.

5. I wish to thank my colleague, John Heapes, for this subliteral narrative.

6. A psychoanalytic colleague of mine has suggested that removing my sport jacket was in fact "seductive." More factually, I would say that it may have been *perceived* as seductive.

CHAPTER 11
DREAMS AND DREAMING:
THE SLEEPING SUBLITERAL MIND

1. Haskell, R. E. (1986). "Cognitive Psychology and Dream Research: Historical, Conceptual and Epistemological Considerations." In *Cognition and Dream Research,* R. E. Haskell (ed.) (special book issue of *Journal of Mind and Behavior*) (New York: Institution of Mind and Behavior, 1986), p.1; see also my "Dreams and Dreaming Research" *Academic American Encyclopedia* (New York: Grolier, 1992).

2. Haskell, R. E. "Dreaming Cognition and Physical Illness" Part I, *Journal of Medical Humanities and Bio-Ethics 6* (1985) 46–56; Haskell, R. E. Dreaming Cognition and Physical Illness Part II," *Journal of Medical Humanities and Bio Ethics 6* (1985) 109–122.

3. Hall, C. and Van de Castle, R. L. *The Content Analysis of Dreams* (New York: Appleton-Century-Crofts, 1966).

4. Gutheil, E. *The Handbook for Dream Analysis* (New York: Liveright, 1951).

5. Freud, S. [1900] *The Interpretation of Dreams* (1st English ed.) (London: George Allen & Unwin, 1954), p. 418.

6. Ibid. p. 414.

7. Florin was a coin of British origin, and kreutzer was a German coin. Both were used in Austria during Freud's day.

8. Haskell, R. E. "Cognitive Structure and Transformation: An Empirical Model of the Psycholinguistic Function of Numbers in Discourse," *Small Group Behavior 13* (1983) 165–191.

9. Freud, *The Interpretation of Dreams*, p. 415.

10. Ibid. p. 417.

11. Unfortunately, I didn't systematically collect and catalogue these dreams. Consequently, I don't have the full contextual data about the group and the dreamer that I would need to analyze them in more detail.

12. See Haskell, R. E. (1986). "Logical Structure and the Cognitive Psychology of Dreaming," in *Cognition and Dream Research* R. E. Haskell (ed.). Also special double issue of the *Journal of Mind and Behavior* (New York, Institute of Mind and Behavior, 1986), pp. 215–248.

13. Hobson, J. A. *The Dreaming Brain* (New York: Basic Books, 1988); Hobson, J. A., and McCarley, R. W. "The Brain as a Dream State Generator: An Activation-Synthesis Hypothesis." *American Journal of Psychiatry, 134*(12) (1977) 1335–1348. In this classic article, the authors stop short of saying that synthesis implies meaning.

14. Crick, F. H. C. and Mitchison, G. "The Function of Dream Sleep" *Nature, 304* (1983) 111–114.

15. See Crick, F. and Mitchison, G. (1986). "REM Sleep and Neural Nets, in *Cognition and Dream Research* R. E. Haskell (ed.) (New York: Institute of Mind and Behavior, 1986), pp. 99–119. (Also published as special double issue of *The Journal of Mind and Behavior 7*, 1986, 2:3).

16. Watson, J. D. *The Double Helix: A Personal Account of the Discovery of the Structure of DNA* (New York: W.W. Norton, 1980).

17. See again Haskell, "Cognitive Psychology and Dream Research: Historical, Conceptual and Epistemological Considerations."

18. Ibid.

19. Haskell, "Dreaming Cognition and Physical Illness, Part II."

CHAPTER 12
SUBLITERAL THERAPEUTICS:
THE NEW PSYCHOTHERAPY OF ROBERT LANGS

1. See Langs, R. J. *The Bipersonal Field* (New York: Jason Aronson, 1976); Langs, R. J. A New Dawn for Psychoanalysis. *Voices: The Art and Science of Psychotherapy 18* (1982) 575–612.

2. As I mentioned in chapter 2 (see end note # 5), I had been aware of the literature on the use of metaphors in psychotherapy, but this is not the same as what Langs suggests.

3. See for example, Langs, R.J. and Badalamenti, A. "A Stochastic Analysis of the Duration of Speaker Role in Psychotherapy," *Perceptual and Motor Skills 70* (1990) 675–689.

4. Langs, R. *The Evolution of the Emotion Processing Mind: With An Introduction to Mental Darwinism* (London: Karnac Books, 1996).

5. Langs, R. *Clinical Practice and the Architecture of the Mind* (London: Karnac Books) (1995);
    Langs, R. *Empowered Psychotherapy* (London: Karnac Books); Langs, R. *Science, Systems and
    Psychoanalysis* (London: Karnac Books Brunner/Mazel, 1992).

6. Langs, R. *Unconscious Communication in Everyday Life* (New York: Jason Aronson, 1983).

7. Smith, D. L. *Hidden Conversations: An Introduction to Communicative Psychoanalysis* (London:
    Tavistock/Routledge, 1991).

8. The reader should be aware when reading Langs' work that because of his strict defini-
    tion of confidentiality, the examples of derivative in his books may not be actual examples
    from patients. But according to Langs, the examples are true to the original data.

9. Smith, *Hidden Conversations*, p. 146. For convenience in referring to and tracking down
    these examples, I use Smith's examples here so the reader can easily go to a single source
    for the examples used and as an introduction to communicative psychoanalysis.

10. Ibid. p. 146.

11. Ibid. p. 143.

12. Ibid. p. 146.

13. Ibid.

14. Ibid. p. 147.

15. Langs, *Evolution of the Emotion Processing Mind*.

16. I would like to thank Dr. Smith for his clarifying this point on Langs' theory and also
    other points on psychoanalysis in general.

17. Smith, *Hidden Conversations*, p. 52.

18. Ibid. p. 54.

19. Ibid. p. 60.

20. Freud, S. "The Disposition to Obsessional Neurosis." In the standard edition of the com-
    plete psychological works of Sigmund Freud. Translated and edited by James Strachey.
    (London: Hogarth Press, 1913) p. 320, cited in Smith, *Hidden Conversations*, p. 60.

21. Myers, P. "Sándor Ferenczi and Patients' Perceptions of Analysis." *British Journal of
    Psychotherapy* 13(1) (1996) 26–36.

22. Cited in Smith, *Hidden Conversations*, p. 142.

23. Ibid.

24. Ibid. p. 264.

25. Ibid. p. 142.

26. See Kissin, B. *Conscious and Unconscious Programs in the Brain* (*Psychobiology of Human
    Behavior*, Vol. I) (New York: Plenum Press, 1986).

27. See Bucci, W. *Psychoanalysis and Cognitive Science: A Multiple Code Theory* (London:
    Guilford, 1997).

28. See Dawes, R. M. *House of Cards: Psychology and Psychotherapy Built on Myth* (New York: Free
    Press, 1994).

29. For readers interested in following up on this area of research, the following is a representa-
    tive sample in chronological order: Dollard, J. and Miller, N. *Personality and Psychotherapy*
    (New York: McGraw-Hill, 1950); Shevrin, H. and Dickman, S. "The Psychological
    Unconscious." *American Psychologist 35* (1981) 421–434; Dixon, N. F. *Preconscious Processing*
    (New York: Wiley, 1981); Bowers, K. S. and Meichenbaum, D. (eds.) *The Unconscious
    Reconsidered.* (New York: Wiley-Interscience, 1984); Erdelyi, M. *Psychoanalysis: Freud's Cognitive
    Psychology* (New York: W.H. Freeman 1985); Kissin, B. *Conscious and Unconscious Programs in
    the Brain* (*Psychobiology of Human Behavior*, Vol. I) (New York: Plenum Press, 1986);
    Greenwald, A. G. "New Look 3: Unconscious Cognition Reclaimed," *American Psychologist 47*
    (1992) 766–779; Kihlstrom, J. F. "Commentary: Psychodynamics and Social Cognition—
    Notes on the Fusion of Psychoanalysis and Psychology," *Journal of Personality, 62* (4) (1994)
    681–696; Shevrin, H., Bond, J. A., Brakel, L. A. W., Hertel, R. K. and Williams, W. J. (eds.),

Conscious and Unconscious Processes: Psychodynamic, Cognitive, and Neurophysiological Convergences (New York: The Guilford Press, 1996); Bucci, W. *Psychoanalysis and Cognitive Science: A Multiple Code Theory* (London: Guilford, 1997).

30.   From Pinker, S. *How the Mind Works* (New York: W.W. Norton, 1997), p. 299.

APPENDIX
OVERVIEW OF ANALYSIS,
AND VALIDATION OPERATIONS

1.   Adapted from Robert E. Haskell. An analogical methodology for analysis and validation of anomalous cognitive and linguistic operations in small group (Fantasy theme) reports. *Small Group Research* 22 (4) (1991), pp. 443–474.

2.   See Herbert Feigl. Some major issues and developments in the philosophy of science of logical empiricism. In *Minnesota Studies in the Philosophy of Science* eds. Robert H. Feigl and M. Scriven. Minneapolis: University of Minnesota Press, 1965) pp. 3–37; Lachman, R. J. Lachman L., & Butterfield, E. C. *Cognition Psychology and Information Processing* (Hillsdale, New Jersey: Lawrence Erlbaum, 1979); Nagel, E. *The Structure of Science: Problems in the Logic of Scientific Explanation* (New York: Harcourt Brace Jovanovich, 1961), p. 271.

REFERENCES

ARTICLES AND BOOK CHAPTERS

Abelson, R. P. "Computer simulation of hot cognitions, in *Computer Simulation of Personality: Frontiers in Psychological Theory* eds. S. Tomkins and S. Mesick (New York: Wiley, 1963), pp. 277–298.

Baars, B. J., Cohen, J., Bower, G. H., and Berry, J. W. "Some Caveats on Testing the Freudian Slip Hypothesis: Problems in Systematic Replication," in *Experimental Slips and Human Error* ed. Bernard J. Baars (New York: Plenum Press, 1992), (pp. 289–313).

Beck, B. E. "The Metaphor As Mediator Between Semantic and Analogic Modes of Thought," *Current Anthropology 19* (1978) 83–96.

Beck, B. E. "Metaphors, Cognition, and Artificial Intelligence," in: *Cognition and Symbolic Structures*, ed. Haskell, R. E. (Norwood, New Jersey: Ablex, 1987) pp. 9–30.

Bormann, E. G. "Fantasy and Rhetorical Vision: The Rhetorical Criticism of Social Reality," *Quarterly Journal of Speech 58*, (1972) 396–407.

Brean, H. "Hidden Sell Technique is Almost Here: New Subliminal Gimmicks Now Offer Blood, Skulls, and Popcorn to Movie Fans," *Life Magazine*, 44, No. 13 (March 31), 1958, p. 102.

Broen, W. E. and Storms, L. H. "Lawful Disorganization: The Process Underlying a Schizophrenic Syndrome," *Psychological Review 73* (1966), 265–279.

Crick F. and Mitchison, G. "REM Sleep and Neural Nets," in *Cognition and Dream Research*, ed. R. E. Haskell (New York: Institute of Mind and Behavior), pp. 99–119 (Also published as special double issue of *The Journal of Mind and Behavior 7*, 2:3).

Crick F. H. C. and Mitchison, G. "The Function of Dream Sleep," *Nature 304* (14 July 1983) 111–114.

Crosby, F., Bromley, S. and Saxe, L. "Recent Unobtrusive Studies of Black and White Discrimination and Prejudice: A Literature Review," *Psychological Bulletin 87* (1980), 456–563.

DeMause, L. "Historical group fantasies," *Journal of Psychohistory*, 7 (1979) 1–70.

Blumenthal, A. "Psycholinguistics: some historical issues," in *Structures and Transformation*, eds. K. Siegel and G. Rosenwald, (New York: John Wiley, 1975). pp. 1–15.

Dunphy, D. "Phases, Roles, and Myths in Self-Analytic Groups," *Journal of Applied Behavioral Sciences 4* (1968), 195–225.

Farrell, M. P. "Collective Projection and Group Structure: The Relationship Between Deviance and Projection in Groups," *Small Group Behavior 10* (1979), 81–100.

Feigl, H. "Some Major Issues and Developments in Philosophy of Science of Logical Empiricism," in *Minnesota Studies in the Philosophy of Science*, eds. H. Feigl and M. Scriven, (Minneapolis: University of Minnesota Press, 1956), pp. 3–37.

Fine, H., Pollio, H., and Simpkinson, C. "Figurative Language, Metaphor and Psychotherapy," *Psychotherapy: Theory, Research and Practice 10* (1973), 87–91.

Fodor, N. "The Psychology of Numbers," *Journal of Clinical Psychopathology*, 8 (1947), 525–556.

French, L. P. "Toward an Explanation of Phonetic Symbolism," *Word: Journal of International Association 28:* (1977) 305–322.

Galin, D. "Implication for Psychiatry of Left and Right Cerebral Specialization," *Archives of General Psychiatry 31* (1974), 572–583.

Gertner, D. "Structure Mapping: A Theoretical Framework for Analogy," *Cognitive Science 7* (1983), 155–170.

Gibbard, G. and Hartman, J. "The Significance of Utopian Fantasies in Small Groups," *International Journal of Group Psychotherapy 23* (1973), 125–147.

Gick, M. L. and Holyoak, K. J. "Analogical Problem Solving," *Cognitive Psychology 12* (1980), 306–355.

Greenwald, A. G. "New Look 3: Unconscious Cognition Reclaimed," *American Psychologist, 47* (1992), 766–779.

Gresson, A. "Postmodern America and the Multicultural Crisis: Reading *Forrest Gump* as the 'Call Back to Whiteness,' " *Taboo: The Journal of Culture and Education 1* (1996), pp. 11–33.

Gresson, A. "Coda: 'Cognitive Elitism' Versus Moral Courage," in *Measured Lies: The Bell Curve Examined,* eds. Kincheloe, J., Steinberg, R., and Gresson, A. (New York: St. Martin's Press, 1996) pp. 433–440.

Hartman J. and Gibbard, G. "A Note on Fantasy Themes in the Evolution of Group Culture," in *Analysis of Groups,* eds. G. Gibbard, J. Hartman, & R. Mann (San Francisco: Jossey–Bass, 1974).

Haskell, R. E. "Vico and Jaynes: Neurocultural and Cognitive Operations in the Origin of Consciousness," *New Vico Studies 11* (1993), 24–51.

Haskell, R. E. *Dreams and Dreaming Research,* in *Academic American Encyclopedia* (New York: Grolier, 1992).

Haskell, R. E. "An Analogical Methodology for the Analysis and Validation of Anomalous Cognitive and Linguistic Operations in Small Group (Fantasy Theme) Reports," *Small Group Research, 22* (1991), 443–474.

Haskell, R. E. "Analogical Transforms: A Cognitive Theory of the Origin and Development of Equivalence Transformation, Part I, II," *Metaphor and Symbolic Activity, 4* (1989), 247–259.

Haskell, R. E. "Structural Metaphor, and Cognition," in *Cognition and Symbolic Structures: The Psychology of Metaphoric Transformation,* ed. R. E. Haskell (Norwood, New Jersey: Ablex, 1987), pp. 241–255.

Haskell, R. E. "Social Cognition and the Non-Conscious Expression of Racial Ideology," *Imagination, Cognition and Personality, 6* (1) (1987) 75–97.

Haskell, R. E. "A Phenomenology of Metaphor: A Praxis Study into Metaphor and Its Cognitive Movement Through Semantic Space," in *Cognition and Symbolic Structures: The Psychology of Metaphoric Transformation* ed. R. E. Haskell (Norwood, New Jersey: Ablex, 1987), pp. 257–292.

Haskell, R. E. "Giambattista Vico and the Discovery of Metaphor," in: *Cognition and Symbolic Structures: The Psychology of Metaphoric Transformation,* ed. R. E. Haskell (Norwood, New Jersey: Ablex, 1987), pp. 67–82.

Haskell, R. E. "Structural Metaphor and Cognition," in *Cognition and Symbolic Structures,* ed. R. E. Haskell (Norwood, New Jersey: Ablex, 1987), pp. 242–255.

Haskell, R. E. "Cognitive Psychology and Dream Research: Historical, Conceptual and Epistemological Considerations," in *Cognition and Dream Research,* ed. R. E. Haskell (special book issue of *Journal of Mind and Behavior*) (New York: Institution of Mind and Behavior, 1986), pp. 1–29.

Haskell, R. E. "Logical Structure and the Cognitive Psychology of Dreaming," in *Cognition and Dream Research,* ed. R. E. Haskell (Also special double issue of the *Journal of Mind and Behavior*) (New York: Institute of Mind and Behavior, 1986), pp. 215–248.

Haskell, R. E. "Cognitive Structure and Transformation: An Empirical Model of the

Psycholinguistic Function of Numbers in Discourse," *Small Group Behavior 13* (1983), 165–191.

Haskell, R. E. "Thought-Things: Levi–Strauss and the Modern Mind," *Semiotica: Journal of the International Semiotic Association, 55*, 1/2 (1985), 1–17.

Haskell, R. E. (1985). Dreaming Cognition and Physical Illness," Part I. *Journal of Medical Humanities and Bio-Ethics 6* (1985), 46–56.

Haskell, R. E. "Dreaming cognition and physical illness," Part II, *Journal of Medical Humanities and Bio Ethics 6* (1985), 109–122.

Haskell, R. E. "Empirical Structures of Mind: Cognition, Linguistics and Transformation," *The Journal of Mind and Behavior 5* (1984), 29–48.

Haskell, R. E. "Cognitive Structure and Transformation: An Empirical Model of the Psycholinguistic Function of Numbers in Discourse," *Small Group Behavior 13* (1983), 165–191.

Haskell, R. E. "The Matrix of Group Talk: An Empirical Method of Analysis and Validation," *Small Group Behavior 2* (1982), 419–443.

Haskell, R. E. "An Analogic Model of Small Group Behavior," *International Journal of Group Psychotherapy 28* (1978), 27–54.

Haskell, R. E. "The Analogic and Psychoanalytic Theory," The *Psychoanalytic Review 55* (1969), 662–680.

Haskell, R. E. "Anatomy of Analogy: A New Look," *Journal of Humanistic Psychology 8* (1968), 161–169.

Herrnstein R. and Murray, C. *The Bell Curve. Intelligence and Class Structure in American Life.* New York: The Free Press (1994).

Hobson J. A. and McCarley, R. W. "The Brain as a Dream State Generator: An Activation-Synthesis Hypothesis," *American Journal of Psychiatry, 134*(12) (1977), 1335–1348.

Honeck, R. P., Riechmann, P., and Hoffman, R. R. "Semantic Memory for Metaphor: The Conceptual Base Hypothesis," *Memory and Cognition, 3* (1975), 409–415.

Kihlstrom, J. F. , Barnhardt, T. M., and Tataryn, D. J. "The Psychological Unconscious: Found, Lost, and Regained," *American Psychologist, 47* (1992), 788–791.

Kihlstrom, J. F. "Commentary: Psychodynamics and Social Cognition—Notes on the Fusion of Psychoanalysis and Psychology," *Journal of Personality, 62* (4) (1994), 681–696.

Lacan, J. "The Insistence of the Letter in the Unconscious," in *Structuralism*, ed. J. Ehrmann (Garden City, New York: Doubleday Anchor Books, 1966).

Langs R. J. and Badalamenti, A. "A Stochastic Analysis of the Duration of Speaker Role in Psychotherapy," *Perceptual and Motor Skills 70* (1990), 675–689.

Langs, R. J. "A New Dawn for Psychoanalysis," *Voices: The Art and Science of Psychotherapy 18* (1982), 575–612.

Lazarus, R. S. "Thoughts on the Relations Between Emotion and Cognition," *American Psychologist 37* (1982), 1019–1024.

Marks L. E. and Bornstein, M. H. "Sensory Similarities: Classes, Characteristics, and Cognitive Consequences," in *Cognition and Symbolic Structures*, ed. R. E. Haskell (Norwood, New Jersey: Ablex, 1987).

Mcdonald, K. A. "Americans Have Interest in but Ignorance of Science, Study Finds," *The Chronicle of Higher Education 17* (July 1998), p. A22.

Mohrmann, G. P. "An Essay on Fantasy Theme Criticism," *The Quarterly Journal of Speech 68* (1982), 109–132.

Morocco, C. "The Development and Function of Group Metaphor," *Journal for the Theory of Social Behavior 9* (1) (1979), 15–27.

Myers, P. "Sándor Ferenczi and Patients' Perceptions of Analysis," *British Journal of Psychotherapy 13(1)* (1996), 26–36.

Norman, D. A. "Categorization of Action Slips," *Psychological Review 88* (1981), 1–15.
———. "Twelve Issues for Cognitive Science," *Cognitive Science 4* (1980), 1–32.
Oppenheimer, J. R. "Analogy in Science," *The American Psychologist 2* (1956), 3.
Piaget, J. "The Affective Unconscious and the Cognitive Unconscious," *Journal of the American Psychoanalytic Association 21* (1973), 249–261.
Ricoeur, P. (1979). "The Metaphorical Process as Cognition, Imagination and Feeling. In *On Metaphor,* ed. S. Sacks (Chicago: University of Chicago Press, 1979), pp. 141–157.
Shepard, R. N., Kilpatric, D. W., and Cunningham, J. P. "The Internal Representation of Numbers," *Cognitive Psychology 7* (1975), 82–138.
Shevrin H. and Dickman, S. "The Psychological Unconscious," *American Psychologist, 35* (1980), 421–434.
Sperry, R. W. "Brain dissection and consciousness." In *Brain and Conscious Experience,* ed. J. C. Eccles (New York: Springer-Verlag, 1966).
Trabant, J. "Parlare Cantando: Language Singing in Vico and Herder," *New Vico Studies 9* (1991), 1–16.
Tuckman, B. W. "Developmental sequence in small groups," *Psychological Bulletin 63* (1965), 384–399.
Zajonc, R. B. "Feeling and Thinking: Preferences Need No Inferences," *American Psychologist 35* (1980), 151–175.

BOOKS

Arieti, S. *Interpretation of Schizophrenia* (New York: Basic Books, 1974).
Baars, B. J. *The Cognitive Revolution in Psychology.* (New York: Guilford Press, 1986).
Baars, B. J. ed., *Experimental Slips and Human Error* (New York: Plenum Press, 1992).
Baldwin, C. S. *Ancient Rhetoric and Poetic* (Gloucester, Massachusetts: Peter Smith, 1959).
Bales, R. F. *Personality and Interpersonal Behavior* (New York: Holt, Rinehart & Winston, 1970).
Bergson, H. *Creative Evolution* (New York: Henry Holt, 1923).
Boon, J. *From Symbolism to Structuralism* (New York: Harper Torchbooks, 1972).
Bowers, K. S. and Meichenbaum, D. eds., *The Unconscious Reconsidered* (New York: Wiley Interscience, 1984).
Brown, R. *Words and Things: An Introduction to Language* (New York: Free Press, 1958).
Bruner, J. *Acts of Meaning* (Cambridge, Massachusetts: Harvard University Press, 1990).
Bucci, W. *Psychoanalysis and Cognitive Science: A Multiple Code Theory* (London: Guilford, 1997).
Buchanan, S. *Poetry and Mathematics* (New York: John Day, 1929).
Campbell, J. *The Hero with a Thousand Faces.* 2nd ed. (Princeton, New Jersey: Princeton University Press, 1968).
Carroll, L. *Through the Looking Glass* (New York: Random House, 1946).
Cassirer, E. *Mythological Thought* (London: Yale University Press, 1955).
Cassirer, E. *The Philosophy of Symbolic Forms, Vol. I, Language* (New Haven: Yale University Press, 1955).
Chaika, E. *Understanding Psychotic Speech: Beyond Freud and Chomsky.* (Springfield, MA.: Charles C. Thomas, 1990).
Chomsky, N. *Language and Mind* (New York: Harcourt Brace Jovanovich, 1972).
Chomsky, N. *Syntactic Structures* (The Hague: Mouton, 1957).
Cooper, L. *The Rhetoric of Aristotle* (New York: Appleton-Century-Crofts, 1960).
Culler, J. *On Puns: The Foundation of Letters* (London: Basil Blackwell, 1988).
Danesi, M. *Vico, Metaphor and the Origin of Language* (Bloomington: Indiana University Press, 1993).

Dantzig, T. *Number: The Language of Science.* (Garden City, New York: Doubleday Anchor Books, 1930).

Dawes, R. M. *House of Cards: Psychology and Psychotherapy Built on Myth* (New York: Free Press, 1994).

Dixon, N. F. *Preconscious Processing* (New York: Wiley, 1981).

Dollard, J. and Miller, N. *Personality and Psychotherapy.* (New York: McGraw-Hill, 1950).

Durkin, H. E. *The Group in Depth.* (New York: International University Press, 1964).

Edelman, G. M. *The Remembered Present: A Biological Theory of Consciousness* (New York: Basic Books, 1989).

Ellenberger, H. *The Discovery of the Unconscious: The History and Evolution of Dynamic Psychiatry.* (New York: Basic Books, 1970).

Erdelyi, M. *Psychoanalysis: Freud's Cognitive Psychology* (New York: W.H. Freeman, 1985).

Foulkes, S. H., and Anthony, E. J. *Group Psychotherapy* (Baltimore: Penguin, 1957).

Freud, S. *The Interpretation of Dreams,* 1st English ed. (London: George Allen & Unwin 1954). [Orig. published 1900].

Freud, S. *Jokes and their Relation to the Unconscious* (trans. by J. Strachey) (New York: W.W. Norton, 1963).

Freud, S. *The Psychopathology of Everyday Life* (trans, by J. Strachey) (New York, W.W. Norton, 1960).

Fromkin, V. A. *Speech Errors as Linguistic Evidence* (The Hague: Mouton, 1973).

Gadamer, H. *Truth and Method* (New York: The Seabury Press, 1975).

Gardner, H. *The Mind's New Science: A History of the Cognitive Revolution* (New York: Basic Books, 1985).

Gazzaniga, M. S. *Social Brain* (New York: Basic Books, 1985).

Goleman, D. *Emotional Intelligence* (New York: Bantam Books, 1995).

Gordon, D. *Therapeutic Metaphors* (Cupertino, California: Meta Publications, 1978).

Gresson, A. *The Recovery of Race in America* (Minneapolis: University of Minnesota Press, 1995).

Gresson, A. *The Dialectics of Betrayal: Sacrifice, Violation and the Oppressed* (Norwood, New Jersey: Ablex, 1982).

Gutheil, E. *The Handbook for Dream Analysis* (New York: Liveright, 1951).

Hall, C. and Van de Castle, R. L. *The Content Analysis of Dreams* (New York: Appleton-Century-Crofts, 1966).

Haskell, R. E. ed., *Cognition and Symbolic Structures: The Psychology of Metaphoric Transformation* (Norwood, New Jersey: Ablex, 1987).

Hilgard, E. E. *Divided Consciousness: Multiple Controls in Human Thought and Action* (New York: Wiley Interscience, 1977).

Hobson, J. A. *The Dreaming Brain* (New York: Basic Books, 1988).

Jaynes, J. *The Origin of Consciousness and the Breakdown of the Bicameral Mind* (New York: Houghton Mifflin, 1976).

Johnson, M. *The Body in the Mind: The Bodily Basis of Meaning, Imagination and Reason* (Chicago: University of Chicago Press, 1987).

Jung, C. G. *Dreams* (Transl. by R. F. C. Hull) (Princeton, New Jersey: Princeton University Press, 1974).

Kahn, D. *The Codebreakers: The Story of Secret Writing.* (New York: Scribner, 1996).

Kasanin, J. S. ed. *The Language and Thought of Schizophrenia* (New York: W. W. Norton, 1964).

Kissin, B. *Conscious and Unconscious Programs in the Brain* (Psychobiology of Human Behavior, Vol. I) (New York: Plenum Press, 1986).

Kuhn, T. *The Structure of Scientific Revolutions* (Chicago, University of Chicago Press, 1970).

Lachman, R. J., Lachman, L., and Butterfield, E. C. *Cognition Psychology and Information Processing.* (Hillsdale, New Jersey: Lawrence Erlbaum, 1979).

Lakoff, G. and Johnson, M. *Metaphors We Live By* (Chicago: University of Chicago Press, 1980).

Langacker, R. W. *Foundations of Cognitive Grammar, (Vol. II), Descriptive Application* (Stanford: Stanford University Press, 1991).

Langer, S. *Philosophy in a New Key* (New York: Mentor Books, 1942).

Langs, R. *The Evolution of the Emotion Processing Mind: With an Introduction to Mental Darwinism* (London: Karnac Books, 1996).

Langs, R. *Clinical Practice and the Architecture of the Mind (London:* Karnac Books, 1995).

Langs, R. *Empowered Psychotherapy* (London: Karnac Books, 1993).

Langs, R. *Science, Systems and Psychoanalysis* (London: Karnac Books Brunner/Mazel, 1992).

Langs, R. *Unconscious Communication in Everyday Life* (New York: Jason Aronson, 1983).

Langs, R. J. *The Bipersonal Field* (New York: Jason Aronson, 1976).

Lazarus, R. S. *Emotion and Adaptation* (New York: Oxford University Press, 1990).

Leach, E. *Claude Levi-Strauss* (New York: Viking Press, 1974).

LeDoux, J. *The Emotional Brain* (New York: Simon and Schuster, 1996).

Levi-Strauss, C. *The Raw and the Cooked: Introduction to a Science of Mythology, I* (New York: Harper Row, 1969).

Levi-Strauss, C. *The Savage Mind* (Chicago: University of Chicago Press, 1966).

Levi-Strauss, C. *Structural Anthropology* (New York: Basic Books, 1963).

Litz, A. W. *James Joyce* (Princeton, New Jersey: Princeton University Press, 1972).

MacLeish, A. *Poetry and Experience* (Baltimore: Penguin Books, 1964).

Mann, R. *Interpersonal Styles and Group Development* (New York: Wiley, 1967).

Marks, L. E.., *The Unity of Senses: Interrelations among the Modalities* (New York: Academic Press, 1978).

Martindale, C. *Cognition and Consciousness* (Homewood, Illinois: Dorsey Press, 1981).

McLuhan, M. *Understanding Media: The Extensions of Man* (New York: McGraw-Hill, 1964).

Miller, G., Galanter, E. and Pribram, K. *Plans and the Structure of Behavior* (New York: Holt, 1960).

Mills, T. *Group Transformation* (Englewood Cliffs, New Jersey: Prentice-Hall, 1964).

Montague, A. *Man's Most Dangerous Myth: The Fallacy of Race,* 4th ed. (Cleveland: World, 1964).

Mullahy, P. *Psychoanalysis and Interpersonal Psychiatry: The Contributions of Harry Stack Sullivan* (New York: Science House, 1970).

Nagel, E. *The Structure of Science: Problems Is the Logic of Scientific Explanation* (New York: Harcourt Brace Jovanovich, 1961).

Neisser, U. *Cognition and Reality: Principals and Implications of Cognitive Psychology* (San Francisco: W. H. Freeman, 1976).

Ornstein, R. E. *The Right Mind* (New York: Harcourt Brace, 1997).

Palmer, R. *Hermeneutics* (Evanston, Illinois: Northwestern University Press, 1969).

Piaget, J. *Play, Dreams and Imitation of Childhood* (New York: W.W. Norton, 1962).

Pinker, S. *How the Mind Works* (New York: W.W. Norton, 1997).

Pinker, S. *The Language Instinct: How the Mind Creates Language* (New York: William Morrow, 1994).

Plato, *The Republic* (Trans. by Benjamin Jowett) (New York: P. F. Collier & Son, 1901).

Plato, *Phaedrus.* (W. E. Helmbold and W. G. Rabinowitz, trans.) (New York: Bobbs-Merrill, 1956).

Plato, *Meno. In Great Dialogues of Plato.* (trans. by W. H. D. Rouse) (New York: New American Library, 1956).

Plotkin, H. *Evolution in Mind: An Introduction to Evolutionary Psychology* (Cambridge, Massachusetts: Harvard University Press, 1998).

Polanyi, M. *The Tacit Dimension* (Garden City, New York: Doubleday, 1966).

Pollio, H. R., Barlow, J. M., Fine, H. J., and Pollio, M. R. *Psychology and the Poetics of Growth: Figurative Language in Psychology, Psychotherapy and Education* (Hillsdale, New Jersey: Lawrence Erlbaum, 1977).

Reber, A. S. *Implicit Learning and Tacit Knowledge: An Essay on the Cognitive Unconscious* (New York: Oxford University Press, 1993).

Ricoeur, P. *Freud and Philosophy: An Essay on Interpretation* (New Haven: Yale University Press, 1970).

Rossi, E. ed., *The Collected Works of Milton H. Erickson.* (New York: Irvington, 1980).

Sagan, C. *The Demon-Haunted World: Science as a Candle in the Dark* (New York: Random House, 1995).

Sartre, J. P. *Being and Nothingness* (Trans. H. Barnes) (New York, 1956).

Schutz, W. *Here Comes Everybody: Body Mind and Encounter Culture* (New York: Harrow, 1971).

Shevrin, H., Bond, J. A., Brakel, L. A. W., Hertel, R. K., and Williams, W. J., eds., *Conscious and Unconscious Processes: Psychodynamic, Cognitive, and Neurophysiological Convergences* (New York: The Guilford Press, 1996).

Simonov, P. V. *The Emotional Brain: Physiology, Neuroanatomy, Psychology, and Emotion* (New York: Plenum Press, 1986).

Slater, P. *Microcosm: Structural, Psychological and Religious Evolution in Groups* (New York: Wiley, 1966).

Smith, D. L. *Hidden Conversations: An Introduction to Communicative Psychoanalysis* (London: Tavistock/Routledge, 1991).

Snell, B. *The Discovery of Mind* (New York: Harper & Row, 1960).

Stekel, W. *The Interpretation of Dreams* (New York: Liveright, 1943).

Vico, G. *The New Science* (T. G. Bergin and M. H. Fisch, trans. and abridgers) (London: Cornell University Press, 1948) (Original work published 1744).

Waller, J. *Face to Face: The Changing State of Racism Across America* (New York: Plenum/Insight Books, 1998).

Watson, J. *The Double Helix: A Personal Account of the Discovery of the Structure of DNA* (New York: Atheneum, 1968).

Webb, E. J., Campbell, D. T., Schwartz, R. D., and Sechrest, L. *Unobstrusive Measures: Nonreactive Research in the Social Sciences* (Chicago: Rand McNally, 1966).

Weimer, W. and Palermo, D. S. eds., *Cognition and the Symbolic Processes* (Hillsdale, New Jersey: Lawrence Erlbaum, 1974).

Weiskrantz, L. *Blind Sight. A Case History and Implications* (New York: Oxford University Press, 1986).

Werner, H. and Kaplan, B. *Symbol Formation: An Organismic Developmental Approach to Language and the Expression of Thought* (New York: Wiley, 1963).

Whitaker, D. S. and Lieberman, M. *Psychotherapy Through the Group Process* (New York: Atherton, 1964).

Whitehead, A. N. *Science and the Modern World* (New York: Macmillan, 1963).

Whyte, L. L. *The Unconscious Before Freud* (New York: Mentor Books, 1960).

Yalom, I. *The Theory and Practice of Group Psychotherapy* (New York: Basic Books, 1970).

BROADCAST MEDIA

ABC, 7 September 1977
CNN, Burden of Proof, 7 August 1998.
CNN, 20 August 1998 (Evening news, EST)
CNN, 13 September 1998, 1:16 pm, EST.
The Merv Griffin Show, 14 September 1977.

INDEX